DEC  2016

# LAST GIRL
# BEFORE FREEWAY

ALSO BY LESLIE BENNETTS

The Feminine Mistake

# LAST GIRL
# BEFORE FREEWAY

The Life, Loves, Losses, and Liberation of
Joan Rivers

LESLIE BENNETTS

Little, Brown and Company
New York Boston London

Little, Brown and Company
Hachette Book Group
1290 Avenue of the Americas, New York, NY 10104
littlebrown.com

First Edition: November 2016

Little, Brown and Company is a division of Hachette Book Group, Inc. The Little, Brown name and logo are trademarks of Hachette Book Group, Inc.

The publisher is not responsible for websites (or their content) that are not owned by the publisher.

The Hachette Speakers Bureau provides a wide range of authors for speaking events. To find out more, go to hachettespeakersbureau.com or call (866) 376-6591.

Photographs on insert pp. 1–3, 9–11, 15 © Melissa Rivers and Sheboygan Productions, LLC; p. 4 © Chicago Tribune/TNS/ZUMA Wire; p. 5 Michael Ochs Archives/Getty Images; pp. 6, 7 bottom Photofest; p. 7 top Dan Grossi/AP Photo; p. 8 top NBC/Photofest; p. 8 bottom CBS via Getty Images; p. 12 top Richard Drew/AP Photo; pp. 12 bottom, 13 top Ron Galella, Ltd./WireImage; p. 13 bottom Michael Weinstein; p. 14 top Broadimage/REX/Shutterstock; 14 bottom © Ken Babolocsay/Globe Photos/ZUMAPRESS.com; p. 16 © Staff/TNS/ZUMAPRESS.com.

ISBN 978-0-316-26130-2 (hc) / 978-0-316-43306-8 (large print)
LCCN 2016938566

10 9 8 7 6 5 4 3 2 1

LSC-C

Printed in the United States of America

*This book is dedicated to everyone who has lost love or work or money or success or youth or beauty or hope: may Joan's indomitable spirit encourage you in your bleakest hours, inspire you to triumph over any odds, and remind you to keep your sense of humor along the way—as it has done for me.*

# CONTENTS

# Contents

# LAST GIRL
# BEFORE FREEWAY

# PROLOGUE

$S$he sat on the bed, the gun in her lap. Everything seemed hopeless. "What's the point?" she thought. She couldn't think of one.

Only a few months earlier, Joan Rivers had everything she ever wanted: fame and fortune, the job of her dreams, a loyal husband, a loving child, a lavish estate—and a future that beckoned with enticing possibilities. After years of struggle, she had not only succeeded as a comedienne but had made history as television's first and only female late-night talk show host.

And now she'd lost it all. The first lady of comedy was fired from her job and publicly humiliated. Her husband—unable to bear his own failure as her manager and producer—killed himself. Their daughter blamed her mother for his death.

Reeling with grief and rage, Rivers then discovered she was broke. She had earned millions of dollars and lived a life of baroque luxury, but her husband had squandered her wealth on bad investments. She was $37 million in debt, and her opportunities for making more money had vanished.

At the Bel Air mansion where five telephone lines once buzzed relentlessly, the phone never rang. Nobody wanted to hire her as an entertainer. Suicide wasn't funny, and her husband's tragic death turned her into a professional pariah. Even her social life evaporated. No one invited her to anything.

As her fifty-fifth birthday approached, she couldn't see any reason to keep on living. It was hard enough for young women to succeed in show

3

business, but for an aging has-been, resurrecting a ruined career seemed impossible. Her home once sheltered a happy family; now the rooms echoed with silence. In her fancy peach-colored bedroom, she was alone.

"This is stupid," she thought.

And then her Yorkshire terrier jumped onto her lap and sat on the gun. Rivers knew her way around firearms; she often packed a pistol, and she felt no hesitation about using it. Once, when an assistant accidentally surprised her in the middle of the night, Rivers thought she was an intruder and accosted her with trigger cocked. "Your time's up," she said calmly, ready to fire.

Maybe that was the answer now: one moment and the act would be done.

But then a terrible thought occurred to her: If she killed herself, what would happen to Spike? The diminutive Yorkie was very cute, but he was also mean and cantankerous. He didn't like anybody but his mistress, and he was ridiculously spoiled; his favorite food was a rare roast beef sandwich, no mayo or mustard. Joan's daughter referred to him as "a tall rat."

Without Joan, who would protect and pamper the tiny dog she loved so much?

"Nobody will take care of him!" she realized, aghast.

As she sat on her bed, staring down at the gun, no oddsmaker would have bet on Rivers's future. In the history of show business, no middle-aged woman had ever done anything remotely comparable to what she was about to do.

But Rivers didn't shoot herself, and she refused to give up and slink into oblivion. Written off as a lost cause, she started over, invented new opportunities for herself, and went on to achieve the impossible. Working with maniacal fervor through her sixties and seventies and into her eighties, she re-created herself as a cultural icon, a vastly influential trailblazer, and a business powerhouse who built a billion-dollar company.

In the process, she rewrote her entire life story. Raised to believe in the classic fairy tale of happily ever after, she had been desperate to find the requisite husband. When she finally got married at thirty-two, she was overjoyed to have a loyal helpmate who looked like the black-suited groom on a wedding cake—and even more thrilled when baby made three.

In her thirties and forties, Rivers achieved her very own, uniquely modern version of the American dream, a forward-looking combination of classic male goals and conventional female aspirations. Like a successful man, she earned wealth and fame, but she also had a happy family—the *Good Housekeeping* seal of approval for any woman, no matter how accomplished.

Together, Rivers and her husband created a marital mythology that enshrined her as the star but credited him as the essential power behind the throne. But as the years went on, appearance diverged from reality—at first by a little, and then, terrifyingly, by a lot. Unable to keep up with his voraciously ambitious wife, the man in charge became increasingly depressed about his own lack of success. Instead of elevating her to the heights she craved, Mr. Right ended up playing the pivotal role in taking her down.

When she had to start again in midlife and go it alone, reality forced her to embrace a very different narrative. Her steady climb to the top had turned into a dizzying roller-coaster ride that ricocheted between spectacular triumphs and soul-crushing failures—a Dickensian saga of alternating extremes that included deep loves and tragic losses, stinging betrayals and enduring devotion, agonizing rejections and the adulation of millions, economic terror and riches beyond the wildest imaginings of all but the rarefied few.

None of it was what she expected. She grew up chubby and plain, with drab hair and thunder thighs and a horsey face that remained resolutely unpretty even after the requisite nose job. Fiercely jealous of Elizabeth Taylor, only a year older but a movie star even as a child, Rivers never got over her anger that she herself wasn't beautiful.

But that seeming handicap proved far less important than she assumed. Throughout her life, Rivers believed that beauty was the key to women's happiness and success—and yet talent and ambition gave her rewards that far exceeded anything earned by the pretty girls she envied so bitterly.

She thought she needed a man to prop her up—but when she finally took charge of her own life, she became much more capable than the men she depended on. Convinced that a woman's worth is measured by the intensity of men's desire, she saw aging as the ultimate enemy—and yet she achieved her greatest renown long after passing the sell-by date society decrees to be the expiration of female sexual viability.

In her later years, Rivers claimed that Spike saved her life when he sat on her gun that day, but in truth her fate was preordained by the fanatical determination she always recognized as the core of her identity. "Even in my darkest moments, I knew instinctively that my unyielding drive was my most important asset," she wrote.

That drive inspired her philosophy of life, which was as ferocious as it was uncompromising: "Never stop believing. Never give up. Never quit. Never!"

And she never did. After her life fell apart, it took her years to dig her way out of the wreckage. The process was hard and humbling, but it ultimately produced an outcome that no one, not even Joan herself, could have foreseen.

When she died at eighty-one, she was, improbably and amazingly, at the height of her fame—not only as a comic who battled her way back from oblivion, but as an insatiable overachiever who had fought her way into a dozen other fields as well.

After a sixty-year career, she was still doing stand-up comedy every week of her life, but she had also been an Emmy Award–winning talk show host; a radio host; a reality star online and on TV; the best-selling author of memoirs, fiction, and self-help books; a playwright and a screenwriter; a film star and a Tony-nominated actress on Broadway; a Hollywood movie director; a Grammy Award–winning recording artist; a CEO and designer whose company sold more than a billion dollars' worth of jewelry and clothing on QVC; and a philanthropist who commenced her enduring support of AIDS patients at a frightening time when that commitment was a rare act of public bravery.

As a snarky fashion arbiter on the red carpet, Rivers played a key role in creating a multibillion-dollar industry that employed countless designers and stylists and hair and makeup artists and publicists and photographers and all the other minions of the voracious media that now feed off an endless round of celebrity galas and awards ceremonies, spawning a perpetual ratings bonanza of televised critiques.

All that frenetic activity made Rivers an icon to an enormous and wildly diverse audience. In her later years, her fans ranged from the little old Jewish ladies who were her actual contemporaries to the Middle American housewives who bought her rhinestoned bumblebee pins on QVC to the millennials of every race, religion, background, gender identity, and sexual orientation who followed her insulting, obscene commentary on *Fashion Police*.

Rivers never set out to be a revolutionary, but the things she said—as shocking as the toads jumping out of the nasty daughter's mouth in the French folktale—had long since made her into one. When she started out in stand-up comedy, women simply didn't do most of the things she ended up doing—let alone talk about them. But if polite society said it was taboo, Rivers couldn't resist making fun of it.

Appalled by the hypocrisy of the prevailing social mores, she mocked the double standards that judged men by different criteria than women. If she was fixated on finding a husband, she was also merciless in lampooning the relentless pressure on women to land a man.

When Rivers made it onto *The Jack Paar Show*, she explained, "I'm from a little town called Larchmont, where if you're not married, and you're a girl, and you're over twenty-one, you're better off dead."

Being Jewish only exacerbated the problem. On *The Tonight Show*, Johnny Carson asked her when Jewish parents start to harangue a daughter about her marital prospects.

"When she's eleven," Rivers replied.

Men had a lot more latitude. "Jews and Italians get very nervous if a daughter hits puberty and there's no ring on her finger," she observed. "A son can be ninety-five."

A woman's worth was measured by her youth and desirability, but men need offer little more than a pulse. "A girl, you're thirty years old, you're not married—you're an old maid," Rivers said. "A man, he's ninety years old, he's not married—he's a catch."

When her parents moved to the suburbs in the 1950s, the talk of Larchmont was the arrival of the New England Thruway, which bisected the town. As one of her signature comedic bits, Rivers conjured a vivid image to convey the endless humiliations her mother inflicted on the spinster daughter nobody seemed to want.

"I'm the last single girl in Larchmont," Rivers said. "My mother is desperate. She has a sign up: 'Last Girl Before Freeway.'"

Her mother expected Joan to do what she herself had done: get married, have children, and become a housewife obsessed with domestic perfection. And yet Joan's mother was miserable; her husband didn't earn enough money for the family to live the way she wanted, and their home-life was riven with bitter fights that forever scarred their children. Growing up in an explosive atmosphere of recriminations and regret, Joan vowed that she would never depend on a husband to support her.

What Joan wanted was fame—but achieving glory seemed even more remote than finding a nice Jewish husband. Ever since she played a pretty kitty in a preschool play, she had planned to be an actress, but she wasn't pretty, and no one thought she had any talent. After graduating from Barnard, she was rejected by all the casting agencies, even when she crept in through the door on her hands and knees and crawled all the way to the receptionist's desk to reach up from the floor and offer a rose with her white-gloved hand.

But finally one secretary laughed and said she was funny and maybe she should try comedy. When Joan started begging for the chance to do stand-up in Greenwich Village clubs, nobody thought she was any good at that either.

Behind their hard-won facade of middle-class gentility, her parents were frantic with worry. They couldn't understand why Joan refused to settle for a normal life. Her conviction that she was destined for stardom seemed delusional, and they were doubly mortified when she performed at their beach club and bombed so badly they had to sneak out through the kitchen door rather than face their friends. Whatever "it" was, the universal consensus was that Joan Alexandra Molinsky didn't have it.

Hurt and angry at their lack of faith in her dreams, Joan was undeterred.

When an agent named Rivers told her that Molinsky wasn't an acceptable name for a performer, she became Joan Rivers on the spot. Bemoaning her failures in coffeehouses and comedy clubs, she portrayed herself as a wallflower who was perennially rebuffed by men. Even in the grubbiest dives, she was booed off the stage and fired before the second show.

But slowly, Rivers learned how to handle an audience, a challenge that demanded the ferocious control of a lion tamer. If audiences were tough, her peers were worse. Comedy was a man's world, and the men wouldn't let her in.

So she refused to take no for an answer. Bulldozing through previously impenetrable barriers as if they were made of toothpicks, she crashed her way into innumerable clubs run by hostile men who didn't want her. If they didn't consider her pretty enough to seduce, she taunted them with her relish for defying their judgments. Girls were supposed to be virgins until they married, but Rivers closed her show with a startling come-on: "I'm Joan Rivers, and I put out."

If women weren't allowed to share their experiences, she forced people to hear about them anyway. When she was eight months pregnant with her daughter, Ed Sullivan forbade her even to mention pregnancy on the air. Women were supposed to remain pristine on their pedestals, impersonating sanitized mannequins unsullied by corporeal reality. Rivers shocked her audiences by talking about what it feels like when a woman visits the gynecologist: "An hour before you come in, the doctor puts his hand in the refrigerator."

Audiences gasped, but she was just getting started; by the time she was a senior citizen, she was regaling people with jokes about the effect of age on female genitalia. "Did you know vaginas drop? One morning I look down and say, 'Why am I wearing a bunny slipper? And it's gray!'"

By then she was an international icon whose extraordinary career had been forged from an attention-grabbing hybrid of traditional female concerns and bold new transgressions. Pathologically afraid of gaining weight, she starved herself into an acceptable degree of emaciation; for decades, she ate only Altoids when she went out to dinner with friends. But she also became a ruthless enforcer of such strictures. Lashing out at women who let themselves go, she made headlines for lambasting her childhood nemesis.

"Elizabeth Taylor's so fat, she puts mayonnaise on aspirin."

"Elizabeth Taylor pierced her ears and gravy ran out."

"Mosquitoes see Elizabeth Taylor and scream, 'Buffet!'"

Until the end of her life, Rivers savaged other women for not conforming to the dictates of popular fashion, and her cruelty made some listeners recoil. As a cultural assassin, she even kept up with the times; her targets evolved from Elizabeth Taylor to Lena Dunham, but the rage never left her. And yet she was equally fearless about violating the social taboos that had long kept women in a Victorian stranglehold.

In doing so, she helped to shatter those taboos—but even as she did so, she continued to personify the contradictions that define women's lives. Until the week she died, Rivers performed outrageous comedy routines poking fun at the foolishness of men—but her entire life was shaped by her grief and anger at the male values that deemed her inadequate, no matter how hard she worked to live up to them.

She mocked the sexist and ageist attitudes that hold women back, but she remained hostage to the fears that made her into a virtual poster girl for grotesque excesses of plastic surgery. Mutilating her entire body with surgical interventions, she plumped up her sagging face with injectable fillers until she was unrecognizable as the plain young woman who had been catapulted to celebrity by a single star turn on *The Tonight Show Starring Johnny Carson*.

And yet even as she conformed to the cultural straitjackets circumscribing women's behavior, Rivers played a significant role in destroying them. During her lifetime, the modern American women's movement built a freeway to the future that liberated millions of women and girls from the limitations of the past. Although Rivers never set out to become part of a social justice crusade, she was by nature the quintessential iconoclast, compulsively rebellious and utterly fearless in her willingness to thumb her nose at such restrictions. Like a large boulder dropped into a still pond, her defiance had a ripple effect that spread out in ever-wider circles, rocking every boat it encountered.

Rude and transgressive, Rivers's humor freed the women who followed her, liberating them to tell the truth about their experiences and their bodies and their feelings, to say whatever they wanted and reject other people's ideas about what a woman can't do, onstage or onscreen or anywhere else. Her boldness helped pave the way for the legions of aspiring comediennes who now throng stages all over the country, no longer deterred by the naysayers who tell them they're not pretty enough or fuckable enough—let alone that women aren't funny.

But Rivers was more than a role model for women in the entertainment industry. With stunning candor, she shared her own financial, professional, romantic, marital, and emotional struggles in self-help books and on motivational speaking tours. Unlikely as it seemed, the famous diva who lived in an apartment so lavish it was routinely compared to Versailles had also managed to make herself into everywoman's sympathetic best friend, an intimate confidante and sensible adviser whose strength and determination provided encouragement for ordinary people overwhelmed with their own challenges. As she put it in the subtitle of one of her books, "I've survived everything…and you can too!"

Both she and Elizabeth Taylor grew up at a time when the story of a woman's life was defined by the man she married. Taylor won renown as the most beautiful woman in the world, but her career was in decline by the time she hit middle age. Today she is primarily remembered for being beautiful—and for marrying eight times. Between them, Taylor and Rivers had a total of ten marriages, but neither of them ever found that a man was the answer.

As for beauty, Rivers would have traded all her achievements to become one of the swans she envied, but instead she used her midlife catastrophes to create the startling new accomplishments that made her a cultural powerhouse in old age.

For her, the real answer was success. She never saw herself as a feminist groundbreaker; all she ever wanted was to make people laugh so she could feel loved in return. No matter how many triumphs she accumulated, she still felt unappreciated—but when she died, in 2014, the outpouring of emotion was so overwhelming that no one could fail to realize she had won the love of millions.

Headlines around the world recognized her as a history-making pioneer who left a legacy of expanded opportunity for all those who followed. An inspiration for anyone struggling to overcome heartbreak and tragedy, she had long since become a living embodiment of courage, ingenuity, and re-silience for every woman who faces unexpected hardships—or who yearns for something more substantial than a life story defined by how she looks and whom she marries.

Fierce and indomitable, the ugly duckling was the one who helped to change the world.

## Chapter One

# NOBODY EVER WANTED IT MORE: "BUT SHE HAS NO TALENT!"

In school, she didn't have friends. At lunch, she couldn't find anyone who wanted to sit with her. During recess, nobody chose her for their team in any sport.

Such slights made her feel bad, but from her earliest childhood, Joan Alexandra Molinsky was consoled by the incandescent memory of the unforgettable moment when she discovered the solution to all of life's disappointments.

The epiphany arrived like a bolt from the heavens when she won the role of a kitty in the preschool play. Performing in front of an audience, she was struck by "the ecstatic sense...that I could say, 'I want to be somebody wonderful and walk out onstage and be the princess,' and the world would say, 'Yes, you are the princess!'"

When everyone applauded, she was suffused with a joy she had never known—a miraculous high she spent the rest of her life trying to recapture. People accepted her! They enjoyed her! They thought she was beautiful!

That night she wore her kitty cat hat with the bunny fur and pink felt ears to bed, where she sat in her best pajamas and waited expectantly for her parents to bring their dinner guests upstairs, certain that the grownups would again make a fuss over her and say, "Aren't you darling!"

She didn't stay darling for long. As a very small child she was an angelic blonde, but the golden ringlets soon drooped and darkened to a dull mouse brown, her nose grew, and the tiny princess got so pudgy she would never stop despising herself for having been overweight as a child.

But she had found the magic escape from her self-loathing, from feeling inadequate and unwanted. She had learned how to make people love her, even if only for a few precious moments—and she was hooked forever.

From then on, the pretty kitty story represented the emotional truth at the core of her very existence—the Rosebud moment that defined the rest of her life. But in other regards, Joan Rivers's public story of origin—like so many other aspects of her carefully constructed identity—was a shrewdly designed facade that obscured a considerably less photogenic reality.

When she started to appear on television, she always said she came from Larchmont, a New York suburb that was noted for its "impeccable gentility," as she put it with airy nonchalance, as if she was born to the little black dress and WASPy strand of pearls she wore like a uniform for her early TV performances.

But even in a black dress and pearls, Rivers couldn't resist the temptation of juicing up her impact with some showbiz pizzazz, so she always added a tacky feather boa. In the photographs of her first ever appearance on *The Tonight Show*, the bedraggled boa is crumpled in a forlorn heap, like a limp, mangy bird that happened to die on her lap while she was bantering with Johnny Carson.

Her life story offered an equally curious amalgam of disparate elements. Far from the leafy green suburbs, Joan was born in 1933 in Brooklyn, where she spent her childhood. She and her older sister, Barbara, were raised in Crown Heights, at the intersection of Eastern Parkway and New York Avenue, on a block of houses known as Doctor's Row. Their father, Meyer Molinsky, was indeed a doctor. But he grew up poor in a family of struggling Russian immigrants, and he never figured out how to be a successful businessman—a failure that had harrowing consequences for his family.

Trying to establish a practice during the Depression, he seemed perpetually unable to manage the financial demands of running an office, so he would skip out on the rent by disappearing in the middle of the night after emptying everything he owned into a truck at 3 a.m. A soft touch who cared more about having people love him than about paying the bills, he charged a dollar a visit and accepted a cake or gefilte fish if his patients said they couldn't pay, even if they were driving a new car and he wasn't.

"If somebody was sick, he would just take care of them. Money didn't mean anything," said Larry Ferber, a longtime friend of Joan's and the former executive producer of her daytime television talk program, *The Joan Rivers Show.*

Unfortunately, money was what meant the most to Meyer's socially ambitious wife. Beatrice Grushman came from a family of well-to-do merchants in Odessa, and she raised her daughters on enthralling stories of her own enchanted Russian childhood, of lavish parties with peacocks strolling on lush emerald lawns and liveried waiters twirling trays of gold flatware and pears filled with caviar. But all their riches were left behind when their lives were overwhelmed by Russia's prerevolutionary turmoil. After sewing jewels into the sable lining of her coat, Beatrice's mother fled with her children to America.

As a young woman in New York, Beatrice worked at a sewing machine in a blouse factory, stuffed her shoes with newspaper when the soles wore out, and lived in a cold-water flat, where she slept on two chairs pushed together while her bed was rented to boarders. Humiliated by her family's straitened circumstances and haunted by their loss of privilege, she developed a lifelong obsession with the trappings of wealth. She spent the rest of her life trying to create the appearance of class, which to her mind was signified by materialistic excess and exaggerated formality.

"Both my parents were almost pathologically terrified of poverty," Joan wrote in her first memoir, *Enter Talking,* which was published in 1986. But instead of bonding over shared trauma, her parents dealt with their fears in disastrously conflicting ways. While the debt-ridden Meyer agonized over every penny they spent, Beatrice filled their home with damask and brocade, dressed her daughters in silk pajamas from Paris, and squandered $2,000 the family didn't have on a mink coat that sent her husband into paroxysms of helpless rage.

"Elegance was her religion," Joan said. "My mother wanted MD to stand for 'Make Dollars.'"

Although there were never enough dollars to satisfy her, Beatrice refused to curtail her extravagance. No matter how many screaming fights the Molinskys had over money, no matter how many times Beatrice stormed out of the house in disgust and then slunk back home because she couldn't support herself, her compulsive spending forced her husband to live perpetually beyond his means.

The consequences were painful for everyone. To the outside world, the Molinskys were the very embodiment of midcentury success—a nuclear family with a doctor father, a beautifully dressed mother who gave impressive dinner parties, and two healthy children. But behind closed doors, the atmosphere was poisonous. Beatrice's ferocious quest for status caused unbearable financial pressure that doomed the entire family to live in a state of unrelenting stress. The result was an excruciating tension between the refined image they strove so hard to convey and the terrifying economic insecurity that always threatened to overwhelm them.

Furious at Meyer's failure to provide a more opulent lifestyle, the haughty Beatrice subjected his every move to withering scorn. When he said or did something she considered common, she was contemptuous: "Well, you come from kikes!"

When she told him disdainfully to put his napkin on his knee, he would say, "Go to hell!"—and put the napkin on his knee.

When Beatrice couldn't pay the bills, she made secret trips to the pawnshop to sacrifice her wedding ring and gold bracelet yet again. She was so desperate to maintain her fabricated self-image that she never even told her husband the truth about her own background.

"Incredible as sounds, my father during their entire forty-eight years of marriage did not know she had ever been poor and always believed that Beatrice had been rich in Russia and rich in America," Joan wrote.

An emotionally absent workaholic obsessed with his practice, Meyer paid little attention to his family. He was the breadwinner, but Joan identified with her frustrated mother, and her anguish at Beatrice's powerlessness would shape the course of her life.

"I knew then that I was not going to let that happen to me," Joan said. "I was going to be what was called in those days a career girl, and would never, never let myself be dependent on anybody—and I never have."

Joan got another lesson in the power of money when she went away to summer camp at twelve. She was so certain she would be given the lead role in the camp play that when someone else was cast as Snow White, Joan went ballistic. "My reaction was overpowering rage, with no sane way to release it," she recalled.

Convinced that Phyllis Bernstein got the role because her father donated a new curtain for the camp stage, Joan organized her fellow campers in protest, demanding auditions and fomenting a strike. Even though the camp was owned by a friend of her mother's, Joan was expelled and sent home.

The mortifying debacle served as a bitter lesson: "If you had money, you could be Snow White!" But it was also an inescapable reminder of her own deficiencies. How could she have mustered enough social power to goad an entire camp into an uproar, and yet still lack the interpersonal skills to win friends and make people like her?

Quite by accident, Joan had discovered one way to make people like her when her father took her on a fishing trip with several other doctors. To her surprise, she found she could make the group of adult men laugh by telling a story in a funny way. The experience was a revelation: "This is power!" she thought. In *Joan Rivers: Exit Laughing*, a Comedy Hall of Fame documentary that aired on PBS, she explained, "Laughter gave me power."

But for the most part, Joan was a social dud, and the problem got worse as her peers expanded their get-togethers to include boys as well as girls. The first time Joan found herself in a group playing spin the bottle, the boy who got stuck with her in a darkened room immediately said, "Let's forget this." When the next boy ended up alone with her, he grabbed her nose and twisted it instead of kissing her—"which makes you realize you are not attractive," Joan said wryly.

She was tormented by the sense of having been "cheated by fate," which had, in her opinion, promised her a life of kitty hats and

17

princesshood. But if Joan craved the adulation of a crowd, her mother had other goals in mind.

Despite the family's chronic inability to keep up with its financial obligations, Beatrice decided, as her daughters moved through adolescence and their Brooklyn neighborhood deteriorated, that it was time to improve their standing in the world. In the classic migration of urban strivers determined to create a new identity that reflected comfort and privilege, the Molinskys bought an impressive house in a suburb that seemed like the epitome of the American dream.

Originally known as a summer resort for wealthy New Yorkers, Larchmont had, by the late 1950s, become a desirable haven filled with stately Victorian, colonial, and Tudor homes on the scenic streets bordering Long Island Sound, whose tranquil waters made the Larchmont Yacht Club an important gathering place for the sailing world.

Most of the beach clubs, like the surrounding country clubs with their manicured golf courses, were inhospitable to Jews, but the Molinskys didn't come to Larchmont for the boats or the greens. When they bought their dignified Georgian house, Beatrice told her daughters it was their "picture frame"—a trophy acquisition designed to serve as "a home to impress the boys who came there," as Joan later put it. Beatrice was determined to launch her daughters into advantageous marriages, and Larchmont was an appropriate setting to attract the kind of husbands she envisioned.

Joan had a very different vision: she just wanted to escape suburbia and get famous. Even as a teenager, she was savvy enough to realize she would have to buy her own ticket out of town, so she went to work selling jewelry at Wanamaker's department store. When she'd saved up enough money, she took her mother out to dinner at a nice restaurant. "We had never before sat down relaxed and ordered anything we wanted," reported Joan, who was thrilled to be able to leave "a major tip" that made her feel she was "very hot stuff"—and very unlike her father, whose anxious penny-pinching ruined every family outing.

The experience crystallized the lesson that would drive her for the rest of her life. "I thought, 'Money is power. Money is wonderful.' I have not changed my opinion," she wrote forty years later.

Despite its manifest influence, money was ultimately a means to the desired end. For Joan, the ultimate point was what she referred to, always in capital letters, as "THE DREAM." Although the reasons were apparent to no one but herself, she possessed "a permeating confidence that I had been born a great dramatic actress and my classmates would be sorry they had not appreciated me. I once wrote in my diary, 'One day when I'm famous, I'll laugh in their faces when the boys ask me to dance and please God don't let that be too far off.'"

As far as Joan was concerned, she was J. Sondra Meredith, a brilliant thespian who was destined by fate to become one of the great actresses of her time. She practiced her own private melodramas in front of the bathroom mirror, imagining herself as a brave American who pretended to be a little French girl so she could smuggle documents past the Nazis on a death-defying mission. But as Joan later observed, lots of girls dream about becoming stars, and most don't devote their lives to the single-minded pursuit of applause—so why did she?

"The answer is the difference between a dream and an obsession," Joan wrote in *Enter Talking*. "Performing became a psychological need at age fourteen, when I first experienced the full, intoxicating rush that happens onstage and all my fantasies were confirmed."

This time around, nobody handed her the chance, as some benevolent fate had done so many years earlier when she was given the role of the pretty kitty. As a homely but determined teenager, she had to create the opportunity for herself, which she did by taking on the responsibility of organizing the class plays, reviving the discontinued school tradition of an annual variety show, and making sure she was a featured performer.

She made the most of her turn in the spotlight: "Suddenly this chubby girl who had never been worth much attention was mesmerizing and manipulating the entire school and faculty and all the parents. For a moment I was the supreme princess, somebody dazzling, somebody else." That night she wrote in her diary, "Golly, I feel wonderful!"

Those precious moments confirmed everything she had first intuited in prekindergarten—that the most enveloping kind of love could be found onstage and experienced through the applause of a crowd. But in the coming years, such highs would be few and far between as Joan struggled to navigate the widening gap between her ecstatic fantasies and her parents' real-world expectations.

When she finished high school, Joan wanted to go "right into drama school at the Pasadena Playhouse next door to Hollywood." Her mother's reaction was unequivocal: "Absolutely not." Joan was expected to go to an eastern university, so she followed her older sister to Connecticut College for Women, a private liberal arts college in New London.

In that environment, Barbara excelled as usual: she got high marks, was invited to dine at the Colony Club, and dated Yalies who had gone to Andover and Exeter. Joan tried to emulate her social success, but the results were very different. Ever enterprising, she wrote letters to boys all over the eastern seaboard, but even when she landed a date, it was an unpleasant experience for all concerned.

When she trotted down the dormitory stairs to meet one blind date, "the guy frowned, turned to his friend, and said, 'Why didn't you tell me?' A moment like that—and there were many—rakes every open wound and makes you feel like nothing," Joan recalled years afterward.

Instead of inspiring lust or longing in members of the opposite sex, Joan was made to feel that her looks provoked only revulsion. After going to the beach with another boy, she took off the little robe she was wearing so they could go swimming. Her date said, "Oh, my God."

"The anguish was not just the disappointment in those boys' faces, it was also my embarrassment—really shame—at not being like the other girls who got the invitations, got the votes of approval," Joan said.

To make matters worse, her parents would come to visit her at college, driving up in a Cadillac she knew her father had received from a patient who repossessed cars, with her mother wearing the mink coat that her father had screamed about and a diamond bracelet, bought on time at Macy's, that had also precipitated angry scenes. Joan didn't have enough money to travel to Yale for her next blind date, but she was forced to smile and nod as her parents took her dorm mates out to dinner and pretended to be as affluent as they looked.

"I hated myself for playing along and joining their hypocrisy," Joan recalled later. "Maybe that is why in my comedy I try to puncture the hypocrisy all around us, why it is almost a crusade with me to strip life down to what is really true."

Although she still felt like a social outcast, she finally carved out a small niche for herself by directing a school play and finding a best friend. After two years at Connecticut College, she transferred to Barnard, where she discovered a more congenial tribe of artsy girls and theater nerds in an environment where "idiosyncrasies did not make you strange, they made you chic. Every girl was very, very bright and very, very neurotic. It was wonderful."

As much as Rivers appreciated her college experience, she was not content to make her way in life as a plain old Barnard alumna following her graduation in 1954. After she became a public figure, she always let interviewers know she was a member of Phi Beta Kappa, which is widely considered to be the nation's most prestigious collegiate honor society—and an automatic signifier of intellectual distinction. When coverage of Rivers didn't specify that she was Phi Beta Kappa, it usually mentioned that she graduated with honors. If you google "Joan Rivers Phi Beta Kappa Barnard," more than thirteen thousand entries pop up.

Like many other aspects of the Molinsky family history, this particular "fact" turns out to be untrue. "Joan did not graduate Phi Beta Kappa—and no honors either," said Debora Spar, Barnard's current president, after checking the college's academic records. Much as Rivers resented her parents' efforts to embellish their status, she did the same thing with her own academic record.

One might suspect that Joan falsely claimed to be Phi Beta Kappa in order to compete with her accomplished older sister, but that assumption would also prove to be incorrect. When her sister—then known as Barbara Cushman Waxler—died in 2013, her obituaries specified that she too had earned such academic honors. "Barbara received her BA in economics from Connecticut College for Women, where she graduated Phi Beta Kappa," reported Main Line Media News, as did Philly.com.

But Joan wasn't the only Molinsky to burnish her image with a more impressive intellectual pedigree. After checking its records, Connecticut

College discovered that Barbara Molinsky, who graduated in 1951, wasn't Phi Beta Kappa either, according to Deborah MacDonnell, a spokesperson for the college (which shortened its name in 1969, when it began admitting men). Both Molinsky girls spent their entire lives claiming to be Phi Beta Kappa, but neither actually earned that distinction.

Joan's real interests were elsewhere, and finishing college finally liberated her to pursue the goal she had cherished for so long. As a newly minted graduate, she applied to become an apprentice at the Westport Country Playhouse in a program run by the Theatre Guild. Joan saw Westport as "the Tiffany of summer stock companies," and she was overjoyed when she was accepted.

But to her own astonishment, instead of sashaying triumphantly into Westport as J. Sondra Meredith, she took to her bed and lay there in a fetal position for days, unable to face the challenge she had longed for all her life. When her chance finally came, she couldn't bear the possibility that she might try to live out her dream and fail. After days of making increasingly ridiculous excuses, she finally gave up and told her mother, "I can't."

"In the end, it was an almost conscious choice to preserve my childhood fantasy and keep my secret self-image out of danger," she observed later.

And so, having sabotaged the theatrical career she had hungered for, she took a course in typing and shorthand and found a job in the executive training program at Lord & Taylor. She did so well that she was hired away by Bond Clothing Stores to be a fashion coordinator.

Founded in Cleveland, Bond was the largest retail chain of men's clothing stores in the United States during the 1930s and 1940s. Best known for selling two-pant suits, Bond expanded to include women's clothing during the 1950s, when the chain operated nearly a hundred outlets around the country. In New York City, the flagship store was Bond Fifth Avenue at Thirty-Fifth Street and Fifth Avenue, but it was the Times Square store that was dubbed "the cathedral of clothing." For Joan, Bond would provide a fateful turning point that helped to determine the course of her life.

As she progressed in her working girl career at the store, her love life was also looking up. She fell madly in love with a friend of her cousin's named David Fitelson, on whom she'd had a crush since girlhood. When

he decided that he liked her too, she was astonished, and even more incredulous when he announced that she was his girlfriend.

To Joan, everything about David was dazzling. He was studying history
at Columbia University and planning to be a poet. His father was an at-
torney with the Theatre Guild, and the family personified the kind of
cultural cachet Joan admired and envied. A Chagall and a Matisse hung
in the living room of the Fitelson house in Greenwich Village. The garden boasted a Henry Moore sculpture. A silver cigarette case from Mary
Martin gleamed on the table.

The Fitelson family's sophistication notwithstanding, Joan's parents
were unimpressed with the prospect of David as a mate for their daughter.
To them, he was a spoiled, disreputable bohemian who wouldn't be able
to support a wife in the style to which they expected her to become accustomed. Joan was supposed to marry a doctor, a lawyer, an accountant—
not some wild-eyed, impractical urban Heathcliff who loved her with the
kind of dramatic fervor that epitomized grand passion in her eyes. Joan
and David fought with operatic intensity and great regularity, and after
every explosion he would write an elegy, which Joan thought was very
romantic.

Far less romantic, even to a besotted Joan, was the fact that he was always broke. He would drive to Larchmont in the middle of the night with
no money to buy gas, expecting her to pay. He was the love of her life, but
their fights were so terrible that on one particularly memorable occasion
she screamed, "You're a lazy rich man's son waiting for the inheritance!"—
and then jumped out of a moving car. And yet their mutual attraction exerted such an overwhelming pull that they couldn't seem to leave each
other alone. He vowed he would never let her go.

So when David finally went into the Army, Joan figured she had the
six weeks of his basic training to get herself married to someone else. As
if sent to her by central casting, James Sanger materialized to fit the bill.
The son of the merchandise manager at Bond, "he was the royal prince
and we were the buzz of the store," she said proudly.

Joan decided that Jimmy was just what her parents wanted for her: a
Columbia graduate and a businessman, already well-to-do and destined

for success. Instead of constant emotional chaos and a future of impoverished disillusionment with David, a life with Jimmy seemed to promise a nice apartment, a maid, a country club, and a mink coat—everything that she had been raised to want, and that, in truth, a significant part of her actually did want.

Joan told Jimmy that they should get married immediately. She was twenty-two years old, and so sure she was making a mistake that she had to take a tranquilizer before the wedding—"but I knew what was expected of me and was going to do it," she said.

Her acquiescence did not signal her acceptance. "I was furious about having to get married," she admitted long afterward. "I was Phi Beta Kappa, and all they wanted me to do was get married!"

Her anger at such social expectations was compounded by her parents' implicit disparagement of her other prospects. "Her mother thought Joan would never marry, so she said, 'Listen, nobody else is coming along, so you'd better grab this guy,'" reported Blaine Trump, who became a close friend many decades later. "Joan said it was a disaster."

Like her parents before her, Joan found herself mismatched in a marriage as ill-conceived as it was hasty. It became clear almost immediately that neither partner understood what they were getting into when they said "I do." Jimmy—who obviously had no idea what Joan was really like—turned out to be "furious that he had an ambitious wife." He kept telling her, "I want to be the boss," and they fought constantly.

Six months after the wedding, Joan left for good. In those days, even when both parties wanted to escape a marriage, the options for doing so were tightly constrained; until the movement to reform divorce laws gained traction in the 1970s, no-fault divorce didn't exist, so one partner had to prove that the other was to blame in order to terminate a marriage.

So they got the marriage annulled on the grounds that Jimmy didn't want children but had neglected to tell Joan. Ending a marriage was scandalous no matter how it was done, and Joan's parents were understandably appalled; in 1955, nice Jewish girls who wore white gloves and aspired to mink coats and country-club memberships didn't jump into and out of a perfectly respectable marriage, let alone all in the same year.

The Molinskys would have been even more upset had they realized what the whole debacle really meant. As far as Joan was concerned, her doomed attempt at establishing a conventional grown-up life "closed the door, not just on Jimmy Sanger, but on ever being Mrs. Westchester and Mrs. Doctor's Wife and Mrs. Normal Citizen in society." She had tried; she had done what her parents wanted her to do. And she had failed.

From now on, she was going to pursue her own dreams, not theirs. Fortunately for the entire family, neither Joan nor her parents had any idea of what a long, difficult, painful, embarrassing journey this would turn out to be—or of the widening gulf that would separate them as the rebellious child battled her way into a hostile future.

In order to do so, she had to find a new support network, and so she began what would become a lifelong process of creating her own surrogate family with friends who understood her goals and sympathized with her hardships.

The son of a burlesque comedian in the Catskills, Lou Alexander grew up in the Borscht Belt branch of show business, and all he wanted was to follow in his father's footsteps. In the late 1950s, after getting out of the service, he started trying to make it as a stand-up comic in his own right. One day his wife, a model named Beth Hamilton, told him that someone she worked with at Bond had asked to meet him. The young woman's name was Joan, and while she had a job in a clothing store, what she really wanted to learn about was comedy.

"At the store, the models would walk around and they would do a whole thing about what you're wearing, like 'This is an off-the-shoulder pinstripe' or whatever," explained Alexander, who was two years older than Rivers. "Joan did the narration of the clothing, but she said to Beth, 'I'm not going to do this. I want to be a comedian.' Beth said, 'I'm married to a comedian,' and Joan said, 'I want to meet your husband.' I was working at a club called the Golden Slipper in Mineola, Long Island, and Joan came out with her boyfriend to see me."

Although Alexander knew the bare facts of Joan's history, she wasn't forthcoming about her marital misadventure. "She was divorced from her first husband, but she never talked about that," he said. "I knew she wasn't doing very well, because she had on a brassiere that was held up with a safety pin."

But she knew what she wanted. "She said, 'Can you give me some pointers on how I can get into the business?' I said, 'Whatever you see me doing tonight, take it and use it as a girl thing instead of a guy thing.' So she wrote down all kinds of notes. Then she said, 'How do I get started?' I said, 'Go to Greenwich Village and work for nothing. Tell them you want to break in. If they like your act, they throw change—quarters, dimes, nickels—and that's your money."

Alexander promised to come and watch Joan perform when she got onstage, which he did. "I went down to Cafe Wha? in Greenwich Village and saw her," he reported.

Founded in 1959 as a club on Macdougal Street, Cafe Wha? was a popular venue for aspiring musicians and comedians, many of whom went on to have legendary careers, including Bob Dylan, Jimi Hendrix, the Velvet Underground, Peter, Paul, and Mary, Woody Allen, Bill Cosby, Richard Pryor, and Bruce Springsteen.

When Alexander first saw Joan onstage, her lack of experience was so apparent that his initial notes focused on the basics of communicating with an audience. "The material wasn't that good, and she talked too fast," he explained. "She was speaking so fast I said, 'It's very hard to understand what you're saying. As soon as you get to the punch line, say to yourself, "One, two, three…"—and then say the punch line.'"

The next time he watched her perform, he was in for a surprise. "She's doing her act, and she says out loud, 'One, two, three!' She's supposed to say it to herself!"

Alexander has told this story before, but it was reported as if the joke were on Joan, the clueless novice who was so green she didn't realize she wasn't supposed to say the numbers of her little countdown out loud. And yet this interpretation seems absurd: Joan was a woman who would go to any lengths to make someone laugh. In this case, it seems clear that her intended target was Lou Alexander, whom she was so eager to impress that she was willing to sacrifice the entire room to crack up her mentor with a private joke that only he would get.

It worked. "How could I not laugh at that?" Alexander said. "I fell on the floor."

The joke was not only calculated but totally unexpected, its impact compounded by the irresistible frisson of marking its intended audience as part of a select group of knowing insiders—a group that, in this case, numbered only two. No one else knew why the joke was funny, or even that it was a joke—but to Lou and Joan, it was hilarious.

The experience convinced him that Joan had the one irreplaceable attribute of any comedian. "You can't teach somebody to be funny," he said. "There's gotta be something there to start with. Joan was a little bit outrageous, a little bit out there."

Driven by a compulsive need to transgress, she seemed willing to sacrifice almost anything to make people laugh, from propriety and good taste to her dignity and her femininity. The reward certainly wasn't riches; when Joan got started, a working comic like Lou Alexander was lucky if he earned enough to pay for food and shelter. "I was making sixty dollars for four shows in two days at the Golden Slipper," he reported. "Joan said, 'Can I make that kind of money?'"

"Everything's relative," Alexander replied dryly.

Despite her family's emphasis on material wealth, Joan was not discouraged by such hardships. Trying to placate her parents by making some money, she juggled office temp jobs with an endless round of largely fruitless efforts to land an acting gig. She was fired from so many jobs that she resorted to a fervent prayer: "Please, God, if you're going to make me a failure, fine—but don't make me a failure at something I don't want to do."

She was no more successful on the rare occasions when she landed a role in some kind of stage show. After assuring the director that she had lots of relatives who would come see her in a play, which seemed to be the primary qualification for being cast, Joan was thrilled to be included in an Off-Broadway production called *Seaweed*. She was told that the job didn't pay any money but could be useful as a showcase. When it turned out that the only available part was Man in Black, Joan suggested that the role be changed to Woman in Black.

And so the character became a lesbian, and Joan found herself impersonating a young woman in love with another female character, who was played by "a skinny high school girl with a large nose and a pin that said 'Go Erasmus!'" The Brooklyn girl with the big nose was named Barbara Streisand, but she would later change her name to Barbra and become one of the biggest stars in the world.

*Seaweed* didn't turn out to be Streisand's big break—or Joan's. "The actual performance is a blur—the mind protects itself," Joan wrote in *Enter Talking*. "I do remember I had a big love scene where I told Barbra I loved her very much and she rejected me and I had a knife in my hand and tried to kill her and then myself. I also remember a horrendous lot of coughing, like a tubercular ward, and knowing this whole thing was insane and wanting to turn and wink at the audience, sitting there in overcoats."

The only review appeared the next day in *Show Business*, which called *Seaweed* sophomoric and ridiculous and added that the performances couldn't be evaluated because the material was so bad.

The Molinskys' reaction was equally scathing. Joan's father told her that *Seaweed* was "the worst piece of garbage I ever saw, and these people are garbage. You're crazy." Joan's mother said she was wasting her life on acting and should give up and go to law school like her sister. Both were baffled by Joan's obstinacy. As far as they could tell, no one on the planet thought Joan had what it took to make it—except Joan.

"What makes you think you can be a success?" her mother asked in desperation. "How do you know you have talent? Has anyone ever said you have talent? It's absolutely, utterly ridiculous. You're talented in so many other ways; why throw your life away in the one area you have nothing?"

In her memoir, Rivers related such painful experiences in great detail, but it seems she took as many liberties with the truth as she had in describing her ostensible academic honors. When the author James Spada published *Streisand: Her Life* in 1995, he reported that Rivers fabricated virtually everything about her alleged appearance with Streisand—including the name of the play, which was actually *Driftwood*, and the lesbian romp Rivers claimed to have had with the future megastar.

"'There was no lesbianism in my play,' says *Driftwood* playwright Maurice Tei Dunn. 'I can't imagine where Joan got that. In those days, it would have been suicide in the theater. Barbara and Joan never had a single exchange together. They were never onstage at the same time. That picture of them together in Joan's book was posed during rehearsals.'"

What Joan didn't exaggerate was the unanimous dismay that greeted her own performance. When it came to her viability as a potential talent, all available evidence suggested that her parents' concerns were warranted—and yet Joan remained implacable.

Busy going nowhere as a dramatic actress, she was also trying to get onstage as a comic, but when she managed to land a gig, the reception was even worse. She was thrilled when Lou Alexander introduced her to an agent named Harry Brent, who booked her as an emcee at a place called the Show Bar in Boston. Brent informed her that her stage name was Pepper January, and she'd be known for "comedy with spice."

The Show Bar turned out to be a seedy strip club where Pepper's castmates were named Dyna-Mite and Aurora Borealis, the Shooting Star. Trying to maintain some semblance of dignity, Joan told the strippers that she had gone to Connecticut College. "Oh—me too," said one of the strippers, who astonished Joan by naming the dormitories where she had lived.

When Joan went onstage, another shock awaited her. Looking down at the audience, she saw, "almost at my feet," a Yale student she had dated—"the blond son of the owner of Peck & Peck," dressed in a Brooks Brothers gray flannel suit and rep tie. "I do not know which of us was more astounded and upset," Joan said.

The audience wasn't any happier. As she launched into her routine, men started screaming, "Get the fuck off! Bring on the girls!" Joan's set was so bad she was fired before the second show of the night, which meant she didn't get paid.

Back in her cheap hotel, which smelled of urine and peanuts, she couldn't stop crying. "I was seeing myself as my parents saw me, facing the truth that theater had not worked and comedy was not working," she said. She took a long shower in a tub so filthy she kept her socks on. "Standing in that dirt-blackened tub, I no longer knew whether the thing inside me struggling to come out was talent or only an obsession. But even at that moment I could still feel it there, enormous inside me, still constantly pushing. It wanted to get out and I wanted it out—and could not find a way to release it. I was giving birth to a baby and someone had tied my knees."

When she got home to Larchmont and acknowledged her failure to her parents, they told her that "this foolishness has got to stop." Her mother said, "You're making your father and me ill." Joan didn't stop, and she kept trying valiantly to fit in, even at strip clubs. "I used to buy pasties and put them on over my dress," she said.

But then Harry Brent managed to book her into a strip joint in Springfield, Massachusetts. When she came off the stage, the boss said, "Get your stuff and get the fuck out of here."

At this point Brent gave up and told her he wouldn't handle her anymore. He was, however, keeping the rights to "Pepper January, comedy with spice"—because "great names and logos don't come easy," he said.

"When you are not even Pepper January, then you are truly nothing," Joan observed. No one seemed to think she was going to make it. Nobody except her boyfriend, an Italian wannabe actor named Nick Clemente whose father was connected to the mob, ever encouraged her at all. And yet no matter how many times she failed, she simply refused to give up.

But it was a long time before Joan's perseverance began to pay off. As she learned more about comedy, she also realized how bad she was at it. "I knew my act was terrible," she admitted. She admired the sophisticated comedy of hip talents like Mike Nichols and Elaine May, but it didn't occur to her that she might draw from her own everyday humor to create jokes or sketches that were more original than the tired old gags endlessly recycled by generations of hacks.

In the spring of 1959, she finally met a kindred spirit, an aspiring comedy writer named Treva Silverman—"a dream sister who had graduated from Bennington College, done her thesis on James Joyce's *Ulysses*, and known since day one that she belonged in show business," Joan said. "We were two salmon swimming upstream together."

Through her new soul mate, Joan got to know a group of comedy-obsessed twentysomethings who, like Treva, wanted to be writers rather than performers. They were all students of comedy, their role models were the legendary wits of the Algonquin Round Table, and their goal was to make it to Upstairs at the Downstairs, Julius Monk's satirical revue at the old Wanamaker mansion on West Fifty-Sixth Street—a far cry from a gig in the Catskills.

Hanging out with such smart young things, Joan was exposed to a very different world than anything she had known, and a different sort of people. Up until then, she spent much of her time with her incongruously inappropriate boyfriend. A great comfort, Nick gave her unfailing emotional support even when no one else did, but he was a former Marine who lived with his parents in Brooklyn, where his father was a housepainter who also worked for the Mafia, according to *Enter Talking*. Joan knew he wouldn't fit in with Treva's cabaret crowd any better than he would with her own very Jewish, very status-conscious parents, so she kept each part of her world quite separate.

Treva's friends also introduced Joan to a different approach toward her work. They were obsessed with the craft of writing, and Joan began to focus on developing her material and shaping it to her own individual persona instead of conforming to a generic mold. In addition to making fun of herself, she ridiculed society's expectations of women—a topic that became a staple of her work in jokes about traditional female roles: "I hate housework. You make the beds, you do the dishes, and six months later, you have to start all over again."

A quarter of a century after meeting Treva and her friends, Joan wrote about what an important influence they had on her own development as a comic. "Treva even gave me one line I still use: 'If God wanted me to cook, my hands would be aluminum,'" Joan reported in *Enter Talking*.

As she began to drop old routines from her act and replace them with new material, she also assumed a new identity. When a theatrical agent named Tony Rivers said he couldn't send her out as Joan Molinsky and she had to change her name, she came up with a new one on the spot. "Okay, I'll be Joan Rivers," she said.

And slowly, a new persona began to emerge. "In the course of all that bombing in cheesed-out clubs, I gradually saw my mistakes and tried not to repeat them—it is the bad that teaches you, makes you think; good takes care of itself and only gets better," she said. "However, no matter how many times I bombed and cried, I could not wait to get to the next job. Hope always lived in the next show."

But when she bombed in front of all her parents' friends, the Molinskys finally reached their breaking point, and the public humiliation Joan inflicted on them touched off a shattering explosion that left her homeless.

The Molinskys were members of the Riviera Shore Club in New Rochelle—"not the best beach club, but one my parents could afford," said Joan, who described its decor as "high Bronx." Even there, the Molinskys felt compelled to elevate their status by pretending they had a cabana when they had only a locker.

Joan was nonetheless gratified when her father suggested her as the professional entertainer for one of the club's regular Saturday night dinner shows. The manager agreed, mainly because a recent appearance by the comedienne Totie Fields had depleted his budget and he needed to find free entertainment.

But when Joan took the stage, the crowd quickly progressed from muttering "Oh, it's Joan Molinsky—you know, Dr. Molinsky's daughter. No, not Barbara—Joan!" to "How long do you think she's going to go on?" and "Shouldn't we leave now and avoid the traffic?" Drenched in flop sweat, Joan finally fled the stage and ran to hide behind the kitchen door, shaking—only to be confronted with her parents.

The manager saw the Molinskys "dying of embarrassment and led them out through my escape route," Joan reported. "Coming through the kitchen was my father, confused and shocked, looking as though somebody had sat on him. With one outstretched hand, he was trying to steady my mother, dressed in very high-heeled satin shoes, a lace Bergdorf Goodman dress, wearing the good pearls and clutching a little Judith Leiber bag...On her face was the look that must have been on somebody's face at the first sight of Hiroshima."

After trying to sneak out without having to face anyone, the whole family was further humiliated when they were forced to wait for their car in front of the club, along with everyone else. "Mostly they just looked away and said nothing," Joan recalled, although a few women came over to her mother and said sorrowfully, "I'll call you tomorrow."

At home, Joan went up to her room, but the window was open and she could hear her parents talking on the terrace below. "She has no talent. What can we do?" her mother said. "She is throwing her life away."

Her father was equally desolate: "The people expected more, even from an amateur."

Joan finally exploded. "I went crazy. I ran down the stairs and out the back door…[and] screamed at them, 'I don't care what you say! You don't know! I do have talent! You're wrong!'"

Her mother told her she had to give up. Her father told her she was associating with "a bunch of derelicts and fairies." Joan yelled, "It's my life! It's my choice how I live it!"

When her father said she could go to hell, she told him he didn't know what the hell he was talking about—whereupon her mother told her she wasn't allowed to swear at her parents and her father said she was turning into a tramp, just like her friends.

Then her mother played the fatal trump card: "Joan, if you're going to live in our house, you're going to live by our rules."

Joan took the bait. "In that case, I won't live in the house! You can't tell me what to do. I'm too old. I've been married and divorced."

Her father shouted, "You want to leave? Leave! Who wants you? It's our house—just get out!"

"You got it," Joan screamed, and ran off in her pedal pushers.

She got into her car and waited, but nobody came to retrieve her. After waiting for a very long time, she drove down the driveway at a snail's pace, but her parents still didn't come after her. She drove around Larchmont aimlessly, but couldn't figure out where to go. Eventually she drove into the city and found herself in front of the YWCA at 1 a.m. At last, she did what she always did when she ran out of other options: she called Nick Clemente, waking up his parents. As usual, he rushed into Manhattan to rescue her.

Also as usual, her white knight lacked the wherewithal to give her anything more than reassurance, so she slept in her car until Nick pawned a friend's sister's typewriter to get enough money to pay for a room at the YWCA for a week. After the week was up, the two checked themselves into a succession of hotels under various fake names, ordering roast beef dinners from room service and then sneaking out without paying the bill. When they ran out of hotels, Joan worked at office temp jobs to scrounge up enough money for a room in a women's residential hotel.

As the weeks went by, she lived on Orange Julius and date-and-nut-bread sandwiches at Chock Full o'Nuts, making calls to advance her nonexistent performing career from a phone booth in Grand Central Terminal. Haunted by the constant barrage of evidence "that I was a moron whose instincts had been wrong since I was three years old," she still refused to face the possibility that she might never realize THE DREAM.

"I could not endure the reality that I might end up Joan Molinsky, an unattractive, nondescript little Jewish girl, run-of-the-mill, who might just as well have stayed in Brooklyn and married the druggist and had a normal life," she said. "I had come from normal life, from real life, and nobody there had been happy. I knew I had to be special, had to have a life different from anything I had ever known, and if I ended up ordinary Joan Molinsky, I would always be unhappy and make my husband and children unhappy."

Although Nick Clemente was endlessly supportive, he—unlike Joan—didn't seem to mind being broke. One night they were debating whether they could afford a hot dog at Howard Johnson's when Nick made the mistake of saying that money didn't mean anything. This made Joan furious, but when she pointed out that they were cold and hungry and tired and unemployed and couldn't buy dinner, Nick did not rise to the occasion by saying that maybe he could get a job.

Since Joan needed to make her rounds as an aspiring actor during the day, she goaded him by announcing that she would get a night job and become a hooker. Nick replied that she might be able to get five dollars for a trick, "but only under the boardwalk at Coney Island at night."

Not surprisingly, the fight ended up with Nick storming out to seek moral support and alcoholic solace from his friends Sal and Guido, who eventually convinced him that if he really loved Joan, he should call her family. So he telephoned Barbara in Larchmont and told her that Joan had decided to become a prostitute, which prompted Mrs. Molinsky to pick up an extension and scream at Nick that it was all his fault, whereupon he screamed back that it was, in fact, her fault. Sal decided the Molinskys were abusing his friend, so he grabbed the phone, yelled "Listen, you fuckers!," and hung up.

At this point Nick called Joan and said, "I think maybe I made a mistake."

When he told her what he'd done, she said she was going to jump out the window of the women's residence. Nick promptly hung up and told Guido, "I gotta go—she's gonna jump!"

Guido said he knew "a big black guy who had a car," which launched an against-the-clock car race worthy of a French farce. Ten people set out at breakneck speed in three different cars, all heading for the same destination from different directions, with each of them frantically running every red light in their effort to reach Joan in time to prevent her suicide. In one car were Nick, Sal, Guido, and the big black guy; the second car held Joan's mother and father and sister; and the third, a chauffeur-driven limousine, contained Joan's Aunt Alice and Aunt Fanny, two dowagers in pearls who had been summoned to the rescue by Joan's hysterical mother.

When all of them converged at the women's residence, Joan's mother shouted at Nick that he was a bum, and the big black guy yelled back at her to defend Nick until Joan's mother demanded to know who he was— whereupon the big black guy grabbed Nick's arm and retorted, "I'm his brother!"

Meanwhile, Dr. Molinsky ignored the hotel clerk's agitated protests that no men were allowed upstairs, charged up to Joan's room, and started trying to wrestle her back down the stairs as Joan clung to the railing in her bathrobe, screaming and crying hysterically.

Dr. Molinsky finally halted Joan's resistance by announcing that she had two choices: come home to Larchmont at once or he would commit her to Bellevue that very night.

"All along my father was convinced I would end up a whore and now it had happened," Joan wrote years later. "Why would the Italian lover lie? And the only reason his daughter would turn to prostitution would be insanity. I knew he meant it—and that he could do it. I had lost."

When they got back to the lobby, Joan's mother was shrieking "What have you done to my daughter?" at Sal and Guido, who were drunk, while Aunt Fanny poked at them with her cane. When Mrs. Molinsky went back to yelling at Nick that it was all his fault, Sal shouted, "Don't yell at my buddy!," and the black guy said ominously, "Don't worry, I'll call some friends!"

"Three Jewish ladies, none over five feet tall, in mink coats and Delman shoes, were screaming and swinging Hermès pocketbooks at three rough Italian boys," reported Joan. Weeping with rage, she ran to Nick and sobbed, "How could you do this?"

But when he lifted his arm to comfort her, Aunt Fanny cried out, "My God, he hit her!"

Aunt Alice finally imposed a truce by announcing that Joan would spend the night with her while the Molinskys would go home. Joan asked Nick to come with her so they could talk, but Guido said, "You're not going. She's not Italian." As Nick struggled to leave, Guido grabbed him by his coat and held on until Nick broke free and ran off, coatless, with Joan. Nick had sold out the Italians to a Jew, and Guido never spoke to him again.

Ever the dutiful boyfriend, Nick went to Aunt Alice's apartment on Park Avenue, where he and Joan "sat on her Chippendale sofa under her Vlaminck, surrounded by her wonderful English antiques," while Aunt Alice negotiated a deal: Joan would go home and behave herself, Dr. Molinsky would not have her committed to Bellevue, and her parents would accept her goal of becoming a performer.

So life went on, and what happened that night was never mentioned again—but on the rare occasions when Joan's parents encountered Nick Clemente, Mrs. Molinsky always asked him, "How's your brother?"

The crisis left Joan feeling defeated; she saw her father as having won, and his threat to have her committed to Bellevue as a powerful weapon that transformed him from a parent into a policeman. From then on, she tried to avoid him as much as possible.

And yet the truth was that Joan won what really mattered to her, which was the security of living in her parents' home while retaining the freedom to keep on trying to make it in show business. Constant rejection and her parents' wrath hadn't dissuaded her, nor had poverty and homelessness. While her talent had not yet struck anyone as exceptional, her fanatical, incomprehensible, inextinguishable ambition certainly did.

For the first half of her life, Rivers avoided therapy because she was afraid it might help to resolve her issues—"and there goes the act!" But she didn't need a psychiatrist to understand what motivated her. In 1983, when *People* magazine asked where she got her drive, she replied, "From being the second child and a fat child. My sister was prettier, smarter, and better than I was in every way."

Over the course of a long career, Lou Alexander met most of the iconic names in comedy as well as countless wannabes. After performing as a stand-up comedian for twenty-two years, he became an agent and later worked with Budd Friedman, the founder and original proprietor of The Improv, a Manhattan comedy club that later became a franchise with other clubs around the country. Alexander knows the world of comedy intimately—and yet even by those standards, Joan is unique.

"I've seen many, many people when they got started in this business, and I've seen a lot of people break in. But I've never seen anybody, man or woman, who wanted it more or loved it more than Joan Rivers," he said. "I never saw anybody who was that diligent. She could have a high temperature and she'd go onstage. There is nothing that would stop her. She was willing to give up anything to make it."

## Chapter Two

# DYING IS EASY. COMEDY IS HARD.

For the rest of her life, Rivers's recollections of her early years in the business remained vivid and harrowing. "All of us in comedy have had our Show Bars, our hideous low points that almost destroy us—except that we come back to have more of them—walking out on stages hundreds and hundreds of times when lights are broken, when microphones do not work, when audiences are hostile, when our material stinks," Rivers wrote in *Enter Talking*. "That is what makes you tough. But the process gives terrible war wounds that are forever open, leaving you a victim for the rest of your life."

"If you have reached the top in comedy, you are, in your own way, a killer—but every killer is bandaged. And the anger is never out of you," she added. "Why was Totie Fields so angry? Why did her contract require twelve coffee cups, exactly twelve, in her dressing room? Because twenty-five years ago she could not get even one cup. After years of being pampered, I am still angry. I am angry because of the Show Bar."

When Rivers wrote those words in the mid-1980s, at what then appeared to be the height of her career, she went on to list a host of other indignities that still rankled from countless other sleazy venues, for "the nights I had to get dressed in filthy toilets, for all the disgusting dressing rooms where there was no toilet paper in the john, where the soap had hair embedded in it, where cockroaches ran across the dressing table, where my paycheck had $1.25 deducted from it for two cups of coffee."

But slowly and incrementally, progressing in tiny steps that often appeared undetectable as forward motion, the seemingly hopeless succession of terrible experiences began to pay off. "What makes a comedian finally jell? I know the answer to that now," Rivers said decades later, enlightened by the wisdom of hindsight. "The act evolves out of yourself—but not intellectually. It gathers emotionally inside you, in a strange way a by-product of struggle, of a willingness to do anything, try anything, expose yourself to anything...This is paying your dues, appearing again and again and again on every sort of stage, in front of every kind of audience, until you gradually, gradually acquire technique and a stage identity, which is not you, but has your passion, your hurts, your angers, your particular humor. This is a birth process and it can be very painful."

Through all the soul-crushing rebuffs, what keeps any comic going is the irresistible promise of the reward that shimmers perpetually on the horizon like an enticing oasis offering sweet relief from all of life's hardships—if only one could get there.

In *Why We Laugh: Funny Women*, a documentary that featured interviews with more than a dozen female comedians, Rivers was moved to tears by her own description of what it feels like for a comic to elicit the desired response from an audience.

"There is nothing like walking on a stage and turning to the audience and saying, 'This is what happened to me today, and it was wrong!'—and they say, 'Yes, it was wrong!' It's having a million mothers out there that say, 'You're the best! You're the funniest!'" Rivers said, starting to cry at the very thought. "It's a very tough existence for all of us in real life, and we have an hour and a half when we're going to forget what's tough. Comedy is such a warm blanket to put around everyone."

The comic Judy Gold was more succinct in describing what it feels like to win the laughter of an audience: "I guess it's like a crack high," she said. "When I got the first laugh, and then got another, it was like God had spoken to me."

But it takes years of practice to master the craft of extracting that reward from a volatile and demanding process. Every audience is different, and comedians must learn how to manipulate everyone watching them with the kind of assurance that puts listeners at their ease. Only hard-won experience can give a performer the necessary skills and confidence—not to mention the judgment to tailor the comedic content to a specific audience.

Although comics have always stolen material from one another, it's the individuals who create a distinctive style with original material that make the biggest impact. For Rivers, another crucial step toward success was learning to draw from her personal experience in developing her own characteristic brand of humor—and finding an effective stage persona to deliver it.

This took her a while to figure out. When she auditioned for the agent Irvin Arthur, he said, "That was terrific. The only trouble is, you just did his act."

Arthur gestured toward the friend sitting next to him, who turned out to be a comedy star named Dick Gautier. Rivers and Gautier had never met, but Rivers had copied down his routines from *The Ed Sullivan Show* and performed them so often she'd forgotten where she got them. Gautier asked her politely to stop doing his act, whereupon Arthur suggested she try writing her own.

After she had accumulated enough fresh material, she shaped it into a new act called "The Diary of Joan Rivers" and started begging anyone she knew to get her a booking. At last she wangled a gig at the Cherry Grove Hotel on Fire Island, an experience that produced a major epiphany.

"I finally found the audience that would keep me in show business until I could, so to speak, go it alone," Rivers said. "Basically, it was people who were smart, realistic, literate, up-to-date, with a taste for the camp and the outrageous—and the best of these, I learned at Cherry Grove, were the gays. There has been nothing nicer than five hundred gay faces looking up at me onstage."

Others would discern a deeper connection. "Gay people hated themselves the way Joan hated herself," said Sue Cameron, a former *Hollywood Reporter* columnist who describes herself as bisexual. "She identified with their pain, and they knew it; they were immediately in sync. They use humor to get out of their pain, and so does Joan. They make all these jokes, but inside they feel abandoned, like second-class citizens."

Some audiences were less appreciative. Rivers always felt she deserved more opportunities than she received, but many observers simply disliked what she was offering. At times they were won over by what she described as "a tremendous eagerness to please combined with hopefulness—the quality which makes puppies charming."

But others were put off, both by her style and by her substance. When *Off Broadway Reviews* assessed her performance at an engagement in a Greenwich Village club called Phase 2, the verdict was withering. "There are two main things amiss with Miss Rivers's approach: her material is tired and her delivery is frenetic…Her frantic and strained efforts are only nerve-racking and do not disguise, but rather point up, the material's essential aridity."

The gig at Phase 2 did succeed in bringing Rivers to the attention of Jack Paar's talent coordinator, and Rivers was ecstatic when he finally booked her for the television show, which was her parents' favorite. As was increasingly the case, she drew her material from the ongoing Molinsky family psychodramas.

"I told Jack Paar my mother desperately wanted me to get married, so she painted the entire kitchen pink, because she had heard pink made you look young and terrific. She even bought a pink stove and a pink refrigerator—which was true—but nothing happened for my sister and me. However, three maids ran off with A&P delivery boys," Rivers said.

She also told Paar she was dating a guy whose father was in the Mafia, and she loved going out with him because Italian men are so masculine. "You've never seen a gay Italian, because any time they turn gay, they make them into nuns. That's why so many nuns have mustaches," she said.

Jack Paar stared at her, aghast. "Do you realize Italian people are watching this show?" he asked.

After the show, the talent coordinator told her it was a good performance and they would have her back. But Paar said, "Never again. I don't believe one word she says. She's a liar."

Stunned, the talent coordinator told him, "Jack, they're jokes."

Paar replied, "We don't do jokes."

Rivers was devastated, but for once her parents were supportive. Her father wrote Paar a letter, earnestly telling him that Joan was a doctor's daughter and had gone to the finest schools and was not a liar. "He and my mother really believed that Jack Paar was their friend and once he understood that I had been telling the truth, everything would be repaired. It was so sweet," Rivers said. "They never received an answer and they never watched Jack Paar again."

As it turned out, Rivers had to leave the country to acquire some sustained experience onstage. At the end of 1960, she was included in a USO show called Broadway USA, which toured Army bases in Korea, Japan, and the Pacific Islands. "It was the first time I had ever had friendly, forgiving audiences night after night," she said. Her performing skills improved with constant practice, and by the time she arrived back in New York, she felt like a professional for the first time.

And then one night, when Hugh Downs was guest hosting *The Jack Paar Show*, the talent coordinator called her back and gave her another chance to perform on television. Unfortunately, Downs was as baffled by her sense of humor as Paar had been, and the appearance went so badly that Aunt Fanny phoned Joan's mother afterward and demanded, "When is that girl going to stop? Bea, when is she going to stop?"

"Nobody cared that I was terrific on Guam," said Rivers, who received a further blow when her sister confessed to having taken all the money Joan had sent home from overseas. Instead of depositing it in Joan's account, as she had promised to do, Barbara had used Joan's earnings to get her teeth capped. "I was a beggar again," said Rivers, who went back to office temp jobs once more.

But the following year, Rivers finally got an important break. An agent at William Morris arranged for her to audition for Second City, an improvisational comedy troupe in Chicago that began in the 1950s with such young actors as Mike Nichols and Elaine May. Its later alumni included comedic icons who ranged from John Belushi, Dan Aykroyd, Bill Murray, and Gilda Radner to Stephen Colbert. But when Rivers auditioned, she was familiar with neither improvisational techniques nor the company's work.

Foolishly, she brought her mother to her appointment, figuring it would take twenty minutes and they could go to brunch at Schrafft's afterward—only to be forced to wait for five mortifying hours while a succession of prettier girls were allowed to audition ahead of Joan. When she was finally given her chance, Rivers was startled to find that instead of being handed a script, she was told to improvise something—perhaps a description of what was actually going on in the room.

Hungry, tired, and humiliated at being treated with such disdain in front of her mother, she lost it. "My head swam with fury," she wrote in *Enter Talking*. "I had no chance to get this job, had nothing to lose, and years of accumulated hurt exploded out of me and my voice trembled with rage. 'In this room there is a cheap ugly little man sitting behind the telephone without the manners to get off and watch somebody who has been waiting five hours. And the other man, so superior, is saying, "We don't have scripts." Well, I am sorry! I didn't know you didn't use scripts. I guess I was too busy doing my rounds, trying to make a living as an actress, to know what you are doing in Chicago.'"

She went on and on, "feeling light and alive with anger and recklessness, blasting them…and who the hell did they think they were, so arrogant. I was insane now, screaming, 'I don't care about you, don't care about your goddamn show. You can go to hell'…I grabbed a glass ashtray and flung it, skidding it along the table onto the floor. Then, suddenly, I was empty. I said tiredly, 'That's what I think is happening in this room.'"

The next day, Rivers and the William Morris agent were equally astonished to learn that Second City had chosen her for the available opening in the company. But instead of being overjoyed, Rivers found herself overcome with fear. When she arrived in Chicago, she checked into her hotel and then fell apart.

"Only that night in Boston after the Show Bar had I ever cried like that—racking, heaving, convulsive sobs that went on and on till they hurt, and still I could not stop," she recalled.

She had spent so many years enduring constant rejection while continuing to insist, "I can do it!" And now, when someone finally told her, "Okay, do it," her reaction was panic, as it had been so many years earlier when she was accepted for the Westport summer theater program and found herself too afraid to go.

But this time, instead of running away from her dreams again, she pulled herself together, went to work, slowly made friends, and learned how to perform improvisational comedy—a discipline that taught her invaluable lessons which would influence her comedic style forever.

"At Second City, we worked with the reality of the moment," she explained. "In a play, if water starts dripping through the ceiling and hitting you on the head, you continue with Bernard Shaw. In real life you would stop what you are talking about and discuss the water and deal with it, and at Second City, whatever your partner did, you used it, responded to it, as you would in real life. That is one reason I talk to people in the audience—so I can work off them as a piece of reality, use them to trigger inspirations, make them into my Second City partner."

Among the most important things Rivers learned at Second City was that she hadn't been wrong to trust her instincts instead of heeding the countless naysayers who told her to give up on her dreams. "I finally in Chicago came to believe, totally—for the first time in my life—that my personal, private sense of humor, my view of the world, could make smart adults laugh," she said. "Those improvs washed away the scars of the Paar show and the awful times in front of terrible audiences... In Chicago I felt a comedy ego beginning to grow, which gave me the courage to begin tentatively looking into myself for comedy. Though I did not take my first toddler steps as a comic for another year, I was really born as a comedian at Second City. I owe it my career."

It was at Second City that Rivers began to develop the character of Rita, whom she described as a "man-hungry loser"—the desperate single girl persona that enabled her to explore many of the romantic, sexual, and marital subjects that would inform her work for decades to come.

And yet even at Second City, Rivers never really fit in. Many of her fellow company members had emerged from the University of Chicago with a cerebral comedic style that was very different from her own. "They were always accusing me of going for laughs. 'Too jokey, too jokey,' they would say," she reported. "The whole Second City intellectual snobbery made me furious—their contempt for comics in general, their scorn for me in particular because I had actually played strip joints."

But Rivers was growing stronger by the month—learning how to perform, paying her bills, making her way alone in a new city, coping with the vicissitudes of life without being constantly propped up by the ever-obliging Nick Clemente. When Christmas arrived, she was thrilled to be able to bring her family out to Chicago, treat them to dinner, take them to plays and the ballet, give them money to shop at the better stores, and even pay for their taxis.

"Of course, there was a thread of triumph in my pleasure," she admitted. "I enjoyed being in charge, proving, after all the battling about my career, that I was right and they were wrong. I loved playing the star in front of them, smiling with a becoming mix of pleasure and modesty when people in stores and on the street said, 'You're the girl from Second City, right? We enjoyed the show.'"

When her family left Chicago, Rivers gave her mother some money. Despite years of strenuous opposition to Joan's career, her mother's farewell was more sharp-eyed showbiz critique than mushy maternal gratitude. Appraising her daughter's face, Beatrice said coolly, "You've got to get your nose thinned. It doesn't work onstage."

Buoyed by her success at Second City, Rivers finally decided to go back to New York, where she assumed she would move on to greater heights—but her return proved an unexpectedly humbling experience. In Manhattan, out-of-town credits were viewed as meaningless, and nobody seemed to care that she'd been a star in Chicago.

And yet coming home to Larchmont was surprisingly pleasant, even though Rivers was nearing thirty. After a time away, she appreciated the rent-free security of her parents' house. Now that her ambitions had been validated with some real-world confirmation of her ability, her relationship with her parents improved.

The precise nature of that ability remained unclear, however; as usual, Rivers didn't really seem to fit in anywhere. "I was stalled in New York because I still had no slot," she said. "My act was too ordinary for a so-phisticated nightclub, was not slick enough for the Copacabana, was not dirty enough for strip joints, and was not ethnic enough for the Catskills. I was not like the other girls developing comedy acts, because when Ruth Buzzi, Jo Anne Worley, and Joanne Barretta came onstage, audiences knew instinctively they were funny because they looked funny—Jo Anne Worley screaming with her boas...From the first second I came onstage, audiences were confused. They did not know what to expect from a girl wearing a little black dress and a string of pearls, looking ready not for comedy, but for a date with an aging preppy."

Rivers continued to believe that "the ones with talent always make it," and that perseverance was the most crucial factor in propelling a fortunate few to the top. "To maintain success, stamina is more important than talent," she said. "You have to be a marathon runner."

Rivers's unrelenting efforts to improve her act made a big impression on her coworkers.

During the 1960s, she sometimes opened for the cabaret singer Mabel Mercer, a headliner at Downstairs at the Upstairs, the ground floor room at the New York club Upstairs at the Downstairs. David Finkle, who wrote songs and later produced a revue for the club, was struck by Rivers's unrelenting efforts to improve her act, and after she died he published some of his long-ago memories in a column that was headlined "What Joan Rivers Can Teach Us All About Work."

"She was industry armed with tape recorder," recalled Finkle, who writes a column called "The Aisle Seat" for a website on arts and politics called *The Clyde Fitch Report*. "While onstage she was the yuk-machine dynamo we all know, she was nothing but single-minded determination off...She recorded every show she did. The implication was that she listened to every session. Working so tirelessly off the audience, she never knew when an ad-lib would be eminently worth saving. Not having it caught on tape would be criminal. She might forget it otherwise."

Rivers was still trying to figure out what her kind of humor might be—a challenge compounded by the fact that men could get away with far more than women could, onstage as well as off. But her modus operandi was already clear, and the patterns she established in the 1960s would stay with her for the next half a century; until the night before she died, she regularly performed stand-up in the small clubs where she tried out new material.

Rivers brought the same enterprise to her unending quest for more exposure. "She would call me three times a day, volunteering to come on my show," said the television and radio host Joe Franklin, who had a talk show for forty-three years.

But no amount of exposure would ever be enough if the material didn't galvanize audiences, and a crucial breakthrough was provided by Lenny Bruce, the pioneering stand-up artist whose no-holds-barred approach had an explosive impact during a repressive era. By 1961, Bruce had already run afoul of the law on drug and obscenity charges—the latter for using the word "cocksucker" in a San Francisco performance.

Bruce was just getting started. In the 1964 criminal trial *People v. Bruce* in New York City, Chief Justice John Murtagh wrote that several of Bruce's performances at Café Au Go Go were "indecent, immoral, and impure" because he had used such words as "ass," "balls," "cocksucker," "cunt," "fuck," "motherfucker," "piss," "screw," "shit," and "tits" "about one hundred times in utter obscenity." Murtagh also complained about mention of Eleanor Roosevelt's "tits," Jacqueline Kennedy "hauling ass" at the moment of her husband's assassination, sexual intimacy with a chicken, the masked man Tonto and "an unnatural sex act," and Bruce having "fondled the microphone stand in a masturbatory fashion," among other offenses.

As a young woman, Rivers seemed his polar opposite. She had been bold enough to mock the social biases affecting women in settings like dinner parties:

"We have an extra man."

"Bring him!"

"He's dead."

"Bring him! We'll prop him up and say he's quiet!"

And yet Rivers was still "very priggish" at that juncture, in her private life as well as in her public persona as a comic. "My mother had taught me that a lady does not swear, does not discuss sex and bodily functions," she said. "Onstage, I never swore or did sex jokes and in private I had no vices—did not curse, smoke, or drink alcohol."

When Rivers saw Bruce perform at the Village Vanguard in 1962, the experience changed her life. He not only refused to honor the prevailing taboos—he ridiculed all of them. He made jokes about niggers, kikes, guineas, micks, and spics, and told the audience that it was only the taboos against such slurs that gave them their power and viciousness.

"His words—violent, obscene, wise, astonishing, appalling, liberating— rose and fell, paused and rushed, in musical cadenzas of blasphemy," said Rivers. On the most basic level, Bruce was "hysterically funny, with total control of his audience." But what really resonated for her was his fearlessness—and its contrast with her own uptight, anxious pretensions.

"I was seeing myself through his eyes, confronting my own hypocrisy, the way I had lived the Molinsky lie of phony riches and, while hating it, used it myself as a facade and a refuge," Rivers wrote in *Enter Talking*. "Sitting in that nightclub, breathing the hot, heavy, smoky, electric air, I saw the essential tragedy of my family—their pretense of wealth was so central to their lives, they could not ever admit the lie, even to each other, could never let down and laugh behind closed doors and say, 'Can you believe this? We haven't got a nickel and look how we're living, and everybody thinks…' Then it would have been our secret joke, our shared hoax binding us all together, and everything at home could have been wonderful."

The electrifying experience of watching Bruce onstage would revolutionize Rivers's approach toward her work. "The revelation that personal truth can be the foundation of comedy, that outrageousness can be cleansing and healthy, went off inside me like an enormous flash. It is still central to my stage performance," she said in *Enter Talking*, which was written nearly a quarter of a century later. "Hypocrisy, pretending to be something you are not, will eventually turn into lies, one lie piled on another piled on another until your life is built on quicksand—until you become my mother and my sister, who always had to be the Molinskys of Larchmont and never found a way in life based on reality, never had the foundation to be happy. That is what my act is all about. If audiences can be honest and laugh about some parts of their lives—the problems of getting older, being fat, having the child leave home, being a woman, being ordinary—then they can be honest and laugh about all parts of life."

By the time Bruce died of an overdose in 1966, he had been blacklisted by nearly every club in the United States, so fearful were their owners of being prosecuted for obscenity. But Rivers always credited him with having provided the turning point in her development as a comic, and she claimed to have stopped doing many of her usual routines from that day forward.

Even so, the journey toward the kind of honesty she aspired to achieve was halting and painful.

"Though I understood what was wrong for me, I did not grasp what was right," she said. "The truth had been clear and compelling in Lenny Bruce's mouth, but I did not realize how difficult it would be, how terrifying, to find it and say it for myself. Personal truth means to me talking about your pain, which means stripping everything away, showing all of yourself, not some corner of your life okay for audiences to see. But the risk is awesome."

For Rivers, those insights were increasingly infused with the realization that she could also use her gender in ways that would startle people. "The country was ready for something new—a woman comedian talking about life from a woman's point of view," she wrote in *Enter Talking*.

In doing so, Rivers was also acting out her own very personal drama of primal rebellion. "My mother was such a lady," she said in *Joan Rivers: Exit Laughing*. "I think my whole act is about shocking my mother—to this day."

For Rivers, Bruce certainly demonstrated how shocking a performer could be, but he gave her another gift—a message of validation that encouraged her to persevere despite constant rejection. One night when she bombed at The Bitter End, Bruce sent her a note that read, "You're right, they're wrong." Rivers was ecstatic, and from then on she carried the note around in her bra to remind her of having received such a powerful message of encouragement from an artist she idolized.

Years later, when both she and George Carlin had become major stars, Rivers told him, "You know what kept me going? Lenny Bruce came over and saw me and sent me a note: 'You're right, they're wrong!'"

Carlin replied, "He sent me the same note."

While that news must have been deflating, Rivers chose to focus on Bruce's generosity: "I think he sent it to every comedian around. How sweet, in a way."

As time went on, Carlin established a similar tradition with younger comics, whom he encouraged with his own characteristic advice: "Keep kicking them in the nuts."

Carlin's formulation was as male-centric as the comedy world itself, but it was a classic female heartbreak that supplied the final catalyst for Rivers's professional metamorphosis. Her affair with David Fitelson had ended when she married Jimmy Sanger so precipitously, but she and David met again at Joan's cousin's wedding years later—and they discovered that their feelings for each other were as strong as ever. When they renewed their relationship, it instantly became as stormy as it had always been in the past; their fights were just as epic, and the whole dynamic was so toxic that Rivers described the constant emotional uproar as "a disease."

She finally summoned the strength to break up with him yet again, but after three weeks of anguished separation, Fitelson came to the house in Larchmont, pushed his way into the living room, swore his undying love, and said he couldn't live without her. So he and Rivers got back together.

Their reunion was brief. A month later, she learned some shattering news: during the three weeks when they were separated and Fitelson realized he couldn't live without her, he had managed to impregnate someone, Rivers reported in *Enter Talking*. At long last, Rivers and the great love of her youth broke up for good.

"I have never again in my life endured such pain," she recalled. "I had lost the one man I had wholly loved. I had lost my visitor's pass into the glamour of his father's house on Morton Street filled with the theater at the topmost level, lost my best friend, lost a living piece of a precious era of my childhood, lost the object of an intense physical attraction, lost my girlish illusion that when I met the man I loved, my life from that moment would automatically be a fabulous romance forever. I was left now with an endless, desolate emptiness."

Unable to let go of every last trace of him, Rivers continued to wear a much-loved present Fitelson had given her, an old raccoon flapper coat of his father's from the 1920s. For her next performance at the Showplace, she wore it onstage and "stood there, empty, lost, fighting against tears, looking through the audience in the hope that he was there. Suddenly the terrible, raw truth came from my mouth. 'I've just broken up with somebody and I think I'm going to die.'"

She was enough of a performer to follow that up with some funny material about an affair with a married professor who impregnates his wife after getting engaged to his girlfriend. She also told a joke about the raccoon coat that became a staple of her act. Asking the audience if they liked her coat, she said it was an engagement present from her professor. "But I knew something was wrong when he told me to wear it in Jersey—during the hunting season," she said.

As the waves of laughter washed over her, Rivers felt as if a dam had broken. "I knew in that moment I had found the key," she said. "My comedy could flow from that poor, vulnerable schlep Joan Molinsky, the nerd I felt sorry for, who made me so ashamed I struggled to hide her like a retarded sister, shut away in an upstairs bedroom. At last I had become hurt enough, upset enough, angry enough to expose her onstage— and in my act from that night on, the pain kept spilling and spilling and spilling."

Joan's pain was hardly unique, as other comics readily acknowledge. "I think most of us have something terribly wrong, i.e., unhappy, inside us to go up and take the mike to start with," said Brett Butler in *Why We Laugh: Funny Women.*

"There is an element of crazy," Kathleen Madigan said. "Not like somebody you hide in the attic, but it's a very weird life to agree to. If the crazy train came, I'm on it."

For many comics, one common denominator is an unhappy childhood. "People who do this usually have to, usually because they did not get enough love from one of their parents," added Natasha Leggero in *Why We Laugh*.

"We're all dented cans, and with some of them, you open them and you get botulism," Lisa Lampanelli observed.

"I don't know any comic who hasn't had a rough time," said Judy Gold, who was six feet tall by the time she was thirteen. "We don't belong, whether it's in your family or school. I was called names my whole life— Bigfoot, Sasquatch, Orca, Yeti. There's nothing you can say to me I haven't heard. I never got hugged or kissed, or got 'Great job, Judith!' This is how we've coped our entire lives."

For such misfits, the ability to make other people laugh seemed to provide salvation. "The beaten down and stomped upon end up with a better sense of humor," said Madigan.

As Patricia Marx observed in *Stand-Up Comedians on Television*, "We laugh until we hurt; they hurt until we laugh."

"Comedy only comes from a place of tragedy or anger or being hurt," Rivers said in the documentary. "The worst thing that can happen to a comedian is to fall in love and be happy. You're screwed; get out of the business!"

Rivers believed that women were meant to get love through the one irreplaceable asset she lacked, and she never got over the unfairness of being sentenced to a life deprived of the power of physical beauty. Many female comics see that deficiency as having played a formative role in shaping their comedy. "I think that for a lot of women, comedy is compensation for not being beautiful," said the feminist film critic and author Molly Haskell. "Desperation and compensation are the two traits you find over and over again in women comics. Essentially it's an act of aggression: 'I'm going to make you love me, goddamn it!'"

"With women, a lot of it is because we hate our looks," said Lisa Lampanelli. "If you're not going to get acceptance as a sex symbol, you're going to figure out how to have a personality and say, 'Let me develop that instead of looks, so I can at least get in the game.' If you're funny, and you are making fun of yourself, you figure, I can get me before they get me. A lot of self-hate about looks drives you into doing comedy about that. Not being beautiful is way hard. I always hated my-self. If you told me I could look like Audrey Hepburn and only live till sixty, I'd say, 'Sign me up.'"

Rivers felt the same way. She knew that if she'd been gorgeous, she wouldn't have needed to make people laugh. "The very pretty little girl is not the funny little girl," she said. "Tell me one good quip that ever came out of Angelina Jolie's mouth."

Because she was funny, Rivers succeeded in building an extraordinary life of worldwide acclaim and vast wealth—but she never stopped seeing her greatest strength as a poor second best to what was really important.

*Why We Laugh: Funny Women* was released in 2013, a year before she died. The documentary opens with a quick take in which Rivers admitted that her own priorities remained, at eighty, what they had been at twenty.

"If I had to choose between funny and beautiful? Beautiful," she said.

Then she gestured dismissively, waving her perfectly manicured hand as if to banish her words so they wouldn't be overheard by the other comics who were interviewed for the film.

"Don't tell them. Fucks the whole hour," Rivers said.

## Chapter Three

# DICKS AND BALLS: BREAKING INTO THE BOYS' CLUB

When Rivers first started doing comedy, she had no illusions about the inhospitable nature of the territory. "Comedy is masculine," she said in an interview for the video documentary series *Makers: Women Who Make America*. "You're out there and you've got to be in charge. I'm a lion tamer."

Comedy had been known as a male preserve for generations. "It was always a boys' club," said Lou Alexander, who started doing stand-up in the 1950s.

Thirty years later, little had changed. "If I had twenty-six headliners a year, probably twenty-two were men," said Caroline Hirsch, who opened the comedy club Carolines in 1981. "It's a very aggressive art form, and there's nothing feminine about it."

As a result, few women even considered trying to break in. "I thought you had to be an old man in a suit telling jokes about your wife," Natasha Leggero said in *Why We Laugh: Funny Women*.

In the same documentary, Jenny Yang reduced the problem to its essence: "Stand-up comedy is all dicks and balls," she said.

Until very recently, many men viewed this state of affairs as immutable. In 2007, the late Christopher Hitchens wrote an infamous *Vanity Fair* essay called "Why Women Aren't Funny," which posited that "humor is a sign of intelligence" and offered his explanation for women's deficiency. Men have to cultivate wit to impress women enough to sleep with them,

Hitchens claimed—whereas women don't need to appeal to men that way because men already want to sleep with them.

Except for female comics, whom Hitchens described as "hefty or dykey or Jewish, or some combo of the three." He admitted that men find such women threatening: "They want them as an audience, not as rivals," he wrote.

Even for men, developing a career in stand-up was an arduous challenge. For one thing, making it meant accepting a difficult life of constant travel. "The Internet is creating new stars, but not stand-up comics," said Rick Newman, the founder of Catch a Rising Star, which helped to launch the boom in comedy clubs during the 1970s and '80s. "To be a stand-up comic, you have to get onstage and do it all the time. You can't call it in, and you can't do it periodically. You don't stay good unless you're in front of an audience."

For women, the rigors of the road were exacerbated by the barriers men maintained at every venue. "There's now a comedy club in every major city, but in the 1960s, there were only a few places down in the Village that would put on a comedian, and there were very few that would put on a woman," said Newman. "The feeling with a lot of agents and managers and network people was that women couldn't be funny. They weren't even willing to listen."

The issue wasn't simply a question of who got to perform; gender defined the very essence of what was recognized as comedy. Men wielded the power to decide what was funny, and their biases dictated the limits of what women were allowed to talk about. "People just didn't buy into their material," said Newman. "It was so prejudiced it was awful. Men could talk about masturbation, but a woman couldn't even make a bodily reference."

"It was okay for guys to discuss their dicks and blow jobs, but it was never okay for women to discuss their sexuality, even though you might be following a guy talking about his shit," said the comic Judy Gold in a panel called "Women Aren't Funny: Debunking the Myth," at the 2014 New York Comedy Festival.

*   *   *

For decades, men maintained their stranglehold on most forms of entertainment, serving as decision makers, gatekeepers, content producers, critical arbiters, and the only consumers who really counted. Fish don't know they're in water, and no one questioned the universality of "the male gaze"—a term that wasn't even coined until 1975, more than twenty years after Joan Molinsky graduated from college, when the feminist film critic Laura Mulvey articulated the concept to describe the all-pervasive ways in which the arts and popular culture were structured around the perceptions of a male viewer. As Mulvey pointed out, the male gaze depicts the world in general and women in particular from a male point of view, evaluating everything in terms of masculine tastes and attitudes.

It was many years before this insight began to influence the larger society, let alone to expand its cultural outlook to any significant degree. Until very recently, it was just a given that Hollywood only wanted to make movies aimed at young men; the male executives who controlled the decision-making process simply didn't care about other demographics—even though their stated reasons were often fallacious, as the robust box office grosses of many successful movies aimed at women and older audiences have demonstrated.

But for decades, the handful of female pioneers who dared venture into comedy were forced to play by the rules that men decreed. "The women who were funny were told exactly how and why and when they could be funny," Kathy Najimy said in *Why We Laugh*. "I'm sure there was a well of other crazy comedy, point of view, and observation inside them, but it was like, 'If you're going to be funny, it's got to be on our terms.'"

Such cultural restrictions extended to other disenfranchised segments of the population. "Whatever group is not the 'right' group, that is peripheral and therefore stereotyped by the dominant group, has to work within the stereotype," said Gloria Steinem, who was "the only girl writer" on the satirical television show *That Was the Week That Was* in the early 1960s. "Black comedians were playing off the stereotypes that gave us Stepin Fetchit, so they were presenting themselves as subservient and not smart."

Stepin Fetchit, a character known as "The Laziest Man in the World," was the stage persona of Lincoln Perry, the first black actor in history to become a millionaire. During the 1930s, Perry parlayed the character into a successful film career, but Stepin Fetchit later came to be seen as an embarrassing anachronism that perpetuated negative stereotypes of African Americans.

If the rules of comedy forced black people to downplay their intelligence and industry, women had to sacrifice their femininity. From Moms Mabley to Phyllis Diller to Totie Fields, early comediennes portrayed themselves as sexually undesirable and unattractive, fat, old, or so ridiculous as to seem like crazy bag ladies.

"The only way a woman could come to the public was to at least begin with your stereotype, and make fun of your relationship with your husband, or whatever," said Steinem, who was hoping to become a comedy writer and dating Mike Nichols when she first met Rivers during the 1960s. "You had to start with an acceptable secondary position. If women wanted to have men as an audience, they had to make it super clear that they were laughing at themselves, not at men."

Because Rivers's predecessors accepted such strictures, she found herself following a "long tradition of women comedians who hid their intellect or attractiveness to court audience acceptance," Roz Warren wrote in *Revolutionary Laughter: The World of Women Comics.*

But Rivers's deepest yearning was to be pretty, and in comedy, this presented her with a real dilemma. "Phyllis Diller was happening right before me. But even Phyllis was a caricature, and I didn't want to be a caricature," Rivers said. "I was a college graduate; I wanted to get married."

Diller was actually quite attractive in real life, but she developed a comedic persona with fright wigs, cigarette holders, and exaggerated makeup and costumes that made her look more like a deranged drag queen than a reasonably good-looking woman in her forties. The prim Barnard girl in black dress and pearls was not prepared to go that far. "Rivers, in contrast, took the spotlight as a chic, well-dressed woman who was up-front about being both smart and funny, not to mention gutsy, irreverent, and outrageous," Warren wrote.

"Joan was the first one who wasn't a clown," Judy Gold said.

Although Rivers didn't turn herself into a freak, she made other sacrifices to establish a comic identity of her own. "Joanie had a lush figure, but she used to pretend she was flat-chested, like she couldn't get a man," Lily Tomlin said in *Why We Laugh: Funny Women*.

That strategy became a hallmark of Rivers's career, and from then on much of her humor revolved around her ostensible lack of sex appeal. She was so bosomy that she subsequently underwent breast reduction surgery, but you wouldn't have guessed that from her jokes. "I was so flat, I used to put Xs on my chest and write, 'You are here,'" she claimed. "I wore angora sweaters just so the guys would have something to pet."

And this: "They show my picture to men on death row to get their minds off women."

After she married Edgar Rosenberg, Rivers continued that theme with a slew of jokes about her deficiencies as a marital sex partner, claiming that she had to write "This end up" on her chest so Edgar could tell her front from her back.

Such self-mortification wasn't required of men, according to Shelly Schultz, who booked Rivers for her first appearance on *The Tonight Show* and later became a talent manager. "Everything Joan did was about self-deprecating herself," he said. "Johnny Carson wasn't self-deprecating. Jack Benny wasn't self-deprecating. Bob Hope wasn't self-deprecating. But women felt they had to be self-deprecating."

In truth, men's views of Rivers's appeal were more varied than her act suggested. Some men shared her negative opinion. "As far as I know, nobody ever wanted to screw her," said Schultz. "I never heard anybody say, 'I sure would like to fuck that chick.'" Other men were more generous in their assessment. "I thought the young Joan Rivers was very attractive—cute and very sexy, sensual," said Larry King. "I would have dated Joan, but a lot of her humor was defensive. I don't know why she played herself as ugly, but it was her shtick."

In those days, no one commented on the fact that the concept of women's sex appeal—particularly the fixation on their breasts—was itself a creation of the male gaze, as Merrill Markoe pointed out in *Why We Laugh: Funny Women*.

"'I'm so ugly'; 'I'm so flat-chested'—that's not a female point of view. What do women care if they're flat-chested? It's only men who care if they're flat-chested," said Markoe, a television writer and stand-up comic best known for her work as the Emmy Award–winning head writer for *Late Night with David Letterman*, where she created many of the show's signature elements.

Since many men seem unable to accept humor and physical attractiveness in the same female package, some women suspect that sex appeal is so distracting that it simply overrides all other considerations in the male brain. "I've got sisters who are fucking gorgeous, and guys don't even hear you when you look that good," Brett Butler said in *Why We Laugh*.

Others suggest different reasons why men are disturbed by the combination of wit and sexual allure. "Men definitely find female comedians threatening, mostly because they think if they date you you're going to go onstage and tell everyone how small their penis is," Natasha Leggero observed.

The price women pay is often social as well as professional. "Women comedians talk about how they can't be too funny because men won't continue to date them," said Rick Newman. "No ifs, ands, or buts, men are afraid of being ridiculed. Men are very threatened about being put down in front of other people, especially when it's done with a sense of humor at their expense."

Such insecurities are deeply rooted in patriarchal culture. "If you're going to have a male-dominant system, to maintain the system, you have to teach men to dominate," Gloria Steinem said. "So they come to believe that at a minimum, control is part of masculinity."

Many studies have found that men are inordinately afraid of being mocked by women; even among high school students, being ridiculed by a woman ranks as a male's greatest fear, whereas a female's greatest fear involves being the victim of male violence.

"If women are extremely funny, even if it's just taking over the dinner table, men feel small and threatened," said Caroline Hirsch. "The woman who commands the table is in the power seat, and a lot of men can't take it."

According to Judy Gold, such dynamics help explain why gay women have flourished in comedy. "Why are there so many lesbian comics? We don't care what men think, and guys don't give a shit what we think," she said. "We don't thrive on being attractive to men. I don't need to put on lipstick and be sexy to get attention. I want attention for what I'm saying, not because I have a hot ass."

But gay or straight, women in comedy share an even more important attribute, as Helen Hong noted in *Why We Laugh*. "The one thing people don't know about female comedians is that we have balls of steel," she said. "You just can't see them. They're invisible."

That attribute emerged with striking clarity as Rivers developed her identity as a comic. But in the early days, audiences were often unimpressed despite her fierceness. "She overcame the prejudice against women, and we have to give her full credit for that. But in the beginning, when she was slugging her way to the top, I just thought she was terrible," said the gossip columnist Liz Smith. "She would hunch over in the footlights and talk to the front rows. She was famous for having no real talent, except to turn a comic phrase."

Whatever they thought of her talent, Rivers's peers were always amazed by her courage. "Joan was so bold," said Newman. "Back in the 1960s, she really was a new breed of comedian. She did a different style of comedy than women had done—in-your-face, bluntly honest. Women weren't supposed to do that kind of comedy. She truly was groundbreaking. She opened up the door—and not just for women."

"Joan not only did things women didn't do; she did things men wouldn't do," said Billy Eichner, the creator and star of the comedy game show *Billy on the Street*. "She was more fearless than most."

As time passed, Rivers's hapless-little-girl persona began to evolve in new ways. "Back when she was doing clubs in the Village, I always thought of her as a female Woody Allen, because she was so self-deprecating and so vulnerable and so Jewish," said Cary Hoffman, the longtime owner of the comedy club Stand Up NY. "That was before she broke the barrier of feeling free to say anything about anybody. People started doing esoteric intellectual comedy, and Joan was the first woman to go in that direction. Totie Fields would do a stereotypical dumb blonde joke, doing sign language, but Joan was taking a different, more intellectual approach."

She was also learning how to channel her aggression as an effective tool. "I was against putting women on in late shows, because many females could not handle the drunken audiences as well as a male could," Hoffman said. "Stand-up is first of all about controlling an audience, before you get a laugh. But Joan learned how to control them. Even seeing her on *Ed Sullivan*, I was amazed at her power."

As Rivers developed her comedic persona, she broke fresh ground in other areas. "Rivers did something new: she spoke the truth about women's feelings," Roz Warren wrote in *Revolutionary Laughter*. "For the first time, a woman comic revealed what women really thought and felt. Rivers talked about all the secrets women usually kept hidden, making audiences laugh at such taboo topics as having an affair, going to the gynecologist, having a baby, and faking orgasms. Tame by today's standards, a joke like 'When I had my baby, I screamed and screamed—and that was just during conception' both shocked and delighted sixties audiences."

"She talked about sex and about women in a way that, for its time, felt tremendously edgy," said Billy Eichner. "She talked about withholding sex, about not having sex, about not liking sex. Men had been whining about their wives for many years—'Take my wife, please!'—but Joan turned that on its ear and you saw things from the woman's point of view. This was a new tone."

But integrating a woman's perspective into a male world proved endlessly challenging. In the early 1960s, Rivers briefly dealt with the gender problem by joining forces with Jim Connell and Jake Holmes in a new comedy act called Jim, Jake, and Joan. At their first meeting, Rivers said, "Who's going to play Joan?"

"When nobody laughed, I should have realized we were in trouble," she observed in *Enter Talking*. The trio started performing as an opening act for the Simon Sisters, a folksinging duo featuring Carly Simon and her sister Lucy. Although Jim, Jake, and Joan eventually became headliners at The Bitter End, Rivers disliked what she saw as their "sophomoric humor," and she wasn't particularly enamored of her partners either. "We began to realize that we did not like each other very much," she reported.

When she left the act, she asked Freddie Weintraub, the manager who had put it together, if he would continue to manage her alone, but he refused. "I don't see you ever making it as a single," he said.

After years of knocking on doors, Rivers was still receiving such verdicts with dismaying regularity. Shelly Schultz had seen her in Jim, Jake, and Joan, but when she auditioned for *The Tonight Show*, he gave her "the standard brush-off: 'Thank you, but your material is just not right for us,'" Rivers reported. When she persisted, he told her, "We just don't think you'd work on TV."

Rivers finally persuaded an agent named Roy Silver to come see her perform at The Duplex, and afterward Silver called a friend at William Morris to ask why she couldn't get an agent. "Because everyone has seen her. She's been on the Paar show twice, and there's absolutely no interest in her anywhere," the William Morris agent said.

That view was widely shared. After Irvin Arthur saw Rivers at The Duplex, she pestered him to tell her what he thought until he finally said, "What can I tell you? You're too old. Everybody's seen you. If you were going to make it, you would have done it by now."

Rivers was crushed, but as he turned to leave the club, Arthur added, "Hey, I could be wrong. I told the same thing to Peter, Paul, and Mary."

Although Rivers refused to give up, she did hedge her bets by securing a paycheck with steady work as a writer. Getting hired by ABC's *The Phyllis Diller Show* seemed like a coup until Diller dropped out of the show. After that, Rivers found another job, with Allen Funt's *Candid Camera*.

And then one day Roy Silver called to tell her that Shelly Schultz had agreed to put her on with Carson. After seven years of banging her head against a very hard wall, and after auditioning for and being rejected by *The Tonight Show* seven different times (or eight, as she sometimes claimed), Rivers finally got the crucial break that turned her into an overnight success on February 17, 1965.

For comedians then and for decades to come, *The Tonight Show Starring*

*Johnny Carson* was the holy grail. When Carson began his thirty-year run as host of *The Tonight Show* in 1962, the show quickly became an all-important launching pad for aspiring comedians as well as the template for a new kind of television programming.

"Johnny Carson didn't invent late-night TV, but he might as well have," explained Carson's obituary in *USA Today* when he died in 2005. "For it was his *Tonight Show* that perfected the art of wee hours talk, comedy, and music, setting a gold standard punctuated by his genius for effortlessly wringing a laugh out of a well-chosen grimace or tie-straightening gesture…He made stand-up comics' careers with a mere gesture, a 'Nice stuff' compliment that spoke volumes, or an invitation to come sit and chat. Jerry Seinfeld, Roseanne Barr, David Letterman, and Carson's successor, Jay Leno, among many others, vaulted to stardom by warming his couch."

In Rivers's various accounts of her history, she always stressed the long, uphill battle to get on *The Tonight Show,* and she often credited Bill Cosby with having suggested that Carson book her. That version is not accurate, according to Schultz. "I don't think the idea of revisionist history is unique to Joan Rivers, but Joan made up these tales," he said. "Here's the bad news: they catch up with you sooner or later. Joan said that here's how she got on *The Tonight Show:* Bill Cosby was on as a guest, there was a comic on the show who died, and Bill leaned over to Johnny and said, 'Joan Rivers could do better—why don't you put her on?' That never happened. Joan just wanted to associate herself with Bill's comedy persona. She was the queen of changing history. She never saw history as a succession of events as they were. She always rewrote history with her own idea of how she succeeded."

According to Schultz, Roy Silver, who managed both Cosby and Rivers, persuaded him to take a look at Cosby. When Schultz booked him on *The Tonight Show,* the young black comic was a huge success. "He was so likable, so cute, you just wanted to embrace him as a person," Schultz said.

"Then Roy called me again and said, 'Come see this chick Joan Rivers—she's funny.' And she was adorable. She was homely and plain, but she had some funny stuff, and you couldn't help but like her. She had the same quality Cosby had. There's a word in Yiddish—*haimish*—that means humane, or warm. She was *haimish*. So I came back to *The Tonight Show* and said, 'Roy Silver has this girl, a goofy little broad from Brooklyn.'"

According to Schultz, he then helped to shape Rivers's debut in a process that was standard operating procedure. "The way we worked on *The Tonight Show* was this: nobody just came on," he said. "The interview was written. The response by the guest was written. The retort by Johnny was written. This was a fail-safe show. So I brought Joan in and worked with her to prepare her spot. A stand-up spot is six minutes, and she had a hodgepodge of material, so I said, 'Take this out. Put this in.' Show night comes a couple of nights later, she comes on and she kills them—destroys them. She was so good Johnny waved her over to sit down."

Whatever the differences in their recollections, all concerned agree that when Rivers finally got a shot on the show, everything clicked. She was introduced as a girl writer, her chemistry with Carson was immediately apparent, all her material worked, and those few minutes changed her life forever. By the time she finished her appearance, Carson was wiping his eyes. "He said, right on the air, 'God, you're funny. You're going to be a star,'" Rivers marveled afterward.

By the next day, she was. "Rivers Stay Near Our Door" was the headline in an effusive column by Jack O'Brian in the *Journal-American*. "Johnny Carson struck gleeful gold again last night with Joan Rivers, another comedy writer who was an absolute delight," O'Brian wrote. "Her seemingly offhand anecdotal clowning was a heady and bubbly proof of her lightly superb comic acting; she's a gem."

And suddenly, the endless struggle was finished. A lifetime of battling against the people who told her no, who said she couldn't do it, who thought she wasn't good enough—all the rejections and hardships wiped away as if by a magic wand. "Ten minutes on television, and it was all over," Rivers said.

That single appearance produced a "miraculous, instantaneous career turnaround" that transformed Rivers from a pitiable never-was has-been into a hot new star anointed by King Carson.

Her success stood out in other ways as well. "It's very hard in the world of comedy to become a star without a vehicle," said Cary Hoffman, who became a talent manager after a long career as a comedy club owner. "Robin Williams would have had a hard time becoming a star without *Mork & Mindy* and *Good Morning, Vietnam*. For Ray Romano, it was *Everybody Loves Raymond*. Without a vehicle, it's just you and a microphone and your thoughts. But Joan never did her own sitcom. She never did a great film. The vehicle was Joan. And Joan became a star."

Rivers's auspicious debut launched an enduring relationship with *The Tonight Show*, which served, for many years, as the foundation for her burgeoning career. Carson—the white-bread all-American boy from Iowa and Nebraska, a user-friendly WASP who epitomized genial Midwestern masculinity—proved the perfect foil for Rivers's edgier, far more ethnic comedic persona. A few years later, when Rivers was trying to broaden her national profile, agents at William Morris told her she was "too New York" and "too Jewish" to succeed in the heartland. But on *The Tonight Show*, Carson was the consummate straight man, and the combination of his easy paternal affability and Rivers's jittery, eager neuroticism worked brilliantly whenever the two performed together.

At a lunch interview with me, Shelly Schultz described Rivers's appeal in the early days of her career. "Joan knew nothing about show business. How green was she?" He held up a piece of asparagus from his plate and wiggled it. "But she knew what she wanted to be, and she was very determined, and she was funny, and she was sweet. She didn't look like a bitter old chick. She was always creating new stuff; she was very prolific. So we'd create a spot, and she never bombed—not even close. She always came on with fresh stuff."

When Henry Bushkin first met Johnny Carson, they went to see Rivers perform. "She was appearing in a little club, and he wanted to go see it," said Bushkin, who became Carson's lawyer and was one of his best friends for nearly two decades. "That's when I first met her. She was demure, wearing her little black dress, and it almost looked as if her hair was ironed."

Rivers invited Carson to join her onstage, where their easy banter proved that their comedic chemistry wasn't confined to the television studio. "He had been drinking, and he went up and they did a few bits onstage, and it was terrific," said Bushkin. "There was some sexual innuendo: she said, 'I'm using the coil now.' Johnny says, 'A coil?' She says, 'It's the new birth control device.' He says, 'Does it work?' She says, 'Yes, but every time Edgar and I have sex, the garage door opens.' That was the early Joan. It's not the nasty Joan. She was almost happy. She didn't strike me as attractive at all, but I thought Johnny really liked her as a person, and thought she was a terrific comedienne. There was nothing other than great like for her."

But if Carson was generous about his protégé's growing success, other members of the boys' club failed to rejoice at the sudden ascent of a female rival. "They were hostile because they didn't want competition," Schultz explained. "Comics are difficult guys who are very competitive. They dis each other, and they're more competitive with women. A woman comes in and presents herself with a different persona, and she stands out. A chick like Joan Rivers comes on, gets on *Johnny Carson*, and explodes. These guys who've been banging around for fifteen years are really pissed off. 'That ain't funny! What's funny about that?' It's funny because it's coming from a young woman, and she's delivering it, but it's a very hostile environment. It's like being on the road with ISIS: they also want to cut your neck off."

Would-be rivals weren't the only men who expressed their hostility. For the careers of female comics, the cost of male resistance is impossible to quantify, but its toll can be discerned in lost opportunities, critical double standards, wage gaps, and other professional obstacles. For Rivers, the penalties also included an ugly threat of violence from Jerry Lewis, one of the biggest names in comedy.

For nearly sixty years, Jerry Lewis hosted an annual Labor Day telethon to benefit the Muscular Dystrophy Association. After observing that the long-running event had been good for Lewis's career, Rivers offended the legend by voicing her revulsion at the way he used the children's disabilities as fodder for his own melodramatic histrionics.

"He was standing there with a child next to him saying, 'This kid is gonna die.' And I said, 'I will never do this telethon again,'" Rivers said. "You do not say in front of a little boy who is going to die, 'This child is going to die.' Who are you? You unfunny lucky, stupid asshole."

Enraged, Lewis responded by sending her a letter that read, "We've never met and I'm looking forward to keeping it that way. If you find it necessary to discuss me, my career, or my kids ever again, I promise you I will get somebody from Chicago to beat your goddamned head off."

Lewis added a postscript: "You do know that you're not allowed to threaten people. So if you go to [the police], show them this letter, they'll arrest me. But I want you to never forget what it said. Here's the number of the police chief of Las Vegas. Call him if you want to!"

For once, Rivers was scared into silence. "Done. Never talking about him again! I don't want to have my knees broken over Jerry Lewis," she told one interviewer. "Do you understand you can be arrested for that? That is a real threat. We hired guards, my husband and I, and we didn't take him to court…My last words are not gonna be 'But I was only kidding.' You're not happy, you want me to shut up? I'll shut up. Fine!"

But Lewis neither forgave Rivers nor forgot his threat, which he brought up many years later in a 2014 SiriusXM Town Hall interview with Maria Menounos. "I always feel bad when somebody passes away— except if it was Joan Rivers," he said. "She set the Jews back a thousand years."

Despite Rivers's promise, she proved characteristically unable to keep her mouth shut. When Anderson Cooper mentioned Lewis's warning on CNN, Rivers said, "Well, when did we last laugh at Jerry Lewis? Look, the French think he's funny. Those idiots."

On another occasion, she added, "I don't think there's ever been a female comic who's liked Jerry Lewis."

When Rivers began her career, the disdain of such male titans could prove an insurmountable barrier to women's success. By the time she died, female comics were able to shrug it off as irrelevant.

Tina Fey summed up the prevailing attitude in her 2011 best seller, *Bossypants*. "Whenever someone says to me, 'Jerry Lewis says women aren't funny,' or 'Christopher Hitchens says women aren't funny…Do you have anything to say to that?'" she wrote. "Yes. We don't fucking care if you like it."

Performers aren't the only ones who have changed; so have audiences—and neither feels compelled to defer to the dictates of condescending men. Armed with economic autonomy and the freedom to make their own choices about how to spend their money and time, women have created a growing demand for content very different from the male-centered entertainment that prevailed when Rivers was young.

"I don't give a fuck whether the men think we're funny. Women think we're funny," said Blair Breard at the panel "Women Aren't Funny: Debunking the Myth."

The executive producer of the Louis C.K. show *Louie*, Breard added, "I write content for me. We control the money, and we control the content."

In *Why We Laugh: Funny Women*, Whoopi Goldberg passed along some words to live by for the next generation. "The best advice ever given to me was 'Fuck 'em if they can't take a joke,'" she said.

## Chapter Four

# STARDOM AND WIFEDOM: HAPPILY EVER AFTER?

The early months of 1965 made Rivers into a success, erasing all the professional disappointments that had dogged her for more than a decade. To her astonishment, the second half of that same year made her romantic dreams come true as well—and once again Johnny Carson's *Tonight Show* provided the means to a fairy-tale ending.

Most women don't envision Prince Charming as short, stocky, bespectacled, pretentious, and middle-aged, but for Rivers at thirty-two, Edgar Rosenberg was the willing, appropriate Jewish husband she'd spent the last decade searching for—the answer to her mother's most fervent prayers.

Although his actual job was in public relations, Edgar fancied himself as an independent producer, and he was working with Peter Sellers to develop a movie about a traveling clown. When the script needed a rewrite, Edgar asked *The Tonight Show* to recommend a comedy writer. He and Rivers were introduced, and Edgar took her and her manager to lunch at an elegant French restaurant. Then he set up another meeting to discuss the script, arrived in a limousine, and whisked Rivers off to the Four Seasons.

Ever her mother's daughter, she was deeply impressed with Edgar's British accent, his incessant name-dropping, his Cambridge education, and his personal style. "I could see that this forty-year-old winner producer in a Dunhill blue suit and Lanvin shirt had class—a classy way of talking, a classy way of dressing," she said.

Edgar also seemed very successful, at least to Rivers: "He was producing five movies for the United Nations and was Mr. Big—called Monsieur Le Patron on the movie set in France, telephoned by the likes of Cary Grant, Ava Gardner, Sean Connery, and Joe Mankiewicz."

Such credentials were somewhat misleading. Eight years older than Rivers, Edgar worked as an employee at a public relations firm where he handled accounts that ranged from the Rockefeller brothers to Encyclopedia Britannica. After convincing the *Today* show to do on-location broadcasts that promoted such products as scuba diving equipment made by a client of his, Edgar came up with the idea of creating a series of television movies about the United Nations. He convinced his boss, Anna Rosenberg (who was not related to Edgar), to let him form a production company called the Telsun Foundation, and he persuaded such stars as Yul Brynner, Peter Sellers, Edward G. Robinson, Rita Hayworth, Eva Marie Saint, and Marcello Mastroianni to participate.

To Rivers, such names were dazzling, and she was even more impressed when Edgar invited her to work on the clown script with him and another writer at a Caribbean resort where Sellers was supposed to join them after a few days. "I was thrilled," said Rivers.

But nothing in her background had prepared her to deal with such jet-set getaways. When she arrived at Round Hill, "an incredibly posh enclave of cottages" in Jamaica, she was embarrassed to realize she had packed inappropriately: instead of breezy beach cover-ups and sandals, she had brought sweaters with pleated skirts, panty girdles, and stockings with matching leather pumps and bags.

The other guests, Joe Mankiewicz's son and his wife, soon had a fight and left, and Sellers and the second writer were both waylaid by other plans. So Rivers found herself unexpectedly alone with her host, whom she continued to address as Mr. Rosenberg.

But Mr. Rosenberg seemed oddly uninterested in working on the job at hand, which puzzled her. Rivers was very eager to prove herself as a screenwriter, so she tried to behave like a professional associate rather than a date—which seemed appropriate, since Edgar made no physical overtures or even verbal expressions of warmth. And yet she did enjoy his dry sense of humor and his erudition, which was intimidating: "He had seen everything, heard everything, read everything, and, worse, retained everything," she said.

Rivers also felt a deeper sense of connection. "There in Jamaica the British public school accent and reserve came off as courtliness, an elegance that was extremely appealing because it reminded me of my mother and was what she wished she had married," she observed.

Looking back, she recognized that Edgar sensed an equally profound kinship with her. "He understood right away what my life was all about, knew that the mouthy girl onstage was not the real me, knew the real me wanted to live well and have beautiful things," Rivers wrote in her second autobiography, *Still Talking*. "I realize now that he understood because he had the same dream, the same consuming obsession with show business and success—and the same insecurity and hunger for respect. He had spotted a soul mate."

On her third day in Jamaica, Rivers went for a swim and then returned to her room, whereupon Edgar appeared in the doorway. "Suddenly, when I saw him, I had a deep sense of well-being, of coming home, a certainty that he was what I had been looking for, that this was absolutely right! Yes, so quickly," she said. "It was as if…in a split second, with one step forward, we went from absolutely nothing to everything. We made love, and then, as though it were the natural order of events, he proposed and I accepted. Everything fit. Here was a man I could trust, who was going to take care of me. We were a good match—he gave me class, I gave him warmth. We filled each other's gaps—he was the intelligent one with the English accent, and I was the performer, full of the fun he did not know how to have."

Believing that they had found their destiny, the new couple rushed headlong into commitment without giving themselves any time to get to know each other. Rivers convinced herself that all signs were auspicious: when she brought her betrothed home to Larchmont to meet her parents, Edgar and her mother got along immediately. "They were both formal and set great store by dignity. They were loners who had almost no friends and trusted very few people. They wanted the finer things. As

Edgar used to say, 'We're both snobs.' I was about to marry my mother,"
Rivers concluded.

Even by the clichéd standards of whirlwind romance, they formalized
a shared future with dizzying speed. Three days after they returned from
Jamaica, Rivers and Rosenberg were wed by a judge in a Bronx court-
house, where Rivers wore a twenty-six-dollar dress from Bloomingdale's.

Years later, Rivers marveled at how surreal those events seemed and
how much she had changed since then. Looking back at herself as a
giddy bride, she admitted that she felt "absolutely no relationship to
that girl. She still believed in happy endings," Rivers observed wryly.
"She was naive about the treachery, about the pitfalls, the backbiting, the
meanness, the stupidity in big-time show business. The success that was
happening for her seemed absolutely right and logical. She had worked
hard and, by God, was a rising star with a wonderful, successful husband.
Well, the movie should have ended there."

Real life turned out to be vastly more complicated than the romantic
mythology that shaped Rivers's dreams, in which Prince Charming provides the solution to all of a girl's questions about the meaning of life.
During their twenty-two years together, Rivers and Rosenberg presented
a solidly united front to the world, and she was unwavering in her support
of her husband. It was only after his death that she admitted the fateful
truth she recognized far too late: that the seeds of their destruction were
an integral part of their relationship from the outset.

"Looking back, I think Edgar and I were, from the beginning, headed
for tragedy," she wrote in *Still Talking*.

They first bonded over their shared interests, and on paper the new
couple seemed to have a great deal in common. Both were so driven to
succeed in show business that their hunger resembled an addiction—but
their underlying needs were very different.

Rivers was eternally propelled by her insatiable need for approval—
and she didn't require a psychiatrist to explain where that came from. She
spelled it out very clearly in *Still Talking*.

She had always felt emotional distance from her father, whom she saw
as perpetually too busy to pay attention to his children. But it was her

mother's lack of demonstrativeness that imbued such a hunger for visible affirmation in Joan.

"My mother, Beatrice, a formal, queenly woman, was my rock of security, always there for me, solid, always taking my side, defending me, totally loyal. Her children, by God, were the best. If she saw any faults in me and Barbara, nobody heard about them. I adored her," Rivers wrote. "But her love could not come out as tenderness. There were no loving arms encircling us. I remember reaching over and touching my mother's hand in the theater. I do not remember her ever touching mine. Her love was expressed as worry, making sure Barbara and I had everything we should—education, good manners, know-how in society, the right clothes. I was a disappointment to her. She could not understand why I wanted to be an actress. In her mind I should be like my sister, Barbara...My mother did not realize my need for the love and approval that can well up from an audience."

For Rivers, performing satisfied her deepest cravings. "Show business is the ultimate wish fulfillment, the dream of being eternally beautiful, eternally talented, eternally loved, and wealthy," she said in *Still Talking*. "Once you've had that, you spend the rest of your life trying to keep it coming."

When Rivers met Edgar, he also seemed to be "hooked into that high," she observed. "Edgar was launched into production at the top, and he chased that feeling for the rest of his life."

But it wasn't approval that Rosenberg sought. Born in Bremerhaven, Germany, where his father owned a butcher shop, Edgar and his family spent much of his childhood fleeing from the Nazis, first to Hamburg, then to Copenhagen, and finally to South Africa. The fears, losses, and chronic insecurity he endured in childhood shaped his adult life in ways that his wife understood only in retrospect.

"Whereas my show business addiction is drinking in love on a stage, his drug was to be the boss, answering to no one," she explained in *Still Talking*. "At the time I believed he was simply a strong, take-charge person, but ultimately events turned that need into a flaw that brought us both down. I think Edgar craved control because he had such a hard time handling uncertainty. And I believe the reason lay in his past. Whenever a goal had been in his grasp, it had been yanked away."

Stiff, formal, and aloof, Rosenberg maintained such emotional distance that he hid a critical chapter of his past, even from his wife. It was only in the six months before he died that Rivers learned he had suffered from tuberculosis as a boy in Cape Town. Highly contagious, the disease carried a terrible social stigma until the years following World War II, when antibiotics finally provided an effective treatment. As a child, Edgar had been ashamed as well as bereft when he was exiled to a sanitarium and then nursed and educated at home. His memories of that time were so painful that when he finally shared them with Joan at the end of his life, he begged her not to tell their college-age daughter how traumatic his experience had been.

As the coddled son of a doting mother and her housekeeper, who disapproved of him having a wife, Edgar didn't marry until he was forty. After he met Rivers, he continued to work as a producer, but he soon became her unofficial manager as well.

"Edgar was a tiger for details, and I was not," she said. "Throughout our life together, he ran the business side—balanced my checkbook, filled out the checks for me to sign, picked my photographs, answered the mail, met with the accountants, invested the money that was starting to come in, handled the bank transfers. So I would not be upset and distracted, he solved problems he never told me about. He protected me by reading all the contracts, and amazed the lawyers by spotting the weaknesses...He trusted no one."

As Rosenberg assumed more control over Rivers's career, the arrangement seemed to work for both of them. "The bigger I became, the more power he, as my husband, wielded behind the scenes," she said. "My career became us. Success in life equaled success in my career, and Edgar and I knew how to build my career, but we arrived at our heights in the grip of our pasts. Edgar was driven by his need to prove himself a major player. I was driven by my insecurity, my need to be loved, my easily hurt feelings, my obsession with loyalty, and my need to win. We were united by the anger that waited in both of us, the rage at accumulated half-remembered injuries that set us side by side against the world."

But even in the early days, Rosenberg often alienated people inadvertently. Rivers performed regularly at Downstairs at the Upstairs, and they enjoyed hanging out at the club, but Edgar wasn't popular with his wife's colleagues. "Edgar was the tough one, and the impression I got was that they didn't like him, because he was very demanding," said David Finkle, who also spent time at the Downstairs, as a songwriter and producer. "People like that get the reputation for being difficult from people who are less good at their jobs. I think Edgar was the hatchet man for Joan even then, and I guess she thought, 'This is the kind of person I need to help me get where I want to get.' But he probably was nastier than he needed to be. He was obviously a depressed guy."

Lou Alexander observed the same dynamic. "People I knew who met him didn't care for him," Alexander said. "He had an attitude. He came on very strong. He had to be the bad guy."

As Rivers's friends and associates got to know Edgar, many were surprised by her choice of mate. "I never got it," said Sandy Gallin, who first met Rivers in the early 1960s and later became her manager while she was living in California. "Joan was really smart, and Edgar, I thought, pretended to be smart. He was a star's husband, but he wanted people to think he was a very big producer and had a very big past as a producer in London. I never believed his made-up background. He had this accent, and he was always dressed in his blazer and tie, and it was like, oh my God, you gotta be kidding. I felt sorry for him."

Some industry veterans were openly derisive. "Everyone knew Edgar was full of shit. They would laugh about it," said one.

If Rivers was convinced by Edgar's affectations of class, others found them far less persuasive. "He was a Jewish guy who tried to look like a fancy elegant pompous British guy, but he was in way over his head—way out of his league," said Mark Simone, a longtime New York radio personality who had Rivers on his show "like, four hundred times."

The pros at *The Tonight Show* were equally unimpressed. "She needed a guy, but when she came up with this guy, I almost shit," said Shelly

Schultz. "When she brought him over to the show one night, everyone held their head like a massive migraine went through the staff. He was this short guy—shorter than her—and he was pretentious. He had kind of an unpleasant persona. He was arrogant. He was just not likable. She was kind of giddy—to her, he was Marlon Brando—but we looked at her and said, 'Is she kidding?' This guy had zero going on. He wasn't even funny, which is the biggest crime of all. Be an asshole, but be funny. But he was just an asshole. And he was a total fucking fraud. They said he was a businessman. Guess what business? Nobody knows. She said he was a producer. She was rewriting history. He was a producer of what? We never learned that. Nobody knew who he was. Between us, on the staff, we had a hell of a reach. There were seven writers, three or four talent coordinators—and none of us knew him. None of us ever heard of him in the context Joan described. It was bullshit."

Edgar soon developed an annoying tendency to interfere with the process at hand. To a busy staff trying to put on a show—whether onstage at the Downstairs or on the air at NBC—Edgar's need to control the minutiae of his wife's career was simply exasperating, and many coworkers were doubly infuriated by what they saw as his lack of competence. "There was a line somebody wrote back then—it may have been me," Schultz said. "We decided that Edgar could fuck up a two-car funeral." He raised a hand as if unrolling a sign across his forehead: "F-u-c-k u-p!"

Edgar's old-fashioned formality also seemed out of place in an era when Frank Sinatra and his jaunty Rat Pack personified masculine cool with their sly, knowing bad boy humor and sexual savoir faire. In the jaded, cynical precincts of the entertainment world, Edgar seemed more like the pompous, incompetent detective played by Peter Sellers in the Pink Panther movies.

Henry Bushkin, who published a memoir in 2013 called *Johnny Carson*, is developing the book into a musical whose characters include both Rivers and Rosenberg. "I refer to Edgar in the play as Inspector Clouseau," Bushkin said.

Although they eventually fell out, Carson considered Bushkin his best friend for many years and often joked about Bombastic Bushkin in his monologues on *The Tonight Show*. But even to Bombastic Bushkin, Edgar seemed pretentious and self-important.

"Edgar was a strange man," said Bushkin, who also served as Rivers's lawyer for a time. "Everything with Edgar would be, like, hush-hush, top secret, cloak-and-dagger, but you're making everything far more important than it really is. He was British, fastidiously so, with the cigarette holder and the whole nine yards, but he was strange-looking, and he had these weird, big spectacles. I think Joan was one of the smarter show business people; she didn't miss a trick. But it was hard to reconcile how funny she was onstage with how dull he was. I always thought they were very pleasant as a couple—it was certainly my impression that they liked one another—but we wondered what she saw in this guy."

Barbara Walters, a good friend of Rivers, was equally unimpressed. "I never found Edgar particularly appealing, and he was certainly not a great talent," she said. "The appeal of Edgar was that he wanted to marry her."

Many observers attributed Rivers's decision to the pressures imposed by her religious and ethnic background. "I thought, here's a Jewish chick from Brooklyn who's basically a two-feet-on-the-ground kind of person," Schultz said, "but even though she's starting to have some success, she still needs a guy in her life, because that's just the history of the Jewish family: get married! You're not a success until you have a family. When you come from a very middle-class Jewish family, the mentality is such that when she brought Edgar home, her mother said, 'Oh, perfect—Joan, don't let this one get away!' He wasn't a glamorous guy; he wasn't a wise guy. He was a short Jew who professed his love—a Jewish mother's dream."

Deeply impressed by her new husband, Rivers seemed oblivious to such caustic opinions. She saw her marriage as an advantageous match that rescued her from a life of discouragement and deprivation—"living in a dinky struggle apartment over a deli, wearing struggle clothes," as she put it.

Having achieved her two most important goals, Rivers enjoyed the second half of the 1960s as "a sweet, happy time." She relished her status as the producer's wife, meeting people like David Niven and

Rudolf Nureyev through her husband and going to parties on Sam Spiegel's yacht in Monaco. In return, Rosenberg drove her to gigs in the Catskills and hung out at the Stage Delicatessen after her New York City performances, sharing sandwiches at 4 a.m. with Rodney Dangerfield, Dick Cavett, George Carlin, Dom DeLuise, and Jerry Stiller and Anne Meara.

She and Edgar lived in an apartment on Fifth Avenue, and her career was flourishing; she appeared on *The Tonight Show* once a month or so, going on anytime she called up to say she was ready. She hired Dangerfield to help her write new jokes.

Her only problem was that her new and improved life deprived her of the usual fount of material about frustration and disappointment. Domestic chores were a reliable source of shtick, but that wasn't enough to sustain a career. "My act is complaining about my life, and in those years I was content," Rivers said. "There was no humor in being happy and having a terrific husband."

Turning from desperate-single-girl jokes to clueless-married-woman jokes, Rivers told her audiences that she wore a nightgown with feet to bed on her wedding night. She said she knew nothing about sex because all her mother had told her was that the man gets on top and the woman goes underneath—"so I bought bunk beds."

As innocuous as such jokes were, "people were shocked," Rivers reported. "I was breaking new comedy ground with talk about women's intimate experiences and feelings, with jokes like, 'I have no boobs. I went to nurse my daughter. She sucked on my shoulder. I moved her to the breast and she lost four pounds.' But compared to the standards of today, my act then was extremely mild."

The atmosphere of the time was so repressive that *The Ed Sullivan Show*, where Rivers also performed regularly, forbade her to use the word "pregnant" on the air—even when she was obviously expecting a baby. In that era, many female teachers were forced out of their jobs when their pregnancies became apparent, and pregnancy discrimination hadn't yet become a legal issue that transformed employment practices, as it would years later. The prevailing cultural mores decreed that it was unseemly to mention a woman's pregnancy, or even to allow the public—let alone schoolchildren—to see any evidence of it.

When Rivers got pregnant, she wrangled with Sullivan over mentioning her condition on the air, but he wouldn't budge. She finally had to compromise with the silly line "Soon I'm going to be hearing the pitter-patter of tiny feet," as if her infant would scamper out of the womb wearing ballet slippers.

Since marrying Edgar, Rivers had morphed from a career-obsessed single girl into a contented wife, and she became an equally doting mother when Melissa arrived in 1968. Her desire for a child had come as a surprise: "Edgar had shown no interest in having a child during the first two years of our marriage. I was caught up in my career and had never been the one who went 'Kitchy koo' to that baby in the park... I did not reinvite people who brought their kids over," she wrote in *Still Talking*.

But marriage had not satisfied her unfulfilled emotional needs. "My mother was wonderful, but basically cold," Rivers said. "My father was preoccupied. Edgar was not a sponge for love. I was a touchy-feely person surrounded by repression."

Having a baby seemed to offer the opportunity to love unconditionally as well as to be loved in return, and when she got pregnant, Edgar was also thrilled. "He loved seeing me so happy, and I think, too, he was proud of this proof of his manhood," Rivers observed.

A child provided another vehicle for living out her dreams, and Rivers bequeathed her mother's preoccupation with class to her daughter by choosing a middle name that signified wealth. "She was Melissa Rosenberg," Sue Cameron said. "The Warburgs were one of the most moneyed Jewish families in Europe, so Joan put 'Warburg' in."

Her new status as wife and mother seemed to fulfill all her most cherished expectations. "My career had not yet become the glue that held my life and marriage together," Rivers said in *Still Talking*. "The rock at the center of my tiny universe was still the baby and the home and the marriage."

She felt very fortunate—and for a while, what she had seemed like enough. "I hate to be corny—but I'm so happy!" Rivers told *TV Guide*.

But the change in circumstances required Rivers to update her material, so marital sex became a new staple of her act. Her punch lines had always revolved around her own deficiencies: "My body is so bad, a Peeping Tom looked in the window and pulled down the shade." As a married woman, she focused on Edgar's ostensible lack of carnal interest in his wife: "Before we make love, my husband takes a painkiller," she claimed.

Marriage hadn't solved the underlying problem: "I have no sex appeal," Rivers said. "If my husband didn't toss and turn, we'd never have had a kid."

Her weight was an ongoing theme: "I stepped out of the shower the other day and my husband called me 'Fat, fat, the water rat.'"

And yet there was often a curious disconnect between Rivers's jokes about her sexual ignorance and the promiscuity she alluded to before her marriage. Sometimes her humor was directed outward, skewering the sexual double standards that allowed men so much more latitude than women. "A man sleeps around—no questions asked," she said. "But if a woman makes nineteen or twenty mistakes, she's a tramp."

At other times, she was more explicit about being a sexually liberated single woman. During the early 1960s, her stand-up routine often closed with the punch line "I'm Joan Rivers, and I put out!"—a shocking claim at a time when the sexual revolution was just beginning to gather steam and hypocrisy remained the requisite posture for young women who were supposed to remain virgins until their wedding day.

Rivers usually made herself the butt of such jokes, but Edgar was occasionally relegated to the role of sucker. "When the rabbi said, 'Do you take this man,' fourteen guys said, 'She has,'" Rivers claimed. "My husband bought the horseback riding story, thank God."

As the sixties got under way, Rivers wasn't the only pioneer claiming such new territory. The FDA approved the birth control pill in 1960, and when Helen Gurley Brown published *Sex and the Single Girl* in 1962, it sold two million copies in the first three weeks. The book, which led to Brown's appointment as the longtime editor of *Cosmopolitan*, was a harbinger of the changing attitudes that would soon transform American society. It would be many years before the magazine published regular features on orgasms and blow jobs, but Brown's groundbreaking best seller encouraged women to become financially independent and to have sex before marriage—if not instead of it.

Rivers was always candid about having had premarital sex, but it wasn't until long after Edgar died that she admitted to having been unfaithful during her marriage—a revelation she shared with Howard Stern on his radio show. In a 2012 interview, Rivers confessed that she had had several extramarital affairs while she was married to Edgar—including a one-night stand with Robert Mitchum after an appearance together on *The Tonight Show* in the 1960s, when she was a relatively new bride. Rivers also told Stern that she had an extended affair with actor Gabriel Dell during the out-of-town and Broadway productions of her play *Fun City* in 1971, and that she had "left Edgar over" this affair for several weeks.

Even then, there was at least one more bombshell still to come. In the final year of her life Rivers unexpectedly made one of her most incendiary claims: that she had had sex with the mentor she had once worshipped, the man she was widely regarded as having betrayed by leaving *The Tonight Show* to do a television show of her own—Johnny Carson, from whom she had remained estranged until his death.

When Rivers first appeared on *The Tonight Show*, she was thirty-one years old and Carson was thirty-nine. Already married to his second wife, he was the father of three sons from his first marriage. But his personal life was chronically turbulent and lurid, at least by the standards of the era. When he died in 2005, Carson had been married four times and endured three acrimonious, expensive divorces, accompanied by reports of infidelity.

And yet his romantic profile as a roué provided a striking contrast with the awkward social persona that people were surprised to encounter off the air. On television Carson was always the genial guy everyone loved, but in person he was a painfully shy man who avoided large parties and didn't seem to know how to carry on a conversation.

"I felt sorry for Johnny in that he was so socially uncomfortable," said Dick Cavett, another comic whose career received a crucial boost from *The*

*Tonight Show*. "I've hardly ever met anybody who had as hard a time as he did."

The screenwriter and director George Axelrod, who wrote *The Seven Year Itch* and often appeared on the television show *What's My Line?*, had a similar view of Carson. "Socially, he doesn't exist," said Axelrod. "The reason is that there are no television cameras in living rooms. If human beings had little red lights in the middle of their foreheads, Carson would be the greatest conversationalist on earth."

Carson's extreme social discomfort led him to devise various stratagems to avoid the ordinary interactions most celebrities learn to finesse. With interviewers, he typically refused to talk about his childhood, his personal life, politics, or controversies. When journalists tried to ask him questions, he offered a list of prepared answers:

Yes, I did.

No, I didn't.

Not a bit of truth in that rumor.

Only twice in my life, both times on Saturday.

I can do either, but I prefer the first.

No. Kumquats.

I can't answer that question.

Toads and tarantulas.

Turkestan, Denmark, Chile, and the Komandorski Islands.

As often as possible, but I'm not very good at it yet. I need much more practice.

Carson's notorious unease was never visible on the air, where he seemed warm and comfortable. In his appearances with Rivers, he listened to her woe-is-me laments with avuncular kindliness, responding with the sympathy of an older, wiser confidant. In return, she was always obsequious, presenting herself as his surrogate daughter, lavishing him with praise and expressing her effusive gratitude for everything he had done for her. "I adored Johnny Carson," she said in *Still Talking*.

But their ostensible rapport was apparently limited to the brief sessions of bantering for the benefit of their audiences. "Our friendship existed entirely on camera in front of America, and even then, during the commercial breaks, when the red light went off, we had nothing to say to each other," Rivers wrote later.

Although Carson's liaisons with a bevy of other women made headlines over the years, no one ever suggested that Rivers was one of his sexual partners. Those who knew them both were therefore shocked when Rivers, a few months before she died, suddenly claimed to have had "a one-night bounce" with Carson back in the day.

Although he had been dead since 2005, a long-lost Carson sex tape surfaced in early 2014, and gossip websites buzzed with items suggesting that the late talk show host was "hung like a horse." As Rivers headed into the L.A. airport one night, she was accosted by a TMZ camera crew about the sex tape and asked whether she'd like to see what was on it.

"I've seen it," Rivers said airily. "How do you think you got on the show?"

It's hard to think of another eighty-year-old woman who would generate a public sex scandal about herself and her long-deceased professional mentor, but Rivers achieved her apparent goal. Her unexpected revelation generated a round of breathless headlines, including "Johnny Carson's penis...I TOUCHED IT!"

If her claim was true, Carson would hardly be the only entertainment industry power broker to have exercised that kind of droit du seigneur. But their friends didn't believe it. "It never happened," said Dorothy Melvin, Rivers's longtime manager. "Joan would seize any chance, especially in her later years, to get publicity. Johnny was dead, and nobody would refute it. Joan wanted to be talked about, so she said outrageous things."

Men who knew both parties were equally incredulous. "Never happened," Shelly Schultz said firmly. "In my wildest imagination I could never see that. The very idea that she said that—it's all about self-aggrandizement. And to discredit him, maybe. Johnny could have any guest he wanted. If you saw Joan Rivers back then and you were Johnny Carson, she wasn't even on page twelve. She was a cute, scrawny little

Jewish girl from Brooklyn. There was not anybody that I know of who wanted to jump her bones."

Carson was dignified rather than lecherous at work, according to Schultz. "He was discreet, in that he wouldn't do a wink and a nod with us," he said. "He didn't talk salaciously about any of the guests. He never said, 'And I screwed that woman!' He may have, but we didn't know it."

Other Carson associates cited similar reasons for rejecting Rivers's claim. "I didn't believe it for a moment," said Henry Bushkin. "I thought it was just pure Joan. It was all bullshit, but it was theatrical. It gave her something else to talk about, but I can't imagine it to be true. If you saw the women Johnny had one-night stands with year-round, he wouldn't have been attracted to Joan Rivers."

Rivers's friends were just as dubious that she ever had a fling with Carson. "I know she didn't. It just wasn't in the equation," said Robert Higdon, a longtime confidant.

Higdon found her boast about Mitchum equally implausible. "One day she called me up and said, 'Is Robert Mitchum dead? I just said on the radio that I slept with him,'" Higdon recalled. "She said, 'If he's dead it's okay, but if he's alive it could cause some problems.' I said, 'The next thing you'll tell me is you slept with John F. Kennedy!' She said, 'I did. I just never told you.'"

Higdon's explanation: "She's a comedian," he said. "Living inside her head—it must have been a difficult place to be. It just never stopped. She would say these things all the time, and it got to the point where I would just disregard it. People would say, 'I can't believe Joan did that!,' and I would say, 'It was a joke.' Her friend Tommy Corcoran said she had Tourette's disease: she would just say whatever. He would look at me and say, 'It never happened.'"

Rivers herself left ample room for that interpretation. "There is nothing I won't do for publicity," she admitted. "Humiliation does not exist in my vocabulary. I never had the cushion to say, 'I won't do that.'"

Some of Rivers's outlandish statements may have been designed to get attention, but others were motivated by empathy, according to Higdon. "If you said to her, 'My husband beats me with a brick,' she would say, 'I know exactly what you mean—my husband did the same thing, and you have to leave him!' If you said you fell out of a 747 over the Atlantic Ocean, she would say she had done it too and was there to support you. It was compassion: 'I've been there too.' And the person would feel, 'Well, isn't that sweet—she knows my pain!' She wanted everyone to feel included."

Whether or not Rivers indulged in the occasional dalliance, marriage and motherhood formed the core of her personal life during the late 1960s and the 1970s. And her marriage appeared to flourish, even as it gradually changed from an intimate relationship into a quasi-professional one.

Insidious but inexorable, that process progressed as if it were a natural evolution—even inevitable, given the personalities involved. For a while, Roy Silver continued as Rivers's official manager, but Edgar quickly became her unofficial one—"because we both saw him as the one person in my life who was 150 percent in my corner, the man who would protect me from all those people in show business who try to use and exploit you," Rivers explained.

But to entertainment industry veterans, that scenario was a toxic cliché virtually guaranteed to produce an unhappy ending. "This is an old story in show business," said Shelly Schultz. "When a star or a burgeoning star marries somebody, the new mate tries to be the manager. They will eventually become the manager, and that person's career will go into the toilet for a certain period of time. There isn't a wife or a husband of a star who hasn't interfered in the star's career. I'm sure Roy saw the handwriting on the wall. He would say, 'Any minute now!' We joked about it. Edgar was short, and one time we were sitting in a meeting at *The Tonight Show* and somebody said, 'There really are eight dwarfs.' It was like there was a bad odor permeating from somewhere—oh, it's from him! He gave me the fucking creeps."

As Schultz and Silver foresaw, Silver was ultimately replaced as Rivers's manager, and Edgar hired the late Jack Rollins, a top manager who also handled Woody Allen. For the time being, the star's husband continued to play a role behind the scenes, but his hunger for more power gradually skewed the Rosenbergs' professional decisions in ways that would soon warp Rivers's entire career.

## Chapter Five

# WESTWARD HO: CALIFORNIA DREAMIN'

As a girl, Rivers wanted to be Katharine Cornell, the toast of Broadway—not Phyllis Diller or Totie Fields, the disheveled crazy ladies of comedy. No matter how successful she became as a comedian, she never got over the idea that her achievements were a poor second best to respect as a serious actress.

So Rivers was thrilled when she met the director Frank Perry and he wrote a bit part for her in the 1968 movie he made from "The Swimmer," a celebrated short story by John Cheever. The film starred Burt Lancaster, and *The New York Times* gave Rivers a favorable mention in its review—but no further movie offers were forthcoming.

The prospects in television seemed brighter, and the following year the William Morris Agency offered to package a television talk show for Rivers. Unfortunately, her husband seized on that idea as a crucial opportunity for himself as well.

"Edgar wanted to be the show's producer—which meant quitting Anna Rosenberg," Rivers reported in *Still Talking.* "I kept saying to him, 'Are you sure? Are you sure? What's going to happen if the show doesn't work?' To me, he was already a movie producer, and this little half-hour morning show seemed like a comedown. I worried that he was giving up his power base."

At the time, she didn't realize that Telsun was running out of steam and that Edgar hadn't come up with any other films to produce. He didn't want to resume his duties as a public relations employee servicing the company's clients; he wanted to be a big-time producer, and his wife's new gig looked like the ticket to his own success.

"The William Morris TV show package was irresistible because it put Edgar at the top with complete control," Rivers said. "The decision to do the show began the fusion of my career with Edgar's. That was not our plan. It just happened."

For a while, this dynamic seemed to meet the needs of both partners. "I was frightened by the responsibility of carrying a show on my shoulders, and Edgar and I obsessively hashed out every decision," Rivers said. "I had a joke based on the truth—'My marriage is wonderful because when I wake up in the morning, I'm thinking of me and so is he.' Still in bed, Edgar would say, 'I figured out during the night that the contract should read…'"

Rivers liked having everything revolve around her, and she admitted that her career provided the "romance" in her life—and even that she saw it as her "lover." While this relegated Edgar to the role of functionary, she thought their relationship was doing fine. "As my mother used to tell me, nothing is perfect, and this marriage was working," Rivers insisted.

With a notable lack of originality, Rivers's new show was named *That Show,* and she was delighted when Johnny Carson agreed to be a guest on the pilot. She wanted to send him a significant present to express her gratitude, but what to give the man who already had everything?

Why, her most precious possession, of course.

So the Rosenbergs dressed up the infant Melissa and dispatched a nurse in cape and uniform to take her to NBC and deliver her to Carson. The nurse found him in the middle of a staff meeting, handed him the baby, and announced, "Mr. Carson, this is for you."

Rivers reported his initial reaction in *Still Talking:* "The joke around the show was, Johnny went white because he thought maybe the baby was his."

But Carson relaxed when he found the note attached to Melissa, which read, "Dear Mr. Carson—My parents don't know how to thank you for what you did for my mother, so they wanted to give you something they really love, and that's me. My name is Melissa Rosenberg. I weigh twelve pounds. I eat very little. Please bring me up Jewish."

Carson thought the prank was funny, and for a time everything else seemed to proceed just as smoothly. The Rosenbergs managed the schedule of Joan's program so she could tape three shows in one day and two the next, leaving her time to fit in club dates during the rest of the week. In January of 1969, she also became a regular guest host on *The Tonight Show*.

"It was a proud, happy time for everybody," she recalled.

But *That Show* soon lost its luster. There were problems with the syndication process, Rivers grew weary of the grueling schedule, and she was cavalier enough to think this was just the first of many such opportunities. She was relieved when the show ended—but Edgar was "extremely upset" about its termination, which marked the end of his role as producer.

Not knowing what else to do, he continued to piggyback onto his wife's projects. Rivers was still obsessed with the theater, a passion she was determined to pass along to her daughter. "I would take her with me before she could sit on the seat," Joan said.

Unable to persuade anyone else to put her onstage, Rivers wrote a stage comedy called *Fun City* as a starring vehicle for herself. Her husband and Lester Colodny were credited as coauthors of the play, which chronicled the misadventures of Jill, an "up-to-the-minute feminist" who was "active in all sorts of causes" but deficient in the womanly arts of domesticity and romance. There was no mistaking *Fun City*'s autobiographical elements—"Her fiancé wants to marry her...Trouble is, he's Italian and her Jewish mother mistrusts Italians," according to the blurb that advertised the play—and when it flopped on Broadway at the beginning of 1972, its failure dealt Rivers a major psychological blow. She had finally dared to reach for her ultimate dream—and she was definitively rejected.

Instead of consoling his wife, Edgar took a sleeping pill and refused to talk to her. "This was our first failure as a team, the first major stress on our marriage, and we did not band together," Rivers said. "We did not go to each other for comfort. We drew apart."

*The Tonight Show* had always been based in New York, but in 1972 it moved to Burbank, California, further weakening Rivers's commitment to her lifelong home base. Looking out of her windows one night at the glittering lights of Manhattan, the grief-stricken Rivers made a sudden, dramatic decision. "You don't want me, New York, I don't want you. We're out of here!" she said out loud.

And so the Rosenbergs moved to Hollywood, driven as much by anger as by a positive agenda for the future. "We had no idea that as the plane flew over Mississippi toward Los Angeles, Edgar's doom was sealed," Rivers observed later. "After so much struggle in his life, after finally experiencing his dream in New York, he was on his way to the one place in the world where he could never be appreciated for himself, on his way to becoming a star's husband."

For Rivers, the move made sense. "Joan had always wanted to come here, and she decided this was the time to try Hollywood," said Sue Cameron, who was a columnist at the *Hollywood Reporter* when she first met Rivers. "She wanted to break out. She always wanted to be an actress more than anything, and she wanted to star in a sitcom, she wanted to do television movies, she wanted to do all the variety shows."

But Hollywood was unfamiliar territory, so Rivers set about infiltrating the new milieu. "I got a call from her press agent saying, 'Joan Rivers would like you to come to her house for lunch. She's new in town and would like to meet you,'" Cameron reported. "Joan decided I was going to be her guide to L.A., because she didn't really know anybody."

For Rivers, such strategic tactics were standard operating procedure. "Joan always wanted to become best friends with the press," Cameron said. "It's no accident that her friends were people like Barbara Walters, Cindy Adams, and me. She made sure that whoever was the big press deal was her friend. If you had an outlet, even for an hour, she always kept you on her list, because she never knew where you were going to be. She could always get someone on the phone if there was a problem. It was very calculated, but we ended up loving each other."

When the Rosenbergs first arrived in Los Angeles, they moved into a rented house in Coldwater Canyon. "I was greeted by the guy we called Archie the Ice-Skater," said Cameron. "He was a gay guy who had aged out of being an ice-skater, and she gave him a job as her assistant. The table for lunch was set magnificently."

Over time, Cameron became a real friend, forging a bond with Rivers that lasted until her death. Cameron often traveled and vacationed with the Rosenbergs, and such close proximity gave her an intimate view of Rivers's private life—which was very different from the persona she presented for public consumption.

"When she was really Joan, when she went home and there was no one around, she was in a bathrobe and glasses and no makeup, curled up in a corner reading a book," Cameron said. "She would eat her meals on a stool in the kitchen."

But Rivers cared desperately about what people thought of her, and she was very conscious of creating the image she wanted for her new environment. "Her first question was, 'Did I rent a house in the right area?'" Cameron recalled. "She wanted to rent a house in the very best area. I said, 'No, you need to move to Bel Air.' As soon as her lease was up, she moved to Bel Air. Her second question was, 'Where do I get English riding lessons for Melissa?' I got her the name of a riding academy, and from there our friendship just bloomed."

Even the details of her daughter's hobbies had to be just right. "When she called me and said, 'Who is the best English riding teacher for Melissa?,' I had to find out who all the chichi people sent their children to," Cameron said. "When Melissa had riding lessons or a riding exhibition, Joan would dress her in a 'riding to the hounds' outfit, with a black velvet helmet, high boots, jodhpurs, a red jacket, a white shirt, and a little black tie. It's all about Waspiness."

As a hostess, Rivers often seemed to care more about social pedigree than about whether a guest was smart, interesting, or accomplished. "When she gave a dinner party, she made sure there was always someone like C. Z. Guest," Cameron said, referring to the socialite and gardening expert whose husband was related to the Duke of Marlborough and Sir Winston Churchill.

Rivers also worked hard at mastering the domestic management skills of the upper crust. "I remember Joan asking me to lunch, because she had just hired new butlers and cooks," said the writer Jesse Kornbluth, who was divorced from Katharine Johnson, the daughter of the multibillionaire media mogul Anne Cox Chambers.

"Joan knew I had been married to Katharine Johnson, and she wanted me to assess her help," Kornbluth said. "She knew I was an aspirational Jew—like Joan. We're having lunch, and she's saying, 'How is the cooking? How is the service?' I think she felt I had greater expertise—East Coast expertise. Joan knew there was a larger social world than L.A."

And yet no matter how hard they worked at it, both Rivers and her husband had difficulty adjusting to Los Angeles. It was good for some new jokes. The living was easy—"too easy," Rivers complained. "I miss the tension and anger of New York."

Even dying was easier. "They will not declare you dead in California till you lose your tan. You just have to lie there for weeks till you're starting to fade," Rivers claimed.

But winning social acceptance was something else entirely. From school to camp to college and beyond, Rivers had never been gifted at figuring out how to be part of the cool crowd, and that challenge proved particularly difficult in Hollywood. Her idea of proper entertaining entailed formal place settings and finger bowls, but Rivers's personal style—a lifelong legacy from her ever-striving mother—often seemed ill-suited to the informality and casual chic that were prized in Los Angeles. "She was indeed a fish out of water," said Arnold Stiefel, Rod Stewart's longtime manager, who managed Rivers's book and movie projects in those years.

Her partner didn't make things any easier. "Joan without Edgar was a lot of fun, but it was not fun to be with Joan and Edgar," said Sandy Gallin. "It was like she was with her grandfather."

Rivers was also deeply uncomfortable with the prevailing drug culture. She was happy to make jokes about it: "California is druggy, druggy, druggy. If it is white and it is on the table, they are gonna sniff it. I have a friend who OD'd in the beauty shop on dandruff."

But she didn't participate. "She was at a party in Hollywood and somebody offered her cocaine," reported David Dangle, a close friend who ran Rivers's QVC company in later years. "She tries it, and somebody says,

'Do you need a tissue?'—because she had snot running down her face. Her nose was running, and from that point on, she wouldn't do it. You couldn't put a gun to her head and get her to do it, because you lost control."

Whatever problems Rivers experienced in adjusting to California, her husband's were far worse. His stiff, formal persona couldn't have been more different from the bohemian, pot-smoking athleticism of the Hollywood movers and shakers whose habits dictated the prevailing ethos for men. In an environment where masculine style evoked the image of someone like Ryan O'Neal running shirtless beside the ocean in Malibu, Edgar was more like Richard Nixon, who famously wore a dark suit, lace-up shoes, white shirt, and tie to walk on the beach.

But Joan had her career, whereas Edgar increasingly found himself without one of his own. The power brokers who ran the industry found his credentials unimpressive and his personality uncongenial, and he wasn't making any progress toward his goal of succeeding as an independent producer. "His attitude became, 'I'll show those bastards!'" Rivers reported.

Resentful at being slighted, Rosenberg suppressed his anger but refused to share his frustration in any meaningful intimacy with his wife. Neither could admit it, but each was secretly disappointed in the other. "I think Edgar believed he was married to a show business insider who would bring him in—only to find that I was an outsider too," Rivers said. "Like him, I never fit in with the right people, never had that knack."

But even those who accepted Rivers often found her husband charmless. "A lot of people didn't like him," said Rick Newman. "You never heard that Edgar was a great guy."

As a father, however, he couldn't have been more devoted, and Melissa adored him in return. Inside their own domestic world, the Rosenbergs managed to create their own showbiz version of a happy little family. "From the time Melissa was two, she watched Joan perfect her harshly innovative comedy routine," *People* magazine reported in 1993. "The tot would sit in the wings of nightclubs like the one at Caesars Palace in Las Vegas and wave to her mother, who stood center stage performing her routine. 'By age five,' says Joan, 'she knew it verbatim. She'd say, "I hate to cook. I hate to clean. Housework is stupid. No woman was ever made love to because she scrubbed the linoleum.""

Even then, Joan saw her daughter rather than her husband as the emotional core of her life. "Melissa is the one to whom I could give total affection and feel it being absorbed and returned," she said. "I wish I had had ten children...After Missy, I had two miscarriages and a tubular pregnancy. Not having more is my only regret in life. We were going to adopt, and then Edgar changed his mind. I worry now because there's nobody for Missy. When the chips are down, the only one who will take you in is a relative."

The Rosenbergs worked hard to make their daughter feel she was their top priority, even when they were on the road for Joan's nightclub gigs. According to *People* magazine, "'Mom and Dad would fly in from wherever for even minor school events,' recalls Melissa, who attended a trio of private schools in Southern California. Confirms Joan: 'I was even a Brownie troop mother. Now that was a picture.'"

Being raised in Beverly Hills was challenging nonetheless. "I always wanted to be tall and blond, and I'm still having trouble with that," Melissa told *People*.

"Melissa grew up in a society where everyone who walked in the door was beautiful," her mother explained. "Nicollette Sheridan went to her school. Missy always felt short and squat, but we constantly told her, 'You're the best! Go for it!' In third grade swim meets she was three foot two while other kids were six foot two. And I would scream, 'You can beat them!'"

Trying to counter such influences, "Joan purposely chose schools that were not filled with the scions of show business," *People* reported. "'I wanted her to see that other kids' fathers are doctors and businessmen,' says Joan. And there were family rules: when Joan and Edgar were in town, the family had dinner at 6 p.m. During the meal, all phones would be shut off. Then they would talk about everything—school and work, life and art, business problems and solutions. 'We wanted Melissa to know about the good times and the bad,' Joan says."

Within the charmed circle of the family, Edgar thrived, and he also won admirers among family intimates, who were touched by his devotion to his daughter and his high-powered wife. "When I met Edgar I loved him instantly," said Cameron. "I often felt that if they got divorced, I would like to marry Edgar. I am bisexual, and I had a girlfriend at the time, but he was just magical. He was so funny. He was so acerbic—Noël Coward, Malcolm Muggeridge. He was actually funnier than Joan. She had fast, funny one-liners, but Edgar was the guy who said something under his breath that could kill you. I loved this man so much. He was an extraordinary intellect, and his eyes twinkled, but he kept it all in because he wanted Joan to be the star. He looked weak, but he wasn't. He was watching everybody, mentally taking notes. At the end of the day they would go over everything together. He was her partner in plotting her career, and he was fine with it for a long time."

Cameron wasn't the only friend who empathized with Edgar, but even his defenders acknowledged that he was a difficult man. "The entire range of opinions about Edgar has validity," said Dorothy Melvin, who started working for the Rosenbergs as an assistant before she became Joan's manager. "I don't think Edgar ever got his due. Edgar was very kind in a lot of ways that people didn't see, but he was a very tortured person, and he would erupt. He had a career in New York, and he was respected as Edgar Rosenberg, and then they came here and it wasn't the same in L.A. In Hollywood, you have to be thought of as your own person, but Joan was the star of the household, and he was the adjunct. They worked hand in hand, and they were really one person. He never did anything without complete discussion with Joan, and she was very protective of Edgar and fiercely loyal to him. There were a lot of very old-world values in Joan, and she said, 'That's your husband and you have to protect him.' She never did anything without Edgar. She always acquiesced to him."

But his lack of finesse sometimes cost her significant opportunities. In 1983, the writer and author Bob Colacello interviewed Rivers for *Parade*, the Sunday newspaper insert that had such an enormous circulation it was known as the most widely read magazine in the United States. "Edgar gave us such a hard time about the cover photo that the whole thing got canceled," said Colacello.

When he first went to interview Rivers, she was staying at a Holiday Inn in Albany, where she was performing. "I got to her hotel, and she had a pistol and was polishing the different parts," Colacello said. "They had a limousine, and we went to Stockbridge to see the Rockwell museum. She and Edgar were real autodidacts, so on the way back they read aloud to each other from a history of the queen of France. I got a great interview, and Walter Anderson, the editor of the magazine, loved it."

Everything was fine until Edgar picked a fight over the control of his wife's image. "Edgar told me they had done their own cover shoot, but she was in furs and jewels, which was all wrong for the *Parade* readership, where you can't have a cover that looks like royalty," said Colacello. "It was very presumptuous of them to do their own photo shoot, and they were like the king and queen of France with the furs and jewels. So I said, 'We have to do our own shoot.' Edgar demanded photo approval, and Walter said, 'We don't do that at *Parade*.' But we worked out a compromise, and everything was settled until Edgar said to me, 'We want approval of the retouching.' I kept saying, 'Edgar—thirty-five million readers!'"

But Edgar wouldn't budge, and his intransigence finally blew up the whole deal. "Walter Anderson was a nice guy, very easygoing, but when I went back to him, he said, 'Fuck her. I don't want the story anymore. She's just not that famous,'" Colacello recalled. "This wasn't investigative journalism, and nobody was out to get Joan. It just seemed overprotective and annoying. I thought the whole situation was absurd, from the gun, to the performance where she's asking these upstate ladies if they used condoms, to the cultural journey, to the back and forth with Edgar's requests. He lost her the cover of *Parade*. He did a very bad job for Joan."

Whatever her husband's misjudgments, Rivers's career was thriving, and she quickly became an icon to her fellow Jews and to gay men, two of the constituencies that would help form her most loyal fan base. "I grew up in St. Louis, and starting when she was on *Carson*, when I was in junior high school, it was like a holiday in my house when Joan was on," said Andy Cohen, the host of *Watch What Happens: Live* as well as the executive producer of the *Real Housewives* franchise. "I was gay, and she was Jewish. We relate to very strong, glamorous women who pull no punches, and she was fearless."

Rivers stayed busy, appearing regularly on *The Hollywood Squares*, trying out new material at a club in Los Angeles, and going on the road to work as an opening act at major casinos, which quickly became an important part of the Rosenbergs' lifestyle. "Joan was playing Vegas, Reno, Tahoe, and I was always sent up to interview them, so everyone ended up in Las Vegas every weekend," Cameron explained. "She would arrange for me to stay at Caesars, where she was playing. Every Sunday I would walk from my room in my robe and meet Joan and Edgar in their robes, and everyone would read the *L.A. Times* and *The New York Times* and order room service, and we would just sit and read and talk. It was a New York experience. They lived a New York experience no matter where they were. They were always reading, always talking. Joan and Edgar lived a very intellectual life."

But Rivers never stopped looking for new creative outlets. In a brilliant stroke of karmic revenge, she wrote a screenplay inspired by the terrible blind date she had in college with the boy who was so disgusted by his first sight of Joan that he said angrily "Why didn't you tell me?" to the friend who had fixed them up.

That boy became a doctor and married a girl Rivers had known in New York. Years later, the same woman called Rivers in California, and Rivers invited her and her husband to a poolside supper party. At forty, the doctor husband was now fat and bald—and he had no idea there was any connection between the dumpy Joan Molinsky who had once repulsed him and the stick-thin, glamorous star he was now fortunate enough to be visiting in Hollywood.

"He was all over me; everywhere I went, there he was, obviously a cheater, following me into the kitchen to get me alone," Rivers reported. After the party, she joked to her friend Kenny Solms that she should have said, "Does the name Joan Molinsky mean anything to you?"—and whipped out a gun and shot him.

Solms said, "That's a movie."

So Rivers wrote a script called *The Girl Most Likely to…*, which became a 1973 made-for-television movie starring Stockard Channing and Ed Asner. A black comedy, it told the story of "a fat ugly girl who gets thin and beautiful and kills every boy who ever slighted her," said Rivers, never one to forgive and forget. "That script came right from the heart."

In presenting plastic surgery as the solution to the ugly girl's unhappiness, the plot certainly embodied one of Rivers's most cherished fantasies. After being terribly disfigured in a car accident, the central character is treated with reconstructive surgery that transforms her into a beauty. In real life, Rivers didn't resort to murder as punishment for those who had rejected her, but she spent the rest of her life chasing the tantalizing idea that an unattractive woman could undergo a complete metamorphosis and become so beautiful that she was able to avenge her painful past.

As Rivers expanded her career, her husband's languished, and it soon became obvious that his expensive office was unnecessary. So he gave it up and started to work from home—except that he really didn't have anything to work on. Neither Joan nor Edgar wanted him to be a house-husband, but he rejected his wife's suggestion that he get a job, thinking that would be demeaning. Since he only wanted to be a producer, they decided that Rivers would continue to write screenplays and become so successful she could demand that her husband produce the movies.

"Should I have known better by then? Of course I should," she said in *Still Talking*.

But like her husband, she too was the victim of a troubling gap between her aspirations and the realities of her career. The bad news was that her subsequent scripts were turned down and she wasn't offered any acting jobs; the good news was that she did well in Las Vegas. Another performer might have been happy that she was in demand, but Rivers was upset about being pigeonholed as a Vegas comic when she wanted to win recognition as a serious actress or a success in the movie business.

Instead of bonding over their mutual angst, the Rosenbergs let it drive a wedge between them. "Edgar handled his frustration by withdrawing into himself," Rivers said. "He broke my heart. He pretended he was not suffering, but I knew he was…He was miserable. And I was miserable.

With our wounds from *Fun City*, we could not comfort each other. Our marriage was shaky. He resented me for being busy, and I felt guilty for being busy."

When Joan tried to talk about how unhappy they were, Edgar stonewalled her and said there was nothing wrong.

Rivers finally reached her breaking point one night in 1973 when she came back from an engagement at Harrah's in Tahoe and realized she couldn't face going home to her husband—so she went directly from the airport to the Beverly Hills Hotel with Melissa and her governess. A few nights later, she heard a scary noise at the back door of her cottage and thought someone was trying to break in. Instead of reaching out to the hotel staff, she called Edgar, who was there in ten minutes.

The next day Joan went back home, and for a time the pressure seemed to lift; her brief rebellion had shocked Edgar into recognizing the depth of her distress, and he had reassured her by being the husband she could always count on in a crisis. But nothing really changed: they never talked honestly about his failure to establish himself as an independent player in Hollywood, they kept drifting further apart as intimate partners, and they handled their respective disappointments in counterproductive ways that were chillingly prophetic.

"When Edgar passed a certain anxiety threshold, he would check out with denial and a sleeping pill. I, in turn, would lose myself in my daughter and a whirl of feverish activity," Rivers said.

Without an individual portfolio of his own, it soon became a given that Edgar's role in life was to facilitate what both he and his wife referred to as The Career. "We run a factory, and Joan is the product," he said.

That dynamic allowed for a pragmatic division of labor, but it also gave Rivers a free pass to be "the easygoing sweetheart, smiling and joking," while leaving Edgar to do the dirty work of making sure her interests were served. "I was being unfair, letting Edgar be the lightning rod for the hostility that floats around town," Rivers admitted. "But that is built into the star/husband equation...So I let my husband take the heat."

As Rivers made more money, she also yearned to put down roots, and in 1974 the Rosenbergs moved to a twelve-room house on Ambazac Way in Bel Air. Designed by Paul Williams, an influential black architect, the new home was "a micro-Tara."

But at first it was largely empty. Shortly after Rivers moved in, she invited around twenty people for a curious quasi-social event. "We were told to come after dinner for coffee and dessert," said John Erman, a television and film director who didn't know Rivers but was brought by a friend. "There was almost nothing in the living room, and we all had to sit on the floor. Joan sat down and said, 'I need to make money, and I'd like to go around the room and have everyone tell me what they think is the best way to make it.' We all kind of looked at each other and rolled our eyes."

As far as Erman could tell, Rivers was clearly the one calling the shots. "I thought Edgar was kind of a schlep," he said. "He was like the Frog Prince, following in her footsteps."

But over time, as Rivers made more money, she decorated the house as her private romantic fantasy—a tangible testimonial to her own success and the concept of class she had absorbed from her mother's thwarted aspirations. "Joan's lifestyle was like the Queen of Versailles, which she loved because she could afford it," said Cameron. "Her house looked like Louis XIV; it was extraordinarily formal. It was an English colonial, and the living room was Fabergé eggs, Chinese screens, Oriental rugs, damask furniture. The dining room was very English, all dark wood and credenzas and another Oriental rug. The staff at the house called her Mrs. R., for Rosenberg. It was all very old-fashioned, very old-school. Edgar loved Rodgers and Hart, and I seem to remember them listening to Rodgers and Hart at cocktail hour."

Rivers's taste satisfied a deep yearning to achieve what her mother had longed for, but it was distinctly out of step with the ethos of California casual. Years later, after Edgar had died and Joan was getting ready to sell the Ambazac house and move back to New York, the freelance writer Jenny Allen interviewed her for an *Architectural Digest* story. "She clearly loved the house, but she said, 'It isn't really a California house,'" Allen recalled. "It was all French, English, and Russian antiques—period furnishings. She said one of her friends once walked into the house and said, 'Who died here?' There was no Art Deco, no Arts and Crafts—Arts and

Crafts style particularly appalled her—and there was nothing attesting to a career in show business. Not one showbiz poster or Vegas memento. She wanted to be perceived as worldly, generous—a lady."

Rivers took care to differentiate her real-life identity from her stage persona. "It seemed very important to her to make the distinction between her private self and her public act," Allen said. "She said, 'That's just an act—it's not who I am. I'm a doctor's daughter from Larchmont.' She seemed overly self-conscious about making this distinction; she returned to it several times."

When Allen wrote her story for *Architectural Digest*, the first draft began with that observation: "I said, 'Joan Rivers is at least two different people. One of them is the one we see on television, but the other Joan Rivers is gracious, private, ladylike, correct, and elegant.'"

Rivers was quite specific about the inspiration for that old-fashioned identity. "She said her mother was very elegant and obsessed with politesse, and she inherited that from her mother," Allen said. "She used the word 'homage'—she saw her house as an homage to her mother and her mother's taste."

And yet with Rivers, contradictions always lurked just below the surface. "Underneath it all, Joan was like a cross between *Town & Country* and *Road & Track*," Sue Cameron observed. "*Town & Country* was completely visible, but *Road & Track* was her ambition, which ran twenty-four hours a day."

In Los Angeles, the disjuncture between the Rosenbergs' rigidly controlled style and the social mores of the freewheeling, drug-addled 1970s and '80s could be jarring for everyone concerned. "Joan liked to give very formal dinner parties, and when she gave her first dinner party in Bel Air, she wanted it to go perfectly," Cameron said. "The guests were Roddy McDowall and his boyfriend, George Segal and his then wife, Edgar and Joan and me."

Despite Rivers's meticulously planned agenda, the dinner party careened out of control before the first course was over. "Roddy's boyfriend had too much to drink, and he was upset because some trade paper had given him a bad review," Cameron reported. "Even though it wasn't me, he started in with vicious cracks about me, just because I was a trade paper writer, so I represented all the bad people. He got so abusive he went to hit me across the table, and Roddy had to put him in the car, where he passed out. So now there's a beautiful roast with Yorkshire pudding on the table, and we just keep talking like nothing happened. And then Mrs. Segal goes to the bathroom, and she's gone a really long time, and Joan finally says to me, 'Do you mind going to check on Mrs. Segal?'"

Cameron obliged, only to encounter a social challenge that couldn't be ignored. "Mrs. Segal was passed out on the floor from some kind of drug, but her leg was blocking the door, so you couldn't get the door open," Cameron recalled. "So now the whole dinner party is ruined—there's a guy in the car and a woman on the floor. Joan has been Little Miss Perfect the whole time, and she finally throws her fork down and says, 'Fuck it, I'm ordering pizza.'"

Rivers's anger was unpredictable, and she sometimes lashed out in surprising ways; newly ensconced in the exclusive enclave of Bel Air, she loved to play the role of English country house chatelaine, but at heart she was still the aggressive little Jewish girl from Brooklyn.

"Being Jewish was very significant to Joan," Cameron reported. "In Bel Air, the property line of her backyard was directly up against the Bel-Air Country Club golf course, and the Bel-Air Country Club was restricted, like all the clubs in the late 1970s. Joan loved gardening, and one day she was back there pruning her roses, and all of a sudden a golf ball comes flying over. A man comes to the fence and says, 'Lady, can I please have my ball?' And Joan says, 'You Nazi, I'll have your balls cut off!'"

Notwithstanding such eruptions, the Ambazac house was a dream come true for Rivers—but it was expensive to maintain, so she went on the road for several months out of every year to earn enough money to pay for her increasingly opulent lifestyle. And yet no matter how hard Rivers labored to perfect the stage setting for her life in Los Angeles, she continued to be dissatisfied with the marriage that anchored it.

Sue Cameron was stunned one day when Rivers said she'd decided to make a public announcement that she was separating from Edgar. "She wanted me to release this," Cameron said. "The message was that she was in Hollywood now and he didn't really fit in. She wanted a whole new life, and she was interested in dating. So Edgar left. Melissa was eight."

Cameron saw the whole episode as motivated by Rivers's show business aspirations rather than by any romantic yearnings. "It was the call of Hollywood," she said. "It was very exciting; it was something she had to do. It was thrilling for her to be in Hollywood, and be in Vegas and Reno and Tahoe and Beverly Hills, and have all the limos. It was a huge dream. It meant so much to her."

Confronted with an unwelcome separation, Edgar patiently waited her out. "He knew she was going to come back," Cameron said. "Edgar would call Joan every night before she went to bed, to make sure she got home from her date and was all right. He kept that up, and he kept that up. Finally she called me and said, 'Where are you going to find someone who calls in every night to make sure you're okay? Hollywood isn't what it's cracked up to be. I'm going back to Edgar.' I don't think it lasted very long—maybe two months."

But the separation didn't cure the insidious cancer that was eating away at the heart of their marriage. "The more successful Joan became, the more she realized Edgar was a fish out of water in Hollywood, and I think she had less respect for him," said Cameron.

Even so, the family they had created together was now Joan's world, and her mother's death in 1975 sharpened that feeling. In her last conversation with her mother, Joan had been angry, and they had quarreled. Her father was recovering from a heart attack, and Joan wanted her mother to hire a live-in nurse for him when he came home from the hospital. Her mother refused, insisting that she would care for him herself.

"Her mother had a heart attack, and she died that night," Cameron said. "Joan never got to rectify it, and she felt terrible guilt."

A dozen years later, those feelings were revived and immeasurably exacerbated by Joan's overwhelming sense of guilt about her husband's suicide. But the intervening years were a halcyon time in which success seemed to make up for all the rest of life's tribulations.

And success on a grand scale was finally hers.

## Chapter Six

# THE FIRST LADY OF COMEDY: NOTHING IS SACRED

Rivers's humor was always fueled by anger, but in the early years of her career her resentment was usually channeled into lampooning the double standards of a world that was unfair to women in general and to her in particular. Glints of the slashing knives to come could already be seen, but it wasn't until she shifted away from self-deprecation and focused her rage on ridiculing other women that she became a real cultural assassin. Rivers's true feelings hadn't changed—her underlying motivation was clearly driven by jealousy—but the strategic decision to victimize women she saw as rivals who didn't deserve their good luck turned her act into a potent weapon and transformed her career.

Long before the term was ever invented, Rivers made slut shaming a staple of her act. If a woman was beautiful, men desired her—so she must be promiscuous. "You show me a woman with a naturally beautiful body, and I'll show you a tramp," she said.

As an outlet for her suppressed fury, she invented a fictional character named Heidi Abromowitz, and whenever Rivers appeared on *The Tonight Show* she regaled Johnny Carson with regular bulletins about Heidi's sexual precocity. "I'm telling you that at eight she knew more about reproduction than Xerox," said Rivers, who claimed that Heidi was a former schoolmate.

Carson always played along, cueing Rivers with leading questions to elicit fresh news about Heidi's developmental milestones. These supposedly focused on specific skills: "Kissed a boy for the first time to-day. Very disappointing. It's nothing compared to oral sex."

But adolescence posed particular challenges: "When Heidi had her braces removed, the entire football team sent her orthodontist a thank-you note," Rivers said.

She eventually published a collection of such jokes in a book called *The Life and Hard Times of Heidi Abromowitz*, which distilled Heidi's philosophy of life as someone who mindlessly serviced an unending procession of men: "Never put off for tomorrow who you can put out for tonight."

Casting herself as the virtuous good girl, Rivers made a point of contrasting Heidi's trashy behavior with her own: "We both decided we were going to give our bodies to the Harvard Medical School—only I was going to wait till I was dead."

But even a fictional character has limits, so Rivers began to broaden her focus and skewer actual people. She started by generalizing about groups that provoked her disdain. "The thing that really sticks in my mind was the jokes about how horrible female stewardesses were," said Ann Northrop, cohost of the weekly television news show *Gay USA*. "She said that stewardesses ignore women on planes and treat them like dirt because all they want to do is flirt with men and marry rich guys, and they'll throw a drink in your face while they go sit in the lap of a man. She had contempt for those women; it was just a blanket condemnation. To me, that kind of anger at women who had no real power was upsetting."

And yet even when she attacked stewardesses, Rivers acknowledged the sexist and ageist standards that discriminated against them. "They're all single, and they're very busy with the men, but they fire them at twenty-six, so they have a deadline," she said.

As her humor grew ever more cutting, Rivers became increasingly willing to skewer specific individuals, often in person. "You photograph so beautifully," she told Ann-Margret, patting her knee in a joint appearance on the *Today* show in 1978. Then Rivers smiled brightly. "I hope she's not happy. It just kills me," she said.

Rivers avoided therapists in those years, fearing that greater peace of mind could sap her professional drive. But a psychiatrist might have suspected that her hostility toward better-looking counterparts was rooted in sibling rivalry. Rivers grew up with a sister who was constantly praised as prettier, smarter, and more acquiescent, and the preferential treatment bred a lifelong rivalry. Joan's success only exacerbated the tensions with Barbara. "She's very much a Main Line Philadelphia lawyer," Rivers told *People* magazine in 1983. "I think what I do embarrasses her terribly because I'm so unladylike onstage."

As Rivers got older, the primal unfairness of knowing that her parents favored her sibling was exacerbated by her growing anger about the many sources of unfairness every girl encounters in the larger society. By the time she got famous, anger had become the hallmark trait that defined her public persona for the rest of her life. "The way I've always described Joan Rivers is that she's a mean, angry, bitter bitch, and I mean that as a total compliment," said the comic Gilbert Gottfried in the Comedy Hall of Fame documentary *Joan Rivers: Exit Laughing.*

But anger requires a target, and Rivers discovered another rich vein of material in the burgeoning field of celebrity gossip as publications like *People* magazine and the *National Enquirer* became a prime source of inspiration. Sometimes the humor simply violated the boundaries of good taste, not to mention what would later come to be known as political correctness. "I heard Mike Nichols recall a Joan Rivers joke he'd heard her tell in England: 'The day I have multiple orgasms is the day Stevie Wonder hits a hole in one,'" George Plimpton said. "This seems to me tasteless on two counts, which is difficult in a single sentence."

But the jokes about women were always meaner. As far as Rivers was concerned, supermodels were all morons: "You want to get Cindy Crawford confused? Ask her to spell 'mom' backward."

And if an actress was rated a perfect ten, she too had to be stupid: "A woman went to her plastic surgeon and asked him to make her like Bo Derek. He gave her a lobotomy."

Since acting was the lofty occupation that Rivers revered, particular scorn was aimed at anyone who dared call herself an actress while also being beautiful: "Bo Derek turned down the role of Helen Keller because she couldn't remember the lines."

105

Such jokes turned into a lifelong vendetta as Rivers became an avenging fury bent on smearing all the women she envied so desperately—the pretty ones who were chased by men, unlike lumpy little Joan Molinsky, who repelled all the boys. For the rest of her life, beautiful women remained perennial targets, no matter what else they might have accomplished.

Long after Angelina Jolie became a goodwill ambassador for the United Nations and won an Academy Award for best supporting actress, Rivers was still portraying her as an idiot so empty-headed she peed on the floor on command, like a dog.

"I've worked with stupid actresses—I've worked with Angelina Jolie. She saw a sign that said 'Wet floor' one time, and she did! I mean, she's attractive, but not a bright girl—stunningly beautiful, but stupid," Rivers said disdainfully.

It soon became clear that venting such hostility was a good career move: the more venomous Rivers was, the more attention she got. "Joan started coming up with the put-down jokes of other big celebrities, and I said to her immediately, 'This is going to take you to the next level,'" said Sandy Gallin, who was her manager at the time. "Edgar and my partner, Ray Katz, came down on me and said, 'Stop telling her this. It's going to ruin her career. It's absolutely the wrong thing to be doing.' But I thought you have to take chances if you're going to go for it, and she agreed with me."

The new tack generated a publicity bonanza for Rivers. "She was hitting the papers with all her remarks about people who were bigger than her," said Pat Cooper, a veteran comedian who worked with her. "She was jealous of anyone who looked better than her. She was not a bad-looking woman, but in her heart she was bad, and she hated anyone who was good-looking. She attacked everybody. I've never seen her give a compliment to anybody who was beautiful. She was hitting out at all of them. She's a talented girl, but not a happy one. She was born unhappy. She would have liked to be born Elizabeth Taylor or Marilyn Monroe."

When *People* magazine did a cover story on Rivers in 1983, the cover line read, "Can we talk? Nothing is sacred to the first lady of comedy." The actual feature was a short Q and A, but Rivers managed to insult no fewer than three First Ladies, one former presidential daughter, Princess Grace and her "two trampy daughters," and assorted actresses, one of whom was slut-shamed for having "hickeys on her knees" because she was dating a shorter actor.

The country's most admired former First Lady was fair game: "Jackie O. looks like E.T. without makeup," Rivers said.

Nor did Mrs. Onassis's tragic widowhood protect her. "I use her as a great example of what women should do: always marry for money," Rivers said.

After calling herself and Edgar the tackiest couple in America, Rivers pronounced Jimmy and Rosalynn Carter the second tackiest: "When you go to the White House, you want finger bowls, not Rosalynn Carter hitting a pot and yelling, 'Come and get it!'"

Rivers claimed that President and Mrs. Johnson had neglected to invite her to the White House because she insulted their daughter: "I said Lynda Bird had no style. I said, 'I took Lynda Bird into a shoe store, and she put her foot into the size measurer and said, "I'll take it."'"

The same issue of *People* featured a picture of a plump Elizabeth Taylor, whose middle-aged weight gain marked a pivotal turning point for Rivers. On the life-altering day when she first saw an unflattering photograph of her childhood nemesis, Rivers's reaction was comparable to the gory feeding frenzy that ensues when a shark smells blood in the water and targets a weakened prey. Rivers had finally found the definitive outlet for her anger, and the effect was galvanic. "I did not realize that this moment was going to skyrocket my career," she said.

That very night, Rivers performed at Ye Little Club in Los Angeles and delivered a joke about Elizabeth Taylor: "I took her to McDonald's just to watch her eat and see the numbers change."

"That got such a reaction, I went on, 'I had to grease her hips to get her through the Golden Arches.' When I tried those two jokes on *The Tonight Show*, the reaction was an eruption of laughter way beyond anything I had ever experienced," Rivers reported. "I had hit a vein."

"Rivers talked to her audience the way you'd dish with your close girlfriend. That included dissing other gals," Roz Warren wrote in *Revolutionary*

*Laughter: The World of Women Comics.* "Who can forget her infamous quip that in a *People* magazine cover, Liz Taylor looked like she'd devoured her previous husbands? It was mean. It was shocking…And it was hilarious. Because it was exactly what we were thinking ourselves, but were too timid (or too kind) to express."

People often found themselves torn between horror and admiration at the things that came out of Rivers's mouth. "It was a crazy kind of courage," said Gloria Steinem. "It was clear that she was desperate; to me it was like watching an addict. She couldn't help but say anything she thought was going to get a laugh."

Rivers's slash-and-burn tactics helped to establish a whole new persona that had an electrifying effect on her career. "America is, at last, catching up to the savage brand of humor she has been dishing out for more than twenty years," *People* magazine reported. "In her midforties, Rivers's career has never been brighter. This month she hosted *Saturday Night Live* on the heels of a hugely successful twelve-city tour (her Carnegie Hall debut sold out in two days); her latest comedy album, *What Becomes a Semi-Legend Most?*, is climbing up the charts; and she is putting the finishing touches on her autobiography."

Within the world of comedy, the roots of Rivers's cruelty were all too familiar. "I think the comic has an angry and vicious mind," said Shelly Schultz. "My mother used to tell me we didn't know who we were running from, the Nazis or the Cossacks. The idea that you can make humor out of sad or awful things—Joan found that a caustic, nasty streak of humor was what made people laugh the hardest. She developed a persona, and people were just looking for the next mean thing she was going to say. They wanted to hear somebody say something terrible about somebody. If they didn't want to hear it they would have rejected her, but they couldn't get enough."

Ever the sharp-eyed social observer, Rivers didn't hesitate to take on the social taboos of the time. Even abortion wasn't off-limits. "She said, 'I knew I wasn't wanted when I was born with a coat hanger in my mouth,'" one director recalled. "People didn't talk about things like that back then; illegal abortion was verboten, and at the time it ruined people's lives. She broke ground because she dared to say things that other people dared to think were funny—and she got away with it."

That kind of material was based on her identification with women as a group who suffer from many of the same indignities in a sexist culture—a sympathetic and inclusive view of her peers. But as her success grew, her perspective began to shift from victim to oppressor.

As had always been the case, Rivers's looks provided the roiling core of her psychic pain, her rage at an unjust world, and—increasingly—the source of her creativity. Some people grow out of their discomfort with childhood's awkward stages, but Rivers never got over hers, and weight remained a central obsession. "I was a fat tub of lard," she said bitterly. "I am still waiting to wake up pretty."

As she got older, she learned how to starve herself to stay thin; early press coverage of her career as a budding comic mentions the fact that she seemed to live on Life Savers, a habit that was later supplanted by an addiction to Altoids, which constituted a major food group for Rivers in her later decades. "You'd go out to dinner with her and she would say, 'Give me the largest glass of white wine you have and a piece of lettuce,'" said Arnold Stiefel. "She would only drink part of the wine."

But when Rivers got thin, she became increasingly unforgiving about other women's weight problems. She deprived herself in the name of beauty, and she had no sympathy for those who didn't—particularly if they'd been more fortunate to begin with.

"She was really fanatical about the weight thing," said radio personality Mark Simone. "She had been a fat kid, and that's one thing she really hated."

"She had an eating disorder, so she would eat two Altoids and then have dessert," said Andrew Krasny, a tennis announcer who worked as Rivers's assistant and became a close friend. "If we want to be on television and in front of people, we have to learn self-denial, and Joan was very conscious of that."

Rivers saw beauty as such a priceless asset that it was unforgivable for a woman to devalue her looks by failing to take care of them. Such attitudes were hardly unprecedented; when fat shaming joined slut shaming as a staple of Rivers's act, she was connecting herself with a long-standing tradition by ridiculing other women, thereby reinforcing the time-honored trope of women in catfights.

"The culture hasn't changed completely," said Gloria Steinem. "It's still safer to come to the public as someone who makes fun of women's strength in women's appearances. Joan was consciously doing that to other women, because it's okay to do. It's part of the stereotype that women don't like each other, that they are competitive and don't get along. If there's a powerful group up here, and a less powerful group down there, the less powerful group is supposed to compete for the favors of the more powerful group."

For Rivers, making jokes about Elizabeth Taylor's weight satisfied her professional goals as well as her personal needs. The jabs earned Rivers so much publicity that she got hooked on the response, which affected her like a crack addiction. The strategy was a brilliant career move, but it was also deeply gratifying on a purely psychological level. "Dancing on the grave of a former beauty was a gleeful thing for her," said the comedian Margaret Cho, a good friend of Rivers in her later years. "It's the ugly girls' revenge."

At the time, such personal attacks seemed genuinely shocking, and the initial onslaught became an all-out siege that went on for years. The jokes were unrelenting.

"Is Elizabeth Taylor fat? Her favorite food is seconds," Rivers sneered.

"They asked her what she wanted with her hamburger and she said, 'A hot dog.'"

"She's so fat she could moon Europe."

And Rivers made no apologies for her nastiness. "I am delighted to be called outrageous," she said, comparing herself to Lenny Bruce and Don Rickles. "When I say, 'Elizabeth Taylor wore yellow and ten school-children got aboard,' people laugh out of embarrassment and out of the truth of it and because they also are thinking the unspeakable—the unspeakable that some comedians dare to say."

As far as Rivers was concerned, her mission was "blasting people out of their comfortable complacency. I think to survive well, to have some happiness, we must face the world as it really is, face the truth about what we are and what we want," she said.

Some of her peers agreed. "It's the truth, and a lot of people don't want to face the truth," said Larry King. "She was acerbic, and her comedy was rough. It cut people. I don't think she was a warm performer. Don Rickles practically begs for your love, even as he's cutting you, but Joan was biting. You'd go to her house, and she was magnificent; she was warm and a great hostess in person. But her stage persona was different. She broke barriers."

Although thin-skinned herself, Rivers had no sympathy for famous people who might be hurt by what she said about them. She seemed to think celebrities were impervious to such attacks—or should be. "Don't your jokes hurt people?" the journalist Nancy Collins asked Rivers in the 1983 *People* magazine cover story.

"If I thought I hurt anybody, I'd go crazy," Rivers replied. "That's why I pick on the biggies. They can take it."

"What hurts you?" Collins asked.

"Everything. Everything! I'm terribly sensitive. I want to please everybody. I cannot work on a set unless everybody loves me and I love everybody."

And yet she remained willfully obtuse about the effect of her own cruel words on others. Years later, Taylor wrote candidly about how painful Rivers's public ridicule had been for her. "I was dying. But I never said anything, because I didn't want anyone to know," she said. "Unfortunately, many people took my silence as license to be cruel. Comedians used my appearance for routines and one-liners. They went after me when I was totally vulnerable. There's nothing the public likes more than to tear down what it has built up. I was built up as a movie star, and when I became fat the public was alternately thrilled and saddened. If Elizabeth Taylor could look the way I did, anyone could and that seemed a comfort to a lot of people. I could understand the fascination. What I still cannot understand is the deliberate cruelty. The jokes were often vicious and served no purpose other than to incite laughter over my misfortune."

Taylor was equally disdainful about her tormentor's later attempts at self-justification. "Not so long ago I was at a benefit with Joan Rivers, who had been foremost among the entertainers who made my weight the butt of their jokes. When I was ready to leave, she grabbed my hand, saying, 'Elizabeth, you look wonderful! I just want you to think about why I said those things about you when you were heavy.'

"'Okay, I'll certainly do that,' I answered, and tried to get away. She held on to my hand and repeated, 'No, no, I mean it. I want you to really think why I did it.'

"'Okay, Joan, I'll think about it,' I answered as I extricated my hand and walked away. I didn't have to think about it; I knew what she was implying. She was taking credit for my losing weight. But I don't think you can justify cruelty and turn it around into a benediction. Jokes were made about my weight because they got laughs, period. In the end, I lost weight because I forced myself to face the truth."

Even that didn't halt the barbed remarks. Rivers acknowledged that Taylor was a gold mine for her. "Without Elizabeth Taylor, I would not have been able to pay for my house," she said. But she also admitted her annoyance at the star's weight loss. "It upsets me, because one more year as a fat pig and I would've had a brand-new house," Rivers complained.

Taylor was too dignified to return fire, but she exacted a private revenge by playing an exquisitely calibrated practical joke on Rivers—one that was as subtle and classy in its execution as Rivers's jokes had been mean and vulgar.

Rivers delighted in having formal dinner parties at the house on Ambazac Way, which she had decorated in an extravagantly rococo style that featured high-end antiques. "If Louis XIV hasn't touched it, I don't want it," she told *People* magazine.

Eager to show off their home while building a viable social life among Hollywood insiders, the Rosenbergs planned one such evening to include Liz Smith, George Hamilton, and Roddy McDowall, who were close friends with Elizabeth Taylor.

"I'd known Joan for years, and I said to Elizabeth, 'I'm invited for dinner at Joan's,'" Hamilton said. "She said, 'Oh, Sunshine!'—she called me Sunshine—'I want to go!' Elizabeth had never showed any hurt from what

Joan had done, but I just felt she thought it was an easy shot for a co-median to do that. When she heard I'd been invited to Joan's house, she thought it would be a perfect time to show up and do nothing except look terrific."

And by this time, the violet-eyed legend was once again looking terrific. "She loved to eat, she just adored it, and she'd eat whatever she wanted—she'd eat crème brûlée—but then she'd pull herself together for a movie, and the minute she decided to lose the weight, she did," Hamilton said. "Elizabeth and I were doing a western called *Poker Alice,* so she was getting ready for the movie and she looked fantastic. Her waist was so small, she had a dark tan—she loved the sun as much as I did—and of course no eyes were ever that color."

While they were plotting Rivers's comeuppance, the co-conspirators took pains to keep their hostess in the dark about the social thunderbolt that awaited her. "When Joan invited me she said, 'Bring whomever you want, but I need to know the name for the place card,'" Hamilton explained. "Elizabeth said, 'I don't want her to know I'm coming,' so she chose her movie name from *Giant,* where she played Rock Hudson's character's wife, Leslie Benedict. I loved being part of this prank, and Elizabeth had confidence in herself to do it with humor—never maliciously."

On the appointed night with the Rosenbergs, Smith said, "We were sitting having a nice time before dinner when the doorbell rang, and Edgar went to the front door and then called for Joan as if there were a big emergency. Standing at the front door were Elizabeth Taylor and George Hamilton, who were having this much-talked-about fling. George loves to advise women about how to be more attractive, so he had taken her over and said, 'Lose the weight, exercise, change the makeup!'—and now she was ravishingly beautiful again. He just stepped in and said, 'This is Elizabeth Taylor.'"

According to Hamilton, Rivers was momentarily struck dumb with consternation. "She stepped back, and she did not know what to say or do," he said. "She just didn't know how to handle it. It was the first time I had ever seen Joan really off. Elizabeth took the moment and said, 'It's so wonderful of you to invite me!' Elizabeth knew how to make a person feel incredibly at ease—she had charm—and it was as though she walked onto a stage and was going to play this scene out."

And play it out she did, in an evening of excruciating discomfort for Rivers but utter delight for the other guests, who were enthralled. "Joan was aghast, but she had enough class to act normal," Smith said. "Elizabeth gave me a big kiss and said, 'Oh, so nice to see you!' She had the support of Roddy and George, and she was enjoying this to the max. She was so glorious that night, so classy. That was the only time I ever saw Joan non-plussed, and we were all bitchy enough to enjoy it that Elizabeth Taylor had turned the tables on Joan after Joan had said all those horrible things about Elizabeth."

Having co-opted the part of grande dame for herself, Taylor left the role of anxious supplicant to her hostess. "Joan looked like she was the maid in *Downton Abbey*," Hamilton said. "She was following Elizabeth around, try-ing to make her comfortable—and Elizabeth was very comfortable. Joan could recover from a bad audience booing her, but you can't recover from somebody that you're in awe of who you've maligned and taken cheap shots at, who comes in and smiles and steals the entire evening, totally without malice."

The effect on Rivers was devastating. "It was like an animal tranquil-izer dart that night, like a zookeeper shot that thing right between her eyes," Hamilton said. "It was like a complete stop. I didn't see Elizabeth ever say anything bad about her, and she never brought it up—that would have diminished her—but it was the idea that she never brought it up. What a grand gesture! It was done so deftly. Joan felt more humiliated than Elizabeth ever felt."

Joan's husband didn't fare much better. "Edgar was getting smaller by the moment," Hamilton said. "It was like, 'Joan's gotten herself into an-other one!'"

For everyone else, however, "it was an incredible laugh," Hamilton said. "I remember Elizabeth having a smirk on her face. She didn't have any gloat about having done it outwardly, but inwardly, the way she looked was like the cat that ate the canary. She didn't say, 'I showed her!'—not a bit! She didn't need to do that. She just delivered the nuclear bomb."

Despite his loyalty to Taylor, Hamilton admitted that he usually enjoyed Rivers's comedy, spiteful though it might have been. "Joan said what others thought and wouldn't say," he observed. "I always loved insult humor—that kind of Borscht Belt stuff. The bathroom humor anyone can say, but to say what another is thinking—that takes an acute sense of comedy. You lose your breath. Joan crossed all those barriers. She had her own brand of it."

But Rivers's mean girl tactics were not necessarily compatible with her other ambitions, particularly the ones that involved being an elegant hostess with a grand house and an all-star guest list that might include some of her victims. "Joan took no prisoners, but at the same time she had an upwardly mobile social agenda as well," Hamilton said. "She wanted to have a social life that was more than that of a comedian."

The mortifying night when Elizabeth Taylor came to dinner left Liz Smith feeling that she had been "present at an epic event in Joan's life," she said. That evening also seemed to kill off Rivers's enthusiasm for trashing her gracious guest. "She never did attack Elizabeth Taylor again," Smith reported.

Rivers subsequently gave Smith a wide berth, or so the columnist believed. "She didn't particularly appeal to me, and I didn't particularly appeal to her, and I always felt she wanted to avoid me after that, because I was there on the night of her greatest comedown," Smith said. "I felt she just wished I would disappear without her having to kill me, because I had been witness to her humiliation."

But Rivers took pains not to let it happen again, and she went to considerable lengths to prevent Taylor from upstaging her in the future. "Joan did an AIDS research event at Spago with Elizabeth Taylor, and Joan knew that Elizabeth was always late," said Larry Ferber, a television producer who later worked with Rivers. "She had her limo driver circle Spago for close to an hour until they spotted Elizabeth's limo, and Joan got out at the exact same moment, and they walked in together."

George Hamilton has his own theory about the underlying psychodynamics between Rivers and Taylor. "The evening at Joan's house would not have been what it was if not for Joan adoring Elizabeth," he said. "Elizabeth was the face of a generation, or two, that wanted to be her. I think Joan wanted to look like Elizabeth Taylor, and anyone who doesn't have that, I think there's an envy factor. But the truth was that Elizabeth didn't care that much about beauty; she was only the guardian of it. Elizabeth had a world of success in her life, and she didn't need to have someone's opinion of her. But to see her allow it to slide away—I think Joan felt that was wasting it, and she might have felt angry about it. She may have felt that Elizabeth let her down."

Rivers later admitted that this was precisely what she felt. And as far as she was concerned, her fellow females agreed with her. "Audiences have always dictated with laughter what they want to hear," Rivers wrote in *Still Talking*. "When I eventually tried to drop such jokes from the act, people called out, 'What about Elizabeth Taylor?'"

According to Rivers, the reason was the anger they all shared. "We women were furious when the most beautiful of all women let herself go," she said. "As long as she was sexually viable, I could be viable. If she became a slob, there was no hope for any of us. I felt betrayed—and so did women across America."

Such women helped to make Rivers into a gigantic star. No matter what her detractors said, it was hard to argue with success of that magnitude— and in those years there was no disputing her popularity. She was a regular at the casinos in Las Vegas, performing as the opening act for the biggest headliners of the era. After years of serving as substitute guest host for Johnny Carson, Rivers was named the permanent guest host of *The Tonight Show* in 1983. During that same year, she not only attended a state dinner at the White House with President and Mrs. Ronald Reagan, but also achieved the hallowed dream of generations of performers by headlining at the ultimate venue.

"I walked out on the stage of Carnegie Hall, and as I reached center stage, the audience stood up and cheered," Rivers wrote in *Still Talking*. "I began to cry. The tears running down my face were from longing—

the longing requited at last, to be on that stage, to be so validated after over twenty years of my parents saying, 'No. Show business is not right for you,' after fifteen years of telling bookers and agents, 'I am good! I can do that.'"

Her mother had died too soon to witness such important validation. "How I wished she could have known her daughter was somebody," Rivers said.

But the rest of the world certainly knew it. "One critic wrote, 'Ignorance of Ms. Rivers's skyrocketing ascendance into the ether of hype virtually amounts to contempt of one's fellow man,'" Rivers reported. "The signals of stardom were all around me. Money was flowing in."

The early comedy albums of the 1960s—*The Next to Last Joan Rivers Album* and *Joan Rivers Presents Mr. Phyllis and Other Funny Stories*—were followed by the best-selling *What Becomes a Semi-Legend Most?*, which was nominated for a Grammy Award for the best comedy album of 1983. Rivers's fellow nominees were Bill Cosby, Monty Python, Robin Williams, and Eddie Murphy. Although Murphy won the Grammy, it was clear that Rivers had joined the big boys in the big leagues.

She had also become a successful author. After publishing her first book, *Having a Baby Can Be a Scream*, in 1974, Rivers waited a decade before writing her next one. When *The Life and Hard Times of Heidi Abromowitz* came out in 1984, it was a best seller.

During that heady period, Rivers constantly strove to expand her reach, but she wasn't successful at everything. In New York, she had always regretted her failure to make it as a theater actress, and in Hollywood she was frustrated by her inability to sustain any lasting credibility in the movie industry. Not that she didn't try. Ever a workaholic, Rivers spent years creating a movie comedy called *Rabbit Test*, which starred Billy Crystal in his film debut as the world's first pregnant man and featured Rivers in a bit part as a nurse. Rivers wrote and directed the movie, and Edgar served as producer. But *Rabbit Test* seemed ill-fated from its inception. It was initially turned down by every studio, but the Rosenbergs raised money to make it on their own, only to see the project founder when the financing kept falling through. Rivers was so determined to prevail that she decided to mortgage their house, whereupon Edgar refused. When she threatened to divorce him, he capitulated—and suggested that they also mortgage her father's house in Larchmont, which she could do without his knowledge.

After battling innumerable obstacles every step of the way, the Rosenbergs finally finished the movie, which was released in 1978 to devastating reviews. The headlines were as predictable as they were negative: "*Rabbit Test* Flops as Farce." "Rivers's *Rabbit* Flunks the Test." "*Rabbit Test* Nauseating, but…"

"Miss Rivers has turned to directing without paying much heed to whether a whole movie constructed from one-liners is worth even the sum of its parts," wrote Janet Maslin in *The New York Times*' review of the film. "In her case, it's not—and the one-liners weren't all that sparkling to begin with. When it winds up on television, which is where a movie this visually crude belonged in the first place, *Rabbit Test* may improve slightly: constant commercial interruptions may help distract attention from the movie's continuity problems, which are severe. And the coarseness of its comedy may not seem so insufferable to an audience willing to sit still for *Laverne & Shirley*."

Rivers never directed another movie—but she had her career in comedy to fall back on, whereas Edgar was once again left with nothing to do. In his IMDb list of professional credits, Edgar's résumé jumps from his 1978 credit as producer of *Rabbit Test* to his 1985 credit as executive producer of a mock tribute called *Joan Rivers and Friends Salute Heidi Abromowitz*, the unsuccessful television special the Rosenbergs made from Joan's latest book.

Despite such a long gap, Edgar continued to function as his wife's factotum. In public, Rivers always claimed that he relished that role. When *People* magazine asked her in 1983 whether Edgar was ever jealous of the attention she got, Rivers replied, "No, because we both realize that I'm a product. He says 'Let's make the product better,' not 'That bitch is getting too much adulation.'"

She also acknowledged that Edgar relieved her of the more unpleasant aspects of her own celebrity. "People think he's the son of a bitch, but I'm the one who says, 'You tell them to go to hell,'" Rivers admitted. "Edgar just makes the calls."

But Edgar's failure to achieve recognition for himself was a source of growing frustration for both of them. The biggest problem was his own dissatisfaction. If he had resigned himself to leading a quiet life behind the scenes, supporting his high-powered wife while accepting the lack of independent validation as an individual, the Rosenbergs' lives might have played out very differently.

Instead, he never stopped hungering for a more important role that would bring him public prestige in his own right—and his quest to achieve such success through his wife's opportunities would ultimately destroy his life and her career.

But neither of them knew that yet—nor did they suspect that they were nearing the end of what would, in retrospect, look like an idyllic era for their family. As that period drew to a close, the Rosenbergs even seemed to have weathered their daughter's adolescence—almost always a perilous time for Hollywood offspring.

Controlling as ever, Rivers had handled the challenges with her usual determination. "Once, Rivers had TV viewers call a 900 number and vote on whether or not Melissa should buy a convertible," *People* magazine reported in 1993.

Joan also tried to influence her daughter's romantic choices. *People* continued: "'Remember, I wanted to set you up with one of those *21 Jump Street* guys,' Joan says as Melissa rolls her eyes. 'And what about the boy whose father owns North Carolina?'"

When Melissa was seventeen, she asked for contraceptives, and Joan took her to the gynecologist. "'And then I slipped her $250 [for a hotel room] so that it wouldn't happen in the backseat of a car,' she admits. 'It's tricky because you know you're opening up a can of worms. Melissa was starting to feel adult emotions now, and I worried, "Is this boy nice for her?" But at least she was going to have safe sex,'" *People* reported.

Whatever form Melissa's rebelliousness took, she wasn't in jail or in rehab, unlike many other children of stars. Never one to take anything for granted, Rivers was grateful for her good fortune, both domestic and professional. Life seemed fine, and she knew that her family owed its privileged circumstances to her own determination.

"I don't know where the drive comes from, but I'm very blessed to be a workaholic," she told Jane Pauley on the *Today* show in 1986.

That was disingenuous; Rivers understood quite well why she needed to keep getting up in front of one audience after another: "I want them to love me," she said.

And she was equally clear about the rewards of that need—and how much she was enjoying them. "I'm a happy lady," she said. "I'm a lucky lady. I have no complaints except my thighs."

## Chapter Seven

# VICTIM AS ENFORCER: TERRORIZING WOMEN INTO SUBMISSION

Rivers's metamorphosis into a ruthless verbal assassin helped turn her into a cultural icon, and her uncompromising toughness won respect even from men who once disdained her girlish attempts to break into comedy. "She didn't take shit from anybody, and I think everyone was a little afraid of her," said Rick Newman. "You didn't want to get on the wrong side of Joan Rivers. Verbally, she could just destroy you."

There was no denying that Rivers had figured out a winning formula—one that became the foundation of a very successful commercial brand that endured beyond her death and left a lasting legacy. In a world where gladiators once killed one another to entertain the masses and people still pay to watch men's brains get battered at football games and boxing matches, it's not surprising that audiences revel in the comedy of cruelty. They have always taken particular pleasure in seeing women trash other women, and Rivers delighted in feeding that appetite.

One of her justifications was the implication that she only punched up, since she started out by skewering the most beautiful and famous women. "While Rivers has been criticized for putting down other women, if you examine her material, you'll learn she always plays fair," Roz Warren wrote in *Revolutionary Laughter*. "She's just as tough on herself as she is on others, she never picks on anybody who can't defend herself, and she only mocks upward."

But that wasn't really true, and Rivers grew ever more spiteful toward younger, less successful women as she expanded her attacks beyond the lucky few. To Rivers, the cardinal sin was the failure to try hard enough to conform to the dictates of beauty. She herself was willing to endure any discomfort to make herself more attractive, so other women had no excuse if they weren't making the same kind of sacrifice.

Her disdain for such slackers extended even to civilians with no obligation to please the public. "One night I was walking in front of the Plaza Hotel with a woman and she said, 'I can't walk in these heels anymore,'" reported Mark Simone. "It's eleven thirty at night, and here comes Joan Rivers, trotting down the street wearing five-inch heels. She said, 'You young girls—you spoil yourselves! You wear sneakers till you get to work. I'm eighty-one, and I can walk in these heels, and mine are twice as high as yours!'"

To the end of her life, Rivers remained resolutely retrograde in many ways, as much a prisoner of a sexist society as a freedom fighter. A lifelong victim of the double standards that judge women more harshly than men, she also became one of their most lethal enforcers, and she was particularly vitriolic toward women who were homely or overweight. Instead of applauding them for liberating themselves from the strictures she had always railed against, Rivers was enraged by their apparent refusal to knuckle under.

"She was such a trailblazer, but she was very old-fashioned, and she felt resentment at the ones who were making it as fat, or not pretty," said the comic Judy Gold. "It came from jealousy and self-hatred. She was seeing these people who weren't going to conform, and it pushed her buttons: 'I had to do this! I had to do that! And now you're walking around like that?'"

Rivers found such resistance maddeningly provocative. "She was like the queen of insecurity, trying to not only conform herself, but to make everyone else conform," observed Gloria Steinem. "But I see her more as a victim than as a perpetrator. I suspect that the insecurity inside her was an unfillable black hole."

Perpetually tortured by her memories of childhood plumpness, Rivers's overriding obsession had always been the quest to stay thin. "I think she was anorexic," said Sue Cameron. "She basically never ate; she just ate Altoids. She was hungry, but she would talk herself out of it: 'I'd better not do that.' In her mind, she was still fat Joanie Molinsky, trying to get a man, and she hated herself. Her whole identity was about being fat, and she never realized she wasn't fat anymore. She would always have a friend sit next to her so she could give her food to them. She would whisper under her breath, 'Take my steak.' 'Take my fish.' She would push food onto your plate so it would look like she was eating. It made me gain weight. I never saw her finish a whole meal, ever. She might have a lettuce leaf. It was awful."

To Rivers, starving herself represented a triumph over the physical self she had detested since childhood. "I think it meant control over biology," said Margaret Cho, who forgave Rivers her constant harangues about losing weight. Cho saw Rivers's criticism as a well-intentioned attempt to help a friend be more successful by getting thin. "She valued it, because you would have more power in a world that values that more."

Rivers didn't always win her own battles with the temptations of the flesh. "She was a secret Reese's Peanut Butter Cup addict," Cameron said. "She kept them in the freezer."

But Rivers labored ceaselessly to stay in shape. "She exercised all the time," said Bill Reardin, a longtime television production executive who started working with Rivers in 1989 and remained friendly with her until she died. "You were talking to her on the phone and she was huffing and puffing on the treadmill."

Having worked so hard at self-improvement all her life, Rivers was particularly incensed by Lena Dunham, whose success was not based on her looks and who didn't conform to Hollywood's mandates on female beauty. Dunham didn't seem to care if people thought she was too fleshy—and she went out of her way to flaunt her defiance. On her groundbreaking HBO television series *Girls*, Dunham quickly became infamous for nude sex scenes that attracted disproportionate attention precisely because her body was so different from the hard-bodied ideal favored by the entertainment industry.

Some hailed Dunham for her bravery, which seemed like a radical act of subversion in the context of the unforgiving standards that usually prevail on camera. But Rivers's response was as headline-grabbing as it was punitive. "Joan had an issue with overweight people," Linda Stasi wrote in the *Daily News*. "In fact, she disliked them so much she tried to get HBO charged with crimes against humanity for letting Lena Dunham get so naked so often."

Relentlessly trashing other women, Rivers was celebrated in many quarters for her particular brand of bitchiness. "Joan's humor was drag queen humor, which is fear-based," said Jason Sheeler, a reporter and editor who specializes in fashion and the entertainment industry. "It's the guys who were always made fun of, so they make fun of themselves first. They say, 'I'm just being honest and saying what everyone else is thinking.'"

But even those who enjoyed the jokes were sometimes put off by the human cost of such attacks. "Joan could be pretty awful, just by flat out calling people ugly," Sheeler admitted. "Whoopi Goldberg once said, 'The three words I hate are "fat," "ugly," and "stupid."' She said that on *The View*, and it totally changed my life."

To experts on the mental health of young women, hurt feelings are not the only danger posed by fat shaming. "I hated it. I just find that appalling and always have," said the late Lynn Grefe, who was president and CEO of the National Eating Disorders Association, the leading national non-profit advocacy group in the fight against eating disorders. "I'm dealing with people with feeding tubes because somebody told them they were pudgy when they were eight years old. I don't think people understand that fat shaming is as bad as making fun of people missing a leg. We've proven that it contributes to the development of eating disorders, and eating disorders have the highest death rate of any mental illness."

Grefe counted herself among those dismayed by Rivers's increasing vituperativeness over the years. "She used to tell jokes, and she just seemed like a comedian, but later on it was making fun of people. Her humor was all at other people's expense, and there's a big difference between those two things," Grefe said. "As time went on, she only got worse. In her later years, she looked desperate for attention. She was a bully. Rather than hit yourself, you go after other people to make yourself look good. With Rivers, fat shaming was a lot of it, but it was all body shaming and envy—talking about beautiful women to make herself feel better."

And yet Rivers's aggression had other effects as well—some of them distinctly liberating. Western society has long prescribed a wide range of social strictures that discourage women from expressing anger. As Rivers gave vent to her stored-up rage, the effect on some women was electrifying.

*The Girl Most Likely to...*, her movie about an unattractive girl who undergoes plastic surgery and kills all the people who once humiliated her, resonated with other girls who identified with the protagonist's pain. "I was homely, and it was my fantasy to become beautiful and kill everyone," said the comic Kathy Griffin. "*The Girl Most Likely to...* was really influential for me."

As Rivers's comedy grew ever more insulting, Griffin was amazed. "I remember thinking, she's known as a person who puts down people," Griffin recalled. "There was that quality of 'Oh my God—what's she going to say next?'"

Reactions to such humor varied; people who came from similar backgrounds viewed it as normative. "Nobody in my family thought Joan Rivers was mean, because I came from a family where we were like the dueling Griffins," Griffin admitted. "It was the kind of humor you'd now call snark."

But others found it deeply transgressive. "It's really hard to shock me, and I was really shocked by her," said Margaret Cho. "She was so hardcore. Joan taught me how to be nasty. I loved her for that."

For Cho, Rivers embodied a thrilling message of female autonomy in a world of toxic male domination. "Korea is very patriarchal and really sexist, and I came from a family of women who were so submissive to their husbands, who were terrible—cheaters and child molesters who abandoned their families and left the women behind with the children while they went gallivanting around," Cho said. "Joan wasn't afraid of making fun of men, which to me was incredibly invigorating and hopeful. She signified a kind of womanhood that I aspired to, that I hadn't experienced before."

The victim of rape and incest while growing up, Cho was raised to believe that women simply accepted such crimes. "All the women in my family did was apologize to men, cook for them, take care of them, and get abused, physically and sexually," she said. "For them, to disrespect men was to court certain death. Joan showed incredible disrespect to men, which to me was power. She had so much strength, and she didn't pull any punches."

Rivers was also a powerful inspiration for young women interested in performing. "Joan Rivers is one of the reasons I got into stand-up comedy," said the comic Joy Behar. "She taught me I could get paid to trash the people I love."

Lisa Lampanelli always wanted to be a comic but held off until she "hit thirty and said, 'It's now or never,'" she recalled. When she listened to albums by Don Rickles and Joan Rivers, she was galvanized by what she heard. "I thought, 'These people got balls,'" Lampanelli recalled. "I just love women who say too much and then you got to defend it. I love fearlessness and nonapologetic humor. I thought, 'This Joan Rivers is crazy—but in a good way.'"

Until Rivers elbowed her way into the spotlight, such ballsy comedy was seen as quintessentially male. From Jack Benny, Fred Allen, Bob Hope, and Don Rickles to Daniel Tosh and Ricky Gervais, insult comedy has been practiced by generations of men who slam offensive slurs at everyone from other performers to their own audiences. Such verbal assaults are readily accepted in comedy, in which it's considered an honor to be abused as the subject of a roast, and even performers who don't specialize in insult techniques often use them to silence or deflect hecklers.

But the rules are different for women. Social science research has documented a wide array of double standards requiring women to be more likable in fields that range from business to politics to entertainment. Women who fail to tone down their aggression and conform to female gender stereotypes run a high risk of being disliked—even if they're fictional characters in films or novels: critics often denigrate female artists for creating female protagonists they deem insufficiently appealing.

Rivers typically walked a fine line between aggression and ingratiation.

"One day we had Joan Collins on the show, and Joan Rivers said, 'Oh, she's back there with six sailors,' and Joan Collins almost walked," reported Larry Ferber, the executive producer of *The Joan Rivers Show*. Anxious not to lose her guest, Rivers rushed to placate her. "Joan Rivers said, 'I was joking! I respect you!' And they became friends."

But Rivers never stopped insulting a long line of victims, and in emulating the tactics used by her male counterparts, she paved the way for the female successors who have since incorporated insult comedy into their own material, from Kathy Griffin to Sarah Silverman and Lisa Lampanelli.

Having discovered that trashing celebrities was a reliable crowd-pleaser in her stand-up act, Rivers went on to parlay that principle into lucrative television content. The entire premise of *Fashion Police*—which assembles a panel of commentators to critique the outfits of stars who appear on the red carpet at awards ceremonies—is based on the entertainment value of bitchy cracks about the sartorial missteps and physical flaws of famous people. Rivers was always the show's most merciless critic, and the poison darts she aimed at hapless luminaries won her many new fans in her final years.

But others were put off by Rivers's evolution from a gentler Joan into one of the world's most uninhibited mean girls. Early in her career, Henry Bushkin and Johnny Carson went to see Rivers do stand-up at a club, and both men loved her act. "She was terrific," Bushkin said. "Her material was sex stuff, family stuff. It was self-deprecating humor, not sarcastic."

But Bushkin often found himself recoiling as Rivers's humor grew sharper over time. "I never appreciated the latter Joan, quite frankly, because I thought she was too nasty and sarcastic—unnecessarily cruel, for no reason," he said. "I much preferred the more self-deprecating fun stuff, like, 'Every time I go in to buy trashy lingerie, they say, "Do you want it gift wrapped?" They think it has to be for someone else.' To me those were her funnier days."

As her excesses grew more frequent, even her longtime fans were horrified. "She went too far sometimes," said Lou Alexander, one of her first mentors. "She made fun of the three girls who were held captive in Ohio and raped. That was wrong. I said to myself, 'Joan—wrong!' These three girls were raped and didn't know if they were ever going to see their families again. There's nothing funny about that. How can you make fun of these three poor girls living that way with a monster?"

To many people, Rivers's jokes about Ariel Castro and his kidnapping victims represented her callousness at its worst. In an offhand comment, she had compared the living quarters of the three captives to her own accommodations while staying with her daughter and shooting a reality TV show: "Those women in the basement in Cleveland had more room," she said.

But when her initial remarks were criticized, Rivers was not contrite. "They got to live rent-free for more than a decade," she said. "One of them has a book deal. Neither are in a psych ward. They're okay. I bet you within three years one of them will be on *Dancing with the Stars*."

When questioners kept pressing the issue, Rivers became exasperated. "I'm a comedienne," she said. "I know what those girls went through. It was a little, stupid joke. There is nothing to apologize for. I made a joke. That's what I do. Calm down. Calm fucking down. I'm a comedienne. They're free, so let's move on."

Resolutely defiant about such criticism, Rivers always defended a comic's right to make fun of absolutely anything. If people complained, her usual replies were irritable rather than placatory: "Oh, give me a break!" and "Grow up!" She felt no compunction about any of her jokes, no matter how insensitive or hurtful. "If it was offensive, Joan would say, 'Good. Comedy is not funny unless it's a little bit dangerous. You get up there and you have to surprise people and wake them up,'" said Valerie Frankel, who coauthored Rivers's book *Men Are Stupid...and They Like Big Boobs*.

Some people accepted that rationale. "It was cruel, but it's not wrong," said Bill Reardin. "It's her job to make people laugh. There's tragedy, yes, but she said, 'Get over it. Let's not mourn.' It was a principle, and it should be a principle with any comedian that you can't start censoring comedians. I don't think it's particularly nice to poke fun at people's physical characteristics, but I'm not a comedian."

Others were not convinced. "She thought, 'There's nothing I can't use;

there's nothing I will not say. I will not edit myself about anything,'" Lou Alexander said. "She would get into fights with a lot of people. She said, 'What do I care?' But there were certain times she left a bad taste."

To some extent, Rivers was just playing the odds. "She made me laugh more than any other person, but sometimes I would think, oh my God, someone's going to shoot her!" said Sandy Gallin. "She did go too far, but she got away with it. For the 50 people in the audience who may have been offended, there were 950 people who were on the floor, rolling."

When people accused Rivers of crossing some invisible line, she attributed her aggressiveness to the wounds she herself had suffered. "I am tasteless," she acknowledged. "If you are a current comic and do not offend somebody, you are doing itsy-bitsy cutesy-wootsy pap. If 10 percent of the people hate me, I will be fine. I always want to have one couple that gets up and leaves. That means I am still on the cutting edge. However, my whole humor is actually based on the loneliness and hurt of being left out, of being thrown over—which I always fear and dread…In my pain, in my upset and anger, I am railing at the world."

Although concessions were rare, Rivers occasionally did agree to back down. "We had a writer on *The Joan Rivers Show* who was the mean Joan Rivers—he wrote most of the Elizabeth Taylor jokes—and at one point we started to do Delta Burke fat jokes," recalled Larry Ferber, the show's executive producer. Ferber and a plus-sized woman who worked on the show went to Rivers to express their concern, and the woman told her, "I don't think it's wise to be doing this; you're offending women in the audience."

"And Joan stopped," Ferber said. "She respected the women in the audience, and she respected someone she worked with who happened to be large."

But for the most part, people simply avoided tangling with Rivers, afraid of her lacerating tongue. One of the few to take her on was the comedian Pat Cooper.

"She was working at Caesars Palace, and she was ripping everybody off, and she was rude to Elizabeth Taylor, and nobody's standing up to this girl," Cooper said. "She's a bully. So I wrote this little cartoon book and put it in a big basket of fruit and said, 'Only big people can give it and take it. I know you're one of the big people.'"

Titled "Justice for All: Pat Cooper vs. Joan Rivers," the cartoon pamphlet named some of her regular victims in its dedication—"to the Elizabeth Taylors, Queen Elizabeths, Karen Carpenters, Princess Grace and children, Nancy Reagans"—and added, "This book was written to 'balance the books.'"

Cooper's portrait of Rivers was scathing. "Joan Rivers is the only woman with scar tissue on her tongue," one cartoon said. "Jake LaMotta was the Raging Bull, Joan Rivers is the Raging Bullshit," said another. "Her favorite food is Elizabeth Taylor's garbage," read a third.

The pamphlet portrayed Rivers as venomous from infancy to adulthood. "Baby Joan's teething ring" showed her in diapers tonguing a cobra. When little girl Joan asked her father if she could go out to play with the other children, he said, "Sure, but first put on your muzzle." As an adult, she was loveless—"If she was a hooker, she would still be a virgin," one cartoon read—and friendless, according to a picture that showed her sitting at Thanksgiving dinner with a large turkey and a table surrounded by empty chairs. Cooper also took shots at Rivers as a professional, depicting her at a talk show microphone with the caption, "Joan has a new sponsor...rat poison."

Rivers failed to discern whatever humor Cooper thought he was conveying. "I get this phone call: 'You son of a bitch! You oughta drop dead!'" Cooper recalled. "I said, 'You're the real bully—but you're a coward. You won't tell them to their face.' And I hung up on her. Then my wife calls Joan Rivers and says, 'You got some nerve to abuse my husband who was nice enough to send you a basket of fruit! My husband says it the way it is—you can't take it! He thought you'd have a little humor!' And so Joan apologizes to my wife. She says, 'How would you like to have lunch with me? You sound like a nice lady.' My wife comes back and says Joan felt a little embarrassed that she would call; she said, 'He must be a hell of a guy if you defend him.' I get a call a week later, and they offer me two jobs with Joan Rivers."

Although Cooper did work with her again, he also ended up telling her off again and denouncing her as a bully. But even that was not the last of their interactions. A few years later, he had an interesting exchange with Edgar Rosenberg.

"I did her show on Fox, and her husband, Edgar, said to me, 'Pat, have patience,' because he knew I knew," Cooper reported. "He said, 'You're the only one who ever stood up to her.' He was a gentleman, and he was respectful to her, but I don't think she gave a damn. She's the boss. I don't remember her giving him credit. And she blamed him for the Johnny Carson thing. Why blame someone else when you're an idiot? She's hurt a lot of people who are nice people."

Rivers's cruelty was highly selective. "Joan's attitude was, if you're rich and famous, you're a target, but she would never do that to an ordinary person," said Larry Ferber.

But Rivers's penchant for kindness was equally selective—and it could be just as over the top. Despite her eager embrace of the theater of cruelty, she was well-known for being nice to strangers who approached her. Some stars are rude and dismissive with fans, but Rivers—who found their attention as necessary as oxygen—was always delighted to give an autograph, take a picture, and ask about people's lives.

Jesse Kornbluth helped Rivers write the commencement speech she gave at the University of Pennsylvania when Melissa graduated in 1989. To develop material for the speech, Kornbluth asked Rivers a series of questions, one of which was, "Joan, how do we treat the little people?"

"Why, we treat them better," she said. "We only shit on people at our level or higher."

Kornbluth once saw Rivers at a lunch where he mentioned that his wife and daughter never missed *Fashion Police*. Rivers asked how old his daughter was, and Kornbluth told her she was twelve. He assumed that was the end of it: "Joan playing to a crowd—my daughter would never hear from her," he said. "But a few weeks later, a package arrived with a *Fashion Police* badge, a bracelet from the Joan Rivers collection, and a lovely handwritten note. And I thought, 'The little people—we treat them better.'"

Kornbluth was also impressed with the effort Rivers made to express her appreciation for those who rendered support services. In a later essay for the *Huffington Post*, he reported that every time he went to dinner at Rivers's apartment, she would "call for the waiters, cooks, and kitchen staff to come out. She would thank them. And the guests would applaud. I never saw another New York hostess do that."

Such gestures extended beyond the home. Before Rivers started performing at the Laurie Beechman Theatre, she did stand-up at a nightclub called Fez and at the Cutting Room, both of which eventually closed. "On the final day at Fez, she comes in followed by people with hand trucks," said Chip Duckett, who produced her live shows in New York. "She had a bottle of wine for each person, with an individually signed label—fifty or sixty people, including every server and every bartender. She did the same thing at the Cutting Room when it closed. She personally thanked everyone who cleaned a bathroom at those places. She treated everyone with that kind of respect. You show me anyone else in show business who would do that."

Rivers's reasons were doubtless multidetermined: ingratiating herself with fans and coworkers and cultivating new customers with free gifts might both be seen as shrewd brand-building activities that would ultimately redound to her own benefit. In other circumstances, however, her version of noblesse oblige could be so generous as to appear genuinely altruistic.

"She did a lot of things anonymously," said Dorothy Melvin. "She would read about a child in the Midwest who had a prosthetic leg stolen from their car, and she anonymously sent money to replace the leg. This woman really cared about people."

Rivers's compassion sometimes resulted in an enduring connection. "Joan was at the Riviera in Las Vegas, and it was the middle of the night after the second show, and we went to the coffee shop to relax," said Melvin. "There was a girl named Lynn who bussed the tables. She was a high-functioning person with Down syndrome, and the waitress was berating her. Joan was always protective of the underdog, and she got so angry she yelled at the waitress. She said to the hostess at the coffee shop, 'If anybody abuses that girl, I will go to Walter Kane and I will have her job!'"

Kane was the entertainment director of Howard Hughes's hotel-casinos, and Rivers was more than capable of making good on her threat. But she didn't leave it at that.

"Then she went back and sat Lynn down with us and started talking to her," Melvin reported. "Lynn was getting married, and her fiancé worked at the Hilton, and they were going to Disneyland on their honeymoon. Joan said, 'Did you have a nice wedding shower?,' and Lynn said, 'No. I don't have friends.' The next morning we started calling every entertainment office—the Sands, the MGM Grand—telling them that Joan was giving a wedding shower for this girl, and everyone had to come and bring a gift. She wanted one woman to come from each office. She gave Lynn a wedding shower at the Riviera."

Nor did Rivers relinquish her role as fairy godmother after the wedding. "Every year, Joan would say, 'Did we have the Razens yet this year?'" Melvin reported. "And every year, once a year, we had Lynn and her husband, and Joan would pay for a limo to pick up Lynn and her parents and take them to a good dinner and bring them backstage after the show. Who does that? It was so kind. We also had her son, Chadwick Twain—they lived at the corner of Chadwick and Twain—until he died in a swimming pool at the age of two. She never forgot them in all those years. That was the ultimate kindness."

Unlike many donors, Rivers didn't perform such acts for recognition. "She never looked for credit for any of her philanthropy," said Arnold Stiefel.

But it gave her great pleasure to spread her wealth on behalf of chosen beneficiaries, just as it had at the beginning of her career when she was able to fly her parents to Chicago and pay for their dinners. Having fought so hard to establish her career, Rivers spent much of her middle age thinking she had surmounted life's most difficult challenges and could look forward to a future of taking pleasure in the rewards.

She had no idea that the worst was still to come—let alone that it would destroy everything she had built for herself in all those years of struggle.

## Chapter Eight

# THE TEMPTATION OF JOAN: POISONED APPLE

More than three decades after it happened, show business veterans still argue about the legendary feud that Rivers created with Johnny Carson when she left *The Tonight Show* to create a rival program. After appearing with Carson on April 25, 1986, to plug her new memoir, *Enter Talking*, Rivers announced that she had signed on with the fledgling Fox network as host of her own talk show. But she hadn't told Carson beforehand that she was leaving, and many people saw that choice as an epic betrayal by an ungrateful former acolyte. Others defended it as a normal rite of passage that was unfairly penalized by a jealous mentor and a sexist industry all too eager to punish an uppity woman for having the temerity to strike out on her own.

To this day, everyone from the general public to those who were intimately involved in the saga still debates the respective roles of loyalty, duplicity, incompetence, rank opportunism, and bungled communications in creating a cold war so lasting that Rivers was banned from *The Tonight Show* for nearly thirty years. After Carson retired, Jay Leno and Conan O'Brien abided by their predecessor's fiat, and Rivers's long exile ended only when Jimmy Fallon succeeded Leno as the host in 2014, a few months before Rivers died.

The feud was as petty as it was mean-spirited. "When *The Tonight Show Starring Johnny Carson* went off the air in 1992, I asked them if we could use some clips of Joan Rivers with Johnny Carson, and they said no," reported Larry Ferber, the executive producer of *The Joan Rivers Show*, the daytime talk show Rivers was doing at the time. "They put rumors out that she was a bitch, that she was difficult. A couple of weeks later, there was something in the papers that [said] 'She's at it again—Joan Rivers is trying to steal material from *The Tonight Show*.' Joan was so hurt."

As with most long-running vendettas, the bad blood between Carson and Rivers is often oversimplified by partisans on both sides. But the situation might have been even more complicated—and its underlying cause far more malignant—than anyone understood until now.

After Rivers's death, Carson's former producer and Rivers's former manager ran into each other by accident at a shopping center in Los Angeles. They hadn't spoken in nearly thirty years, but when they started to compare their respective pieces of the jigsaw puzzle, both were stunned by the unfamiliar picture that emerged.

Was it conceivable that the real culprit had remained hidden until this late date?

With the possible exception of that one bad actor, whose motives are very much open to question, it seems clear that nobody else on either side ever wanted such a rupture to occur. In the mid-1980s, when Rivers's career was flourishing, she remained deeply grateful to Carson for launching her career, and she certainly had no desire to alienate him in any way.

That said, there's also no question that her own actions subsequently turned a heartwarming story of patronage given and longtime affection received into a breach so bitter and familial it evoked *King Lear*. Rivers never meant for that to happen, and she felt grief as well as anger about it for the rest of her life.

The ugliness of the estrangement was variously blamed on putative villains who ranged from Edgar Rosenberg to the billionaire mogul Barry Diller to Rivers herself. But the new suspect has potentially transformed the entire equation with a chilling alternative scenario.

Could a relatively minor player, one apparently motivated by sheer malevolence, have provided the pivotal plot point—a secret memo ostensibly prepared by NBC brass that excluded Rivers from consideration as Carson's successor—with a gratuitous act so vicious it seems to have been imported from another play entirely? Was the move that wrecked Rivers's career and ended her husband's life actually triggered by a behind-the-scenes Iago as stealthy as he was malicious?

And finally—most heartbreakingly—could the whole catastrophe have occurred because that bitter, twisted person was trying to be funny?

Since the field in question is comedy, the question of who and what is funny provided the larger context for the debacle from the outset. Johnny Carson reigned as host of *The Tonight Show* for nearly three decades, and many people—most of them comedians—served as guest hosts over the years.

Joey Bishop hosted a total of 177 times, mostly in the 1960s, and Rivers racked up 93 hosting credits during the 1970s and 1980s. Other guest hosts ranged from Bob Newhart, Jerry Lewis, and David Letterman to Kermit the Frog, but it was Carson's worshipful "daughter" who began to outshine the star and draw higher ratings.

"Of the various comedians and personalities who substituted for Carson, including David Brenner and Bill Cosby, the most successful was Joan Rivers," Daniel Kimmel wrote in *The Fourth Network: How Fox Broke the Rules and Reinvented Television*. "Her shtick was that she was a chic Jewish suburban housewife, and she complained about her marriage, being a mother, and—somewhat shocking in its day—sex. What made her different was that the few women stand-ups around then, like Phyllis Diller, played somewhat grotesque characters. Rivers, with her aggressive repartee and stylish outfits, looked like someone you'd see at a supermarket or a PTA meeting. By 1983, the fifty-year-old Rivers had achieved stardom."

That was the year Rivers was officially designated as Carson's permanent guest host, a role she had essentially been filling for the previous year. No matter where else she performed, *The Tonight Show* served as the underlying platform for her career and the source of her greatest visibility, and her perceived success as Carson's understudy supplied a vital part of her self-image. She never stopped being grateful for his role in making her a star, but she understood quite well that she would always be the acolyte. "It sounds stupid, but eighteen years later it's still very much master-servant," she told *People* magazine in 1983. "He comes to see me, and it's the boss coming. He gave me everything."

In some ways, of course, they were two of a kind. No matter how much recognition performers achieve, Rivers knew how much of their self-esteem and sense of well-being are derived from ongoing success. Once accustomed to constant adulation, they usually have a difficult time giving it up. As a stand-up comedian, she readily admitted that she too was dependent on applause for her sense of self-worth.

"When I am rejected by an audience, I feel total self-hatred," she said. "I want to stop the act and spit in my own face. The larger the audiences, the worse I feel."

Long experience with the titans of the industry had also taught her what a tough bunch they were. "Nobody wants to admit these great icons are killers," she said. "When I dared cross Johnny Carson to go to Fox, he came on like a gutter fighter—and let his representatives do the talking. To succeed in this rough business we all have to be killers—myself included. God knows what any of these people came out of and how hard they had to fight, what humiliations they suffered. Johnny Carson once said, 'I started in Bakersfield doing magic off the back of a truck to guys standing in cornfields.'"

Rivers recognized the competitiveness inherent to the breed—including her own. When she published *Still Talking* in 1991, she was pushing sixty, but she wasn't anywhere near ready to cede the field to up-and-coming rivals. "I really hate to be admired by young comics," she wrote. "I am not ready. I am still one of you guys. I have not peaked yet. I do not know my full potential—maybe stage or movie acting, maybe directing or writing. I suspect no star, no matter how big, wants to be put on a pedestal. Then you are a monument to yourself, by definition part of the past. I still think of myself as absolutely the present."

The dynamics of Rivers's relationship with Carson were also complicated by gender, whether or not they ever had the sexual encounter she subsequently claimed. Men of his generation didn't expect younger women to threaten their dominance, particularly when the woman in question was a disciple and the man was the undisputed king of an industry where he had reigned for decades.

In later years, Rivers herself would invoke gender in trying to explain their estrangement, as if she were the favorite daughter of a Lear-like monarch who felt abandoned. "Johnny banned me," she said. "He was very angry I left and I really never say this, but I think it was because I was a woman... I left and a wall came down, and I think because he really liked me the best."

Carson was only eight years older than Rivers, but both her partisans and his believed that he was totally sincere in championing her career the way he did. "When you go back to how he put her on the show, you saw Johnny's enjoyment of all his guests, but you always felt he was looking at Joan through different eyes," said Dorothy Melvin, who was the Rosenbergs' assistant for years before becoming Joan's manager. "It was the pride of a parent: 'I enjoy you so much, you're giving me pride and joy, I'm having the best time just looking at you!' You could see it in his face. And she adored him—until she felt he turned on her with the memo."

If Rivers had been single, it is entirely possible that she and Carson would have remained friends until he died—even if a would-be Iago had tried to poison their relationship. But with Edgar Rosenberg as her anxious, insecure, endlessly striving partner, Rivers was vulnerable to the lure of any proposal that seemed to offer her spouse more power and respect.

Still deeply in thrall to a lifetime of indoctrination that women should put their husbands' needs before their own, Joan was just as desperate to see Edgar succeed as he was. He prided himself on being the ultimate defender of his wife's interests, but when it came to his own thwarted ambitions, his capacity for self-delusion was as powerful as his need for external validation.

In 1986, the fatal opportunity for self-destruction was provided by the legendary, formidable, fearsome Barry Diller.

Now the chairman of IAC/InterActiveCorp and Expedia Inc., Diller originally began his career in the mail room of the William Morris Agency after dropping out of UCLA after one semester of college. As ruthless as he was brilliant, Diller quickly made a name for himself as a cold-blooded power player; in 2012, Business Insider described him as one of the leading "executives who rule by fear."

Starting in 1974, Diller served for a decade as chairman and CEO of Paramount Pictures. He left in 1984 to become chairman and CEO of Fox, the parent company of Twentieth Century Fox. Two years later, the Fox Broadcasting Company was launched as a commercial broadcast television network that was intended to compete with the existing big three: ABC, NBC, and CBS.

When the Rosenbergs began their dealings with Diller and Fox, Edgar was already in a weakened state, and had been for quite a while. In 1984, at the age of fifty-nine, he suffered a heart attack that was triggered by an argument between Melissa and her parents over where she should go to college. When she was accepted at the University of Pennsylvania, her parents were thrilled by the prospect of her attending a prestigious Ivy League institution. But Melissa insisted she wanted to stay in California, live with a girlfriend, and go to UCLA. Her parents were horrified, a screaming match ensued, and Melissa ran out of the house with Joan in hot pursuit.

"Melissa and Joan were in the driveway, and Melissa wanted to go somewhere, and Joan didn't want her to go, and I heard Edgar say, 'Dorothy! Dorothy!'" Dorothy Melvin reported. "I ran back in and Edgar was a gray that I'd never seen in my entire life. He was upstairs standing on the landing, leaning on the railing, and I ran screaming for the security guard, who was trained in CPR."

They realized that Edgar was having a heart attack, and the security guard started doing CPR. "Melissa was hysterical, screaming and screaming," Melvin said.

Although Edgar survived the heart attack after undergoing triple bypass surgery, he suffered from weeks of life-and-death complications that left him deeply debilitated. Like her mother before her, Melissa eventually capitulated to parental pressure and headed for college in the Northeast, but the terrible fight that precipitated her father's collapse left her with an enduring burden of guilt and anxiety.

As for Joan, the crisis provided a terrifying reminder of how much she had come to depend on her husband. "After Edgar's heart attack, suddenly I realized that I drew all my strength from Edgar," she said.

And he was no longer the tower of strength she had relied on. "Depressions plagued him, and he retreated to his bed for hours—or he was swept by mood swings. Some emotional governor was missing. The rage that reached back to his childhood was now on a hair trigger," Rivers reported. "He came out of the hospital with his mind muddled, distracted and forgetful. I still think his brain might have been damaged during those episodes when he was brought back from death. He had trouble grasping complexities and remembering details. His memory was so undependable, he carried his own phone number in his wallet. When he did stumble mentally, his embarrassment and self-disgust were profound."

Everyone knew that Edgar was vulnerable to another heart attack, and the fear of a recurrence haunted the Rosenbergs for the remainder of their time together. "For both of us, death was now a palpable presence, waiting just out of sight," Rivers said.

Despite Edgar's apparent recovery, his behavior changed in ominous ways, further eroding his wife's trust. "The keystone of Edgar's character was the need to keep himself and the world around him in control. So any loss of control—helplessness—left him vulnerable and terrified, put him in a downward spiral," Rivers wrote. "His sense of impotency fed his fear, which increased his frustration—which came out as anger—which increased his loss of control—which multiplied the fear and anger—which made people avoid him—which made him even more isolated and angry. He was driving himself crazy—and driving everybody around him crazy too. The one element that gave him a sense of power, even manhood, was money."

So Edgar threw himself into a frenzy of spending, redecorating the Rosenbergs' house with lavish expenditures and buying Joan such treasures as a Fabergé pin once owned by the czar's sister, along with Marie of Romania's necklace of Fabergé eggs. Alternately seduced by the extravagant gifts and dismayed at her husband's lack of judgment, Rivers was too afraid of fighting with him to try to control his excesses.

She dealt with her marital problems in a state of what she called "constructive denial," choosing to believe that this difficult period would pass while focusing on her own independent life as a performer. When she was on the road, she had fun; escaping her tortured spouse was a relief. "After twenty years of marriage I was happy because I was not with my husband," she said. "That is a terrible, terrible truth to admit to yourself. I was barely able to face it and felt guilty and frightened and pushed away the thought because there was nothing I felt I could do to change the situation."

But going home felt like coming back to "a prison." Edgar was "resentful and competitive," cutting her off in the middle of a sentence in social situations and tyrannizing her with petty forms of control like monopolizing the television remote control. "He would not let me read *Time* and *Newsweek* until he had read them, even if that took him a week—so I had to take out duplicate subscriptions," Rivers said. "Any book he bought I could not read first—so two copies of the same book sat on our bedside table."

And yet Edgar continued as his wife's Svengali, the manager who wielded the power to control key decisions about The Career, as they still referred to Rivers's professional life. When the opportunity they had both coveted suddenly appeared on the horizon like a tantalizing Trojan horse, the stage was set for their mutual destruction.

"He was a man too unstable to be the 'rock' in command of my impulses, persuading me with pros and cons and practical consequences," Rivers said. "His natural caution had increased to paranoia, and his priorities were reversed, details becoming more important than fundamental issues. This man, fighting for his sanity, still searching for a source of ego and self-respect, was the husband who would soon be leading us into the jungle of Fox Broadcasting Network, a place populated by men able and willing to kill us."

In July of 1985, flying back from London after doing a series of BBC television shows, Rivers dozed off while Edgar read a *Newsweek* cover story about Rupert Murdoch, the publishing magnate who had bought Twentieth Century Fox Film Corporation, along with six Metromedia VHF television stations: in New York, Los Angeles, Washington, Dallas,

Chicago, and Houston. Fox was planning to use those stations as the nucleus of a fourth broadcasting network, and Edgar realized that Fox, in order to get attention for its new network, would need a big name to head a high-profile show—a name like Joan Rivers.

At the time, the Rosenbergs were increasingly unnerved by their dealings with NBC and Carson Productions. Rivers's contracts had always paralleled Carson's, but when he signed his latest two-year contract, Rivers was offered only a one-year deal. Rivers felt vulnerable, as well as taken for granted and implicitly disrespected by the men who controlled the decisions, both at NBC and in Carson's personal empire.

"Edgar started calling John Agoglia, the NBC executive vice president of business affairs, almost a year before they were to pick up Joan's contract, asking for a deal," explained Sue Cameron, whose résumé included a stint as a network executive at ABC in addition to her years as a columnist and TV editor for the *Hollywood Reporter*. "Month after month, John would make up some excuse, so Joan and Edgar were beginning to get very nervous."

Cameron believed they had ample reason to worry. "Joan's ratings were consistently higher than Johnny Carson's, and Johnny was feeling threatened, so Johnny ordered the network not to renew Joan's contract," she said. "John Agoglia knew the network was going to screw over Joan. It's absolutely true; I had inside sources at every network, and I verified it with NBC. Johnny wanted Joan out. She was too popular."

So when Edgar suggested that he and Joan approach Fox to discuss alternative possibilities, Rivers told him to go ahead, expecting that nothing would come of such talks, but thinking they would keep her agitated husband busy for a while.

Some of Carson's associates blame Edgar for creating the whole problem. "The Fox show came about because Edgar went out looking for it," said Shelly Schultz. "Why would anybody in their right mind do that—go up against a guy who loved her and fostered her career, who gave her every shot there was to get? You could give Edgar the benefit of the doubt and say he didn't know any better because he was a rank amateur, or you could say it's because he was stupid."

But Schultz doesn't absolve Rivers. "There's an old mafioso saying: 'The fish stinks from the head down,'" he said. "Why would Joan agree to do that? She knows firsthand how good Johnny is to her. Maybe she was under the spell of this Edgar; maybe he said, 'This is my chance to be a big producer—and your chance to be a big star.' Whatever it was, it was ill thought out. She should have told Edgar, 'No, I can't do this.' She should never have had a show opposite Johnny Carson. She should never, ever have betrayed him like that, because his show was responsible for her career. She shouldn't have let it get to the point where there was even an offer, but Edgar was stupid, and Joan went along with it because she wanted to satisfy Edgar's need to be useful. Johnny would have been okay with her having her own show. As a matter of fact, it would have been a feather in his cap for somebody he mentored—just not in his time slot. That's terrible. It's kind of like your mate cheating on you; it's the ultimate betrayal. She should have said no. But Edgar was in need of being very important, as opposed to being Mr. Joan Rivers. He was an opportunist, and he convinced her to do it."

When friends tried to warn them against the move, Edgar turned against them. "I said, 'This is a terrible mistake. Do not make this deal,'" Arnold Stiefel recalled. "I didn't think it was a good move, and I would have asked her to resist. But by then I was in the doghouse."

As the talks with Fox got serious, Rivers found herself confronted with a frightening choice between staying with Carson and leaving NBC to strike out on her own. Both courses of action would risk her future security, but in very different ways.

At this pivotal moment, as in so many plots that feature a mysterious letter of possibly fraudulent origin, a fateful document suddenly appeared—one that Rivers mentions only in passing in her account of events but that looms far larger in light of later developments.

Although Carson turned sixty in 1985, associates say he had no intention of retiring anytime soon. His advancing age inevitably inspired gossip about who would eventually succeed him, and there was no shortage of candidates. But Carson didn't end up leaving *The Tonight Show* for seven more years, and his departure was not regarded as anything remotely close to imminent when Rivers started worrying about her own future with the show.

As the sole permanent guest host and a ratings winner in her own right, she was justified in thinking she deserved to succeed him, even though no woman had ever commanded a late-night talk show in the entire history of television. But the Rosenbergs were unable to get any kind of reassurance from the Carson camp or from NBC executives, and what they perceived as stonewalling made them both feel increasingly insecure.

"When Johnny is gone, so are you," Edgar warned his wife, pointing out that NBC had never even bothered to make Rivers exclusive to the network.

"They think nobody will ever want me," she replied sadly.

Some close friends believe that Edgar's fears greatly exacerbated the problem. "He was totally devoted to keeping her in a state of 'us against them'—totally paranoid," said one.

But in this case, Edgar wasn't the only one fomenting trouble. In *Still Talking*, Rivers described the moment that sealed her doom this way: "Then a friend—a real friend, Jay Michelis—smuggled me a list prepared by NBC naming the ten successors if Johnny retired. My name was not on it. I almost died."

Jay Michelis was NBC's West Coast vice president for corporate and media relations, and the list he showed the Rosenbergs seemed to provide incontrovertible evidence that NBC and Carson were planning to betray Rivers and reward her years of loyalty by choosing a man to take over *The Tonight Show* instead of her. The Rosenbergs took their suspicions to the network brass, who claimed they were unfounded—but those assurances failed to allay their fears. "When we confronted NBC, the president, Brandon Tartikoff, denied such a list ever existed. But we had seen it," Rivers wrote. "Edgar said, 'There's no future for you here. You've been deluding yourself.'"

Many of the men associated with the show scoff at the very idea of such a memo. "There was no reason for NBC to compile a list—none," said Shelly Schultz.

But other industry observers believe it's entirely possible that gender bias—whether conscious or unconscious—really was the underlying explanation for why Rivers was overlooked as Carson's successor. "I think the reason she wasn't on the list was that she was a woman," said Larry Ferber, who worked on the talk shows of Dinah Shore, Sally Jessy Raphael, and Mike Douglas, as well as on Rivers's daytime program.

Other experienced professionals saw additional reasons why Rivers might not have been a sure bet to succeed Carson. "One, they didn't know if a woman could work every night," said Sandy Gallin, Rivers's manager during most of her time in California, although she fired him before she left *The Tonight Show*. "They thought she could hold the audience for one or two nights, and then a week at a time, but they didn't know if her personality was too abrasive if she did it every single night. Two, was she controllable enough, or would she have done material they couldn't control and didn't approve of?"

As 1986 began, the Rosenbergs kept reaching out to NBC and Carson executives to discuss their plans for renewing Rivers's contract—only to be stonewalled. In *Still Talking*, Rivers reported that crucial calls were not returned, including those to Henry Bushkin and to John Agoglia. The apparent brush-off convinced them that Rivers's humiliation was just a matter of time.

The resulting atmosphere of fear and mistrust provided the perfect opportunity for Barry Diller to make an all-out pitch for Rivers to come to Fox, a move that seemed to serve the needs of both sides. "Rivers was looking for a safety net if she were to jump from *The Tonight Show;* Fox wanted a marquee name that would give their new network instant credibility," Daniel Kimmel wrote in *The Fourth Network*. "It was a match made in television. Rivers would do a nightly, one-hour show from Los Angeles, mixing comedy, music, and interviews. In essence, Fox would clone *The Tonight Show* with one of its guest hosts behind the desk."

But Rivers was terrified of breaking her ties with Carson, and she agonized endlessly about whether to take such a risk. "A show business career is like riding a shimmering soap bubble, beautiful almost because of its fragility," she said. "If you are a television personality, the bubble is kept filled by visibility, reputation, freshness, currency, celebrity, excitement—

what Carson provided. Without *The Tonight Show,* I would be floating free in show business, a world of knives. Even the biggest stars have no shield. We are all piece workers, always anxious and supersensitive, knowing that our only resources are talent and smarts."

Her insatiable drive was another factor in the equation: no matter how good things were, Rivers seemed constitutionally incapable of saying to herself, "This is great, and it's enough." For her, nothing was ever enough.

"I thought she had the perfect setup with *The Tonight Show:* as much exposure as she needed to support Las Vegas, concerts all over the country, everything she wanted to do," said Sandy Gallin. "But she was always pushing ahead, always striving to do better, always looking for the next thing, always looking to improve a deal, always looking to do something new, always writing, producing, directing, doing stand-up, always looking to improve and do better, become bigger—and never, ever satisfied with what was going on. She was unbelievably ambitious, she was climbing the ladder of success 24/7, and she was tireless in doing whatever work was necessary to do it. She never took a rest. She was obsessed with it."

Barry Diller, who was friendly with Carson as well as Sandy Gallin, did a masterful job of manipulating the Rosenbergs' hopes and insecurities. He assured Rivers that Carson was getting old and tired and would leave his show within a year or two—but that Rivers would not be chosen as his replacement. He convinced Rivers that NBC was treating her badly but that he completely understood her and her needs and would make all her dreams come true.

"He was charming beyond charm," Rivers said. "I was completely taken in."

She wasn't the only one. "Barry was the savior—Prince Charming," said Dorothy Melvin, who worked for the Rosenbergs at the time. "When he was wooing them, they really felt very positive about it. Barry's offer was lifesaving. They were starting a new network and Joan would be the queen of television. The reality was that she was already the queen of television."

That wasn't the only mistaken perception. "Joan and Edgar felt this was what was going to save Joan's career—which was never in trouble,"

Melvin said. "That's the horror of it. But Joan was the most insecure person I ever met. I think she never felt she was good enough, or that people took her seriously. She felt she was fat and ugly, so it was very easy to send Joan that memo and frighten her into thinking she was losing her position in television."

And so the Rosenbergs made the fateful decision that would ultimately destroy them both. On the surface, it looked like a dream come true. In exchange for bringing Rivers's star power to Fox, the Rosenbergs demanded artistic control, a three-year contract giving them complete autonomy, and serious compensation—what Edgar called "fuck you money," the kind of insurance policy for the future that would let Rivers go to Williamstown, Massachusetts, and do summer theater for $125 a week if she wanted.

Diller responded by offering a deal that "gave us everything we wanted," Rivers said. Her show would be given production resources equivalent to those of *The Tonight Show,* and the Rosenbergs would have approval rights on staffing, format, guests, and producer. Rivers would receive $5 million a year for three years, amounting to $7 million after taxes. Rivers had heard that Carson made more than $8 million a year, but he also owned his own show and received half the profits. Although Rivers's deal with Fox was nowhere near as lucrative as Carson's deal with NBC, it was enough to assuage her fears about her future security—and for Rivers, that was a deciding factor.

"A girl who had lived with nothing but money problems from the time her eyes were open—had lived in a low-grade panic of escaping and getting by and then insecurity—was being told she didn't have to worry about money anymore," Rivers said. "There was no downside."

Famous last words. At the time, Rivers saw the move to Fox as an appropriate end to her years of apprenticeship, a well-deserved graduation that would mark the final step in ascending to the peak of her own independent career. But the Fox deal also brought a life-changing benefit for Edgar: he would be the executive producer of the new show.

"If truth be told, this gave Edgar the chance to have a career of his own, so this was very enticing to Edgar as well," Melvin said. "It was very hard for Edgar in Hollywood, and this was his chance to be important; he was finally going to get to be in charge. He was going to be a producer. Acceptance was so important to him, but as brilliant as Edgar was, he was someone who didn't see the forest for the trees. He may have thought he was doing the best for Joan, but he was also doing the best for Edgar."

Did he realize how much his ulterior motives might have influenced his judgment about the wisdom of accepting the Fox offer? That decision made sense only if the incriminating NBC list was authentic, but Edgar's hunger for a power position of his own may have prevented him from even considering that crucial question. Would Rivers have taken the risk of leaving NBC if her husband's need for independent validation had not been a pressing concern? Without Edgar by her side, urging her to abandon Carson and reach for the brass ring, she might not have dared to jump on her own.

But Edgar's needs overrode other considerations, both at home and in the Rosenbergs' calculations about The Career. A show for Joan that gave him the power and prestige he craved seemed like the magic solution to all their problems.

"I believed that would save my marriage, would pull Edgar out of his unpredictable anger, level out his highs and lows, renew his mental acuity," Rivers said in *Still Talking*. "Already he was beginning to be the old Edgar, happy to get up in the morning, happy to go to work, happy to go to all the meetings I thought were boring then. The possibility that the show would not work never crossed my mind."

Perhaps it should have; Rivers was already ignoring the warning signs of potential peril.

The Rosenbergs believed that Rivers's defection to Fox was a huge story that deserved a "gigantic press conference" with a lot of hoopla, but Diller disagreed. He wanted to break the news to selected reporters, along with other news about new stations and additional plans for the Fox network.

In that dispute, Diller ended up letting the Rosenbergs do what they wanted, but he wasn't happy about it. "Okay, make it a zoo—make it a circus," he said. Although Rivers got her way, she later admitted that the contretemps might have poisoned her relationship with Diller from the start. His willingness to concede such decisions to the Rosenbergs would soon prove to be short-lived.

Looking back, Rivers saw the disagreement about announcing the show as the first sign of many that Diller was inexperienced with station-level television. In her view, his success in the movie business had made him overconfident about his decision-making prowess, and he failed to recognize the areas where his lack of experience impaired his judgment in an unfamiliar arena. "He did not know what the affiliates wanted, was unrealistic about ratings, had no feel for the late-night audiences, and little understanding of the necessary staff," she said. The Rosenbergs felt that their own intransigence was a reasonable reaction to a boss who didn't fully understand the challenge they were facing.

But Diller was used to being regarded by friends and foes as the smartest man they had ever met—and he was equally accustomed to receiving due deference. Charm and diplomacy were never Edgar's strong suit, and his social skills were compromised by his years of ill health. Like two elks bashing each other's antlers in a nature documentary about the rituals of male dominance, the two men found themselves in conflict almost immediately. Unfortunately, Edgar seemed to be the only one who failed to recognize who was the alpha male in the contest.

His lack of judgment manifested itself immediately. At the contentious meeting where they disagreed about how to introduce Rivers's new show, Rivers said, "Edgar was treating Barry as an equal, challenging him. And nobody talks back and forth with Barry, except maybe Rupert Murdoch. Suddenly Diller lost his cool. 'Shut up,' he snapped at Edgar. Though Barry immediately apologized, he had done the unforgivable. It was awful. Winning Barry Diller's respect was Edgar's fantasy. To Edgar, Barry represented the Hollywood establishment that had denied us our breaks. Also, the show was Edgar's ticket to being important to himself. So when Barry turned on him, particularly in front of me, the hurt and humiliation must have been unbearable. From that moment forward Edgar's attitude was 'I'll show you.' That 'Shut up' was a flash of Diller's contempt for

Edgar from the very beginning…To Barry, he was merely a star's husband, superfluous, an unnecessary evil."

Edgar's miscalculation was also obvious to others. "Edgar felt comfortable butting heads with Barry Diller, but you don't butt heads with Barry Diller," said Dorothy Melvin. "His name is on the paycheck, and he can pull that card anytime he wants. You have to know who you're working for. It was hard for Edgar to accept that he wasn't in charge. He had Joan as his wife, but Barry was the one in charge."

Rivers came to believe that her husband and her employer were quite similar, despite their apparent differences. "I think Barry and Edgar were destined to collide, partly because their natures were so alike," she said. "I think both were unhappy men, insecure at center but very intelligent, and fighters who used fear to keep their antagonists off-balance. Both had to be right, both had to be important, had to win—and everybody should know they had won. Both were control and detail freaks. When events were out of their control, both of these perfectionists were deeply disturbed."

But in fighting for what he perceived as his wife's needs, Edgar immediately began to create unnecessary showdowns that generated a growing sense of ill will, alienating those whose support was necessary to make the new show a success. "Another pattern was begun: victories not worth the trade-off of anger," Rivers admitted.

The combination of Edgar's unpleasant personality and inept managerial style quickly tainted his wife's budding professional relationship with Diller and other Fox associates. "There are these telltale things that are very small that register later, and you say, 'There were signs,'" Diller observed.

Edgar's role in destroying his wife's relationship with Carson presents a somewhat murkier picture; some observers hold Rivers fully responsible for her actions, while others remain convinced that she was fatally misled by bad advice from her paranoid, controlling, insecure husband.

And then there are those who see Carson as the ultimate villain. "Joan deserved to have that show, but she knew he wasn't going to give it to her, so she got her own show," said Pat Cooper, who detested Rivers but doesn't absolve Carson. "Johnny Carson was not a nice man. He was an evil man, if you ask me. Off the air, he was the biggest prick that ever walked down the street. He was a pig. He peed on my leg at Jilly's one time."

With so many powerful personalities, strong emotions, and competing interests poised to collide, the stage was set for an epic conflict. It turned out to be one for the history books.

# Chapter Nine

## A THANKLESS CHILD:
## "HOW SHARPER THAN A SERPENT'S TOOTH"

During their negotiations over starting a new show, Fox had forbidden Rivers to tell anyone about their deal until the press announcement, which was scheduled for Tuesday, May 6, 1986—eleven days after her final appearance on *The Tonight Show*.

Rivers had sent Carson a copy of her new book, *Enter Talking*, which was dedicated to Edgar, "who made this book happen," and to Johnny, "who made it all happen."

But she hadn't told Carson about her Fox show, even though some in her inner circle urged her to do so. "I kept saying, 'You need to tell Johnny—you should be the one to tell Johnny,' but I wasn't the manager then, so I didn't have credence at that time," said Dorothy Melvin. "Johnny gave her so many breaks, and this was very unfair to Johnny, so I knew it would stun him and make him furious—rightfully so."

Despite intense secrecy and many precautions, word of Rivers's impending move finally leaked the day before the scheduled announcement, when the gossip columnist Rona Barrett notified the Rivers camp that she was going to use the item on the radio that night. According to Rivers's chronology of events, Diller finally gave her permission to call Carson and tell him she was leaving *The Tonight Show* to start her own show at Fox.

But it was too late. Brandon Tartikoff, the president of NBC, had already heard the rumor and called Garth Ancier, a former employee who was now the head of programming at Fox, to ask whether Rivers was doing a new show there. Ancier was evasive, and Tartikoff, recognizing what that meant, called Carson to tell him the bad news. By the time Rivers phoned Carson, he was furious with her.

"When she called him, she said, 'Johnny, it's Joan,' and he hung up—which made her angry too," Melvin reported. "She felt she should have been given the chance to talk to him about it. She felt like the victim. How could he not understand, when he was considering all these people but her? How could he not expect her to go elsewhere?"

Carson had a very different take on Rivers's defection, according to Henry Bushkin, who said he was the first person to inform his boss. "Some reporter called me, and I called Carson to tell him she had signed a deal with Fox, and then I called her new lawyer," said Bushkin. "I was outraged. Carson's reaction was, 'She fucked me!' He was pissed. It was not that she took another show—it was that she did it without talking to him or telling him first, so he wouldn't look like the victim of betrayal. He said, 'I'm never talking to her again,' and he never did. This was totally in character for him; once he was through with people, he never spoke to them again. That's what he was like."

The resulting breach would be discussed for decades to come, with its various nuances dissected in excruciating detail, but one of the most succinct descriptions was offered by Bill Carter, who was then the media reporter at *The New York Times*.

"Carson cut her off like a traitorous child," Carter wrote in *The Late Shift: Letterman, Leno, and the Network Battle for the Night*, his 1994 account of the men who vied for control of late-night television in that era. By the time Carson retired, they were indeed all men, but it is a reflection of the author's perceptions as well as the overwhelmingly male-dominated television scene that Rivers is mentioned on only two pages of a 320-page book. Moreover, *The Late Shift* contains no description of Rivers's long-running success as Carson's substitute host, nor of his potential succession by a woman, nor even of the larger issue that persists to this day: the absence of female hosts in late-night television.

From the moment Carson refused to take Rivers's call, the judgments by most industry insiders reflected harshly on her, even among putative allies. Rivers always maintained that Diller had muzzled her until it was too late to make things right with Carson, but Diller disputes that claim, insisting that it was her choice.

"I thought she had the obligation to go to Carson and talk to him about this," Diller said. "She really should have gone to him in advance, not the day before. I just thought it was the right thing to do. She had a history with him, and it was a very good history."

Diller also held Rivers responsible for preventing him from communicating with Carson in a timely fashion. "Johnny Carson was a good friend of mine," he said. "We had an almost weekly poker game that went on for some twenty years. I had no issue with saying to him straight-out, 'We're going to have a competing show.' I really wanted the ability to tell him myself, but I was precluded from that by her. She told me—or Edgar came back and told me—that [Johnny] would break it publicly, and that there would be unforeseen consequences."

To the extent that Diller blames Rivers, however, he really means Rosenberg. "I think it was her husband, the beast Edgar," Diller admitted. "I don't really know.

Rivers's former manager Sandy Gallin also attributes much of what happened to Edgar's modus operandi. "I think Edgar gave her very bad advice on a lot of things. He turned everything into a little mystery and made everything extremely difficult," Gallin said. "They were always so devious about their planning. Everything was secret."

When the news of Rivers's departure from *The Tonight Show* broke in the media, Carson was shrewd enough to be restrained in his public reaction. "I think she was less than smart and didn't show much style," he told the Associated Press.

Carson subsequently said much the same thing to Diller. "He never considered her a friend, but he felt it was professionally extremely discourteous," Diller said.

Even Rivers's friends agreed. "I think he had a right to be angry," said Gallin. "He made her career, and for years he was so loyal to her—and then she announces she's going on opposite him!"

But somehow Rivers had failed to anticipate Carson's rebuff, and she was crushed by it. "Joan was devastated that people had the impression that she betrayed Johnny Carson," said Melvin. "She never wanted to be the villain. She always wanted to be loved."

Bushkin believes Carson would have been gracious if Rivers had handled the situation differently. "He told me many times that he would have wished her well had she come and talked to him. He would have told her she was making a mistake, but he would have wished her well," Bushkin maintained. "Carson didn't have a particular relationship with Dick Cavett or anyone else. He did have a relationship with Joan Rivers. He considered her a pioneer in women's comedy, and a brilliant comedienne. He took pleasure in her success. Real affection existed between the two of them. Had she met with him and told him, I have no doubt that after her show ended she would have gone back on *The Tonight Show*."

Other industry observers shared that assessment. "She didn't call before signing the deal," said the New York radio personality Mark Simone. "The fact that he heard about it before she told him—that was the problem. Joey Bishop was in exactly the same position, and he never had a problem with Carson, who said, 'I understand.' They remained close friends. The same thing happened with Dick Cavett, who told me about it. Dick Cavett and Joey Bishop handled it the way you're supposed to: they talked to him and asked for his blessing. If things had been handled properly with Carson, Joan would have been able to come back."

And yet even his former associates concede that Carson didn't necessarily see Rivers as a viable successor for *The Tonight Show*, despite his professional respect for her. "Johnny's point of view was that she can't sustain for more than a week at a time, because of the nature of her act," Bushkin said. "People are going to get tired of it, annoyed with it. They're going to want a break. There was nothing sexist about it. She didn't wear well. She'd do Elizabeth Taylor fat jokes, and you start getting into a dangerous area in that some people find it offensive. Carson was right—it didn't work—and the rupture was totally unnecessary."

Others believed that ethnic prejudice may also have played a role. "She has higher ratings than Johnny, he's not going to want her around—but I think it's also true that Joan was high in certain markets," said one industry insider who, like Rivers, was Jewish. "It doesn't matter if San Francisco and New York and Los Angeles love her. You get to the Bible Belt, and they may not love her, because she's a loudmouthed Jew with a filthy, vulgar mouth. The big advertisers want a chicken in every pot, and that's what they really look at. I don't think she was relatable to everyone."

Bushkin also thinks Rivers was childlike in expecting her patron to feel a purely parental pride about her success. "She was finally getting her own shot to fly away, and she felt Johnny would be happy because he was always happy when people from his show went on to be successful," he said. "Maybe she was quite naive in a way."

But at *The Tonight Show*, the reaction was simply outrage at Rivers's apparent treachery. "She never went to Johnny and said, 'Hey, I've got this wonderful opportunity, and I hope I have your blessings, but I wanted you to know,'" the former *Tonight Show* executive producer Peter Lassally said on the *American Masters* special "Johnny Carson: King of Late Night." "She never did that. She never even mentioned it. He was furious with her, and I think rightfully so. It was that simple, but she just didn't do it. After all the loyalty he showed her, it was a terrible decision."

Among those who knew the Rosenbergs, many simply figured Edgar was the guilty party. "Reports were that Edgar called me and I didn't return his phone calls. That's not true," Bushkin said. "The reality is probably that Edgar told Joan he called me, so he could put the blame on me, but he never did call me. I think he was the total reason it got screwed up. I think it was totally manipulation by Edgar. When the shit hit the fan, I think he told her he called me and I didn't call back. It's speculation, but I think Edgar felt Carson would get so pissed and possibly convince her not to do it. I sort of adopted Johnny's attitude: I really felt betrayed as well. I felt the whole process was so badly planned—the secrecy, the lack of courtesy in the attempt to explain why she did it. Edgar had a penchant for not being obvious about anything; everything was designed for quiet and secrecy. No question I think it was Edgar."

But Bushkin also acknowledged that Carson—who grew up with a famously unsupportive mother and subsequently married four times—had emotional issues of his own, particularly when it came to women he perceived as denying him his due. As a child, Bushkin said, "Carson turned to magic because he never got the applause at home, and he liked the applause. When you become a star, you become narcissistic by definition. If you are craving the adulation of the audience, that's all you care about; that's what you live for. So he develops narcissistic personality disorder on steroids, because he's been fucked up by his mother, who was fucked up in her childhood."

The result was that "Carson hated women," Bushkin said. "Look at Carson's relationships with women. He had no respect for the women in his life—and the respect waned the more independent they became."

And Rivers had become independent enough to constitute a threat—which prompted many to suspect that Carson was simply unable to tolerate the prospect of being bested by a woman. "He was jealous of her, because her ratings were higher than his," said Steve Garrin, a producer and voice-over artist who managed Pat Cooper and Joe Franklin in their later years.

Such observers saw sexism as the root of Carson's ire, which reflected a double standard. "I don't think he would have treated a man like that," said *Gay USA* host Ann Northrop. "I think it was not only childish, but it was very misogynistic behavior."

Carson may have had particular difficulty in his relationships with women, but he had trouble with others as well. "Johnny Carson was one of the most emotionally crippled guys I ever met," said Liz Smith. "He was really antisocial. He was afraid of being friends with people. If you said anything about him, he would just sic that big Hollywood lawyer on you."

In his relationships with men, Carson typically surrounded himself with employees and hangers-on; if he couldn't tolerate women who jeopardized his status as top dog, he didn't gravitate toward men who were his equals either.

Knowing this, some think he was simply unwilling to tolerate challengers of either gender. "Dick Cavett wasn't a threat to Johnny Carson. Joan Rivers was. I don't think it was sexism," said Bill Reardin, a longtime television production executive at NBC, Tribune Broadcasting, and other companies, who worked with Jack Paar, Geraldo Rivera, and Dick Cavett, in addition to Rivers.

The darkest interpretation was one that cast Carson as a knowing villain who had figured out a diabolical way to sabotage Rivers while escaping any of the blame. "Johnny was a very sick Machiavellian puppy, and he could have orchestrated the whole thing," said Sue Cameron. "Joan didn't want to go to Fox, but Johnny ordered John Agoglia to not renew her contract with *The Tonight Show*. John Agoglia's wife was a good friend of mine, and she said John had to keep stalling, and it was terrible because he couldn't renew the contract. It was brilliant, and there was nothing Joan could do. Johnny could then say, 'She betrayed me,' and get really angry at her. But it was all a lie. It was really horrible, what happened to her. It wasn't that Joan was ungrateful. She really revered Johnny, and she kept wanting to be absolved by him for something that she didn't do."

As time went on, Rivers seemed unable to resolve the question of how much responsibility she should take for what happened with NBC. She expressed some contrition when she wrote about the disaster in *Still Talking.* "I think the way Johnny found out was a shame," she said. "He should have heard from me, and I like to think I could have made him understand. It must have been a huge shock."

But she was also convinced that Carson didn't see her as an equal, even when she regularly sold out five-thousand-seat houses. When male protégés like Bill Cosby and Richard Pryor did so, they were acknowledged for having achieved great success in their own right, but they didn't incur Carson's wrath.

So Rivers consoled herself by rationalizing that the outcome would have been the same no matter how she had handled the situation. When Carson finally did retire, she declared that "there was no way in hell I would have succeeded Johnny Carson," and that she was therefore right to have left when she did.

She paid a high price that included ostracism as well as exile from NBC. "I think a lot of people never spoke to her again," said Liz Smith.

But was that fair? Any real verdict on Rivers's culpability ultimately depends on the trustworthiness of the secret in-house memo that NBC executive Jay Michelis leaked to warn Rivers that she was not being considered as Carson's heir. Key players have always insisted that this scenario seems implausible because there was no reason such a list would even have existed.

"I never saw one, I never heard of one, and it was our show," Henry Bushkin said firmly. "If there was a short list to replace Carson, if it was an NBC list, it was never shown to me, and it was never shown to Carson. We had every right to pick the successor. As the lawyer, I would have been severely pissed to think they were assembling a list of possible replacements for Carson without consulting us. Brandon Tartikoff and Grant Tinker were running the network then, and both those guys were very friendly with Carson and myself. Carson Productions owned our version of *The Tonight Show*, so nobody at NBC was telling us what to do. The fact that Joan became the permanent guest host had nothing to do with NBC; it was a decision by Carson Productions. And there was never one moment of consideration of who would succeed Johnny Carson, because Johnny Carson was not ready to stop. This list makes no sense to me."

Bushkin always suspected the Rosenbergs invented the story to justify Rivers's betrayal. "When I heard it, I thought it was just a great excuse: 'I wasn't on the short list, so I had to take care of myself!'" he said. "I attributed what Joan said to showbiz. I think she really jumped at the chance of getting her own show, and the screwup was not talking to Johnny Carson ahead of time. Even if she dreaded talking to him, she should have told him. He never got over it. He wasn't the type to get over things."

Bushkin also disputes the idea that Michelis would have been a player in any top-level strategic planning. "I remember Jay Michelis, but he wasn't very high up at NBC," Bushkin said. "Who knows what he did? But it has nothing to do with us. If this guy showed her a list and she's not on it and Joan accepted that without checking any further, it would have been a dreadful mistake on her part, on her husband's part, on her manager's part. What the fuck? There could have been no list that would have been in any way official without Carson having approved it—and why would there be a list, anyway? Maybe this guy made up the list. I would like to think it's bullshit."

But it seems equally preposterous that "a real friend" of Joan's would have done such a thing to her. Fabricating a list suggests a level of malice that is almost incomprehensible—and yet when Dorothy Melvin ran into Peter Lassally at a shopping center in Los Angeles during the summer of 2015 and they talked for the first time in decades, their conversation suggested precisely that scenario.

By the time Rivers left NBC, she and Edgar had a long history of friendship with the Lassallys, but the relationship had become strained. Rivers's comedic instincts were often at odds with Lassally's sense of what was appropriate for the show, and she felt a growing tension with Lassally and Freddie de Cordova, the executive producer, as she became more successful—and less obedient.

"I think they eventually saw me as their baby who had grown away from them," said Rivers, who also attributed such feelings to Carson. "I believe my relationship with Johnny was permanently shaped by his feeling, on some level, that I was his creation and so could be taken completely for granted. Indeed, I played that role, catering and kissing and thanking—and staying loyal beyond reason."

When Rivers finally defied Lassally, the results were disproportionately damaging, thanks in part to Edgar's tactlessness. In 1984, Lassally instructed Rivers to drop a joke from her monologue, and she told Edgar she couldn't take it out—and that Lassally shouldn't have asked her to do so.

"I was already being driven crazy by the show's censor on questions of taste, and if I let Peter start editing my monologue for humor, he would be another door to fight through before I went in front of the camera," Rivers explained.

A smarter go-between would have recognized the disagreement as a minor annoyance and made it go away. Instead, Edgar made it into an insurmountable problem by telling Lassally that Rivers refused to change the joke because she didn't respect his judgment about comedy. "Peter was helpless and furious," reported Rivers, who realized too late that Edgar had humiliated Lassally in front of his boss. Thanks to her tantrum and Edgar's lack of finesse, she said, "fourteen years of friendship with Peter were gone."

Rivers hadn't wanted to establish a precedent by letting Lassally censor her material on *The Tonight Show*, but she was also convinced that the disagreement involved a larger principle that she considered vital. Throughout her career, she refused to capitulate to anyone else's judgment about what was funny and what wasn't, and she always treated the issue as a matter of life-and-death import.

And for her it was. Ever since the days when she would crawl into an agent's office on her hands and knees, Rivers had viewed the ability to make people laugh as more important to her survival than food or oxygen. An incorrigible practical joker, she would go to extraordinary lengths to get a laugh, and her friends responded in kind.

That pattern could also help explain what happened with NBC, according to Dorothy Melvin, who originally got to know Rivers while working for Sandy Gallin.

"Her pranks were absolutely the best," Melvin said. "She called up Kenny Solms, who was one of her closest friends, and said, 'I don't like you, and you know who else doesn't like you? Edgar doesn't like you, Melissa doesn't like you, Dorothy doesn't like you.' Then she called back with more names, and then she called back with Acme Plumbing and the white pages of the phone book. She filled up his entire answering machine."

Such acid-tinged antics were routine among Rivers and her friends—which may have led to a fatal miscalculation. "She and Jay Michelis played pranks on each other," Melvin reported. "On his birthday, Joan hired a bagpipe player to stand outside his office and play the bagpipes the whole day, and even to follow him to the commissary."

When Michelis smuggled Rivers the infamous list, "it was purported to be an interoffice memo at NBC," Melvin said. "Joan was the permanent guest host for Johnny, and Johnny was nowhere near leaving the show, so the timing didn't make sense. But the memo said, 'These are the people who will be considered to replace Johnny Carson when he retires,' and listed people like Garry Shandling and David Brenner."

Melvin can vouch for the existence of the memo, if not for its authenticity. "I saw it," she said. "I can still see it in my mind's eye. Jay

Michelis sent it to Joan and wrote on the memo, 'You have no home at NBC.'"

The memo seemed to confirm the Rosenbergs' most paranoid nightmares. "Joan was devastated and frightened," Melvin said. "That was her great fear—that she didn't have a future at NBC and it was time to start looking for something new. She thought she was riding the crest of a wave that would last for a long time, and all of a sudden the rug was pulled out from under her. There was a great deal of fear in the household about this, and they were renegotiating her contract at the time, and all of a sudden it was, 'We need to look elsewhere!'"

But Melvin didn't buy the ostensible reason why. "There were ten or twelve men on that list, all people who never got big numbers at NBC. Joan got the high ratings, and nobody on the list had the numbers Joan had," Melvin said. "I never felt it was a real memo, because it made no sense. Why would they want somebody who didn't get Joan's numbers? Johnny was very proud of Joan; he loved her very much. Peter Lassally was her best friend, and it didn't make any sense that these people wouldn't say anything to her."

Melvin was also privy to an intimate view of the falling-out with the Lassallys. "The Lassallys and the Rosenbergs were best friends," she said. "They did everything together. The Lassallys would come with us to Vegas, to Tahoe, to Atlantic City. When all this happened, Peter felt betrayed by Joan and Edgar: 'You're my best friends—how could you do this behind my back?' Joan called [Peter's wife] Alice, and Alice said, 'How could you do what you did?'"

But Rivers felt aggrieved as well. "Joan didn't understand why her best friend didn't tell her what was happening," Melvin said.

So when Melvin ran into Peter Lassally and his wife nearly a year after Rivers's death, the conversation naturally turned to her acrimonious departure from NBC. "I said, 'If it hadn't been for the memo…,' and Peter said, 'What memo?'" Melvin reported. "I said, 'You don't know about the memo? Oh my gosh!' When I told him about the memo, he and Alice sat there with their mouths open. Peter was in shock. He said, 'Dorothy, there was never such a memo. How would I not have been included?' I said,

'I thought you were part of it! I didn't understand why you didn't come to us, but I thought you were probably between a rock and a hard place.' Peter and I were gobsmacked. I said to Peter, 'This is a total bombshell. How could you not have known?'"

Unlike the Rosenbergs, who accepted the ostensible NBC memo at face value, Melvin had always been suspicious. "I have no doubt in my mind that it was manufactured; I'm absolutely convinced of it," she said. "There was no reason for the memo to begin with. Johnny Carson was nowhere near retiring. I don't think Joan questioned that it was real, but I kept saying it to Edgar. They didn't pay attention. Joan just felt Peter was stabbing her in the back."

Melvin now believes the entire sequence of events might have been deliberately set in motion by Michelis, either as outright sabotage or as a disastrously misconceived joke. "Was this all the result of a prank gone wrong, with Jay watching it all spiral out of control and laughing his head off?" Melvin said. "I'm sure if he fabricated it, he was enjoying it. He was very bitchy, and he liked to stir the pot and sit back and see what happened. I can still see his handwriting on the memo—he signed it 'J. M.' in blue pen. He probably sent that and got great glee out of it. Possibly he didn't realize it would blow up the way it did. See what an elaborate web this wove?"

That explanation is consistent with his character, according to Melvin. "Jay was a 'good friend' with an underlying sense of meanness," she explained. "He was downright evil—a mean, bitchy man. He called his secretary Miss Douchebag, and he called Joan Mrs. RosenJew. I was Cycle Slut, because my boyfriend took me on motorcycle rides. The day of Edgar's funeral, the phone rang, and he said, 'Cycle Slut, tell Mrs. RosenJew that I will not be at the funeral, because I will be at my fabulously expensive home in Glendale driving around in my fabulously expensive Mercedes.'"

In response to a tragic death, such conduct seems unfathomably cruel. But if Michelis had engineered the whole catastrophe, he might have had good reason for avoiding the funeral—if not for communicating his regrets as viciously as he did.

"It was just so ugly," said Melvin. "If this was not a real memo, the way Jay Michelis devastated lives, it wasn't just a joke gone wrong. It was a joke that exploded and left such devastation in its wake that it was horrifying."

Many of the players in the feud are now dead and can never tell what they knew or how they would apportion the blame for what happened. The list of the departed includes Rosenberg, Carson, Rivers, and Michelis, as well as John Agoglia and his wife, who were also friendly with the Rosenbergs.

Among the living, some still refuse to talk about the feud, including Peter Lassally, who declined repeated requests to discuss Rivers—or even his chance conversation with Melvin about the NBC list. And so it's likely that the question of Jay Michelis's motives will never be resolved.

In 1988, the year after Fox canceled Rivers's show and her husband killed himself, Michelis died in bed at his home, surrounded by "drug paraphernalia and white powder," as one news report put it. Small quantities of a substance "resembling powder cocaine" were found on a mirror, and a rolled-up dollar bill was found on a coffee table near the bed. Elsewhere in the bedroom, a "small paper bindle with cocaine" was discovered in a wooden box. A toxicological report subsequently confirmed that Michelis had ingested cocaine, but the cause of death was declared to be a heart attack. He was fifty years old.

"Whatever his guilty secrets, they died with him," Melvin said.

In the years since, most people have accepted the conventional narrative that the Rosenbergs betrayed Carson and paid the price. But Melvin remains convinced that the memo was fabricated, and she is heartbroken that Rivers will never know the truth about what might have been a diabolical lie.

"It kills me that I can't share this with her and say, 'This wasn't real,'" Melvin said. "But in my heart of hearts, I feel Edgar knew it wasn't real. I think he just took it and ran with it because it gave him the chance to have his own show, where he could be in charge."

## Chapter Ten

# DEBACLE: THE DEATH OF A SHOW, A MARRIAGE—AND A HUSBAND

When Joan Rivers got her own late-night talk show, it could have been a triumphant cultural milestone with far-reaching consequences—and many women saw it as such.

"It was huge," the comic Lisa Lampanelli said. "Doing a late-night show is a big deal. It means you can do what the big boys do. *Saturday Night Live* was a boys' club. The *Harvard Lampoon* was a boys' club. All of a sudden, there's this girl who's playing with these guys. She was doing edgy material when it wasn't safe for a chick to be doing it."

Rivers certainly tried, but her efforts may have been doomed from the start. Looking back on the disastrous launch of her show at the Fox network, she would later describe the behavior of all the major players as driven primarily by fear. To the executives who had succumbed to Barry Diller's siren call for a major gamble on a new venture, the stakes were nearly as high as for Rivers herself.

"All of them were frightened—terrified that they had left secure jobs for a network that would not work," Rivers wrote in *Still Talking*. "So everybody was under pressure you can't believe—including Barry Diller."

For the Rosenbergs, who thought they'd signed on for an exciting creative challenge they could shape to Joan's strengths and run as they saw fit, the result was frustration and conflict. "To protect themselves, all the Fox people wanted control, wanted to have input into the show, wanted to take over," Rivers said. "They became like a sorority that would not let me in. The more they tried to control everything, the more petty the fights became, everybody grinding private little axes."

Unfortunately, the worst ax-grinder was her own husband. "Maybe the most frightened of all was Edgar, who right from the beginning was nit-picking: 'I insist on this. I insist on that.' So right away the show became Edgar versus Barry—which included Barry's chain of command," Rivers reported glumly.

To their intimates, it seemed that Edgar misjudged the situation from the outset. "He thought, 'I'm a producer now! I can go head-to-head with Barry Diller!'—but nobody goes head-to-head with Barry Diller," said Dorothy Melvin.

Edgar's inflated expectations set the stage for disaster, and the dysfunctional dynamic was quickly compounded by other errors. According to Rivers, Rupert Murdoch insisted that her show debut in early October, "which gave us and Fox just five months to set up the smoothly running machine NBC had assembled through decades. It was a herculean task: ready the studio—build the set, install the lighting, the sound system, the seating—hire a staff with top bookers to corral the guests, get excellent segment producers to preinterview and handle each guest, find first-class writers to think up the nightly monologue and the stunts, recruit a skillful producer and assistant to manage the show."

Faced with innumerable challenges of every size and description, Edgar immediately went to war with Fox over one detail after another, fighting about everything from the space and the set to the producers, the staff, the orchestra leader, and the theme music, which was cowritten by Rivers. In retrospect, she would acknowledge many aspects of her husband's contribution to the debacle.

"Edgar never dealt directly with Diller. He bucked him by being brusque and superior to his lieutenants," she said. "Edgar was brilliant on ideas, brilliant on follow-through, but his missing chromosome was diplomacy. Getting a job done right was more important to him than finesse. And since the heart attack his patience had been stretching tight."

Under physical, emotional, and professional stress, Edgar swiftly made himself persona non grata, which put Rivers in the untenable position of being caught in constant cross fire between her employer and her husband. "She was viewed as having this anchor around her neck called Edgar," said Shelly Schultz. "He had made himself very disliked around the industry at a very high level, because she was operating at a very high level."

Diller finally informed Rivers that Edgar was being destructive and making everyone unhappy, and he asked her to keep her husband away from the show. Rivers resisted, protesting that no one gave her specific examples of the problems he was causing, which left her unable to address them. Despite Edgar's reputation as a maniacal control freak, she claimed that she and her husband simply wanted to be included in the decision-making process. "Diller could have controlled us so easily by giving Edgar a little respect and me some affection," she complained.

Given Edgar's predilection for waging full-out wars over minutiae, that seems unlikely, but such face-saving measures were not forthcoming in any case. Rivers admitted that her husband irritated a lot of people, but she saw him as the loyal warrior who dealt with all the mundane details that Diller's inexperienced staff didn't even know were necessary for the kind of program they were trying to create. "He was wonderful at all the horrible, boring things that make a show work," she said.

In Rivers's accounts of what happened at Fox, all roads eventually lead back to Diller, but she may not have understood some aspects of what was going on behind the scenes. "That show was risky anyway, because it didn't have enough affiliates, so there was no way the ratings could be high. Joan was kind of a sacrificial lamb for Fox," explained Sue Cameron, who was a former network executive as well as a TV reporter and columnist. "Diller only had the owned-and-operated stations, and he needed a big name to get the local stations to give them the time. He used Joan to get the affiliates; he was looking for them to sign on and give him the time slots. Joan was being used, but I don't think she knew it."

Diller's perspective places considerable blame on Rivers as well as on her husband. "When we got into the planning of the show, I wasn't involved very much in that," he told me. "There was a long lead time, and we wanted to make the environment as good for her as we could. Around the only thing I remember during the preproduction stage is that I would hear little things that were bad, and that disturbed me, about her lack of preparation. As far as guest policy and other pieces of the show, there wasn't very much, other than enormous attention to her dressing room. We really wanted her to be comfortable, and we had proposed things that were pretty nice, but I would hear tales about things like that, where there was more attention than there was on preproduction."

Diller was dismayed by such "little signs," he said, but they were soon eclipsed by a much larger issue. "The big sign came when I got word back from the staff that it seemed like Edgar was making the decisions I never thought he would make," Diller said. "I thought Edgar was a business person or manager. We hired a very good executive producer, and then I got these tales back of Edgar taking over the show, in terms of making decisions. Joan was fairly absent; she was not engaged."

On all sides, the new working relationships curdled very fast. In *Still Talking*, Rivers reported that as early as July, the Rosenbergs were already spending a fortune on lawyers who sent combative letters about various points of dispute. The legal bluster infuriated Diller, who responded by lecturing the Rosenbergs on "causing dissension and trouble."

But relations continued to deteriorate. September found Edgar arguing over everything from the number of telephones in the office to the secretaries' deficient shorthand skills to catered dinners for the staff. "The more Fox refused to acknowledge Edgar's demands, the more important they became," Rivers recalled. "Feeling embattled everywhere, he fought back obsessively to get every detail of our production identical to the Carson show."

Still exhilarated by the heady ego gratification of having landed her own show and serious money, Rivers didn't realize how high the stakes were until much later. "I could have stopped all the fighting, could have said, 'Edgar, you're out of here. Barry, do what you want,'" she admitted. "But there is no way I could have banished my husband to being at home alone. I did not realize how seriously we were all crippling the future. There are always birth pains in setting up a new show. I thought that once we were on the air, the trouble would vanish."

But every aspect of getting the show on the air soon turned into a nightmare—including the all-important challenge of booking top guests, which was an uphill battle from the start. The Carson camp put out the word that anybody who appeared on Rivers's program would be blackballed by *The Tonight Show*, and the resulting chill intimidated many of the big names that Rivers coveted for her own lineup. NBC made it very clear that it was waging war on the would-be rival who had the temerity to challenge Carson by copying his show and encroaching on his time slot. "Our job is to destroy you," Jay Michelis told Rivers.

Such tactics took a serious toll. "In a demonstration of just how powerful Carson still was, Rivers found herself one step removed from leper status in Hollywood," Bill Carter wrote in *The Late Shift*. "Guests had to risk the wrath of *The Tonight Show* to go on with Joan."

Although there was considerable crossover in their prospective audiences, Rivers also hoped to appeal to a younger demographic, which meant expanding the range of guests. Carson's *Tonight Show* was increasingly perceived to be "stodgy and out-of-date," as Carter put it. "One headliner comic told his friends, 'When you go on that show, you can smell the polyester.'"

So when *The Late Show Starring Joan Rivers* premiered on October 9, 1986, it immediately signaled some momentous departures from precedent. Just by going on the air as host of her own program, Rivers became the first woman in history to have her own late-night television talk show on a major network—itself a revolutionary idea.

"Anticipation was high," Daniel Kimmel reported in *The Fourth Network*. "Perhaps unfairly, she was expected to compete with her old boss, Johnny Carson, even though they'd only be going head-to-head for half an hour. *The Late Show* would air from 11 p.m. to midnight—an hour earlier in the Central time zone—while Carson didn't start until after the late news at 11:30 p.m."

On her first show, Rivers's guests included Cher, David Lee Roth, Pee-wee Herman, and Elton John. Rivers was thrilled with what she had accomplished, but history would judge her harshly. "She did herself no favors by trying to turn into a hipster, booking rock-and-roll acts half her age

and singing 'The Bitch Is Back' with Elton John," Carter wrote disdainfully in *The Late Shift*.

The ratings returned a mixed picture. "It was foolishness to think
Rivers could beat Carson, especially fresh out of the starting gate,"
Kimmel wrote. "For the October 9 premiere, Rivers actually outdid
Carson in the New York Nielsen ratings as well as in the competing Arbi-
tron service ratings in Los Angeles, but in most places Carson enjoyed the
higher viewership."

As Rivers subsequently pointed out, her show was competing with the
World Series during its first week, and Fox had far fewer outlets than
the major networks. She nonetheless managed to score a 3.2 nationally in
98 markets, compared with 6.4 in 202 markets for Carson. In the coming
weeks, her show began to average a 3.9 rating in big cities while falling
into the 2s at small stations.

But the critics were scathing. "They said things like, 'No need, Johnny,
to lose sleep over the new challenger,' and called the audience 'moronic'
and 'airheads,'" Rivers reported. "Tom Shales wrote in the *Washington
Post*, 'Maybe Rivers should spend less time at the beauty parlor and more
time with her writers. The beauty parlor would appear to be a lost cause
anyway.'"

Fox had promised to give Rivers at least a year for her show to
find its audience, but the network immediately panicked; its ratings
forecasts had been as unrealistic as Rivers's expectation for an immediate triumph. Her hopes of appealing to a more youthful demographic
than Carson's audience also seemed increasingly misguided. "As the ratings started to slump in later weeks, the real question became whether
younger viewers were interested in this type of TV fare at all," Kimmel
wrote.

Diller saw other problems as well. "Joan wasn't a great interviewer,
which was okay, but what I was really surprised about was that she did
no homework," he said. "I thought, these shows aren't supposed to be
judged on their first day, but I was judging the process—and I thought,
oh God, we're really in it. If you watch those first four to six months of
episodes, you could see she wasn't prepared. The interviews were awful,

and there was no week-to-week, month-to-month improvement. I never could figure it out. I thought, okay, she's been essentially in the most horrible environment, stand-up comedy—but that process is completely different from running a show. But instead of giving it up to professionals, because of her paranoia, she turned it over to her husband and became immediately defensive. The mistake we made was because of how good she was on *The Tonight Show*, but *The Tonight Show* was produced by Freddie de Cordova, and it was a totalitarian regime. What I know from Carson was that that show was a precision instrument. She didn't have to do anything, because they did everything."

The opposite of a totalitarian regime, *The Late Show Starring Joan Rivers* was more like a hydra-headed monster, with each serpent fighting to the death for control of the whole organism. "The show was not well reviewed, and then it was a natural implosion that turned to a lot of recriminations," Diller said.

As her corporate overlords grew ever more anxious about her prospects, Rivers found herself under pressure in the one inviolate area where she would brook no opposition: the question of comedic content. She always insisted that no one had the right to tell her what was funny and what wasn't—least of all a bunch of suits.

And they *were* suits, which was another problem. The people telling her what to do were men, but Rivers saw women as the core of her audience, and she felt that the executives opposing her instincts simply didn't understand who she was.

"I don't want to be Carson. I don't want to be Letterman," she told them. "I want to be me, my humor, whatever that turns out to mean." She wasn't used to having to define it, but her best guess was that it meant "silly, acerbic, female-oriented, gossipy, trying anything."

Her nemesis remained unmoved. "Barry, very cool, just kept saying, 'No. It's not funny,'" Rivers reported.

And so in every particular—from the guests to the comedy to the mechanics of running the show—*The Late Show Starring Joan Rivers* became an ongoing battleground. Despite *The Tonight Show*'s opposition, Rivers managed to book celebrities who ranged from Nancy Reagan and Lucille

Ball to Eugene McCarthy and Ray Charles. But the atmosphere behind the scenes was toxic.

"Throughout the fall of 1986 the show was two armed camps with little raids conducted back and forth across battle lines, destructive for all concerned," Rivers said. "To this day I still wonder why Barry allowed the situation to disintegrate so totally."

Edgar was indisputably a big part of the problem. "He did make a fuss about small things, because he couldn't make fusses about big things," said Sue Cameron. "Barry Diller emasculated him, and he was fighting for his own masculinity. He was becoming invisible, and it was very, very hard on him. By that time he knew he wasn't the best producer for Joan anymore, and Joan knew it too. He had her back, in terms of taking care of Joan, but he really wasn't the best producer for the show. That was a very hip show, and it was out of Edgar's bailiwick. Television had become edgier, but Edgar was very old-school. He was a very proper gentleman, but time had moved on, and Edgar hadn't moved along with it."

If Edgar generated much of the conflict, Rivers wasn't exactly a model of statesmanship; rising above the fray with dignity was never her style. Infuriated with Diller and his henchmen, Rivers decided to hide a fish in the executive greenroom, which was nicknamed Diller Acres, and gloat over their inability to figure out where the stench was coming from. "Talk about childish revenge!" she said later. "That's for the third grade, not when you have the house on the hill with servants."

The terrible irony was that the Rosenbergs and their Fox overlords shared the same goal: they all wanted to make the show a success—but no one seemed to know how. "Everyone involved was frantically trying to fix it," Kimmel wrote in *The Fourth Network*. Panic bred angry conflict over each decision, no matter how minor its import, and meetings degenerated into shouts and insults.

Confronted by the Rosenbergs' intransigence on matters large and small, their corporate partners grew increasingly exasperated. "When even the most well-meaning Fox executives tried to make suggestions for improving the program, the Rivers team dismissed them as if they were enemy agents," Kimmel wrote in *The Fourth Network*.

"Did it get petty? You know, I'm sure it did," said Garth Ancier, the former NBC executive who had become head of programming at Fox. "But at the end of the day, it was mostly based on the fact that the show unit was being operated as an armed camp separate from us."

Kevin Wendle, Ancier's number two in programming, saw Rivers as squandering potential goodwill with pointless opposition. "It was a shame, because here was a woman with all this talent, and she was so married to her production team that she didn't want to hear ideas about how to make the show better, really," Wendle said. "She saw any ideas that we came in with as interference. The more we suggested ways to make the show better, the more she resisted, the more friction there came between her and Fox."

The Rosenbergs' paranoia was further exacerbated when they heard that Fox was building a case to break Rivers's contract while simultaneously conducting a campaign to drive her to the snapping point in hopes that she herself would breach the contract.

The disputes deteriorated from the petty to the ridiculous; when Fox prohibited Edgar from riding to the studio with his wife in her limousine, she said she would take Edgar's Mercedes and the limo could follow her. "It was beyond childish," said Dorothy Melvin. "It was a game of who was more powerful."

One tantrum followed another until the bloodlust for winning at any cost eclipsed any sane perspective on what was at stake in a given altercation. "Edgar's friend Tom Pileggi said to them, 'Remember who signs your checks,' which would have been very good advice for them to heed," said Melvin. "For Edgar, everything was about the need to feel important, and Joan was the kind of woman who always thought she had to support her husband. But Joan had totally, completely misjudged Barry. I don't think Joan ever foresaw that this would tear down the entire house of cards, but how could you even begin to think you're going to go against Barry Diller? It was absurd. Edgar should have been very frightened of Barry Diller, but he felt Barry needed Joan in order to build his network. He thought Barry needed them more than they needed him."

When the office bookshelves arrived and turned out to be shorter than

Edgar wanted, he obsessed on the problem until even Rivers had to face the fact that he was cracking under the strain. "That was when I knew I was in deep, deep trouble," she said. "It was the first time in twenty-one years that I could not reach him on a rational level."

Edgar's distress became so visible that close friends grew deeply concerned. "One day he had been looking awful and Joan said, 'I don't know what's wrong with him,'" Cameron said. "I grabbed Edgar, pushed him into a bathroom at Fox, and said, 'What's wrong?' He said, 'I'm very depressed, I have gout, I have ulcers, I have heart issues, I have no energy—I just don't feel well.' He was losing it. I was really, really worried, and I told Joan."

One night Edgar and Joan had a bad fight, and Edgar slept in Melissa's room. The next morning Joan left the house while her husband was still in bed, only to receive an urgent call during a meeting with her segment producers. It was Edgar, who sounded drunk and was mumbling incoherently. She finally made out something he was trying to communicate: "I think I'm having a stroke," he said.

At least that was how Joan described it in *Still Talking*—but Melvin remembers it differently. "Joan was blaming Edgar for the fall of the show, because he butted heads with Barry Diller. So Edgar took a pill and called Joan and said, 'I've just taken an overdose,'" Melvin reported. "He was at the house, and we were out in Burbank Studios, and we went to the hospital in an ambulance with sirens blaring. It was a fabricated suicide attempt—he only took one pill. It was a cry for help."

Whatever Edgar's motives, his wife discerned the deeper meaning behind his impaired state. "I think psychologically he was ill with the fear that he was more and more unnecessary, that I was subtly slipping away from him," Rivers said.

But the Fox show was also slipping away from her. In February of 1987, Rivers was told that she would no longer be allowed to supervise her writers and segment producers, to give them any directions or make any decisions. "I would become a puppet," she said.

Defiant as ever, she and Edgar ignored the directive and continued to function as they had before. But her bosses weren't kidding. On March 20, a routine meeting devolved into a bitter argument that ended when Diller walked in, stripped Edgar of all his responsibilities as executive producer, and banned him from the set.

Enraged, Edgar lashed out at him. "You're a tinhorn dictator," he said. "I'm a rich man. I don't need this!"

"Go fuck yourself," Diller replied.

Rivers's reaction sealed her fate. "I should have told Edgar to shut up," she admitted in *Still Talking*. But instead, "I chose my husband," she said. "And I would do it again."

The reasons were rooted in her lifelong beliefs about the deference a wife owed her husband, no matter what the cost. She and Edgar had been married for twenty-two years, and her identity as a wife was crucial to her sense of who she was in the world. Her staff still called her Mrs. Rosenberg, and Mrs. Rosenberg couldn't imagine putting other interests above those of Mr. Rosenberg when there was a conflict.

"I believe that marriage is a total commitment, that once you say 'Yes' to somebody, that is it—and I had received the same commitment from my husband," Rivers said. "That was one thing I doubt Fox ever understood—that the bottom line of my behavior and marriage was loyalty. There is so little of it in life. It is the only thing you have left when everything else between two people is stripped away."

Her decision made sense to her on an emotional level, but its professional consequences were predictably catastrophic. "We walked out of the meeting with Edgar's dignity and our marriage intact," Rivers reported. "But from that moment on we were dead."

Some industry observers acknowledged that Diller had put Rivers in an excruciating position. "Barry Diller hated Edgar, and Edgar hated Barry Diller," said radio host Mark Simone. "Barry Diller thought Edgar wasn't a good producer, and he was right—but you don't make a wife choose between her husband and her job."

But the Rosenbergs, seemingly oblivious to Fox's needs and long-term goals, had also failed to recognize a crucial fact: that by getting Rivers's show on the air, they had already served their purpose in helping to launch the new network. After that was accomplished, the way they ran the show created so much enmity that they weren't worth the ongoing effort required to sustain the relationship. When Rivers's show began, Fox hadn't yet created any other content, but as the network started to roll out other programs, its trailblazer seemed like more trouble than she was worth.

"Now that they were finally operating in prime time, the Fox executives no longer had an interest in prolonging the pain with Joan Rivers," Daniel Kimmel reported in *The Fourth Network*. "She had done what they had hired her to do—give the new network some instant legitimacy—but hadn't been able to move beyond that. In other circumstances her show might have been given a chance to grow, now that Fox had a prime time on which to promote it, but there was just too much bad blood."

In the end, Fox allowed Rivers only seven months before pulling her off the air. "I think Barry Diller would have given it more time, but the main reason the show got canceled was that he didn't want to deal with Edgar anymore," said Mark Simone.

That view was widely shared. "Half the reason the show went off the air was because they couldn't wait to get rid of Edgar," said Shelly Schultz. "They hated him because he was a crazy man. He was a bully. He thought he was Cecil B. Fucking DeMille. He gave the impression that he invented Joan Rivers. Joan Rivers invented Joan Rivers. Nobody else invented her. She was a natural."

While her departure was being negotiated, Rivers continued to go to the studio and do the show. To settle her $15 million contract, she agreed to a payment of a little over $2 million, which included damages for defamation and emotional stress. Although she recognized that most people would consider $2 million a fortune, the deal represented a devastating defeat to her.

"For that money I never would have left Carson and given up the foundation of my life, lost my status, lost fans, been forced to live forever with the perception that my show was a failure," she said.

That perception also administered the fatal blow to her marriage. "When Barry Diller gave her the ultimatum—fire Edgar or lose the show—she knew it would kill Edgar if she fired him," said Sue Cameron.

"She told me she had to lose the show to save the life of her husband, but she resented him from then on. She was just wild with anger."

And Edgar was unable to absorb the blow. His intimates failed to realize it, but by this point he had been contemplating suicide for some time. "About two months before he died, I was having lunch at Le Dome and he came over to me and said, 'There's something I want to ask you. Promise me you will always take care of Melissa,'" Cameron recalled. "Melissa was absolutely the apple of her father's eye, and I said, 'Of course,' but I didn't pick up on what that meant."

The news that Rivers's program was being canceled broke on May 15, when she hosted her final show. Fox was so desperate to get rid of her that it handled her departure in a way that still astonishes industry insiders. "What was incredible is that Fox dropped Rivers in the middle of the May ratings sweeps," Daniel Kimmel explained in *The Fourth Network*. "The 'sweeps' are the periodic measurements of the home TV audience that are used to establish advertising rates."

Dumping their signature show at such a crucial juncture caused intense consternation among Fox's affiliates. Reported Kimmel: "'You just don't make a change like that in the middle of a ratings book [the report of the sweeps period], and if the Fox people were thinking like broadcasters, they wouldn't have done it,' said one disgruntled general manager—Dennis Thatcher of WOIO, Fox's Cleveland affiliate."

After Rivers left, *The Late Show* carried on for a while with Arsenio Hall as host, and then limped to its final fate with Ross Shafer before being canceled in October of 1988. In retrospect, the verdict on Joan's effort would be succinct: "The show was doomed and disappeared in six months. Johnny Carson had prevailed again," Bill Carter wrote in *The Late Shift*.

Rivers was still angry with Carson, and she felt tremendous fury toward Fox and Barry Diller—but she also blamed her husband. "I was deciding very, very deep in my heart that if Edgar had not been involved, I would have made the show work," she confessed. "I saw myself throwing away everything I had wanted since the day I was conscious in order to save this man's pride. Too, somewhere in myself, I was looking to Edgar to save me—I had always looked to him—and he had failed."

Some cynics just shrugged and concluded that both Rivers and Rosenberg had simply been outclassed by a more lethal opponent. "Barry Diller is not a success because he's not ruthless and smart," Liz Smith said dryly. "Barry is one of the smartest people I've ever met. Joan just encountered somebody who was more ruthless and smart than she was."

As Fox replaced Rivers with a series of other hosts on *The Late Show*, she found herself without work—always the source of her greatest anxiety—and grappling with the question of what her career might be without the Fox program or *The Tonight Show*. Television had always served as the essential foundation for her stand-up bookings, but now she was left without an outlet to give her such consistent national visibility.

She also had to confront the fact that her partnership with Edgar was irrevocably damaged by the demise of their show. The atmosphere at home grew poisonous. "I realized that this man, who had built his life on being my champion, had turned against me. I had become his Barry Diller," Rivers said. "Even the simplest exchanges became loaded and dangerous."

She told Edgar they had to get professional help, but he rejected the idea of marriage counseling, insisting that they could work out their problems on their own. Despite his protests, other intimates sensed the depth of his distress, and Sue Cameron had a terrible premonition. "About two weeks before he died, I woke up crying in the middle of the night," she reported. "In my dream, Edgar had died. I felt his death with my whole body. I was lying there and it was like the life went out of my body."

Exasperated by Edgar's obstinacy, Rivers finally resorted to threatening him: while out of town on a business trip, she said she wouldn't come home until he agreed to accept some form of intensive treatment.

By this time, her intimates thought she was really sick of the whole situation. One confidant was Tommy Corcoran, whom she considered her best friend until his death several years later. "Tommy said Joan had been putting up with so much shit for so many years, and when the Fox thing happened, she was like, 'I can't stand this anymore'—and she left him," said Pete Hathaway, a close friend of both Corcoran and Rivers.

With the threat of separation hanging over him, Edgar finally capitulated, saying that he would do as his wife asked—but only after he made a quick trip to Philadelphia to see his best friend, Tom Pileggi, whom he described as "the brother I never had." Melissa had persuaded him that talking to Pileggi would be helpful, so Edgar flew to Philadelphia, checked into the Four Seasons, and spent three days with Pileggi, going over voluminous records of everything the Rosenbergs owned. As usual, Edgar was focused on getting their affairs in order, which meant attending to every detail.

He and Pileggi also made several trips to an eighty-seven-acre site in Bucks County where they had once hoped to build a controversial development called Two Ponds. One of several real estate projects that Pileggi and the Rosenbergs were involved in, it was eventually abandoned because of intense local opposition.

Beset by medical, professional, financial, and emotional woes, Edgar continued to argue with Joan on the telephone. She wasn't the only one who thought he needed help; his doctor wanted to put him in the hospital in a psychiatric unit, but Edgar refused. At one point he even told his wife, "I'm so depressed I'm going to kill myself," but she didn't take the threat seriously.

"I remember making a flip joke: 'Don't do it till Friday, because Thursday I'm going under anesthesia,'" said Rivers, who had scheduled liposuction to be performed at a hospital in Los Angeles.

As she had hoped, Edgar laughed.

But he made the same remark to Pileggi, who immediately called Joan to say that he wanted to check Edgar into a hospital in Philadelphia. Again Edgar refused, and he made his friend a promise. "I won't do anything foolish," he told Pileggi.

Another remark Edgar made to Pileggi would haunt his wife when its chilling implications became clear after his death: "Pride can kill a man, and that's all I have left." And yet everyone close to Edgar believed that he would never actually commit suicide. "We all thought he was too much of a control freak, had too much pride to say, 'I've lost,' was too rational for suicide—which he used to call 'a permanent solution to a temporary problem,'" Rivers said.

Given Edgar's habitual secretiveness, it was easy to underestimate the depths of his despair. "After his death, his psychiatrist was surprised," said Melvin. "He said, 'We were both big fans of Winston Churchill, and all we ever talked about was Churchill.'"

Edgar finally agreed to check into a hospital soon after he arrived back in Los Angeles, and Pileggi arranged for security to check his hotel room every hour during the night before his flight. Meanwhile, Edgar continued to make his usual meticulous plans for the immediate future. He asked Melvin to arrange limousines to take him from his hotel to the Philadelphia airport and to pick him up at the airport in Los Angeles. He told her to have his accountant meet him at his house at 9 a.m. on Saturday and then to arrange for another limo to take him to the hospital at 10 a.m. "It was a normal conversation," Melvin said.

From Philadelphia, Edgar also made an appointment for a doctor to check him out physically at the hospital before he went into therapy. He even arranged for a security guard to be posted at his hospital room door in Los Angeles.

On Thursday afternoon, he called his daughter from Pileggi's office, told her he was coming home on Friday, and promised not to harm himself. Before leaving Pileggi for the evening, he agreed to meet him the next morning for breakfast, and once again promised not to do anything foolish. He asked his friend to call off the hourly security checks at the hotel so he could get a good night's sleep, and Pileggi agreed.

On his way back to the Four Seasons, Edgar stopped at a barbershop and had his beard shaved off. He also bought a tape recorder and three blank tapes. At the hotel, he phoned Melvin to ask whether she had reconfirmed his flights and limos.

When Melissa called him that evening, she thought he sounded good enough that she didn't need to phone him again later that night. Pileggi called and Edgar reassured him as well, saying, "I'm fine. I'll see you for breakfast." His psychiatrist phoned from Los Angeles, and Edgar said he was coming home to enter intensive therapy.

Then he recorded three farewell messages—one for his wife, one for his daughter, and one for Pileggi—and put them in three separate hotel envelopes, adding his Rolex watch and his gold money clip to the one for Melissa. He marked each envelope with three Xs for kisses. He left tips in other envelopes for the maid, the bellhop, and the maître d' at the hotel restaurant. He put business papers and instructions in a manila envelope and addressed it to Joan Rosenberg. He left out a note listing the people who should be notified of his death, packed his bag, and unlocked the door. He leaned a picture of Joan and Melissa against the bedside lamp.

"Then he swallowed the bottles of Valium and Librium he had been saving," Rivers reported. "Next, completing the combination he knew had killed the columnist Dorothy Kilgallen, he removed the miniature scotch and brandy bottles from the courtesy bar and methodically drank them from a tumbler."

Some of their friends think Edgar was bluffing again. "I don't believe he actually meant to die," Melvin said. "To this day, I'm convinced that it was another cry for help gone wrong. He left the hotel door ajar, and he made it easy to be found. Because the one pill didn't work, he took a bottle of pills. It looked like he fell and hit his head by the nightstand, so he may have been going to call for help when he fell and hit his head and it knocked him out. There was a list of phone numbers by the phone— doctors to call, numbers you wouldn't need if you were going to die. I think it was a big show."

Rivers herself felt as confused as she believed Edgar had been. "I guess I think that during all those days of mixed messages, he wanted in his head to die and in his heart to live," she said. "I think he was throwing out cries for help to bring me back, but people get enmeshed in their stratagems until they don't know if attempting suicide is a game or feel, by God, I've got to do it."

Joan was obviously fed up with Edgar. "She was done," Melvin acknowledged. "She saw that she had no life with him, and she would always blame him for the loss of her show and *The Tonight Show*. As far as she was concerned, he ruined her career. She could see clearly that anything she did to rebuild her career would be negatively impacted by Edgar, and that he just couldn't be part of it—but without Joan, Edgar didn't have anything. And he knew he was losing Joan."

But her husband's perspective was different. "I think Edgar felt very much the victim," Melvin said. "I don't think he felt responsible. He didn't want Joan to leave, and he was not angry at himself. I think it was more of a 'poor, pitiful me.'"

Edgar arranged his death the same way he handled everything else: with compulsive exactitude. "It was a very final action," said Cameron. "Everything was in order. His financial affairs were in bad shape because of a bad deal with Tom Pileggi, and they had huge overhead, but he left Melissa all the money."

Edgar died on August 14, 1987. He was sixty-two years old. Since Joan was in the hospital undergoing liposuction, it was nineteen-year-old Melissa—at home in Los Angeles, where she was getting ready to return to college in Philadelphia at the end of the summer—who received the call that her father's body had just been found in a Philadelphia hotel room.

So it was Melissa who had to call the house staff together and organize the secretaries to notify friends and acquaintances, Melissa who summoned Dorothy Melvin back from a trip to Oklahoma, Melissa who began planning her father's funeral. And it was Melissa who had to break the news to her mother. "I could remember, as if it were a century ago, waiting in the hospital room that morning after minor surgery, and Melissa suddenly appearing, short of breath from running," Rivers wrote later. "She said, 'Daddy's dead.'"

Recalling that day in a 2005 interview with her mother on CNN's *Larry King Live*, Melissa remembered her first reaction as "complete and total disbelief," she told Joan. "Then the thought of getting to you, because we were not in the same place, before someone else did, so that became the pressing moment for me. I remember you were at the end of a very long hallway, and it was like a very sort of Hitchcockian moment when I saw you walking out of a door and it was one of those moments where you feel like you're running but the hallway keeps stretching. It was incredibly surreal. It wasn't happening. I was watching myself go through the motions. It was almost a physical disconnect for me."

Joan's first reaction was to be overcome with guilt. "I moaned over and over, 'Oh my God, oh my God, oh my God,'" she said. "In my head I screamed the words, 'What have I done? What have I done?' If I had made that one phone call to Edgar saying, 'Come home,' he would still be alive. I had killed Edgar as surely as though I had pulled a trigger."

The shock was followed by a surreal numbness that soon gave way to rage when Rivers found herself sitting on the bathroom floor at home, screaming "You bastard!" to the husband who had abandoned her and their daughter.

"She was really furious with him, and what he did to Melissa," said Margie Stern, who became Joan's close friend in later years. "I think he was a failure, and her career was going downhill because of him. Suicide is the ultimate 'Fuck you.' I think he said, 'See you later.'"

Edgar's other intimates were as blindsided as his family. "I went up to Kim Novak's house in Carmel to visit, and her husband called me and said, 'Edgar Rosenberg just committed suicide,'" Cameron reported. "It was terrible; they had to get an escort for me to get on the plane. When I got to Los Angeles, I went right to the house. Joan was sitting on the couch. She wasn't crying or anything; she was just furious. She was so angry at Edgar for deserting Melissa. She said, 'I don't care if he wanted to leave me, but you don't do that to a child.'"

Although Edgar made methodical preparations for his death, he failed to foresee at least one major logistical problem he created by killing himself in a Pennsylvania hotel room. When the medical examiner's office refused to release his body, Joan—in desperation—finally called the First Lady. "Edgar killed himself in Philadelphia and I couldn't get the body out of there," Rivers told the *Daily Beast* in 2014. "My daughter was going mad. I thought, 'I'll call the White House.' It was 2 a.m. there. I said, 'It's Joan Rivers and it's an emergency. I must speak to Mrs. Reagan.' They woke her up...I said, 'I can't get Edgar's body out of Philadelphia.' She said, 'Let me see what I can do.' The next day his body came back to L.A. Nancy Reagan got Edgar's body out of Philadelphia for me. You don't forget that, especially when the chips are down."

Edgar's funeral was held at Wilshire Boulevard Temple, and a thousand people came, from Milton Berle, Elton John, Barbara Walters, and Kirk

Douglas to Cher, Bea Arthur, Jon Voight, and Los Angeles mayor Tom Bradley. But Edgar's best friend refused to attend; when Edgar promised Tom Pileggi that he wouldn't do anything foolish, Pileggi had replied, "If you do, I won't come to your funeral!"—and he kept his word.

Another absentee was Rivers's former mentor, who had introduced her to her husband. "I was amazed that I never heard a syllable from Johnny Carson," Rivers said. "Forgetting that Hollywood is purely a business town, I thought he would have, for a moment, remembered that he had known Edgar even before I did, and let bygones be bygones."

Rivers handled the logistical requirements of her husband's death with her usual correctness. "After the funeral, we came back and Joan did everything perfectly," Cameron said. "We sat shiva for eight nights, and she had a different fabulous restaurant cater it every night. She knew exactly what to do in terms of manners, which is why Melissa did everything perfectly when Joan died."

Joan's deepest grief continued to focus on her daughter. "The only time I saw her cry was about Melissa," Cameron said. "She would hang back in the kitchen, and she grabbed onto the doorjamb and said, 'Look at Melissa—she doesn't have a father! How could he do that?'"

To compound her pain, Edgar's suicide recalled agonizing memories of her mother's death. They had quarreled right before Beatrice died of a heart attack, so Joan felt as though she had precipitated it—and now she felt as if she had murdered Edgar. Her remorse about having told him he couldn't come home was so acute that she couldn't even bring herself to listen to his farewell tape, but she did read a transcript of his final message to her.

"I cannot bear to be shunted aside and be a fifth wheel," Edgar had written. "I know this is not your fault. This is all my doing. I had the heart attack, and I'm a changed person. But believe me, when I fought, I always fought for you."

With Edgar gone, there was no one fighting for Rivers, and her problems quickly multiplied. "A week or two later, she was completely alone, sitting in the kitchen, crying," Cameron reported. "She said, 'I have been blackballed by everyone. I have no nightclub engagements, no personal appearances. They don't think a woman whose husband committed suicide can be funny. I am now a single woman and I have been dropped by every social list; they consider me a threat. I have nothing here.' They really did have big problems. She couldn't get a job as a comic."

Melissa had a strong opinion about whom to blame for their troubles. "Melissa referred to Barry Diller as 'the man who murdered my father,'" Cameron said.

But for Joan, assigning responsibility was more complicated. "She hated Barry Diller, and she was very angry with him, but she also knew he had a valid point," Cameron said. "She recognized that Edgar's behavior was not helpful. She blamed both Barry and Edgar, because they put her in the position of basically having to cancel her own show."

After Edgar's death, Diller made repeated efforts to mend fences. Two years later, Rivers appeared at NATPE, the annual convention for independent television stations, to promote her new daytime talk show. At the end of a long line of people waiting to meet her, she was shocked to see Barry Diller.

"Ten minutes later, when he reached me, he took my hand. 'I wish you luck,' he said. 'I know you do,' I said," Rivers reported.

For public consumption, she claimed to have processed her anger and to feel mostly "a terrible sadness" about what had happened at Fox. Under different circumstances, she said, "Barry and I could have been friends and worked well together."

In 1992, Diller left Fox and purchased a $25 million share in QVC, the television home shopping network where Rivers had started selling her own jewelry and clothing line after Edgar died, when she couldn't find bookings. The QVC venture had since grown into an important part of Rivers's income, and she was initially terrified by the news that the man who came so close to destroying her television career would once again be her boss, at QVC. But Diller quickly reassured her with a gracious telephone call, and their dealings remained amicable.

Looking back on the whole saga now, Diller declines to accept any blame for Edgar's death. "It's absurd," he told me. "I'm the first person to take on almost any guilt, but I feel none—zero. I had so little dealings with them. I would never get on the ground and have a fight with him; all my dealings were basically indirect. The problem was that the show failed. It was my responsibility to order the show up, so if that affected him, yes, it's collateral damage of a kind—but I had no dealings with him and no relationship with him. In the later period, we were adversaries, because the show was failing and we were decision makers. I did at some point take him out of the situation, because it was so destructive. If you terminate somebody, and then they go and commit suicide, yes, you're a causal agent, probably. But if you've acted correctly, and decently—and I have zero issues on that in my history—there are no casualties. This was public: we canceled the show. We did not terminate the show because Edgar Rosenberg was the producer—that's crazy. We removed him, and I may have been the one who had to tell Joan. But I have no responsibility for Edgar Rosenberg's death."

As time passed, Joan apparently decided they were all culpable. "She blamed herself for letting Edgar get involved in the Fox mess when she knew what he was saying was wrong," said her friend Robert Higdon. "She said, 'Edgar was wrong. I knew it, but I couldn't go against my husband.' She was very aware of the fact that it was a mistake in her career, having her husband be her manager, but she was exceedingly loyal and very traditional. She would use the f-word in her act, but she was like Brooke Astor in some ways. If it's your husband, you just don't do certain things; you treat them with respect."

Despite the surface civility Rivers managed to muster in public, the truth was that she bore grudges forever, and her real feelings about Diller were no exception. After the 9/11 terrorist attacks, she often made jokes about the tragedy, and her most shocking was one she aimed at her nemesis. By 2001, fourteen years had passed since Edgar's death, but Rivers remained furious enough to envision her former boss being incinerated at the top of the World Trade Center on that fateful morning.

Caroline Hirsch retains vivid memories of a particularly shocking example. "The joke I will never forget was when she said, 'Did you ever think of who you wanted to meet for breakfast at Windows on the World on 9/11? I would have breakfast with Barry Diller,'" said Hirsch, who now owns Carolines on Broadway. "I was like, oh my God! She still held Barry Diller responsible for her husband killing himself and for ruining her career."

But Rivers also held Edgar responsible. "She said to me once, 'He tried to be a producer, but he wasn't a producer,'" Mark Simone recalled. "He thought he could be a manager, and he botched everything. I think she knew he fucked everything up."

In one of the last interviews Rivers ever gave, a long talk with the *Daily Beast* in 2014, she said, "When I was fired, he knew it was his fault, and he committed suicide. I always think of Samson pulling down the temple. Edgar just took all the columns away and pulled it down. We were all down in the rubble, and he didn't want to dig himself out."

She blamed his decision on cowardice—a luxury she had never permitted herself. "His health was a huge issue, he was just miserable, and he couldn't imagine fighting his way through another surgery, but Joan thought he was a quitter," said Blaine Trump. "She didn't understand weakness."

# Chapter Eleven

# RECOVERY: THE LONG ROAD BACK

The one-two punch of losing the Fox show and her husband effectively vaporized Rivers's career. Seemingly overnight, she was transformed from the Queen of Comedy into a social and professional pariah.

A big professional failure would have been hard enough to survive for a fiftysomething woman who had the temerity to break new ground and defy her longtime mentor. "The Johnny Carson thing was huge: he branded her as a traitor," said Andy Cohen. "She had to completely redefine herself after her husband died. She was not getting booked on Carson or Letterman, and she did not have the sheen of 'I'm one of the top five comedians in the country.'"

But the double whammy inflicted by Edgar's suicide added immeasurably to Rivers's public image problems as well as to her private grief. When he killed himself, the shock among insiders in the media and entertainment industries generated horrified gossip about why he had committed such a violent act and what that signified for his bereaved wife.

"We all were so staggered that he killed himself," said Liz Smith. "Joan and I were not real friends, but Edgar liked me, because nobody ever paid any attention to him. I thought he was a real nice man, but later other friends told me that he had mismanaged her career. I hate to say this, but I think he wasn't good enough for her. I just felt that Joan had arrived and he hadn't kept up. Maybe that's why he killed himself."

Others were even more blunt: one friend said his immediate reaction to news of Edgar's death was that "Joan's life is going to be ten thousand times better without him."

But in the immediate aftermath of Edgar's suicide, such a prospect seemed unthinkable to Rivers. As usual, she tried to put up a good front, and her coping mechanisms revolved around humor—but that strategy was sometimes misconstrued, even by her intimates.

A decade after her husband's suicide, Rivers finally chronicled her gradual return to mental health in *Bouncing Back: I've Survived Everything…and I Mean Everything…and You Can Too!* In the book, she described the painful breach in her relationship with her daughter that began to fester within days of Edgar's death.

"At the shiva, I was still able to laugh, but Melissa went deeper into her shell, which profoundly upset me," Rivers wrote. "She was appalled by my telling jokes just hours after Edgar's funeral. Where were my tears?…What she didn't understand was that my feelings were so overwhelming that I was able to deal with them only in the way that I had always dealt with pain: by laughing through my tears."

But Rivers quickly learned that this tack often generated visible opprobrium. After the week of shiva ended, she and Melissa went to a Los Angeles restaurant one night for dinner. When Joan opened the menu, she commented, "If Daddy saw these prices, he'd kill himself all over again!"

"For the first time since the suicide, Melissa laughed," Joan reported. "Anger left her eyes, and I saw the old sparkle there. I also saw every head in the restaurant turn toward us disapprovingly. Her husband dead a week, and they're laughing!"

Wherever she went, Rivers found herself under scrutiny, and people seemed all too ready to pass harsh judgments on her behavior. "About four months after Edgar died, I was in a coffee shop with friends and one of them cracked a good joke. I laughed hard," Rivers reported. "And then a complete stranger came over and said, one slow cold word at a time, 'I. Knew. Your. Husband.'"

Although some observers respected Rivers's obvious determination to carry on, others apparently felt she should be weeping and rending her garments behind closed doors. "I thought Joan conducted herself in an admirable way," Liz Smith said. "Shortly after the funeral, she went away on a cruise, and a friend of mine told me that on the trip, 'we called her the merry widow.' That began to go around, and Joan was outraged. She called herself that. She made a joke out of everything, including Edgar's death."

Rivers also tried to distract herself with constant activity. "She said, 'Now we're going to go Jewish skiing. Don't say no. Don't be stupid. I'm taking you,'" Sue Cameron reported. "So Melissa and Joan and I and our hairdresser went to Salt Lake City in a limo, and went to Deer Valley, to the Stein Eriksen Lodge."

Cameron was unfamiliar with the rules of Joan's favorite sport, but her friend was happy to explain. "Jewish skiing is this: You get up in the morning and the lodge brings you breakfast," Cameron said. "Around eleven in the morning, you take the tram to the ski area, where you're in a heated shed. Joan's skiing outfit was black ski pants, black suede cowboy hat, black fitted Chanel parka, and jewelry. She looked fabulous. The instructor comes with you, and you go down the bunny hill two or three times, and then it's 'Okay—lunch!' You go and have lunch, and after lunch you go on one more ride, and then Joan goes, 'Okay, time to go home.' There are one or two masseuses waiting for us in the condo, and we all get massages, take naps, and have showers. Max does everyone's hair, and then you go into town and have dinner, and then go to the old vintage clothing store. Park City is where we found two matching Temptations jackets, electric blue with black satin lapels. We each bought one, so we became Temptations for a week."

Despite such diversions, finding work remained Rivers's overriding priority, and she felt real panic when her agent told her no one wanted to book a comedian whose husband committed suicide. Her career was "ice-cold," she said—the hardship she had always feared most.

In truth, it was only two months after Edgar's death when Rivers got the opportunity to perform again. This was her chance to do spin control and set the tone for the next chapter of her career. As soon as she took the stage at Caesars Palace in Las Vegas, she went right for a suicide joke in a preemptive strike.

"I wanted the audience to see I was able to deal with it and so should they—and not have them sitting there through the whole act waiting for it to come up," she wrote in *Still Talking*. "I steeled myself for the first joke: 'My whole life has been so horrendous this year—as many of you may know—because of my husband's suicide and being fired by Fox. Thank God my husband left in his will that I should cremate him and then scatter his ashes in Neiman Marcus. That way he knew he would see me five times a week.' When I had their laughter and their relief, I knew the show was going to be okay."

As time went on, Rivers added other suicide jokes to her repertoire. "My husband killed himself. And it was my fault. We were making love and I took the bag off my head," she said.

She also made similar cracks with Melissa, firmly convinced that they were helpful. When she took her daughter back to college in Philadelphia, Rivers was appalled by the "hovel" where she was living in off-campus housing near the University of Pennsylvania.

"Melissa, I'm glad your father is dead. If he saw this, he would kill himself again," she said.

"We laughed. It was our first healing moment," Rivers reported in *Still Talking*.

But Melissa had her own burden of anger and sorrow to process. "Melissa blamed Joan for her father's suicide," said Cameron. "Edgar was already so depressed that Melissa felt Joan's leaving him at that time pushed him right over the edge. They did discuss divorce before Edgar's suicide, and that's why Melissa got so angry with her mother. She felt her mother was just throwing her father away completely, and she felt that contributed to Edgar's suicide. He couldn't think of a way out, but he was medically depressed, and he wasn't in his right mind when he killed himself. If he hadn't done that, they would probably have been separated for a few weeks and Joan would have taken him back."

In 1993, Rivers told *People* magazine that the painful estrangement from her daughter lasted for a year after Edgar's death. "'The way I see it,' explains Joan, 'Melissa blamed me.' After all, Joan and Edgar had only recently separated when he killed himself. 'But,' says Joan, 'she wasn't going to turn to me by the casket and say, "You killed Daddy!"' Instead, Joan says, anger simmered under the surface as the two 'tried to go on with our own lives and were both so broken that we couldn't help each other...I was totally alone, with no career, no husband, no child. I didn't know what I was going to do. I really thought about suicide myself.'"

*People* added, "For her part, Melissa avoided Joan, blaming her mother and feeling abandoned. 'I didn't want to know [what my mother was feeling],' she says. 'It was her problem. I was going through my own thing.'"

Melissa always believed that her father was misunderstood and his contributions to Joan's career insufficiently appreciated. Her grief at losing him was exacerbated when her mother started to date other men with what Melissa saw as unseemly haste. "Melissa began to criticize me constantly," Rivers reported. "She couldn't understand that I had to be busy all the time to maintain my sanity, something I hadn't always taken good care of."

When one man invited Rivers and her daughter to spend Thanksgiving with him, Melissa was outraged, according to her mother. "'If we're not having dinner at home, I'm not coming!' she cried. 'We belong at home, in California. Daddy's body isn't even cold. Mother, how could you plan a holiday with some other man? How could you!'"

Beset by challenges of every kind, Rivers felt completely overwhelmed. Her husband and her job had vanished, her daughter was furious with her, and she was terrified of the future. She had no one to lean on; her father had died in 1985, ten years after her mother, and Joan felt responsible for her sister, who was widowed in 1977, as well as for Barbara's children. But they lived on the other side of the country, as did Melissa. Without a pressing schedule of professional commitments, Joan didn't know what to do with herself. When she went out seeking respite from sadness, she was racked by wild mood swings—the manic life of the party one minute, a sobbing wreck the next. Her beloved family home seemed big and empty, and she was desperately lonely.

But Rivers also wondered whether her unwelcome solitude might be haunted by Edgar's unquiet presence. She and her staff joked that if Edgar ever came back, the dog would bite him, and the dog suddenly started barking at senseless times for no apparent reason, refusing to shut up even when Rivers tried to wrestle him physically into submission—not usually a difficult task with a Yorkshire terrier.

Other unsettling portents kept intruding on her fragile state of mind. "Every night at ten of seven, Edgar's alarm clock would ring, and nobody could shut it off," Rivers reported. "We would turn up the temperature on the air conditioner and come back to find it down to ice-cold, the way he liked it."

Rivers believed in ghosts, and some in her inner circle insisted that Edgar was manifesting himself to them. One day their bookkeeper mentioned that she'd been pouring coffee when Edgar walked through the kitchen, dressed in his pink shirt and beige pants. Several days later Rivers's assistant said she saw him on his way upstairs, wearing the same outfit.

Torn between fear and indignation that her noncorporeal husband made himself visible to others while neglecting to visit her, Rivers called a Catholic church and asked for an exorcist to come to the house. The priest forgot his holy water, but he went from room to room, praying for peace in the Rosenbergs' home. "I prayed for peace in Edgar's soul," Rivers said.

If Edgar was lurking, however, he wasn't helping his baffled wife to deal with the mechanics of her physical environment. From operating the burglar alarm and the VCR to coping with the business affairs that Edgar always took care of, Rivers realized that she had no idea how to manage many of the practical functions necessary for her to lead an independent life.

Money was another unexpected issue. Before Edgar died, he revised his will and left everything to Melissa, and Rivers soon discovered that she had serious financial problems. "I was $37 million in debt," Rivers told *Esquire* magazine in 2007.

"He was not in his right mind, because of the drugs he was on, and he was making terrible business decisions and investments," explained Martyn Fletcher, Rivers's London hairdresser. "He invested in companies that were going down, and he left her in such terrible financial shape. Joan said if he came back she would kill him again for doing that."

Her accountant said she had to cut her huge overhead, so she started worrying about whether to sell the house or reduce her staff. But Rivers was woefully unprepared to assume responsibility for economic decisions. "Without Edgar, I was a financial idiot," she said.

Feeling that every aspect of her life was spiraling into chaos, Rivers turned to one thing she could control: her body. Compulsively gobbling sweets in regular bouts of stress-related eating, she started making herself throw up so she wouldn't gain weight—and soon became a full-fledged bulimic.

It took years for Rivers to recover fully from the shock, grief, guilt, and anger she felt about losing her husband, and some of the scars would last forever. But staying strong for Melissa was always her overriding concern—and her most powerful hedge against despair. "I decided that for Melissa's sake I had to keep going," Joan said. "Otherwise, I would give her the same message as Edgar—that suicide is the only way out. So I felt she had to see me climb out of the well."

At Joan's insistence, they went into therapy, both separately and to-gether, in Los Angeles and Philadelphia. In the past, Joan had always rejected the idea of psychiatry, afraid that if she explored the demons that drove her, any resolution might sap her drive or deplete her comedic ma-terial. But now, not knowing where else to turn, she found solace in seeing a therapist. As time went on, she became a fervent advocate who credited therapy with facilitating her own healing process and recommended it en-thusiastically to others.

In her self-help book, *Bouncing Back*, she described many of the tech-niques she had used to aid her recovery, starting with a quick exercise to help others suffering from major blows to assess their situation. "Take out some paper or a notebook and in a few short sentences, write down the ba-sic headlines of your challenge or your loss," she recommended. "If I had known to do this after Edgar's suicide, my statement would have looked like this:

"My husband of twenty-two years killed himself. My career is over. I am a widow, and my daughter, the most important person on earth to me, is now fatherless. Despite the fact that we live in a big house and have nice things, we are, because of bad investments, nearly broke."

Her career seemed to have reached its nadir in Los Angeles, and Rivers decided it would be impossible to build a viable new life there. "Hollywood was a company town where nothing mattered except my current low status in the business," she said.

Her personal prospects appeared equally bleak. Like many divorcées and widows, even those whose husbands hadn't killed themselves, Rivers believed she was being dropped from guest lists and frozen out of the social scene by wives who saw a newly single woman as a threat. A lifelong culture vulture and a passionate theatergoer, she found herself visiting New York with increasing frequency, hungry for the kind of stimulation that was harder to find in Los Angeles.

She was deeply attached to her elaborately decorated house on Ambazac, and Melissa was horrified at the idea of selling the family home, but Joan decided it was time to go back where she came from and build a different kind of life for herself. Scouting for a new residence in Manhattan, she found an unusual apartment that was originally two eighteen-foot-high ballrooms, separated by a sliding door, in a Gilded Age mansion at One East 62nd Street. Built in 1897, the property had deteriorated into a certifiable wreck.

"It was now a broken-down warren of cloakrooms, maids' rooms, and musicians' changing rooms, and then vast spaces of no use whatsoever," Rivers said. "It had been on the market for two and a half years without one bid, and by now plaster was falling from the walls, the floor was coming up. There was major water damage. Edgar never would have bought it."

But the idea of "creating something from nothing" and making it into the vehicle for her fantasies proved irresistible. Even her financial woes were recast as an incentive: she figured that taking on such a project would jump-start her motivation to earn serious money as soon as possible. So Rivers bought the place and set about transforming it into the home of her dreams.

Given the decrepitude of the property, its renovation was a lengthy process, so Rivers took up temporary residence in a hotel for the duration. "She had a suite at the Carlyle, but she was such a nester she asked the management if she could recover the sofa," reported the writer Jenny Allen, noting that Rivers filled her hotel room with stacks of books on the bedside table and personal touches like a needlepoint pillow embroidered with the famous Dorothy Parker line "What fresh hell is this?"

Allen was writing an *Architectural Digest* story about Rivers's elaborate house in Los Angeles, and she was struck by the parallels between that place and the new trophy home Rivers was creating in Manhattan. "I'm always interested in women who make a big physical presence in the world, and Joan certainly did that," Allen observed. "The homes she owned weren't just tucked-away private aeries she could nestle in. They were big, and she wanted the town house to be big—as big as her public persona, even though that was in conflict with her private persona."

When Rivers was widowed, she also faced the challenge of creating a different kind of social life for herself. "I met her when she moved to New York," said Blaine Trump, who became a close friend. "Billy Norwich had gotten to know her, and he said, 'Let's have dinner.' I expected a really brassy, crude Hollywood person, but she was very different from what I expected. She really wasn't working, and she'd just been told by Barry Diller that she'd never work in Hollywood again. And she was mad as hell at Edgar. She was angry at the scars it left for Melissa."

Rivers's anger was visible to everyone, but Trump suspected that she also felt a greater sense of personal loss than she was willing to acknowledge. "She really loved him," Trump said. "She really loved that he was 'classy,' that he had taste, that he was sophisticated, that he was worldly. That was important to her."

George Hamilton was another friend who thought Joan was in denial about the extent of her own grief. "She was devastated," he said. "I think she dearly missed him. She felt he'd left her. That was a partnership that ran very deep, I thought. Edgar was more like the master of ceremonies, there to introduce her. There are so many people like that—the strength behind someone. I think Joan had to have him to be herself."

Without her husband or child, Rivers had to find other ways to fill the enormous vacuum created by their absence. In Manhattan, she might have devoted her energy to infiltrating various parts of the entertainment industry, whether in comedy, television, theater, or any of the other cultural worlds she loved so much. Instead, she sought out new friends who—like Edgar when they first met so long ago—seemed to personify class.

"Being part of society meant being accepted," said Blaine Trump, an A-list socialite who was then married to Donald Trump's brother Robert. "I think Joan was so scared by her mother and the idea that 'she's not going to amount to anything' that that never left her. She always gauged her success on how people accepted her. She would say, 'You won't believe it—I was at the A table!'"

As Rivers made new friends, one of the first things they noticed was her thoughtfulness. "You'd be having dinner, and you'd say, 'I haven't read that book,' and she'd say, 'I'll send it to you,'" Trump said. "With most people, it would never arrive, but she forgot nothing. She had a mind like a steel trap."

But her emotional generosity extended far beyond superficial gestures. To a startlingly wide range of people, Rivers was someone who could always be relied upon in a crisis. "I went through a really dark couple of years, and she was the most caring, wonderful friend you could ever have," said Trump. "When you're going through tough times, she was front and center."

After twenty-four years of marriage, Blaine discovered that her husband, Robert, was having a long-running affair with a girlfriend who worked in the Trump family real estate office in Brooklyn. "He had a whole other life with this woman for a long time, and when Joan found out, she went crazy," Trump said. "She invited him to dinner at Isle of Capri, his favorite restaurant, and she just let him have it. She called me afterward and said, 'I just want you to know I did this.'"

Blaine was devastated by her husband's betrayal. "New York society queen Blaine Trump was so despondent when she found out her beloved husband, Robert Trump, was having an affair, she had an 'accidental overdose' on pills, several friends confirmed to Page Six," the *New York Post* reported. "In October 2004, Blaine ended up staying at Mount Sinai for several days after she learned Robert had bought a $3.7 million house on

Long Island for his girlfriend, Ann Marie Pallan, and, to make matters worse, was leaving her for Pallan."

Rivers's response was brisk and bracing. "Joan said, 'Get rid of him! Good! Glad he's gone! It's over. It's done. Move on. Look at this as a positive. Your life is going to be so much happier and better,'" Trump said. "As it turns out, I do have a much better life, and Joan was a big part of the initial healing process. She was a big cheerleader for me."

But healing took time; the Trumps' divorce was bitter and protracted, and it coincided with other emotional blows. "My father died, my best friend died, and there were days when I couldn't get out of bed," Blaine said. "Every day, when things were really rough, Joan would call and say, 'What time do you want to meet?' A lot of people don't know how to help you, but her way of helping everyone was laughter. On the darkest days, she always found the humor in everything. She had to try to make you laugh and bring you out of the absurdity of the pain of life. She would call and say, 'I'm coming over,' and send a pot of fake flowers with a music box. She was always so funny."

Rivers expended considerable effort to comfort a friend in need. "When my father had a stroke and died, Joan called me and said, 'I'm coming,'" Trump said. "I said, 'Don't come.' It was a big trip, but the next day I heard the doorbell ring and the housekeeper yells, 'Miss Rivers is here!' She just wouldn't take no for an answer. I said, 'What are you doing here?,' and she said, 'I just came for twenty minutes. I had to see you and make sure you were okay.' That was Joan. Her friendship was beyond any friendship."

Rivers also invented diversions to distract her friend from grief. "One day she said, 'We're going to Australia, and we'll stop in Hong Kong. I've booked your ticket,'" Trump reported. "I said, 'I can't go.' She said, 'You're going.' And of course I went."

Others tell similar stories. Rivers's London hairdresser, Martyn Fletcher, became a close friend, as did his longtime partner, Digby Trout, a prominent restaurateur. "When Digby found out he had a tumor, she phoned him every day until he died," said Fletcher. "We were supposed to go to Mexico with Joan at Christmas, but I told her he wasn't going to be able to travel. She said, 'If you're not coming over, I'm coming to you.' She flew over to have lunch with him, because she knew she'd never see him again. We went to Cliveden, the Nancy Astor house, and we had the most wonderful lunch. We laughed and talked about all the stupid things we'd done together, and that night she flew back.'"

When Arnold Stiefel was hospitalized in Los Angeles, Rivers was thousands of miles away, but she quickly materialized at his bedside. "This wonderful crazy lady flew in from Canada to see me in the hospital and bring the nurses Joan Rivers jewelry so they would be nice to me," Stiefel said.

Rivers got to know Pete Hathaway when he was a director of European furniture at Sotheby's, and they became good friends. Hathaway later spent time in rehab for alcohol abuse. "Joan was wonderful during what I call my unfortunate incarceration," he said. "I would go to the mailbox and there would be a hologram postcard of spiders. I would turn it over and it would say, 'Don't worry, it's not the DTs! XOXO Joan.' It would just make me laugh so hard. I was living in a sober house in California where the answering machine message said, 'Hello, this is Sober Living by the Sea.' One day I got a message saying, 'This is Suicidal on the sixtieth floor—call me!' It was Joan."

As a widening array of new friendships filled the void left by the absence of her family, Rivers was also making a career comeback. "Everything started falling together again," said Dorothy Melvin. "The jobs were coming to us; she was working. Joan was never content: she was a total workaholic, and she always wanted to work more. But we were doing QVC, and that took off, and we were always looking for new things, and it all just started building. She could never rest on her laurels, and she never felt she was ever on top again, but she was. It was the best time—and we were happy."

Rivers's social circle expanded to include such celebrities as the flamboyant multimillionaire Malcolm Forbes—bold-faced names she wouldn't have known if Edgar were still around. "When we went to St. Petersburg on the Forbes plane for the opening of the Fabergé exhibit at the Hermitage, Joan and I were like merry widows, because I had a partner who died of AIDS," Robert Higdon recalled. "She had a few pieces of Fabergé that were being exhibited, along with things from Forbes and the Queen, so it was a big moment for her. She said, 'Oh my God, I wish Edgar were here!' I said, 'If Sam and Edgar were alive, we wouldn't be here.' She said, 'You're right. Fuck 'em.' I'll never forget how quickly she switched. When Edgar killed himself she moved back to New York and met Forbes and a lot of other people, but she wouldn't have known Malcolm Forbes if Edgar were still alive."

The eternal roundelay of life in New York helped her deal with one of the biggest challenges of all: learning to live an unpartnered life. "Being alone, not dreading another long night of anxiety and fear and remorse, was the last goal to be reached," she admitted. "Gradually solitude became something to be desired."

Not that there weren't men in her life; in the years following Edgar's death, Rivers had several romantic relationships of varying durations and intensities. Her paramours included Spiros Milonas, a Greek shipping magnate; New York lawyer Bernard Goldberg; and the philanthropist and conservationist Orin Lehman, who proved to be the most important.. But in the second half of Rivers's life, it was increasingly her devoted array of friends who provided the emotional support that sustained her on a daily basis.

Rivers was also fortified by a changing perspective. Having weathered such terrible storms, she began to realize that her worst traumas had helped to produce some of her most important learning experiences—and the process of dealing with those challenges had left her permanently transformed.

"I have become my version of an optimist," she said with considerable surprise. "If I can't get through one door, I'll go through another door—or I'll make a door. Something will come up, no matter how dark the present."

In weathering her trials, Rivers also learned the ultimate lesson of life, which is that change is the only constant—and that while the good times don't last forever, the bad times eventually pass too. "I lecture on suicide because things turn around," she said. "I tell people that this is a horrible, awful, dark moment, but it will change, and you must know it's going to change, and you push forward. I look back and think, 'Life is great. Life goes on. It changes.'"

By then she was able to admit the unexpected benefits that evolved from her husband's suicide. "I understand it, and I feel terribly sorry for him, but I wonder if I'd be sitting here today talking to you if he had not killed himself—if we wouldn't have ended up just a very bitter couple in a house on a hill somewhere," Rivers told the *Daily Beast* in 2014. "He would have said, 'That's it, they can all go to hell, and we'll just pull ourselves in.'"

Instead, the loss of her husband had liberated her to grow and establish a truly independent life of her own design. "My personal take was that she felt she was better off without him," said David Dangle. "The marriage was kind of over, and there would never have been a QVC with Edgar around. He was a snob, and he wouldn't have let her do that. He wouldn't have liked the idea of her selling things on television; she was pretty vocal about that."

Forced to fend for herself, Rivers ultimately achieved her greatest success—and her greatest satisfaction. "After he died, because there was nothing, I had to strike out again," she said. "A friend of mine at his funeral said, 'He's freed you.' I thought that was very interesting. And in a way he did, because I had to really start again—thank God."

Although Rivers earned great wealth and fame in her later years, she was so traumatized by her previous setbacks that she didn't feel secure. But the truth was that she achieved so much in her long and varied comeback that it arguably represented the height of her career. "She never felt she was on top again," said Dorothy Melvin. "But she was."

# Chapter Twelve

## REINVENTING A CAREER: "I CAN RISE AGAIN!"

$A$s always, work supplied the essential foundation for Rivers's recovery. The first real breakthrough occurred in 1988, when she surprised virtually everyone by landing the role of Kate Jerome, the mother in Neil Simon's hit play *Broadway Bound.*

"She was a star, but we did not seek her out," said Manny Azenberg, the producer. "She called and said she'd like to play the part. It was unlikely—who would have thought of Joan Rivers to play that part?"

But in some ways, it seemed like a good fit. "If you think about what her status was at the time, her husband was gone, and in the play the husband leaves and the character is alone," Azenberg observed.

The third installment in Simon's semiautobiographical trilogy of plays about Eugene and his brother, Stanley, a pair of aspiring comedy writers based on the playwright and his own brother, *Broadway Bound* traces the dissolution of their family as they discover that their father has been cheating on their mother.

With her children grown and her husband abandoning her after thirty-three years of marriage, Kate is a poignant character. In an Act II monologue about a fleeting encounter with an old-time movie actor that *New York Times* theater critic Frank Rich called the "indisputable peak" of the play, Kate tells Eugene "about the most glamorous incident in her life—a night at the Primrose Ballroom, thirty-five years earlier, when George Raft asked her to dance... It's a mesmerizing journey to a bygone working-class

Brooklyn where first-generation American Jews discovered the opportunities and guilt that came with the secular temptations of a brash new world."

As a girl from her own fractious family of Brooklyn Jews, Rivers brought a visceral understanding to a juicy role. "Kate is a remarkable achievement—a Jewish mother who redefines the genre even as she gets the requisite laughs while fretting over her children's health or an unattended pot roast," Rich wrote. "She's a woman who takes 'her own quiet pleasure' in a world that goes no farther than her subway line, and if her life is over once her dinner table is deserted, she greets her fate with stoical silence, not self-martyrdom…a survivor, not a victim, of an immigrant family's hard path to assimilation."

In the Broadway production, Linda Lavin had already won a Tony Award for creating the role of Kate, and she was replaced by Elizabeth Franz when she left the play. Both actresses were formidable acts to follow, and Rivers could hardly have faced a tougher set of judges than the seasoned professionals whose job it was to choose the next Kate Jerome.

Simon was one of the most successful playwrights in American history, Azenberg was his longtime producer as well as a leading producer and general manager for others, and Gene Saks, the director of *Broadway Bound*, had already won Tony Awards as best director for each of the preceding two plays in the Eugene trilogy, *Brighton Beach Memoirs* and *Biloxi Blues*. Together the three men comprised one of the most successful teams in the theater business.

As gimlet-eyed experts they were not willing to fill a pivotal role with an untested actress—even a celebrity. But when Rivers auditioned, they were unexpectedly impressed with what they saw.

"There was some trepidation—that she wasn't an actress, and that it would be Joan Rivers," Azenberg admitted. "She was a name, but she got the part because she earned it. She did not play Joan Rivers; she acted the text. She came on time, and she commanded our respect because she came prepared. She had seen all the others in the role, and she knew what she was doing. She came almost letter-perfect with the dialogue. If somebody comes like that, you know they're serious—and you also know they're frightened. We liked her, and we didn't have to tap-dance around her. She was good, and she behaved really well. There was no attitude; she was absolutely un-diva."

Most important of all, Rivers was believable as a middle-aged, middle-class housewife from the 1940s. "At the time, she looked like a real person; she hadn't had all that cosmetic surgery," Azenberg said. "There was authenticity. She played a legitimate role as a serious woman, and she knew who that woman was. The woman is a mother, and the husband leaves. The woman's father says, 'What are you looking for?' He says, 'Something else…'—and he's gone. There's no explanation; he just leaves. The loneliness of that character—Joan knew."

For Rivers, earning the role represented the fulfillment of a lifelong dream as well as the best possible therapy. "After twenty-five years, my first love had called me up," Rivers said. "I was ecstatic."

Even better was winning the respect of the critics, however grudging—and some of them were grudging indeed. "Rivers has always struck me as precisely the kind of vulgar, raucous individual, rude, insinuating, and so much else, that I thoroughly dislike," Clive Barnes wrote in the *New York Post*. But in the play, he found her "beautiful and touching," he said. "Her coolly understated acting looked neither contrived nor phony. The shtick-stuck, jokey, elbow-nudging naturalism of television had been abandoned, and Rivers was indeed Broadway bound."

Barnes's final verdict: "I went to scoff and stayed to admire," he admitted.

Joining the cast of *Broadway Bound* gave the stagestruck Rivers the ultimate validation—the prize she had fantasized about since childhood. Becoming part of the theater community felt like "sheer joy," she said, and walking onto the stage every night was simply "bliss."

But the experience also provided a critical turning point in her recovery from Edgar's suicide—not only by giving her meaningful work of the kind she valued most, but also by creating new hope that the future might contain other equally unexpected possibilities.

"*Broadway Bound* saved my life," she said.

As important as the play was to her, Rivers didn't rely on one job. "The first time I met her was about six months after Edgar killed himself, and she was burying her grief in her work," said Steve Olsen, the owner of the West Bank Cafe and the Laurie Beechman Theatre, where Rivers performed in later years. "She was doing the Neil Simon show on Broadway, and she was doing her comedy act at Michael's Pub on Thursday, Friday, and Saturday nights after the Broadway show. She was flying to Los Angeles on the red-eye after the Sunday matinee to tape four *Hollywood Squares* on Monday."

By the time *Broadway Bound* closed, Rivers had gotten another break. She was asked to do a syndicated daytime television talk show for Tribune Entertainment, and that experience turned out to be equally surprising.

Rivers still felt bruised and battered by her treatment at Fox, which she saw as having tainted her reputation. She made no secret of how traumatic it had been, and how scared she was of fending for herself. "The name of her production company was PGHM, which stood for 'Please God Help Me,'" said Bill Reardin, a longtime television production executive.

But at Tribune, Rivers was startled to find herself working for corporate bosses who agreed to her needs, refrained from second-guessing her, and remained supportive. "They gave me respect and returned to me my self-respect as a talk show host," she said.

She also discovered that she still commanded respect from the fellow professionals she needed to put together another show. "I wanted desperately to work for Joan Rivers, because I thought she was a great talent and thought it would be wonderful to work on a show with her," said Reardin, who was thrilled to land an interview with her in 1989.

Knowing Rivers's public persona, Reardin expected a tough cookie—but what he actually encountered was more like a Jewish mother. "For some reason, I was kind of prepared that I wouldn't really like her," he admitted. "I really wanted to work on the show, but I thought she might be horrible to work with. So I walked in, and she's having breakfast, and she puts a hand on my arm and says, 'You've got to eat—what do you want to eat?' She was always very concerned about people, and she wanted to know about them: 'Are you okay? Do you have a boyfriend? Do you have a girlfriend?'"

Rivers's gift for instant intimacy not only put Reardin at ease but drew him into an exclusive and conspiratorial club. "We went over to CBS for a meeting, and one of the CBS executives said, 'Joan, we'd like you to do some test shows and focus groups in June, before your show starts,'" Reardin reported. "Joan stands up and says, 'Look, my husband killed himself, and I'm taking Melissa and going to Europe. I'm not doing test shows in June.' We leave and get in a fancy van, and she slaps my knee and says, 'That suicide bit works every time! I'm going to Europe, but Melissa is not coming with me.' I thought, 'I love this woman!'"

Reardin signed on with the Tribune company as the executive in charge of production for *The Joan Rivers Show*, and he stayed with that show and its spin-offs, *Gossip! Gossip! Gossip!* and *Can We Shop?*, for the next five years. "She was wonderful to work with," he said. "She was just a pleasure. I don't ever remember a harsh word with her about anything. She was so loved by everyone."

That said, Rivers didn't hesitate to do whatever was necessary to get her own way. As Reardin described it, her credo was "Do unto others before they do unto you. Fuck them first, before they fuck you."

And yet he found the experience of working with her to be unexpectedly benign. "When she wanted something, she usually got it," he said. "She would throw a little fit every once in a while if she wasn't getting what she wanted, but basically it was an act. It wasn't every day that she threw a tantrum, but she would knock over a fax machine and go storming out—and as she went by she would wink at me. It was all about acting."

Rivers was equally creative in coming up with a new persona for the show—one that reflected the image she wished to project for her new life in Manhattan. David Dangle, a former actor then working as a costume designer and art director for theater and television, was asked to meet with Rivers about remaking her style. "Sunday morning at 8 a.m. was the only time she had," Dangle reported. "She was this little tiny woman—five foot two when I met her, and a size zero. She was in her late fifties, but she had a great figure."

A different stylist initially got the job, but Rivers was unhappy with the results, and a couple of months later Dangle was called back and hired to redo Rivers's look. "She said, 'I want to look like a New York rich bitch!'" he recalled. "She wanted to look like Blaine Trump, Nancy Kissinger, Betsy Bloomingdale—very WASPy, very New York and Fifth Avenue."

That took some doing. "When I met her, she had had a lot of big 1980s hair, so she changed her hair," Dangle said. "It was a sleek pageboy, and the makeup was toned down. I got rid of the shoulder pads and the flashier California look. She wore beautiful clothes in California, but fashion was changing. It became more elegant, more New York, and I tailored her a lot more."

According to Marlaine Selip, who became the supervising producer on *The Joan Rivers Show*, "David went to places like Le Cirque and drew people, and then he created that look for her. She looked like a million bucks. She had Chanel jewels and tailored outfits and wonderful bags, because she was always carrying stuff. She looked rich. People tuned in just to see what she'd be wearing."

Dangle recalled a gay bar in New York that regularly turned on the show so patrons could see Rivers's opening monologue. "They went to live TV and watched her," he said. "It was because she was hilarious, and also because she was wearing some pretty fabulous things—Galanos, Oscar de la Renta, Michaele Vollbracht, Chanel, Armani, Donna Karan, Helmut Lang. She wanted to be looked at as a New York style icon, and she started becoming known for having great taste. She got a lot of great press for her look, and that was very important to her. She wanted to make a statement: 'Look at me!'"

For Rivers, the metamorphosis echoed the narrative she had reenacted so many times before. "The world kicks her in the can, and she comes back stronger than ever," said Dangle, who received Emmy Award nominations for costume design three times in five years for doing Rivers's wardrobe. "Coming back from the ashes was always a big thing for her: 'I can rise again!' She was leaving California, starting her life again, reinventing herself, building an incredible mansion, becoming a new person. She was about reinventing, reinventing, reinventing—she was a genius at that."

Dangle found Rivers to be easy to work with, but only after he learned to accommodate her preferences. "I'm of the school where you become quiet when you're in somebody's dressing room," he explained. "One day I was quiet and the makeup artist was doing her thing and the hairdresser was doing Joan's hair, and everyone was being very respectful, and Joan finally said, 'It's too fucking quiet—call somebody up and yell at them!' Silence pissed her off. She thrived on energy, chaos, noise. She loved a crisis. She didn't want that funeral parlor tone. She wanted people talking, laughing, complaining, and telling stories. The more chaos and drama, the better, and she loved people fighting."

Rivers was also an inveterate busybody. "She had spectacular hearing," Dangle said. "You could be two rooms over, saying, 'I talked to Bob…,' and she'd be, 'Who talked to Bob?' You couldn't whisper; she heard it. And if she couldn't hear it, she had to know: 'What are you talking about? What did he say?' Constant curiosity."

*The Joan Rivers Show* went on the air in September of 1989, and her staff was impressed with the way she tackled the demands of a live daily program. "She went into it with such verve and vigor, and her general state of mind was good," Reardin said. "She went down in flames at Fox, and she couldn't get a job, she couldn't get hired, and she was broke, although her idea of broke was not my idea of broke. But she's a survivor, and she was determined to be successful."

"She was strong, she was a fighter, and she held it together," Selip said. "She knew it was a challenge, but she was up to the challenge. Her intention was to win: 'I'm not going to roll over and play dead, and we're going to succeed. I'm going to do what I have to do to make sure this wins.'"

But putting on a Joan Rivers show wasn't easy. "In terms of name recognition, you didn't have to sell the host, because everyone knew her, but people had strong opinions," said Randi Gelfand Pollack, the program's booker. "Every time she went off in a monologue and said something, it was like, 'Oh, we're not going to get that guest!' Some people would say, 'I will never do that cunt's show.'"

Rivers's employees were nonetheless struck by the gap between Rivers's public image and the woman they worked with every day. "She wasn't what she seemed; she was much deeper than that," said Selip.

"When I first went in, I didn't realize how smart she was. She loved books, and she read and read and read—all different types of books. She was curious about everything, and she was smart, smart, smart. She just loved knowing what was going on, and she was always very current. She was a really interesting person, and she liked smart, quick-witted people to work with, so everyone could be funny. I learned so much from her. She had broad interests, and she was multifaceted. She wasn't a one-trick pony."

Throughout her life, Rivers remained interested in a range of subjects so broad they often seemed bizarre. When she read a book review that intrigued her, she not only bought the book for herself but sent copies to friends. "There were constant packages going out to people," said David Dangle. "Then she'd ask, 'What did you think about it?' The last few books I got from her were on the weirdest topics. There was Charles Manson's biography; a book about a nineteenth-century aerial artist; a book about the alimentary canal called *Gulp*, by Mary Roach; and a book about the Romanovs and Russian history. Who do you know that's fascinated by Charles Manson, aerial artists, the alimentary canal, and the Romanovs?"

Rivers's fierce work ethic, passionate curiosity, and hard-earned skills paid off with a major reward the year after her show launched, when she won television's Daytime Emmy Award for Outstanding Talk Show Host. Her fellow nominees were Oprah Winfrey, Sally Jessy Raphael, Phil Donahue, and Jeff Smith of *The Frugal Gourmet*, and when she beat them all, she was overwhelmed with emotion.

"I had made it back from the dead," she said. "The instant was entire, immaculate joy, no fear, no guilt. Total happiness…One of the purest moments in my life."

But she also felt genuine grief that Edgar couldn't witness her triumphant comeback. "Two years ago, I couldn't get a job in this business," she told the audience in her acceptance speech at the Emmy Awards. "My income dropped to one-sixteenth of what it was before I was fired. My husband, as you know, had a breakdown. It's so sad that he's not here because it was my husband, Edgar Rosenberg, who always said you can turn things around. And except for one terrible moment in a hotel room in Philadelphia, when he forgot that, this is really for him, because he was with me from the beginning."

She had to stop there, because she was crying too hard to continue. "Welling up in me was the tragedy of Edgar's whole life, the futility of his suicide," she said later. "I wanted to tell him, 'We're back. We're back, you idiot!'"

Edgar's death freed Rivers from the burden of carrying a dysfunctional partner who hindered her career. Despite its tragic ending, her marriage had served an even more liberating purpose: after more than two decades as a wife, she was also able to move beyond the obsession with finding a husband that had warped her youth.

Single again, Rivers no longer viewed marriage as a top priority. "I just remember her being very career-driven," said Selip. "She dated, but I never got the sense that she felt she wouldn't be complete without a man. I think she would have liked that, but it wasn't a must-do. I think there had been an expectation in her life, placed in her when she was young, that she would marry well, have kids, and have a nice life. Back then it was going against the grain to say, 'Hey, wait a minute—I want to do something of my own. I want to be my own person.'"

As a divorced single mother, Selip saw Rivers as an inspiration. "She had a nice life—but it was of her own making," Selip said. "My relationship with her was like, 'Hey, girls can do anything and still have a nice relationship with a man! We don't have to sit here and wait for a man to take care of us!' I don't think she thought anyone was ever going to take care of her. It wasn't like 'Someday my prince will come…' She knew she had to take care of herself."

Although Rivers loved doing the daytime talk show, it elicited mixed reviews, even from its staff. They admired how hard she worked, and gave her full credit for managing with far fewer resources than her male peers.

"There was a period when the Tribune company launched a late-night show with Dennis Miller, and they asked me if I would go to L.A. for three months and fix the show," Larry Ferber recalled. "Both Joan and Dennis were on for an hour daily, but Dennis had thirteen writers, and Joan had one. One of Joan's gifts was spontaneity, and one day she had Leona

Helmsley as a guest. Helmsley was crying these crocodile tears and saying, 'I don't know why they're persecuting me—I'm not Jeffrey Dahmer! I haven't killed anybody!' And Joan said, 'We don't know that, Leona—we haven't checked all the hotel rooms yet!' This was somebody who knew how to listen, and she did it better than anybody."

Even so, the show wasn't a great success. "She was so good, but the content of the show was crap," said Ferber. "She had the most brilliantly wicked sense of humor, and it wasn't being utilized. The turning point came when we had on Angela Bowie and Howard Stern. The talent coordinator said that Howard wanted to meet Joan before the show, but he had a hidden camera and he was going to try to seduce her. So Howard says, 'You're so hot!,' and Joan says, 'So are you!' He completely freaked out. She said, 'I know about the damn camera!'"

But as soon as Stern went on the air, he upped the ante. "Joan was dressed in a beautiful fitted suit, and Stern comes out, and she goes to greet him—and he dips her and grabs her ass," Selip recalled. "She's laughing, and it's so funny because she's going with it. He goes, 'Joan, you are so hot—I can't believe your husband killed himself!' She burst out laughing, because she knew what guts it took for him to say that—and that would be something she would do. They were similar souls. On the show, it was like playing tennis: he would say something outrageous, and she would come right back."

Before the program ended, Stern also managed to one-up his host with her own guest—thereby scoring a publicity bonanza for the show. Angela Bowie, the ex-wife of David Bowie, had written a memoir called *Backstage Passes: Life on the Wild Side with David Bowie*. Its rock star content notwithstanding, Rivers's initial interview was boring.

"Joan was the best listener, but she got nothing out of Angela Bowie," Ferber said. "Stern came out and teased her—'Good interview, Joan! You didn't get anything out of her!' So they brought Angela back, and they double-teamed her. They said, 'Oh, come on, you must have found David in bed with somebody!' She said, 'Well, there was the time I found him in bed with Mick Jagger...' Joan said, 'Yes!' When she walked off, she said, 'I haven't had this much fun in years!' The quote ended up on the front page of the *Daily News*—'Dancing in the Sheets'—and we started to get that kind of press a lot."

An exchange with Larry King elicited another round of headlines. "He had just come from the Miss America contest, where he was one of the judges," Ferber recalled. "Joan said, 'What was it like?,' and Larry said, 'All the girls were so pretty!' Joan said, 'Come on, you can't tell me that out of fifty women they were all beautiful!' He said, 'Well, to tell you the truth, Miss Pennsylvania was a dog!' And that made the headlines, so we really milked it. The next day, we booked Miss Pennsylvania and her mother."

Ferber acknowledged that Rivers had to badger King to get him to say what he did. "Did she dig at it? Yes, she was persistent," he admitted. "But it was great television. It was what Joan was doing at her best, using her interview skills with wit."

Humor was also Rivers's preferred mode at the office, where she cracked as many jokes behind the scenes as she did before an audience. "At that time, the show was on for an hour live at 9 a.m., and we had a briefing at 6 a.m., so we would come in every morning exhausted, because getting up at that hour is exhausting," Selip said. "Joan would have been out the night before—she had incredible energy, and she was out constantly—and she would critique the evening, and we'd laugh and laugh and laugh. If we had taped that, it would have been the show. We would literally laugh for forty minutes in that meeting. She would have been at some stuffy dinner, doing her high-society thing with what she called the fah-fah-fahs—she loved to be in their company, and they loved her because she was so brazen. She'd go, 'Didn't I see you at Erasmus high school?'"

After getting to know the unpretentious Rivers they dealt with at the office, staffers were often disconcerted by the grande dame she morphed into at home. "The first time I was in her house, it was a shock," said Selip. "I was seeing her every morning at work, when she'd be down and dirty, making smart comments—anything goes. And then you walked into this palace, which was beautiful and tasteful. It was regal—it was gold leaf."

Such visible evidence of wealth provided eloquent testimony to how much Rivers had accomplished. "She made all that money herself," said

Bill Reardin. "She would go anywhere as long as there were some bucks in it. At three o'clock in the morning, she'd be going into some sleazebag motel to sleep because she'd had a show somewhere. When she was staying in a hotel, she'd take all the amenities from the hotel room and go out in the hall and take extra soap from the housekeeping cart. She said, 'I don't ever want to run out of shampoo again.'"

Although Rivers took obvious pleasure in her wealth, friends suspected that her pride was mixed with other emotions. "She certainly amassed a fortune, but I think she felt guilty that she was successful, so she always felt she had to give and be good," Reardin said. "I would fight to pick up a check, but I never once succeeded. It was so hard to do anything for her."

When someone did, Rivers always wrote a personal thank-you note. Such rituals helped to keep her busy—a paramount concern now that she was living alone. In New York, she socialized constantly, saw everything on Broadway, consumed cultural experiences, and bombarded her employees with a personal warmth that verged on familial, turning everyone from coworkers to her hairdresser into friends who became a surrogate family.

"I've worked with a lot of famous people, and I've been in Joan's houses more than I've been in the houses of any of the other people I've worked with," Reardin said. "She was always so gracious about having parties for the staff and having me over for dinner. She was never stiff, never intimidating, but she was very elegant. One of the things I learned was that casual, to me, is khakis and a polo shirt, but to Joan, casual is a tie and jacket. If you had nothing to do for Christmas, it was 'Come on over!' It didn't matter what walk of life you were from. So the parties were prominent people from the staff, her daughter, her sister and two kids, and Howard Stern and Lainie Kazan and Phil Spector—he was running up and down the steps waving a gun—and C. Z. Guest and Blaine and Robert Trump and the Gay Men's Chorus. You just never knew who was going to be there."

No one could escape her maternal instincts. On Reardin's fiftieth birthday, he suffered an episode of cardiac distress. "I get to the hospital, and I'm on a gurney, and they're sticking tubes down me," Reardin reported.

"I'm in a room with a curtain, and all of a sudden I hear, 'You can't go in there!'—and it was Joan. I said, 'Joan, what are you doing here?' She said, 'I wanted to take care of you—that's why I'm here!'"

Such attentions won the enduring loyalty of her coworkers. "I really loved her," said Selip. "She was kind, and she was thoughtful."

Having experienced deep grief, Rivers was also solicitous to others who were suffering. "I lost both my parents during that show, and when my mother passed, Joan was in Atlantic City—but she paid a shiva call to my brother's house in Rockland County," Ferber said. "She must have stayed an hour and a half; this wasn't a token call. My mother had brain cancer, and Joan sent flowers to the hospital every single day for two months before she died. That's the kind of person Joan was. She's one of the few people in my life that I will always miss."

Despite her loving gestures, Rivers never pretended to be a saint. "We were doing a show in L.A., and she wasn't happy with some decision, and we were in the producer's office and somebody standing in the room saw a fax machine hurled horizontally across the doorway," David Dangle recalled. "She said, 'Now you know I'm not happy, because I flung a fax machine across the room.' She knew how to make people sit up and listen. She could blow up and scream and be a banshee, but five minutes later it was all forgotten. She didn't have the ability to stay mad at somebody. I hold grudges and stay pissed for a long time, but she would let off steam and get it over with. Everyone was traumatized, because she's Joan Rivers and she's screaming and yelling—but it was healthy for her to be able to get it off her chest. She let the pressure off and then she's fine. One day she screamed at the top of her lungs for about thirty seconds, and then she said, 'I feel so much better! I just needed to do that right now.'"

*The Joan Rivers Show* ended in 1993, defeated by various challenges. Some had to do with its host, whose wit was more serrated than soothing. "I think she did a good job in daytime, and we did some hilarious stuff, but what I realized about Joan was that people either loved her or hated her, and in daytime TV that's hard," said Selip. "You're supposed to be more likable—somebody you could spend time with. She really was a late-night person. You look at Chelsea Handler and the opportunities that

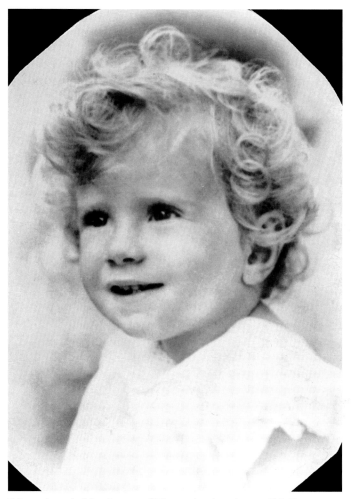

Rivers loved this picture: "The only time in my life I was ever
a natural blonde."

Rivers felt "great sadness" about her mother's 1927 wedding, which sent her, "without love, into a disastrous marriage."

Rivers's father "pinched every penny," and she resented her parents' "facade of affluence built on bitterness."

A year out of college, Mrs. James Sanger married "for security, not love," and soon divorced.

Joan's sister, Barbara, grew up "beautiful and smart and got a law degree at Columbia."

Rivers as a would-be glamour girl.

Rivers poses for a portrait circa 1968 in New York City.

Rivers during the 1960s.

Rivers in 1966, performing "Bride at the Airport," telling her fiancé that her plane was diverted to Denver.

Rivers in Los Angeles in 1965, the year she finally found a husband and became an "overnight" star.

Rivers on *The Tonight Show Starring Johnny Carson.*

In 1967, Rivers wasn't allowed to mention her pregnancy on *The Ed Sullivan Show.*

Edgar Rosenberg as a boy in South Africa.

Mr. and Mrs.
Rosenberg.

Joan and Edgar in California.

Joan and Edgar with Melissa.

Joan took her daughter everywhere, "whether I wanted to go or not," Melissa said.

Rivers and Barry Diller announced her new Fox show in May of 1986.

Winner of the 1990 Daytime Emmy Award as Outstanding Talk Show Host for *The Joan Rivers Show.*

Rivers with "the love of
my life," Orin Lehman,
in 1996.

Rivers's New York apartment, widely compared to Versailles.

Rivers with lots of plastic surgery but no makeup.

Rivers done up as a monument to extreme artifice in 2013.

Joan loved Max
and all her other
dogs.

Joan, Melissa, and Cooper Endicott.

Joan and Melissa on the red carpet at the Academy Awards in 2004.

cable TV presented—if there was cable and Netflix and all the things we have now, Joan would have gone there, but back then there were no options."

The production team tried to come up with other formulas, but their efforts met with mixed success. "We did a separate show called *Gossip! Gossip! Gossip!* where she would sit with gossip columnists and dish," Ferber said. "It was sold to the USA Network, and it was really the grandparent of *Fashion Police.* She started on QVC around the same time, and she was so successful on QVC that the Tribune company, our partner, came up with a concept called *Can We Shop?*—which was disastrous. They hired a merchandise manager, and he would choose the merchandise. One day Joan was selling a toilet bowl cleaner. Do you think this woman ever cleaned a toilet bowl in her life?"

But Rivers felt that no paying gig was beneath her, and the more the better. "Joan was doing *Can We Shop?* plus all her club dates," said Reardin. "She just always wanted to work."

No matter how bad a show was, she was distressed when it ended, and concerned for those whose livelihoods depended on it. "When *Can We Shop?* was canceled, Joan was very upset for me," Ferber recalled. "I said, 'Do you know how much the staff hated that show? We called it *Can We Stop?*' She couldn't stop laughing."

But her coping mechanism was always the same. Whatever the setback, she responded by looking for the next big thing—and she embraced all opportunities with alacrity, no matter how unlikely they seemed. Like a phoenix risen from the ashes, Rivers began to build a new image as an indomitable warrior who coped with the worst and always managed to triumph over any obstacles that confronted her.

## Chapter Thirteen

# ART AND COMMERCE: ALL IN A DAY'S WORK

As Rivers clawed her way back into the limelight, her resilience stunned her friends, foes, and fans. "I watched with amusement and amazement," said Shelly Schultz. "She carried on her career until Edgar convinced her to do something incredibly stupid, which she did, and then her career collapsed. She had a bad reputation, and then she fought her way back—miracle of miracles! There was a saying about her: that this chick would show up on a flatbed truck or in somebody's refrigerator for the right price—it's all about the money."

Rivers's insatiable appetite for remunerative work may have reached its apex in 1994 with an autobiographical television movie that dramatized her stormy relationship with her daughter following Edgar's suicide. She saw nothing wrong with this idea. "I thought it would be a terrific thing to do," she said.

But when it aired, critics and viewers were equally appalled. "Were *Tears and Laughter: The Joan and Melissa Rivers Story* (NBC) not so ghoulishly creepy, it would be an instant camp classic," Ken Tucker wrote in *Entertainment Weekly*. "Joan and her daughter, Melissa, portray themselves in an autobiographical TV movie about the aftermath of the 1987 suicide of Rivers's husband, Edgar Rosenberg. From the opening sequence, in which shots of Joan in a hospital for a liposuction operation are contrasted with scenes of Rosenberg overdosing on pills and liquor, you realize that *Tears and Laughter* will be absolutely shameless. The movie doesn't avoid any awkward moment, from mother and daughter going through Rosenberg's personal effects ("His Filofax!") to Joan's monologue directed at her husband as he lies in his coffin. You watch…and then catch yourself feeling like a voyeur speculating on things that really should be none of our business. Happy viewing."

Viewers agreed. In the movie's IMDb listing, the first headline that comes up is "One of the Worst Movies Ever Made." The second headline calls *Tears and Laughter* "an exploitation of egos," and the third, which describes the movie as "unintentionally funny," adds the following: "Joan Rivers writes such insightful, razor-sharp books about her life and her family that it's an automatic disappointment…What happened to this woman's voice, to her sense of truth? Nearly everything in this biographical drama rings false."

That commenter complained that even "the heated arguments between mother and daughter" didn't come off as convincing, although "they may work as camp"—a prophetic remark, since some Rivers aficionados admit to their gleeful participation in *Tears and Laughter* viewing parties that have retained an enduring appeal over the years, particularly among those under the influence of recreational drugs.

"People quote lines from it all the time," said the actor and theater director Lonny Price. "'I didn't kill Daddy! You didn't kill Daddy! Daddy killed Daddy!' It was unbelievable."

Despite almost universal pans, Rivers retained positive memories of the project in later years. "We had the best time doing it," she said. "It was very therapeutic for me and Melissa. It was wonderful for us, because we bonded tremendously."

Rivers also insisted that the movie performed a public service by helping to destigmatize suicide. "We got sacks of mail saying, 'Thank you! My mother killed herself.' 'Thank you! My brother killed himself.' Nobody ever talked about this before," she said.

Her daughter's memories are less enthusiastic. More than two decades after it was made, the mere mention of *Tears and Laughter* still elicits an expression so pained that it evokes the typical reaction to root canal surgery rather than pride at a major credit on one's résumé. Melissa eventually managed to forgive her mother for the movie as well as for her father's death, but *Tears and Laughter* remains one of the chapters she would rather expunge from her family's historical record.

As the 1990s progressed, there was no shortage of other projects that were driven by dollar signs as well as Rivers's unflagging resourcefulness. The most lucrative was her decision to design jewelry, clothing, and beauty products and sell them herself on QVC, the televised home shopping network whose acronym stood for "Quality, Value, Convenience."

QVC was founded in 1986 in West Chester, Pennsylvania, where the first item sold was a bathtub radio called the Windsor Shower Companion. Four years later, Rivers started peddling her wares on the network, which was far from glamorous at the time.

"In those days, only dead celebrities went on [QVC]," Rivers told the *Staten Island Advance* in 2004. "My career was over, I had bills to pay…It also intrigued me at the beginning."

Although Rivers's QVC business looks like a no-brainer in retrospect, it certainly didn't seem like it at the time. "Everyone told her not to do it," said Blaine Trump. "She said, 'I'm going to do it.' It turned into serious money, and she made a fortune with it. That was the beginning of Joan coming out of the really sad time."

Rivers's relationship with QVC started when "a businessman came to her through her plastic surgeon," David Dangle said. "They were looking for a celebrity to endorse a skin care line, and the businessman had the idea of going to QVC, which was new and kind of tacky and gross. QVC said they were interested, but they said, 'Why don't you do a fashion jewelry line with Joan?'"

The timing was fortuitous. "QVC came at a low point in her career, when work dried up," Dangle said. "Joan didn't say no to a lot of things, and at that point in her life she said no to nothing. Her attitude was 'grasping at whatever I can,' and she very smartly saw that there was something there. She threw herself at QVC, even though her joke was that it was dead celebrities selling things—Carol Channing selling cubic zirconia and saying, 'Diamonds are a girl's best friend!' Joan didn't look at QVC as though 'this is beneath me,' or 'this is a bad career move.' I don't think she was ever a snob."

To Rivers's surprise, the QVC venture took off like a rocket. "They go on the air and it's an instant, insane, brilliant success—everything sells out immediately," Dangle said. "Joan realized, 'I can do this on my own.' The idea was to do fashion jewelry based on Joan's collection of real jewels, and her taste in real jewels. They signed me up to be the product development guy."

When Michael George, the current president and CEO, arrived at QVC in 2006, he asked Rivers about her start with the company. "She said, 'I needed a job, I needed a new opportunity, and I took a chance on QVC,'" he recalled. "She shocked me with her bluntness: 'My husband committed suicide, I got fired from the Fox show, and I needed to work.'"

Rivers's instincts were shrewd: her gaudy taste turned out to be a good fit with the home shopping network's Middle American audience. Her own collection "was initially very Chanel-inspired—pearls, and the bee pin Edgar had given her, which was the very first thing she sold on QVC," reported Dangle.

Her famous bee pin—one of Rivers's signature pieces—was based on a gift that Edgar had had Van Cleef & Arpels make for her. The Rosenbergs saw the bumblebee as a metaphor for Joan herself. "It was diamonds, with sapphires for eyes, and to her it symbolized her body," Dangle explained. "It's chubby, its wings are tiny, and it shouldn't be able to fly—but it does. To Joan, the message was that you can achieve the impossible."

But Rivers was happy to borrow inspiration anywhere she could. "She would go up to Brooke Astor and say, 'I love it—I'm going to copy it!'" said Robert Higdon. "We would be traveling and she would go into jewelry stores and say, 'I'm going to try this.' I would see things come out of QVC that we had seen in Paris or Turkey that summer."

A firm believer in trying as hard as possible, Rivers was always convinced that sheer effort could mean the difference between success and failure. She would never have gone out of the house without doing her hair and makeup, and the products she sold on QVC reflected her determination to maximize her effect by whatever means available. Onstage, she wore a flashy sequined jacket over her black pants and top; going out, she jazzed up even the simplest outfit with an elaborate piece of jewelry—or several. In life, as a performer and in her business, Rivers upheld "the idea that it still matters to dress up with statement pieces," as George put it.

Rivers also made sure her customers understood her philosophy—including its symbol, the bee pin. Her fans knew what it meant to her—and what it could also mean to them if they adopted it as their own inspiration. The message was clear: With enough determination, we can all accomplish great things, no matter what the obstacles!

Having depended on Edgar to manage the business of her career, Rivers began her QVC line with little confidence in herself as a businesswoman. Driven by a sense of desperation and necessity rather than any real faith in her ability, she didn't have an easy time at first. "The first deal she made going in with a jewelry company did not protect her, and she had to fight and buy her way back out of it," said Robert Higdon. "It was yet another mountain she had to climb."

Rivers was encouraged by her initial success in selling her wares, but she had a serious scare in 1992, when Barry Diller left Twentieth Century Fox and bought a $25 million stake in QVC.

"The phone rings one day, and we hear that Barry Diller is taking over QVC—Barry who fired her from Fox," David Dangle recalled. "Within minutes the phone rang and it was Barry Diller, calling to tell her himself. He says, 'Don't worry, it's going to be okay.' He wanted her to know she didn't have to worry. I thought that was pretty classy."

Diller sold his stake in the company in 1995. Since then, QVC has grown into a multinational cable, satellite, and broadcast network received by 235 million households in seven countries—an $8.8 billion empire that shipped 173 million products in 2014, with online revenues of $3.5 billion.

Rivers has represented a significant factor in that success. Over the years, her line has included 7,600 separate items, with jewelry making up 60 percent of the company's sales. "What we do is very item-driven, and one of the things that set her apart as a brand was that she was part of the creation of the product," said Dangle. "Joan was the queen of costume jewelry, and it was her taste and her feedback on the product: 'I like this, but what if we made it bigger?'"

The bee pin proved a perennial favorite, going through many redesigns before being reissued in its original form in 2015 to mark Rivers's twenty-fifth anniversary with QVC. "We've literally sold millions of bees," said Dangle.

Rivers applied the same attention to clothing and accessories. In terms of individual units, the company's most successful Today's Special Value was the Joan Rivers Lavish Luxury Sequin Scarf, which sold more than 88,000 units in one day.

By the final year of her life, the cumulative results were impressive. "We've done over a billion dollars' worth of sales," she told Bloomberg in 2014.

Given the up-and-down nature of her performing career, Rivers was particularly grateful for the consistency of her earnings from QVC, which enabled her to pick and choose among other projects. "She always knew QVC was the goose that laid the golden egg," said Dangle. "Concerts come and go; there are times when you get a big fee and times when you have to lower your get—but QVC was a constant source of income for her. It was an annuity—a very solid revenue stream—and she valued that immensely."

That said, Rivers's profits weren't quite as enormous as they might have seemed. During 2014, *Forbes* reported, "Rivers sold 1.2 million units through the channel, while the Joan Rivers Classics Collection alone generated $4.5 million in sales annually, according to the *Hollywood Reporter*." But when *Forbes* analyzed Rivers's actual income from QVC, its estimate of her take was far less than a billion dollars. "The real punch line: Rivers's personal earnings from her fashion lines were just a fraction of that," *Forbes* announced.

The network certainly made out well, as *Forbes* explained: "Considering $1 billion of Joan Rivers goods over the years, her income could have been an estimated $250 million pretax in that time frame. Though that sounds like a hefty sum, it averages to a relatively modest $10.4 million pretax a year."

But even if Rivers grossed only $10 million a year from QVC, the business provided a vital source of economic security for a woman whose living expenses were perennially over the top. "She used to tell me all the time, 'QVC saved my life,'" said Kenny Bell, the director of programming and special events at the Laurie Beechman Theatre.

Despite her lavish lifestyle, Rivers's colleagues at QVC were struck by her indefatigable commitment to the unglamorous day-to-day grind, which required her to schlep down to West Chester, Pennsylvania, for marathon on-air selling sessions. "She had an amazing work ethic that she never lost—that drive, the sense that you have to earn your way no matter what you do," said Mike George.

The road trip from Rivers's home in Manhattan to the QVC studio took at least two hours, and the on-air schedule was grueling. "She would go on and do fourteen to eighteen minutes on a 7:30 a.m. show, and then do two hours solid from 10 a.m. to noon," said David Dangle. "She'd do a two-hour show from 2 p.m. to 4 p.m., she'd do another hit at 7 p.m., and then 10 p.m. to midnight. She would come down three or four times a month—in the last five years she would be at QVC on forty-eight visits a year. Just looking at her route sheet would make me sick."

But her commitment never flagged. "Some celebrities think they can just endorse a product and that's going to work, but we try to filter those people out, because the customer smells the phony," said George. "Joan's customers got that she was intimately involved with the product."

She took pains to convey that engagement to her audience. "It's the middle of the night, and everyone's buying pins, waiting for the Ambien to kick in—but when other celebrities are on QVC or HSN, it often seems as if they're seeing their products for the first time," said Jason Sheeler, the fashion news director of *Departures* magazine. "They pick up a brooch or a handbag or a scarf, and they're looking at it like, 'What is this? This is shit, but it has my name on it!' Looking at that shit at two in the morning, they're as surprised as we are. But with Joan, she knew. She was always on message with her stuff. Joan was brilliant."

Rivers trolled relentlessly for new buyers, carrying free samples wherever she went. "She walked around with shopping bags of gifts," said her friend Margie Stern. "When I broke my hip, she literally brought a bag of gifts to give to the doctors in the hospital. I finally had to say, 'I don't want any of your crap—just keep it!'"

Rivers was convinced that such largesse could improve the patient's care. "When Robert Higdon had heart surgery, Joan flew out to the Cleveland Clinic and brought a box of bee pins for all the nurses," Blaine Trump reported. "She said, 'I find that when you're in the hospital, bribery works.'"

But Rivers was also trying to broaden her customer base. "Wherever she goes, she's got dozens of boxes of her QVC jewelry she would randomly give to people like waitresses," said Valerie Frankel, her ghostwriter on *Men Are Stupid...and They Like Big Boobs*. "It was generous but calculated. Getting her image out there in a positive way was just second nature."

Some beneficiaries were less than charmed by her generosity. "Her jewelry line was just the gaudiest stuff," said Erin Sanders, a writer who collaborated with Rivers on her Broadway show *Sally Marr...and Her Escorts*. "She would hand stuff out, and I would bring it home and my wife would look at this stuff like I was bringing her a giant turd."

Given her sales record, Rivers's products clearly appealed to a wide range of people. "We typically serve thirty-five-to-sixty-five-year-old women who love to shop and are inspired by shopping, but it's a pretty diverse set of customers, and they're pretty representative of the U.S. population," said Mike George.

"I think QVC draws a more affluent customer than you would expect," David Dangle added. "She's got cable television. She's got a lot of discretionary time. She's a little older. Her kids are probably out of the house, and she's got some discretionary income. Our average price point is in the $50s and $60s, and goes up to $300 or $400—and we have customers who buy dozens and dozens of items a year."

For such women, home shopping represents an opportunity for companionship as well as consumerism. "These customers think of you as a trusted friend who's going to give you good information," said Dangle. "I think they looked to Joan as a girlfriend who was going to give them good advice on what to wear: 'If it looks good on me, it will look good on you.' She never sold schlocky stuff. A lot of people came and went who put their name on schlocky stuff, but Joan knew it had to be good stuff. There was this legendary moment early on when the clasp of a bracelet broke in her hand, and she said, 'Full stop—I'm not going to sell this. If it broke on me, I don't want it to break on you. It's not good enough for you.' She was sly like a fox. QVC was probably freaking out, but she knew the customer would say, 'She doesn't want me to have a bad one!' It was brilliant. I would have just hidden the thing under my pillow!"

As with her comedy act, Rivers also kept developing new material so people didn't tire of what she was selling. "Joan had a classic kind of style, but it never looked dated because it was a modern interpretation with current elements," George explained. "Her line kept evolving and growing. There was always something new and different, whether it was being bold with colors or some interesting new stone, so it felt fresh, but at the same time it didn't feel scary. It was not always the same old same old; you never felt like there was no reason to continue. She kept broadening the reach of the brand."

No matter what she sold, Rivers shared her personal challenges on camera, which was a very effective marketing tool. "People connect with Joan's life story, and she was always real on the air," George said. "Whatever was happening in her life, she'd talk about it. Here's somebody who is amazingly successful, but has led a real life with ups and downs. What matters is that you keep working at it, and the bee pin symbolizes that."

Rivers's laser-like focus on sales sometimes conflicted with her subversive instincts as an entertainer, and she couldn't resist testing the boundaries of what was deemed permissible on the air. "It was very entertaining to watch her sell things, but occasionally it would go too far and I'd get the call: 'We counted three "bitch"es, two "goddamn"s, three "whore"s, and a "dildo"—she's got to dial it back!'" Dangle said.

But Rivers regarded her mandate as something more than making a sale. "Entertainment is a big piece of this business," Dangle said. "QVC rates viewership as well as sales, and she had very high viewership, because whether you bought anything or not, she entertained you. She was making them a ton of dough—sales were phenomenal from the very first day—so they gave her very free rein. She was a brilliant saleswoman."

Rivers also learned to be a competent executive. Despite her self-imposed dependence on Edgar during their marriage, it turned out that she didn't need him, or any other man, to succeed on her own.

Over the years, the names she chose for a succession of companies attested to her growing sense of self-sufficiency. After Edgar died, she called her production company Please God Help Me—a desperate plea from a woman accustomed to having a man she could lean on. As her confidence grew, so did her willingness to go it alone. "She started out at QVC with a bunch of partners, but she finally got rid of them and formed a company called MAM, which stood for 'Mine All Mine,'" said Bill Reardin.

It was actually called JMAM, for "Joan Mine All Mine." Gaining her autonomy was expensive, according to Dangle, the CEO of JMAM as well as of Joan Rivers Worldwide Enterprises. "She wrestled the company back from a bunch of investors," Dangle recalled.

Making it on her own was exhilarating. "She owned this business, and it's a $50-to-$60-million-a-year business," Dangle said. "She was proud that she built this."

Rivers also relished the ability to take care of her loved ones. When her grandson was born in 2000, he inspired his grandmother to name another corporate entity CCF—"which is for 'Cooper's College Fund,'" said Dangle.

Given the scope of her success, some of her friends believe that Rivers never got sufficient credit for her achievements as a businesswoman. "Anyone else who built a billion-dollar company would have been on the cover of *Forbes* magazine," said Sue Cameron.

But no matter how many bumblebee pins she sold, Rivers never stopped looking for other money-making ventures. Her career as an author was another well she continued to plumb, and she had written more than a dozen books by the time she died, both fiction and nonfiction. Their subjects ranged from childbirth to plastic surgery to recovery from trauma. "People really liked her books, because they identified with someone who goes through so many tribulations," said Dorothy Melvin.

"People thought, 'If Joan Rivers can go through losing a husband and pull herself up by her bootstraps and start again, I can do it too.' It gave them hope."

In describing her trials, Rivers often brought a subversive perspective to topics usually treated with saccharine reverence. Her sardonic humor had an electrifying effect on many of her readers.

"When Sara Benincasa was six years old, she found a book in her parents' basement that she knew she wasn't supposed to read," Amanda Hess wrote in a Slate essay after Rivers died. "She read it anyway. 'I was like, "This lady is naughty! This lady's a mom, but she doesn't talk like any mom I've ever heard of!"' Benincasa said. The book was Joan Rivers's 1974 *Having a Baby Can Be a Scream* (styled like a children's book, it was anything but). 'It was a really amazing thing, now that I think about it,' says Benincasa, now thirty-three and herself a comedian and author. 'She planted the seed for what would later become my habit of saying things that women aren't supposed to say.'"

During the ensuing years, Rivers used many different cowriters for her books, which varied as widely in quality as they did in topic. But her first two autobiographies—written with Richard Meryman—were serious and substantive. The first, *Enter Talking*, focused on her childhood and her long struggle to get started in show business—the saga of disappointment and rejection that culminated in a happy ending when Rivers's career finally took off. *Enter Talking* was published in 1986, the final year when her work life and her family life both seemed to be flourishing.

The reviews were mixed. *Publishers Weekly* called it a "tediously detailed autobiography," but *Library Journal* was more encouraging: "Who would expect a book by and about Rivers to be thoughtful, sensitive, and introspective?"

Her life collapsed the following year, and Rivers waited until 1991 before publishing her second memoir, *Still Talking*, which chronicled her falling-out with Johnny Carson, the failure of her Fox show, and her husband's suicide. Although it never made the best-seller list, she claimed it sold more copies than other titles that did, and she told the *Los Angeles*

*Times* she was "furious" that the book was slighted by the press and the publishing industry.

The earnest tone of those two books provided a considerable contrast with *The Life and Hard Times of Heidi Abromowitz*, Rivers's fictional 1984 biography of the slutty character whose exploits she mined throughout her career. Rivers's compass needle as an author seemed to oscillate wildly between serious efforts that genuinely attempted to describe her life experience and jokey books whose mission was simply to entertain and make money.

When Rivers's last book, *Diary of a Mad Diva*, was published in 2014, the *Daily Beast* called it a "gleeful, messy barbecue of famous names, beginning with a quote by Kanye West proudly proclaiming to be a non-reader of books, to which Rivers's dedication on the next page read in response: 'This book be dedicated to Kanye West, because he'll never fucking read it.' There followed almost three hundred pages of jokes at celebrities' expense. One, Kristen Stewart, threatened legal action, after Rivers wrote: 'Many stars do only one thing well. The best one-trick pony is Kristen Stewart, who got a whole career by being able to juggle a director's balls.'"

Rivers claimed she was disappointed when Stewart didn't pursue any legal action against her. "It's a shame, as I wanted her in court and made to touch a doll in the parts where the director touched her," Rivers said.

But whatever else she did, theater remained the holy grail. And of all the creative ventures she took on during a life chockablock with a vast array of professional vehicles, the one closest to her heart may have been the original one-woman show she wrote and performed on Broadway in 1994.

Based on the life of Lenny Bruce's mother, the play was called *Sally Marr...and Her Escorts*. Rivers always credited Bruce as a seminal influence on her development as a comedian, but his life ended with tragic abruptness in 1966, when he was found lying naked on the bathroom floor at his home in the Hollywood Hills, surrounded by a syringe, a burned bottle cap, and other narcotics paraphernalia. He was forty years old.

Rivers also felt a deep identification with his mother, who outlived her son by thirty-one years. Sally Marr was a woman whose son had died of an accidental overdose, a heartbreak that Rivers, whose husband had died of a deliberate overdose, understood all too well. But Marr was also a stand-up comic, dancer, and actress who—like Rivers herself—felt she never got sufficient credit for what she achieved.

Marr died in 1997, a couple of weeks before her ninety-first birthday, but she lived long enough to see the play that Rivers had fashioned from her stories, recollections, and jokes. Shaping that material into a genuinely theatrical experience was a lengthy process that ultimately included two cowriters, Lonny Price and Erin Sanders.

"When I met Joan, she had these tapes where she had interviewed Sally, and she had put together some transcripts, but she didn't really have a play," said Price, a veteran actor, writer, and director who also directed *Sally Marr...and Her Escorts*. "She brought me in to shape it with her. This was a difficult beast to tame; it didn't have any story line or trajectory."

For Rivers, the appeal of the material was obvious. "Joan adored Lenny, and she identified with him," said Price. "She was not politically correct; she said whatever was on her mind, and she always pushed the envelope. She was fearless. Joan was very much like Lenny, and she thought she could play Sally, a Jewish woman of a certain age. Sally claimed she created him—not only as a mother, but also as a comic. She was a very salty, vulgar woman, and I'm sure she influenced him. I think they had a very symbiotic relationship, to a point—and then he tried to separate from her."

For Rivers, who was dealing with her own estrangement from the daughter she adored, the material resonated on many levels. But her schedule was so overbooked that her collaborators had to fight for her attention.

"She kept very busy, so part of the adventure was following her everywhere to grab time to write with her, from QVC to Atlantic City to Vegas," said Erin Sanders, the former dramaturge at Second Stage. "I saw the backside of a lot of casinos."

In shaping the story line, both of Rivers's cowriters had to fight her tendency to turn the show into a stand-up routine. "She was tough as hell,"

Sanders said. "I think she really wanted to be the playwright on this thing, but it was becoming just a series of jokes, which turned out to be the battle for the next two years. She needed a writer, and what I was trying to give her was some structure and dramatic tension—but her drive was always for the comedic moment."

Rivers was also mercurial. "She would read through some pages and say, 'I hate it! I just hate it!'" Sanders recalled. "And within the span of a couple of hours she would say, 'I just love it!'"

The play turned out to be an odd collage of elements. Set in the auditorium of Our Lady of Esperanza High School, it features Marr teaching a night class called How to Die on Your Feet: The Art of Stand-Up Comedy.

"I want you to go home, dig deep inside yourselves, and I want you to come up with your most painful memory," Marr tells her students. "I want you to take that memory and twist it, and I want you to make it funny— because that's what comedy is all about. You want to be funny, you don't start with funny and try to make it funny, because that turns to shit. Comedy comes from pain."

The play incorporated many themes from Rivers's own life, including her stubborn refusal to get off the stage—as when Marr, in an angry confrontation with her son, shouts, "Sally Marr is not retiring!"

But it also featured a disorienting series of curious juxtapositions. Highlights of the comedy class were interspersed with scenes that ranged from Marr teaching her son how to hone his comedic timing to harrowing glimpses of an elderly Marr lying in a coma after suffering a brutal rape by a burglar who nearly killed her.

"Dying's nothing new to me," says the comatose Marr. "I'm in show business. We die every day. I'm used to dying—and let me tell you something. Dying is easy. Comedy is hard."

The play's final message was vintage Rivers. "At the end of the story, she realizes she has no money, and she's sick, but she made people laugh, and that was an okay thing to be doing," said Price. "If you can make somebody laugh, that's not such a bad way to spend your life. That was Joan's story too. It was a bit Pirandello-ish."

When *Sally Marr...and Her Escorts* finally opened, the billboard outside the Helen Hayes Theatre featured a giant photograph of Rivers as Marr, wearing a fur coat that her son had supposedly given her. "She was more than Lenny Bruce's mother," the tagline read.

But the title character was inherently problematic. "Sally Marr was vulgar and disgusting," said Lonny Price. "It was like a Jewish Mama Rose—with less appeal and less charm."

Reviewers were torn between their grudging admiration for Rivers's frenetic energy and their perplexity about the strange concoction she had assembled. In some cases, their views were also colored by a theater world snobbery that seemed to question what a showbiz hack like Rivers was doing at the Helen Hayes in the first place.

"In the category of hardest-working actress on Broadway, the winner is—drumroll, please—Joan Rivers in *Sally Marr . . . and Her Escorts*," David Richards wrote in *The New York Times*. "The play purports to be the story of Sally Marr, a comedian of small repute whose chief claim to show business fame is that she is Lenny Bruce's mother. The woman tearing about the stage in a wardrobe resembling an exploded salad bar is, in her more widely public incarnations, a finely turned-out talk show host and the purveyor of her own line of jewelry. Is Ms. Rivers also a great actress? No, she is not. But she is exuberant, fearless, and inexhaustible. If you admire performers for taking risks, then you can't help but applaud her efforts."

Although it was essentially a glorified one-woman show, *Sally Marr* featured nonspeaking roles by several of the character's "escorts," including the father she worshipped, the husband who left her, and the rebellious son she defended like a tigress.

"As for the sudden explosions of rage or terrible feelings of abandonment, you have the eerie impression they're Ms. Rivers's as much as they're Sally Marr's," Richards noted.

The play tried hard to persuade audiences that Marr was an important figure. "I gave birth to Lenny Bruce and opened the door to modern American comedy," the character proclaims. "So in a way I gave birth to Lenny Bruce, George Carlin, Richard Pryor, Chevy Chase, Robin Williams, Bill Cosby, Eddie Murphy, and David Letterman. No wonder I'm exhausted!"

But when the play opened on May 5, 1994, the critics were unconvinced by Marr's accomplishments and put off by the parallels with Rivers's own history. "It is this play's contention that without Sally Marr, a kind of dirty-mouthed Mama Rose, there would have been no Lenny Bruce," Richards wrote. "Her outspokenness blazed the way for his iconoclasm; from her hatred of hypocrisy sprang his. It is Ms. Rivers, after all, who drives the patchwork script forward with the same manic energy that informs her stand-up routines. Her well-lacquered appearance notwithstanding, she has always had a combatant's mentality. (What is her celebrated call to gossip—'Can we talk?'—but the opening gong in her personal battle against sham?) She may not be Sally Marr, as Hollywood ads used to boast. But like her, she has played the lounges with 'a two-rape minimum,' had a husband abandon her, known crushing failure—and lived to tell the tale. I suspect that's what this oddly confessional evening is really all about."

Some reviewers were more caustic in their assessment. "It is not so much a barrel of laughs as a funeral urn of laughs," Quentin Crisp wrote in *New York Native*. "Ms. Rivers flings herself into the show with an air of desperation, shouting mordant one-liners at other actors, none of whom speaks. All comedians are desperate people, and Ms. Rivers, because of her painful thinness, her harsh voice, and her tragic private—or rather, flagrantly public—life, is a cartoon of a comedian. While one laughs at what she says, one weeps for who she is."

Most of the critics were disdainful about Rivers's most cherished hope—that she would finally win recognition as a serious actress. "The always endearing Joan Rivers is out of her element as Marr," David Kaufman wrote in the *Village Voice*. "She is simply too accustomed to playing herself—or at least her public persona—to effectively play anyone else."

Even her collaborators had to admit that Rivers often misjudged the requirements of a stage performance. "She would not stick to the script," said Sanders. "All of it relied on her to hit her lines, but things often got jumbled up, and it was very frustrating."

Rivers was so used to winging it onstage that she didn't accept the rigor of a theatrical performance. "She paraphrased a lot," said Price. "She wasn't used to having to do it exactly right, because this led to that, so she was not spot-on. She never really learned it. Joan was a natural actress, as all comics are. She was incredibly moving, and she had great access to pain. But she wasn't skilled as a stage actress. She was always ahead of herself; she reached for the phone before it rang."

Rivers also had a tendency to sabotage her performance. "Joan's voice would go on her, and she would take prednisone," said Price, referring to the corticosteroid drug. "The nights she didn't take it, she was really good and connected to everything, but the nights she took it, the performance was off. I made her promise me that she wouldn't take prednisone the night the critics came, but she was afraid her voice would fail, so she took it. She jumped whole chunks of the play. In one scene, she couldn't remember the last line, and it was the cue line for the blackout, so the stage manager didn't go to blackout. She just stood there saying, 'Fuck! Fuck! Fuck!' It was bad. We had worked on this for four years or whatever, and all the big critics were there that night, and she wasn't on her game. I was ready to kill both of us. At that point, I was taken to a bar by the producer."

Until then, audiences seemed to enjoy the play. "It sold pretty well in previews, and she got a standing ovation every night," said Price. "It was a tour de force."

And Rivers was overjoyed when she was nominated for the Tony Award for Best Actress in a Play as well as a Drama Desk Award for Outstanding Actress in a Play. "She wanted legitimacy as an actress, and she was so proud of the Tony nomination," said Price.

But Rivers didn't win, which left her feeling aggrieved that she had "lost out to Diana Rigg, that slut-whore-tramp who happened to do *Medea*, and I had no children to set on fire."

The nominations alone didn't help ticket sales, and her collaborators blamed their lackluster pace on the star's poor theatrical judgment. "She thought it was going to be this megahit, so it was really mismarketed," said Sanders. "We should have started Off Broadway and built a following, but it was marketed to a Broadway audience, who read the lukewarm reviews and said, 'I don't need to see Joan Rivers stink on Broadway.'"

The timing was also unfortunate, since the play coincided with the release of the egregious *Tears and Laughter*. "The movie came out and basically stole all our headlines, because it was 'Joan Rivers is a survivor!'" Sanders said. "Then we open on Broadway as 'Joan Rivers plays Sally Marr as a survivor!' There was a lot of Joan Rivers fatigue at that point."

"The producer's theory was that they could get her for free, and they didn't want to pay for her," Price explained. "She had her own TV show, she was on QVC, she had the play—she was completely overexposed."

When *Sally Marr* closed on June 19, its failure was a terrible blow. "Joan was really crushed," said Blaine Trump. "She worked so hard on that."

That disappointment also coincided with another big change. "She lost the daytime TV show and *Sally Marr* at the same time, and she was devastated," said Price. "She had worked so hard, and she was angry that the public didn't support it. But like the phoenix, as always, she reinvents herself and rises again."

Whatever its other failings, the final verdict on the play might have been the simplest. "With *Sally Marr*, she stopped being funny," said theater writer David Finkle.

Even the show's publicist admitted as much. "It portrayed a hard, tough group of people, and it was depressing," said Bill Evans, who is now the director of media relations for the Shubert Organization. "There was a coldness at the center of Joan, and this show was pretty icy at the center. There was a desperation to it."

Despite her emotional investment in *Sally Marr*, Rivers moved on quickly. "She was the type of person who said, 'Okay, this is a disaster—what's next?'" said Trump.

But Rivers never got over her yearning to make it as an actress on Broadway, and she didn't give up on the idea that *Sally Marr* was the vehicle to help her do so. "In her mind, that was her baby; that was one of her proudest accomplishments," said Robert Higdon. "I think she loved doing it."

Before she died, Rivers was trying to revive *Sally Marr* in some form, and she even made sure that her beloved play accompanied her when she exited the stage for the last time. "They put the script in her coffin," Higdon said.

# Chapter Fourteen

## HOME SWEET VERSAILLES: MARIE ANTOINETTE MEETS AUNTIE MAME

In 1988, when Rivers bought the derelict apartment she would turn into her legendary New York City residence, there were pigeons nesting in it. She had a grandiose vision for creating the home of her dreams, but the transformation of a wreck into a palatial penthouse was an agonizingly long and expensive ordeal.

Housed in a Gilded Age limestone mansion that was built in 1903 by John R. Drexel of the Philadelphia banking family, Rivers's eleven-room condo would combine the top three floors of the seven-story residence at One East 62nd Street, which was designed by Horace Trumbauer in neo-French classic style. Among other amenities, her 5,100-square-foot triplex had five wood-burning fireplaces and two terraces with views of Central Park as well as the cityscape.

Increasingly enmeshed with her socialite friends, Rivers worked hard to cultivate the image of a well-bred grande dame whose gracious conduct was governed by the dictates of Emily Post. But she wasn't above resorting to the manipulative histrionics of a screeching fishwife in the shtetl when such tactics helped to achieve other ends.

"One day she said, 'Do you want to swing by?'" David Dangle reported. "It was two o'clock on a Tuesday, and there were no workmen at the apartment, but there's a foreman sitting with his feet up, reading a magazine. She said, 'What's going on?,' and he said, 'The guys are on vacation this week.'"

Rivers's reaction was comparable to what happens when a stick of dynamite is lit. "She lost her shit," Dangle said. "She went crazy. She threw a paint can on the floor; she tipped over a ladder. There were tears. She literally went nuts on him. 'I'm a widow! I'm living in a hotel!' I didn't know what to do—and then she turns and gives me a big wink, and I realized this was a performance to get this guy back to work."

When the apartment was finally finished, Rivers was forced to confront another challenge. "She was convinced the house was possessed," said Blaine Trump.

Rivers's new residence apparently housed not only a persistent ghost, but an alarming amount of other "negative energy" as well, according to Sallie Ann Glassman, a self-described "mambo voudou priestess" (the spelling Glassman prefers to the usual spelling of voodoo) whom Rivers imported from New Orleans to deal with the problem.

"Joan had seen Mrs. Spencer, the ghost, and she brought in a parapsychologist who had a demon meter," Glassman explained. "It went off the charts. There was one horrible thing after another in that apartment; it was one of the scariest, creepiest places I've ever been, in terms of the energy of it—a very unpleasant place. A lot of people had committed suicide over the years, in the apartment and in the building. Joan was okay with the ghost, but the negativity was really disturbing."

After Glassman performed what she calls a "rather calamitous ceremony," she said, "Everything got better immediately." Just in case Mrs. Spencer wasn't entirely mollified, Rivers also hung a portrait of her in the building lobby and left flowers for her in the ballroom.

With the malevolent spirits dispatched, Rivers was able to focus on her real priority: creating a home that would attest to the immense effort she had made to acquire a discriminating eye. "She had very beautiful, refined taste," said Dangle. "She had important art: Kees van Dongen, Vuillard, Henry Moore, Rauschenberg, Milton Avery. She had knowledge of good furniture. The apartment had an incredible ballroom, incredible boiseries. She wanted to be perceived as being part of that world—a world she didn't feel she belonged in: 'Look at me! I wish my mother was here to see me today!'"

From the leopard-print carpets to the twenty-three-foot ceilings, Greek columns, gilded antique paneling, and crystal chandeliers, Rivers's taste was so ornate that it invariably evoked comparisons with her inspiration, the Palace of Versailles. She herself described her style as "Louis XIV meets Fred and Ginger."

Even the very rich were astonished. "When people would go to Joan's apartment, they couldn't believe it," said Blaine Trump.

"The apartment was like a French salon; I couldn't really fathom that somebody lived there," said an entertainment industry journalist who attended Rivers's elaborate six-course Thanksgiving dinner one year. "It looked like somebody's fabulous aunt's Parisian apartment—high ceilings, antiques, gold everywhere, very stately, old-fashioned, and traditional. There was a needlepoint pillow on a chair in the library that said 'Lonely at the top.' There was a bathroom next to the dining room, and when I went in to wash my hands I was just in awe. The faucet handles were gold. I kept wondering if they were real gold."

The needlepoint pillow actually said "It's just as lonely at the top, only you eat better."

Some observers were reminded of Czarist Russia. "It was like Anastasia's grandmother's apartment," said the actor Charles Busch. "It was not a comedian's apartment. It was dispossessed Russian nobility—an exiled empress."

Others invoked a gaudy Las Vegas—but Rivers was in on the joke. "That apartment was a giggle for Joan," said the writer Jesse Kornbluth. "It amused her to live in Versailles. Why did she want to live in Versailles? Because she could."

"If you want to know how big her palace was, Buckingham Palace has one more closet," said the comic Brad Zimmerman, who often opened for Rivers with his show, *My Son the Waiter: A Jewish Tragedy*. "My place would work very well in hers—as a hamper."

Some saw a deeper meaning in her choices. Rivers spent decades re-creating herself, changing everything from her name to her nose to the entire structure of her face, and the preposterous excess of her home-decorating style just seemed like another iteration of a familiar theme.

"You've got to be a little nuts to do that," said Shelly Schultz. "I guess she pretended she was somebody else, because it was awfully painful for her to get up and think about who she was. She was so demanding. She was so driven, she lived in Versailles because she thought she was the Queen of Sheba."

But New York loves an over-the-top character, and Rivers had found the perfect home. If the exaggerated formality of her social style had seemed weirdly out of place in Southern California, her crystal finger bowls and elaborate place settings were well suited to the residential Fabergé egg where she became famous for her dinner parties.

As always, her plans incorporated her daughter as a central feature in her life. Having sold the California house where Melissa grew up, Rivers took pains to make her daughter feel welcome in Manhattan: the new showplace included "a cheerfully decorated one-bedroom apartment on the first floor that is reserved for her daughter's use during visits," *People* magazine reported.

Rivers was especially noted for her annual Thanksgiving, Christmas, and Seder dinners, to which she invited a rotating array of friends, family members, and colleagues. "They were lovely and fun, and you never knew who the hell was going to be there," said Joan's friend Pete Hathaway, who was particularly struck by the dinner table company of Jean Harris, the infamous private school headmistress who killed her former lover. "I remember Joan put me next to Jean Harris after she got out of jail. I asked her about it, and she looked me in the eye and said, 'I did murder a man. I deserved to go to prison.'"

Whatever the guest list, the dinners were elaborately formal. "One year I had nowhere to go on Thanksgiving, and she invited me," said Lonny Price. "It was so elegant it was like you were in a magazine. I was not used to Thanksgiving being that kind of production. We went around the table, with everyone being asked what they were grateful for—it was very *haimish* and lovely. Every time you stepped into that house it was like you were in a photo shoot for *House & Garden*."

"She had a beautiful, elegant, curated life," Dangle attested. To furnish that life, Rivers was a compulsive shopper and inveterate collector whose mania for acquisition never waned. Always avidly materialistic, she had an unquenchable hunger for expensive property and possessions. Nothing ever assuaged her childhood feelings of deprivation and inadequacy, but she always seemed comforted by her ability to afford such luxuries, and she developed a connoisseur's eye.

"Joan called Sotheby's out of the blue and got me, and she bought a very important piece of eighteenth-century French furniture, a Louis XV ormolu mounted writing table from the collection of Mr. and Mrs. Charles Wrightsman," said Pete Hathaway, then a director of European furniture at Sotheby's. "I was stunned that she was calling about a very important table. I thought, 'Holy shit—she lives really well, and she's got lovely things!'"

Their initial transaction developed into a lasting friendship as well as a business relationship. "Joan collected across the board—eighteenth-century furniture, porcelain, silver, jewelry," said Hathaway, who is now the proprietor of Ragamont House, a catering and event venue in Salisbury, Connecticut. "She had masses of silver, very grand. You name it, she had it: champagne buckets, silver pheasants, candy dishes, nut bowls, silver finger bowls. I've never seen so much silver in my life. When Joan gave a dinner party, the table was just ablaze with silver. I thought her taste was wonderful, but it was very elaborate. She told me that when she did her apartment, she told Louis Malkin, her interior designer, 'I want a combination of Marie Antoinette and Jean Harlow.' She said, 'And I got it!' She loved satins and silks and tassels and gilded things. She lived very grandly, but Joan was very Hollywood, so a lot of it was very theatrical, including the way she would dress for her dinner parties. There was sort of an Auntie Mame, costumey side to the way she dressed."

When Rivers bought a country house in New Preston, Connecticut, owning a second home opened up a whole new range of buying opportunities. "Joan's thing was sixteen sets of china in the country: 'If I have weekend guests, I don't want to see the same china twice,'" Dangle said.

Stockpiling enormous quantities of possessions seemed to give her a sense of security that represented a hedge against any future setbacks. "She would go to Manolo Blahnik and order four pairs: 'If I'm broke, I'm going to have good shoes,'" Dangle reported. "I think the whole idea of being broke stayed with her all her life: 'It might all fall apart, but I'm going to have four pairs of gorgeous $2,600 crocodile shoes.' In the early 1990s, $2,600 was a lot of money. She would find a Chanel shoe she liked and get six pairs."

Rivers also engaged in some competitive gamesmanship to protect her stylistic prerogatives. "If she saw something really great that someone else wore, she would go to Bergdorf's and buy up all of them to prevent anyone else from getting it," said Valerie Frankel, Rivers's ghostwriter on *Men Are Stupid...and They Like Big Boobs*. "She definitely had that side."

But Rivers was as interested in a bargain as she was in couture. "She wasn't a snob; she liked what she liked, and I don't think she was ever a label girl," said Dangle. "She could wear Zara, and she could wear Valentino—whatever made her look good. She could wear a $40,000 Verdura bracelet and mix it with some stuff she bought at the airport. I loved that. It was not just about the designer; you like it because you like it. She liked expensive china, but she also got cheap and cheerful furniture."

As Rivers's finances restabilized, she began to emulate the charitable activism of New York's reigning socialites in addition to their sartorial chic and luxurious homes. The responsibility of noblesse oblige is a bedrock principle with blue bloods on both sides of the Atlantic, and thanks to one of her elegant new friends, Rivers found a cause that remained deeply meaningful for the rest of her life.

"Joan was involved with God's Love We Deliver for twenty-five years," said Karen Pearl, the president and CEO of the organization, a nonprofit charity that delivers meals to homebound people with AIDS. "She was brought in by Blaine Trump, and she fell in love with what we were doing."

Upper-crust WASP women have a long tradition of old-fashioned altruism on behalf of a wide range of causes, but Trump's do-gooder commitment was unusually bold for its time. "Joan asked me what I was doing on Thanksgiving, and I said we were going to deliver Thanksgiving meals for God's Love We Deliver," Trump recalled. "She said, 'I would love to do that,' and that was the beginning of a really important, meaningful relationship with God's Love We Deliver. Every Thanksgiving, she would go deliver meals, and then she'd do Thanksgiving dinner at her house."

Founded in 1985, God's Love began during the early years of the AIDS crisis, when many creative communities were being ravaged by the mounting death toll. For Rivers, this cause was very personal. "Joan was losing her best friends—her hairdresser, her makeup people, some of her business partners," Pearl said. "They were dying from this horrendous disease, and nobody was doing anything, because taking on HIV/AIDS meant taking on the issue of men having sex with men. Joan was outraged, and she felt she had to do something. We were bringing food to people who were otherwise isolated and starving, and Joan thought it was amazing. She was hooked from the beginning."

But AIDS carried a terrible stigma, and many leaders shrank from dealing with it. President Reagan's response to the growing national health crisis was "halting and ineffective," as his biographer Lou Cannon put it.

"Talk about using your voice—Reagan wouldn't even say the fucking word," said the comic Judy Gold.

But Reagan's fellow conservatives had no qualms about expressing their hatred and contempt for the victims. Pat Buchanan, Reagan's communications director, wrote a 1983 op-ed for the *New York Post* claiming that homosexuals "have declared war upon nature, and now nature is exacting an awful retribution." Buchanan's policy prescriptions included the recommendation that homosexuals be prohibited from handling food.

William F. Buckley, the right-wing author and founder of the *National Review*, demanded that HIV-positive people be double-branded. "Everyone detected with AIDS should be tattooed in the upper forearm, to protect common-needle users, and on the buttocks, to prevent the victimization of other homosexuals," he wrote in *The New York Times*.

Other conservative leaders cloaked their hostility in religion—like Reverend Jerry Falwell, the founder of the Moral Majority, who proclaimed that "AIDS is the wrath of God upon homosexuals."

In the prevailing atmosphere of fear and intolerance, Rivers's involvement was particularly noteworthy. "At that time, there was such fear of an AIDS pandemic that people thought we were both nuts," said Trump. "But Joan was fearless. Anytime we needed her to do a fund-raiser, she was there."

That public commitment really stood out during the early years of the AIDS crisis. "Joan never shied away from controversy, and she was the first celebrity to do an AIDS fund-raiser," Pearl said. "I think it was hugely brave, and I don't use that word lightly. AIDS was something nobody wanted to name or touch or do anything about. Joan took on the subject, and there was never a time when she said anything that was not heartfelt or loving. She was a hero then, and I think she stayed a hero for people who were living with HIV/AIDS."

The gay community responded with gratitude and deep affection. "When you're gay and in the closet it's the most painful thing, and Joan was so loving and accepting when AIDS was hush-hush," said Judy Gold. "She had trannies on TV in the 1980s."

In later years, God's Love expanded its mandate to serve patients with cancer, Parkinson's, Alzheimer's disease, ALS, heart failure, multiple sclerosis, and other illnesses. As soon as her grandson, Cooper, was old enough, Rivers began bringing him with her to make holiday deliveries.

"It was very important to her, because she wanted him to understand that there are people in our city who are in great need, and it's an act of honor to be able to help them," Pearl said. "It wasn't done from the perspective of 'I'm better, because I'm doing something for somebody else.' It was more like, 'I'm lucky, because it's a privilege to serve others and make their lives better.' She really meant it—and she didn't just drop stuff off either. She came in and talked to you. She came at this like one person visiting another. She'd be sharing tips with women in their eighties about how it gets harder to get up every day."

Rivers's dedication was so fierce that she sometimes put her commitment to God's Love above her own interests. "One time we had a benefit where Joan was supposed to deliver some lines, and after the show she didn't come to the after-party," said Blaine Trump. "It turned out she'd gone to the emergency room; she had some heart fibrillation, and she didn't want to ruin the show."

When Rivers was a contestant on *The Celebrity Apprentice* in 2009, she chose God's Love as her charity to play for. "She won over $500,000 for us," Pearl reported. "People knew about God's Love because they followed Joan."

For the rest of her life, Rivers never flagged in her commitment to God's Love. But as the years passed, her enthusiasm for other aspects of her New York incarnation began to wane. She enjoyed having a country house, but she grew increasingly weary of the cross-country commute to see Melissa and Cooper in Los Angeles. She wanted to spend more time with them, so she started trying to simplify her life, first by selling the Connecticut house and then by reevaluating her Manhattan lifestyle. She was proud of the gilded showcase she had created, but perhaps it had served its purpose.

"She thought it was stupid to be rattling around in a $20-million-plus apartment that was bought for entertaining when she wasn't entertaining anymore," said Hathaway. "She just wanted a more scaled-down, normal life. When the Plaza went condo, she and Cindy Adams and Barbara Walters were talking about getting cojoined apartments in the Plaza and sharing butlers and maids."

Thinking that she might buy a place in Los Angeles and maintain a smaller pied-à-terre in New York, Rivers put her elaborate apartment on the market in 2009, asking $25 million, and again in 2012, asking $29 million.

The apartment—whose monthly carrying costs were $25,337—didn't find a buyer then, but it did after Rivers died. "It sold for the asking price, which was $28 million," said Hathaway.

The Queen of Comedy had wanted to create a home fit for a monarch. It turned out that the apartment was purchased by Prince Muhammad bin Fahd, the sixty-five-year-old son of Saudi Arabia's late King Fahd.

When the prince took possession of the apartment, he immediately ordered a gut renovation.

## Chapter Fifteen

# HIGH SOCIETY: PUTTING ON THE RITZ

The night Rivers met the man she described as "the love of my life," he was still married to and living with someone else—a Vanderbilt, to be precise. For Rivers, this inconvenient fact was a minor detail she would gloss over in subsequent accounts of her long relationship with Orin Lehman, a philanthropist and conservationist from a prominent New York family.

The very fact that Rivers was hobnobbing with Lehmans and Vanderbilts reflected her new incarnation as a New York society lady. Living in California during the Reagan administration, Rivers managed to befriend such social icons as Nancy Reagan and Betsy Bloomingdale, the wife of Alfred Bloomingdale, an heir to the Bloomingdale's department store fortune. For the next phase of her life as a single woman in New York, Rivers's aspirations centered around the WASP elite of bold-faced names like C. Z. Guest and Blaine Trump, whose seemingly effortless style she admired as the epitome of inherited privilege and superior status.

"She was very much interested in becoming a society girl," said David Dangle, who redesigned Rivers's look to resemble that of the women she envied. "Blaine Trump became her friend, and there were a lot of galas. She wanted that world."

To Rivers, acceptance by the doyennes of Manhattan society—the well-bred "swans" Truman Capote idolized before betraying their secrets in "La Côte Basque," and their successors, the "social X-rays" Tom Wolfe satirized in *The Bonfire of the Vanities*—represented the imprimatur of class she had always hungered to acquire for herself, through success if not by birth.

Another powerful lure was simply the frenetic schedule of their social scene, which offered an endless array of benefits, black-tie balls, ladies' lunches, charitable commitments, and other glamorous diversions that helped to fill up the open evenings that Rivers dreaded.

The occasion where she met Lehman was given by Marylou Whitney, the philanthropist and widow of Cornelius Vanderbilt Whitney. "It was at a party in Saratoga, and all the horse people were there," said Robert Higdon, Rivers's escort that night. "Orin Lehman was Alfred Blooming-dale's cousin, and 'Lehman' was a very aristocratic name."

The scion of a distinguished family, Orin was a great-grandson of Mayer Lehman, a founder of the Lehman Brothers investment house. Orin's great-uncle was Herbert Lehman, who served New York State as a two-term governor and then as a two-term senator.

Orin also had a penchant for marrying into other rich and well-connected families. His first wife, Jane Bagley, was a Reynolds tobacco heiress, and his second wife was Wendy Vanderbilt, an artist.

A Princeton graduate and a war hero, Orin served as an Army pilot during World War II, when he was seriously injured in the Battle of the Bulge. He lost his leg and received the Distinguished Flying Cross and the Purple Heart.

Although he tried going into the family business, five years of working as an associate at Lehman Brothers convinced him not to pursue a career in finance. "I had some money and didn't want to devote my life to making money," he told *The New York Times*.

His attempts to run for elective office were unsuccessful—a liberal Democrat, he lost his races for Congress and for New York City comptroller—but he found his mission in public service. The defining job of his career arrived when he succeeded Robert Moses as New York State's commissioner of Parks, Recreation, and Historic Preservation, a job he held for eighteen years, which made him the longest-serving commissioner in the history of New York State.

As steward of the state park system, Lehman was widely respected for his commitment to conservation. He hiked New York's trails by balancing himself on metal canes, and employees of the park system referred to him affectionately as Father Nature.

In recalling the night he first met Lehman, Higdon said he was predisposed to being charitable —"Orin had crutches, so you're very forgiving to someone"—but Lehman antagonized him immediately.

"At the time, I think I was working for Margaret Thatcher, and he made some sarcastic comment about her," recalled Higdon, who served as a White House aide during the Reagan administration and later became executive director of the Ronald Reagan Presidential Foundation, then of the Margaret Thatcher Foundation, and finally of Prince Charles's Washington-based Prince of Wales Foundation.

"I turned to Joan and said, 'This man is the biggest jerk,'" Higdon reported. "She said, 'I think he's very attractive!' I said, 'Well, then trade places with me.' And she did—and that was that."

Rivers and Lehman proceeded to have an extremely good time, which astonished Higdon. "I think he's the biggest ass I've ever met in my life, but they had chemistry—there's no question about that," he said. "I think there was a huge physical thing with them; she said the physical chemistry was incredible."

But Lehman, who was twelve years older than Rivers and the father of three daughters, was also married and living with his longtime wife— not yet separated, as Rivers would later claim. On that night in Saratoga as well as on another occasion, at designer Arnold Scaasi's house, Higdon said, "There was Orin and Wendy—they weren't separated. In fact, we gave them a ride home. But Orin and Joan went to lunch the next week, and within a few weeks he was part of our lives."

How this happened depends on whom you ask. "When Joan met Orin and he was flirting with her, he was separated from Wendy Lehman," said Blaine Trump. "Joan was an old-fashioned girl, and she called me and said, 'Is Orin married? Because I don't want to go out with anyone who's married.' He wasn't officially divorced, but he was separated, so she thought it was okay to go out with him. She really was a traditionalist."

Orin's then wife tells a different story. "I didn't like Joan," Wendy Lehman said. "I met her before Orin did, and she was very funny and all that, but she was after Orin before she knew I was leaving him."

According to Wendy, she had already decided to end her marriage but had not yet told her husband when he first met Rivers. "We were at a party, and she gave us a ride home, and we had a funny time in the car," she said.

But then Wendy left town on a trip. "I went to Santa Fe to do some casting at a foundry," she said. "When I got back, on the bed was a *New Yorker* magazine and an envelope that size. It had a note from Joan saying, 'I saw this cute article about bats and thought you'd like it.' You know how that goes. They probably had a discussion about bats. She was coming after him."

Soon after that, Wendy told Orin she wanted a divorce. "I had been saying that when our two daughters go off to college, I'm going to be out of here, but I couldn't do it," she said. "I couldn't tell him that and hurt his feelings; it just seemed mean. I didn't want to be mean. I just didn't want to be there anymore."

Wendy found Orin's attraction to Rivers as understandable as it was distressing. "Here he was, seventy-five then, and things were falling apart, and she was offering a cozy armchair, so to speak," Wendy said. "She was funny, and Orin always had a fun time. Where it bothered his friends is that his friends thought she was not up to par with him, intellectually and in terms of manners. I'm sure he had a very nice time, but it bothered me a lot because it embarrassed my children. Joan and Orin were getting their picture taken all the time. He was living with me and going out with Joan and being photographed. I knew Joan, and I sort of thought, 'We girls stick together,' and she should have said, 'If you want to move into a hotel or something…' I felt he should have respected me and respected the children much more. Our daughter was at Vassar, and people would cut out pictures of Joan and scotch-tape them to her door.

"She was on Howard Stern talking about being in bed with Orin—you just don't do that. She could have been nicer to the children and me without making it look like she's trying to get publicity, or like we're fools."

Wendy had anticipated a less public and more amicable transition, but the embarrassment quickly soured any chance of that. "It's hard to hang out at 21 with someone if they're not behaving toward you in a respectful way," she said.

Rivers told a different story, presenting herself as having been "very sensitive to the fact that his divorce was not final," as an unnamed friend of hers told *People* magazine in 1996.

Her new romance astonished her family as much as it did his. "I was mad about Orin," Rivers told *New York* magazine in 2010. "Love of my life. Adored him. People would say, 'Orin Lehman? Blech.' Melissa never got what I liked about him. But he was amazing. A gentleman. He was elegant. He got everything. He was so brave. I loved the bravery. That this man walked! He willed himself to walk. I know it sounds strange, but he was very sexy."

Because Lehman was disabled as well as a dozen years Rivers's senior, some of her gay friends made fun of him as a feeble old man. "Joan had walkers who were incredible social climbers, and when she wasn't seeing someone, they were the ones who would go to the opening at the Met," Dorothy Melvin explained. "They were always saying negative things about Orin: 'He's too old for you! He can't keep up!' But she and Orin had an incredible relationship. Joan had so much fun with him that some people were jealous. They never stopped laughing. Even with one leg, he was incredibly handsome and so quick—and he was hilarious. One night I went to pick him up for something and he got in the limo and I said, 'Orin, your zipper is undone.' Without missing a beat, he said, 'Well, you know, I don't tip the maids.'"

"Oh my God, she loved that man," said Sabrina Lott Miller, Joan's executive assistant. "They had so much fun together, and he would just make her laugh. One day I picked them up, and we were at Budget Rent A Car, and they were making paper airplanes and flying them in the lobby. I'm like, 'If you don't stop, I'm going to put you in the car.' They were like little kids together. She was seriously smitten."

His pedigree was a significant part of the appeal. "She was very proud of the fact that Orin was descended from this great, prominent family," said Pete Hathaway. "That was a great feather in Joan's cap. Orin was one of the very few Jewish men who was accepted in WASP society."

Rivers had always been a divided character, torn between the values of her striving mother and those of a vulgar comedian, and Lehman appealed to the half of her that coveted class. "Joan wanted to date a fancy old distinguished guy," said Mark Simone. "She'd go to Le Cirque with Orin, and the next day she was on Howard Stern talking about her sex life."

To some extent, the unlikely couple may simply have been a case of opposites attracting. "I think she challenged him, in a way," said Higdon. "He was beyond pompous, and he wasn't used to banter; he tried to be very grand, and he spoke with that aristocratic accent she wanted to hear. But Orin and I would banter. I would say in front of people, 'The only reason they're together is because I thought he was an asshole!' But she kept building him up. She put out pictures of him when he was twenty-five years old."

Rivers often invoked Lehman's heroism during the war and the medals he had won for his service. "When I watch him hit a golf ball as he balances on one leg, I tingle with the thought that the human spirit is unconquerable," she wrote in *Bouncing Back*.

Generous as well as solicitous, she delighted in buying him costly presents. "All his suits were by Anderson & Sheppard," said Dangle, referring to the bespoke clothing of the Savile Row haberdashery in London. "She would go order him some more suits."

But her intimates were disturbed by the contrast between her loyalty and her swain's apparent lack of appreciation. "She always used to charter a big motor yacht, the *Big Eagle*, and we'd do boat trips together, but Orin was not easy," said Blaine Trump. "He was difficult and kind of grumpy, but she worked so hard to make sure everything was perfect for him. We would say, 'He has not said one word this whole dinner,' but she just loved taking care of him."

As time passed, however, Rivers's friends began to worry that she was harboring unfulfilled hopes about an imagined future in which Lehman finally reciprocated her devotion. "I think she wanted someone to protect her," Higdon said. "I think she thought Orin would say, 'Let me take care of you.' But he never did. She took care of him. She dressed him, and she served him breakfast every morning. Orin did not live the way Joan lived, and Orin loved that; he wasn't used to it. Joan ran a brilliant house, but I think he took it for granted. This was an arrogant, pompous ass. He tried to act like, 'You're not from an old established family—you're like a showgirl!' But the showgirl is serving him breakfast on a silver tray every morning. What made all of us so angry was that he was so ungrateful."

Exhilarated by her opulent new lifestyle, Rivers adopted the full range of jet-set diversions, from safaris in Africa to cruises on a yacht in the Mediterranean. She was always ready for any challenge. "She was no sissy, that's for sure," said Higdon. "One summer we were in Greece and we both got in the water and something was nipping at our legs. She was such a sport about it; she'd think nothing of it. We were in this horrific storm in Greece, and I was in my cabin, and I couldn't even stay in my bed, so I got down on the floor and crawled down the stairs to get Joan. I have a life preserver around my neck—and she's lying on the bed flipping through a magazine, and Melissa is in the shower shaving her legs."

No matter how adverse the conditions, Rivers's intrepid behavior never devolved into divahood. "She wasn't spoiled and grand that way," said Higdon.

But it was clear to friends that her hunger for luxury was deeply rooted in her childhood anxieties. "I think the way she lived fulfilled her dreams," Higdon said. "As a little girl, she saw something that was pretty, and she wanted it. When she first did her apartment, she didn't have it gilded—and then we went to St. Petersburg. She came home and gilded the columns, the trimmings, the panels on the walls. It looked better, to be honest; it was a grand apartment, and it really gave it that oomph."

And as an adult, Rivers, unlike her ever-frustrated mother, could afford to turn her dreams into realities—except when they involved people who couldn't be bought. As her nine-year relationship with Orin Lehman continued, they took obvious pleasure in each other's company. "Joan was great with Orin, and they certainly seemed to have fun together," said Kip Forbes, the son of Malcolm Forbes.

"One time we were staying at the Ritz in Chicago, and when I came to their suite they were singing old World War II songs and laughing and laughing and laughing," Dorothy Melvin reported.

When Rivers turned sixty-three, Lehman gave her a twenty-carat emerald-cut sapphire ring flanked by two 2.5-carat diamonds as a present. "That ring was major," said Dangle. "It was a giant sapphire, a terrific stone, with major diamonds."

Rivers promptly announced that they were engaged, and she advertised her new status as Lehman's fiancée with a gala event. "She had her engagement party on my father's boat, *The Highlander*, at Chelsea Piers," reported Kip Forbes.

Despite the fate of Rivers's previous marriages, her interest in landing Lehman didn't surprise anyone who knew her. "It was very important to her to be married," said Melvin. "She was a Jewish girl, and that's what we do. In that generation, everyone gets married, and you're looked on as odd if you don't. She wanted to be married again."

Lehman's family took a more cynical view. "Joan was trying to get him to marry her, but Orin was very stubborn—luckily, I guess," Wendy Lehman said. "I think she said to Orin, 'I would like a cocktail ring; it will be a friendship ring.' I think she was trying to put pressure on him so people would say, 'When's the happy day?' So he bought a ring of colored stones, a cluster of stuff, but nothing ever happened."

Although Rivers kept referring to Lehman as "my fiancé," few of their friends expected to see an actual wedding. "He wouldn't commit to anything," said Robert Higdon.

Rivers later claimed she felt no need to make it official. "We didn't want to marry," she said.

But her intimates didn't believe her. "I think she absolutely wanted to marry him," said Dangle. "She would have been Mrs. Lehman in a heartbeat."

Rivers's view of marriage still included traditional gender roles. "I'm from the old school," she said. "When a man marries, he takes care of you. Women should be taken care of."

"Her idea was to have Mr. Astor come in and take care of everything," said Higdon.

But if Mr. Astor wouldn't take care of her, Rivers had the means to take care of herself. Having developed a taste for luxury boat trips, she established her own new tradition by chartering a yacht for annual holiday cruises with family and friends, usually in the Caribbean. Her favorite boat was the *Big Eagle*, a 172-foot custom motor yacht with a crew of ten and six cabins that accommodated a dozen guests.

"Joan would take the boat for two weeks, and it was summer camp for grown-ups," said Pete Hathaway.

Rivers enjoyed being able to spend huge sums on such extravagances, but she never stopped worrying about financial security. "Money was always a very big concern," said Dangle. "It's hard to get to where you think, 'I'm going to have enough.' I don't think she ever got there."

Despite such ostentation, Rivers rarely displayed the sense of entitlement that typically develops over decades of stardom and wealth—but there were times when it got the best of her. In 1999, the late Lynn Grefe was national director of the Republican Pro-Choice Political Action Committee, whose board members included the actress Dina Merrill, the heiress daughter of Marjorie Merriweather Post and Edward Hutton. "We had to do a fund-raiser every year, and Dina said, 'Joan Rivers is a pro-choice Republican—maybe we can get her to speak at our annual benefit,'" Grefe recalled. "So she takes me to Joan Rivers's apartment, and I have this umbrella with me that I got at a consignment store. Instead of saying, 'Hi—nice to meet you,' Joan grabs my umbrella and says, 'I love this umbrella! Can I have it?' I laughed, and she said, 'No, I'm not kidding—I like it.'"

The umbrella was unusual and irreplaceable. "It was a brown umbrella with a scalloped edge, and it had an etched silver handle with a red stone that looked like a ruby on the end," Grefe said. "It was made in the 1920s, and I probably paid ten bucks for it at the consignment store. I was a newly divorced single mother in my forties, and at first I thought, 'She's just kidding, don't take it seriously,' but it didn't come off as funny. I think she just felt I would fall into place and give her the umbrella, but I dug my heels in and said no. Joan says, 'I'm really serious about this. I want this umbrella. Don't you think you should give me this umbrella?'" When

Grefe refused, Rivers was not pleased, and she made it clear that she was doing the benefit solely because of Merrill.

To many observers, Rivers's support for reproductive freedom seemed as paradoxical as her social life, whose components ranged from Nancy Reagan to drag queens. But her predilection for incongruous combinations reached some kind of apotheosis in her supremely unlikely relationship with the British royals.

No matter how successful she became, Rivers always remained a striver who brought a starstruck fan's sense of idol worship to the ultimate embodiment of Anglo-Saxon privilege. "If Joan could have been anything at all in her dreams, she would have wanted to be part of England's royal family," said Sue Cameron. "She decorated like that, lived like that—it was very important to her. I think people revere the royal family as the chicest people in the world, and in Joan's mind, that was what she wanted to be."

Rivers spent years making jokes about Princess Diana and Queen Elizabeth, saying that she had been canceled from a command performance because the Queen "heard what I said about her thighs."

"I'm the only one who ever said to the Queen of England, 'Shave your toes!'" she claimed.

Rivers's jokes about the royals could be as bawdy as her riffs on other celebrities, as in this bit about Queen Elizabeth's less demure sister, Princess Margaret: "Princess Diana and the Queen are driving down the lane when their car is forced off the road by masked thieves. 'Out of the car and hand over your jewels!' After the thieves rob them and steal their car, Diana begins to put her earrings, necklace, and rings back on. 'Wherever did you hide those?' demanded the Queen. 'Where do you think?' asked Diana. 'Pity Margaret wasn't here,' said the Queen. 'We could have saved the Bentley.'"

Despite such cracks, Rivers revered all the royals. "When Princess Diana was killed, she was the first person I called, and she was up and crying, absolutely devastated," said Cameron. "It was like she'd lost a member of her family."

But an actual friendship with any of the royals seemed completely out of reach. Many emblems of success can be bought; all it takes to charter a yacht is a large amount of money. Wealth certainly facilitated Rivers's entrée into New York society, where it can buy seats on boards and access to charitably inclined social sets.

But money can't buy noble birth or intimate contact with the monarchy, and Rivers astonished virtually everyone, including herself, by developing a real friendship with Prince Charles and Camilla, the Duchess of Cornwall. "Joan wanted to be Jackie Kennedy, and what better way for the 'last girl before the freeway' than to be friends with the next king of England?" said Cameron.

Rivers and Prince Charles were reportedly introduced in 2003 while on a painting holiday in the South of France, where they hit it off. "We sat next to each other at a dinner party and got friendly," Rivers said. "He's darling."

Prince Charles was "a big fan" of Rivers, according to Sir Tom Shebbeare, the former chief executive of the Prince's Trust. "He found her very irreverent, antiestablishment—and her being like that around the epitome of the establishment such as the royal family was daring."

"Charles and Camilla have a great sense of humor," Rivers said. "He is so charming and so humorous."

In another apparent case of opposites attracting, the royals seemed titillated by Rivers's propensity for violating traditional notions of propriety.

"Many people are so correct around them, and Joan was so incorrect," said Blaine Trump. "She made them laugh. Joan loved the pomp and circumstance of the traditions of the royal family, and Prince Charles and Camilla absolutely adored her. The English all have potty humor, and Joan was full of that kind of humor. They loved it, and they were real friends."

Rivers still found it challenging to negotiate the gap between their respective sensibilities. Every year Prince Charles sent Rivers a Christmas gift that sometimes consisted of two elegant teacups. Rivers reacted with her usual rude humor.

"One year I took a picture under my Christmas tree with the teacups and wrote, 'How could you send me two teacups when I'm alone?'" she said. "Another time I wrote, 'I'm enjoying tea with my best friend!,' and I sent a picture of me in a cemetery. And he never acknowledges it! He never says to me when I see him, 'Ohhhh, funny funny funny!' So this year I thought, I'm just going to write him a nice thank-you note. And the other day our mutual friend calls and says, 'Just spoke to Charles! He said, "I can't wait to see Joan's note this year!"'"

Although Rivers was thrilled by their association, she understood its limitations; the friendship was close enough to impress people, including herself, but it was not intimate. When asked about her relationship with Charles and Camilla, Rivers admitted, "Not inner circle. Outer inner circle."

As time went on, the bond deepened to include invitations to visit Highgrove House, the family residence of Prince Charles and Camilla in Gloucestershire. By the time they got married in 2005, Rivers was one of only four Americans invited to their wedding. Three years after that, Prince Charles turned sixty, and Rivers performed at *We Are Most Amused*, a birthday gala to raise money for his Prince's Trust charity.

Rivers's ultimate triumph came when she was presented to the Queen. "Joan curtsies, and she was so overwhelmed," recalled Robert Higdon. "She said, 'You just look so fabulous! I just love your pin!' The Queen said, 'Thank you,' in this prim, clipped voice, standing there with her handbag over her arm."

If Rivers managed to behave herself at such times, there were other occasions when she rebelled against royal protocol. "One time at the Prince of Wales dinner, Prince Charles's equerry came up and said, 'Prince Charles would love you to say a few words at dinner,'" Trump reported. "She said, 'Oh my God, I haven't prepared anything!' The equerry said, 'Miss Rivers, just so you know, there will be no "fuck"s in the toast.' So she got up and said, 'I've been told I can't say "fuck."' Being outrageous gave her so much pleasure. She just loved it."

Rivers remained friends with the royal family until she died, but back in New York, her interest in her socialite lifestyle eventually waned. "In the last ten or twelve years of her life, the society thing stopped being something she cared about, and there was the realization that that world completely bored the pants off her," Dangle said. "Is it fun to go to the Met gala and sit with all these women who don't have much to say? Their lives are rather empty, and Joan had a very full life. I don't think she needed to go to another one of those dinners; it was more fun to go to the theater."

And Rivers's passion for such cultural riches was eternal—as was her contempt for anyone who didn't appreciate them. "If you don't go to Broadway, you're a fool," she said in an interview with *New York* magazine. "We're in the theater capital of the world, and if you don't get it, you're an idiot."

## Chapter Sixteen

# BUT IS IT GOOD FOR THE JEWS? SEX, POLITICS, AND RELIGION

During Rivers's lifetime, the modern American women's movement liberated her along with millions of others, breaking down laws and customs that held women back and creating innumerable new opportunities. Although Rivers benefited from those changes, she consistently refused to embrace the goal of equality that inspired them.

"She would say, 'I don't want to be identified as a feminist,'" Kathy Griffin reported. "It would always drive me crazy."

But Rivers's objection was personal rather than philosophical: she feared the label might diminish her appeal as a performer. "She said, 'No one wants to see a feminist! I can see those ticket sales flying out the window!'" Griffin reported. "She said, 'That word isn't always a good word to be associated with. Does that mean men won't come to see your shows?' She felt it was something that could limit her audience base."

Since the definition of a feminist is someone who believes in social, political, and economic equality for women, Rivers's position struck many of her friends as a ludicrous exercise in intellectual dishonesty, since anyone who does not believe in social, political, and economic equality for women is, also by definition, a bigot. "I used to laugh about that and say, 'Look, honey, you're a feminist!'" said Griffin. "She broke barriers; she did everything a feminist does. She was the living embodiment of what a woman can accomplish through true grit and being unapologetic, so you don't get more feminist than that."

Confronted with such denial, Rivers's intimates generally responded by rolling their eyes and focusing on her actual life rather than her professed opinions. "She was a feminist, whether or not she accepted the title," said Margaret Cho. "She was able to empower herself, and she broke through in an era when we didn't hear women at all. She inspired so many women to give voice to their feminism. Women are always trying to be pleasing, but Joan was contrary. She didn't want people to put her in any kind of category; she wanted to define herself in every way. She got to decide who she was."

But who she was remained stubbornly paradoxical. Although Rivers prided herself on keeping up with the times, many of her attitudes were firmly rooted in the past. Gloria Steinem saw her as "a transitional woman," the product of an old-fashioned culture whose life was shaped by social upheaval but who never revised her own thinking, particularly about traditional gender roles.

"Joan was prefeminist to the bone," said Steinem, who was one year younger than Rivers. "She was a kind of queen bee who broke boundaries inadvertently, but didn't see herself as a member of her own community."

To many onlookers, the resulting contradictions were perplexing. Hollywood is often considered a bastion of liberalism, and comics are an iconoclastic breed—but Rivers's politics were distinctly conservative. "Joan was Republican verging on Royalist," said Bob Colacello, the author of *Ronnie and Nancy: Their Path to the White House.*

As with feminism, the roots of Rivers's opinions on politics seemed very personal. "The basis of her thought was money and protection," said Sue Cameron. "She was in favor of the death penalty, and her view was, 'You try to kill me, I'm going to kill you first.' To her, Republican values meant lower taxes and a strong defense. If your motivation is 'I don't want to be broke' and 'I don't want to be killed by an Arab,' and you believe the Republican Party will keep you alive and keep you solvent, that's the one thing that would influence her. She just ignored the social stuff."

For Rivers, personal security came first, and she never felt secure. Sabrina Lott Miller was a firearms instructor and part-time bookkeeper at the Beverly Hills Gun Club when she went to work for Rivers in 1988, and her NRA certification was one of her job qualifications. "Joan would have death threats, and she always felt like she had to have extra protection," said Miller. "She wasn't Annie Oakley, but she could be if needed to protect herself. It was all about security."

Miller has worked for the Rivers family ever since, although Joan once came close to shooting her. "I was staying in Melissa's apartment in New York, which could be accessed through the back stairs in Joan's apartment, and the staff forgot to tell Joan. In the middle of the night, I was coming through the door in the ballroom and there was Joan on the balcony—she had her gun cocked," Miller said. "She was like, 'I don't know who you are, but your time's up!'"

Despite such pugnacity, Rivers gravitated toward women like Nancy Reagan and Betsy Bloomingdale: rich, Republican, rigidly self-controlled wives who concealed their more lethal tendencies behind saccharine smiles and silken manners. As a comic, Rivers broke barriers, flouted the rules, and made fun of gender norms. She also made her own money; having agonized over her mother's financial dependency, she vowed as a child not to rely on a husband to support her, and she never did. But when it came to her social life, she consistently chose the company of pampered wives who expected wealthy, patriarchal husbands to buy their $20,000 handbags and fabulous homes. Rivers didn't hang out with rebellious feminists who questioned establishment politics and traditional sex stereotypes; her friends believed in face-lifts, couture clothes, and lacquered hair that wouldn't budge in gale force winds. "Republican equals the right place setting," said Cameron. "Feminism was just fodder for her act. Feminists had hairy legs and Birkenstocks and bad clothes."

Rivers clearly preferred the protected lily-white world of her powerful, entitled friends over more diverse or iconoclastic milieus—and yet here too she was curiously inconsistent. "She was a bit of a contrarian," Blaine Trump admitted. "She was very conservative, but socially very liberal. She had tons of gay friends, and she thought everyone had the right to be whoever you are and whatever you are—but underneath it all she was very traditional. She was not modern."

Rivers was beloved by gay men long before she stepped forward as a public spokesperson for God's Love We Deliver during the AIDS crisis, so her allegiance to the GOP seemed particularly puzzling when it came to LGBT issues. "She was very early on gay rights and accepting trans-sexuals, very progressive," observed Steve Olsen, owner of the Laurie Beechman Theatre.

Many of her adult fans became obsessed with her in adolescence, when her humor stood out like a beacon that could lead them to more tolerant communities than the ones where they were born.

"When you're a seventeen-year-old boy in a ten-thousand-person town in Arkansas, and the only person you thought might have the same feel-ings you do is a six-foot-seven black man who roller-skated down the interstate and got arrested, you definitely know which famous people are accepting of gay people," said Jason Sheeler, the fashion news director of *Departures* magazine. "You're always looking for subtext, hunting for clues about who would be cool with you, and you would know who was a friend of gays. You knew Joan Rivers was on your side. She was the friend you wanted."

Jeff Cubeta, a New York–based pianist and songwriter who grew up in a blue-collar Pennsylvania family, found Rivers's comedy to be a comforting escape from a difficult reality. "One thing that resonated for me was that I knew Joan didn't have support from her family, and I didn't either," said Cubeta, the son of a factory worker and a hairdresser. "That was some-thing I had to struggle to overcome."

For such fans, Rivers's defiance of social norms was thrillingly trans-gressive. "There was this honesty, a no-holds-barred, I-don't-give-a-fuck attitude," said the comedian and television personality Billy Eichner. "She was also very fashionable and flamboyant and larger than life. It was like she was comedy's answer to Cher."

"She's probably the only female comedian who is a gay icon," observed the actor and director Charles Busch, who is particularly renowned as a drag artist. "She started off with the self-deprecating-ugly-girl comedy, and gay men could identify with her presenting herself as an outcast with humor. She had a mixture of strength, flamboyance, vulnerability, and survival tactics that a lot of those ladies share, from Judy Garland and Liza Minnelli to Streisand."

Rivers always had gay friends, but in her later years she grew increasingly bored with rich Republican wives and gravitated more toward the witty, stylish men who adored her company. "She didn't have to compete as a woman for gay men," said Lonny Price. "It wasn't about her being attractive. She could be Auntie Mame."

Rivers even got herself ordained online by the Universal Life Church so she could perform the marriage ceremony of Preston Bailey, the floral designer of her daughter's lavish wedding. If not as extravagant as Melissa's, his nuptials were flamboyant in their own way. "In 2013, the self-proclaimed 'queen of the gays' officiated at a *King Kong*–themed ceremony for Preston Bailey and Theo Bleckmann atop the Empire State Building," the *Huffington Post* reported in 2014.

But Rivers didn't stop with Bailey's wedding to Bleckmann, a musician and composer. Two months before she died, she was signing copies of *Diary of a Mad Diva* at a Manhattan Barnes & Noble where a couple named Jed Ryan and Joe Aiello were waiting to buy the book. "She mentioned being an ordained minister, and I jokingly asked [Ryan], 'Do you think it's true? Maybe she'll marry us.' And he goes, 'Ask her.' So I did," said Aiello.

Rivers not only performed an impromptu ceremony; she also agreed to do the whole thing again after the couple realized that they hadn't completed the requisite paperwork.

Given the GOP's unrelenting hostility to gay marriage and women's rights, Rivers's identification as a Republican required a tacit acceptance of the viciously discriminatory policies the party has espoused toward two of her core constituencies. To some extent, her iconoclasm was simply a manifestation of her penchant for being a troublemaker. She just loved to provoke people, even if that meant agitating close friends—a pastime she seemed to regard as sport. With one couple whose politics were very liberal, she liked to taunt the husband by saying "schvartze," a pejorative Yiddish word for a black person that is comparable to the word "nigger." Giving Rivers the benefit of the doubt, the couple laughed off such slurs.

"I never believed anything she said about anything," the wife admitted. "It was always joking."

Like Rivers's stance on feminism, many of her views on issues seemed determined more by self-interest than by principle. In 2013, the writers at *Fashion Police* went on strike over wages. They put in sixteen-hour days and worked up to forty hours a week, a schedule that made it impossible for them to hold down other jobs, but they were paid only one-sixth of the Writers Guild's minimum weekly compensation for comedy-variety shows. They wanted to join the Writers Guild of America, West, the union that represents Hollywood writers, but E! had resisted their efforts.

Rivers herself was a member of the Writers Guild, but when the writers sought her support, she was anything but sympathetic to their plight. "She just blew up on us, cussing and screaming," said Todd Masterson, one of the show's writers. "She pounded her fists on the table. She threw a binder on the ground. She stormed out of the room and stormed back in the room."

The guild filed an unfair labor practices charge against E! and Rivers's production company, alleging that the *Fashion Police* writers were owed $1.5 million in unpaid regular and overtime wages. Frustrated by a lack of progress, the writers finally went on strike—whereupon Rivers denounced them publicly as "idiots" and "schmuck writers." After the strike dragged on for more than a year, WGA spokesman Neal Sacharow publicly assigned blame: "One of the biggest obstacles is that Joan Rivers, a WG member and host of the show, not only refuses to stand with the writers but has actively stood in the way of their efforts, even illegally threatening that they could lose their jobs if they unionized," he said.

Rivers avoided expulsion from the WGA by agreeing to stop writing for the show for the duration of the strike and by urging both sides to settle, but her conduct horrified many of those involved. One of the show's former writers, Dennis Hensley, finally landed a gig with a cruise ship, where a play he had written was performed. Its plot revolved around the murder of a talk show host, and the suspects were the show's writers.

In such disputes, Rivers seemed primarily concerned with her own benefit. The catchphrase "But is it good for the Jews?" is a staple of

Jewish humor, but Rivers's choices were often driven by a simpler calculation: "Is it good for Joan?"

At times, however, those who tangled with her were surprised by the virulence of her conservatism. After the 9/11 terrorist attacks, the musician and producer Nile Rodgers recruited more than two hundred musicians and other celebrities to record his song "We Are Family." The director Spike Lee shot the music video, and the late Danny Schechter made a documentary chronicling the recording sessions.

"Nile Rodgers admired Joan Rivers, and he reached out to her," recalled Schechter, a veteran television producer and cofounder of Global Vision, an independent international news syndicate. "The idea was to support an education project to promote tolerance, but her reaction was to denounce it. She attacked it politically, and she was really vicious to the people from WAF who spoke to her on the phone. She cursed them out; it was very upsetting."

The WAF group decided to include her reaction in the documentary. "I felt that was an important element—not everyone was singing 'Kumbaya,' and Rivers spoke for the hardheaded right-wing point of view," said Schechter. "Not only did she refuse to comment, but her lawyer called me and said, 'If you mention this in any way, we will sue you for defaming her.'"

The experience convinced Schechter that Rivers was a "fascist," he said. She was certainly no fan of progressivism; she loathed New York City mayor Bill de Blasio, whom she blamed for a divisive approach that pitted rich against poor. But she may have reconsidered her reflexive Republicanism when it came to other candidates, according to Charles Busch. "She told me she voted for Obama. She kind of whispered it to me," he said.

Many of Rivers's friends saw her conservatism as a function of her strong identification as a Jew. This too seemed somewhat contradictory; Rivers had, after all, changed her surname, gotten more than one nose job, and spent much of her life trying to emulate the WASP elite. "As much as she talked about being Jewish all the time, I think she really would rather have been a WASP," said Sue Cameron.

But such yearnings coexisted with a strong sense of her original identity. "Joan was very proud of being Jewish," Bill Reardin said. "She insisted that our business cards for *The Joan Rivers Show* be what she referred to as Israeli blue, which was the blue from the Israeli flag. Culturally, she was very Jewish."

When she was in her seventies, Rivers got a tattoo on the inside of her left arm that said 6M, for the six million Jews killed in the Holocaust. A rabbi later told her that getting a tattoo was forbidden by the Torah, but she was proud of her visible brand, modest as it seemed to younger aficionados of the art. "She went over to Lady Gaga and said, 'Look at my tattoo!'" Margie Stern reported. "Lady Gaga said, 'You call that a tattoo?'"

The feminist film critic and author Molly Haskell believes that Rivers's Jewish heritage was formative in shaping her humor. "Jewish women were already outside the WASP social contract," Haskell said. "They're not genteel women, with all the traits typically inculcated in gentile women—compliant, unchallenging, uncritical, tamping down their intelligence. There's a tradition of mordant Jewish humor that's very different from the cheery optimism of the Mormons, or the idea that if you can't say something nice, don't say it. Jewish women don't have the same inhibitions that gentiles do. They're not as penalized for speaking out. Jewish mothers are very frank and funny and often brusque."

Rivers's passions included a fierce allegiance to the Jewish state. "Israel was very important to her, and for her, the Republicans had a better stance on Israel," Cameron said. "She was becoming more and more Netanyahu-esque."

Despite her identification as a Jew, Rivers didn't believe in the religious tenets of Judaism, nor did she practice most of its rituals; after her performances at the Laurie Beechman Theatre, her standing order upstairs at the West Bank Cafe was a shrimp cocktail. "I'm never going to say that she was a traditional or an observant Jew in any sense, but it goes to her essence," said Abigail Pogrebin, who interviewed Rivers for her book *Stars of David: Prominent Jews Talk About Being Jewish*. "The whole thing about moxie, about 'Don't tell me I can't do it!'—it's a Jewish mantra, this idea that you can: 'I will show you how wrong you are! Don't tell me I can't join this, go there, be this, accomplish that!' That's been our history, and that was coming out of her pores—and I recognized it, because I was raised like that too. Her beginnings were about defiance, in a way, and I'm not sure your underpinnings ever leave you—the drive, the 'Don't stop,' the 'It's never enough!'"

Pogrebin saw Rivers as representative of her cohort. "Everyone I know who was raised in that similar atmosphere, it's like you are never done, and it could all go tomorrow," she said. "I think Joan falls into the category of 'They did kill us, they still would, and fuck them.' That's a brand of Judaism, and a brand of thinking, that I heard a lot from her generation— although not with as little discretion. She was the most blunt, about her aspirations and about anti-Semites—she had zero tolerance of them. When I go and speak at Jewish Federations all over the country, with women of her generation there's a bit of a siege mentality. Joan is not just a comedian being extreme. She is representative of a certain strand of thinking that I do think is dated now."

Rivers's use of pejorative words like *schvartzes* is offensive by any contemporary standard, but she refused to adapt her behavior to evolving sensibilities, let alone the demands of political correctness. In fact, she delighted in cracking jokes that reinforced Jewish stereotypes.

Some involved sex: "I saw my first porno film recently," she said. "It was a Jewish porno film—one minute of sex and nine minutes of guilt."

Other jokes upheld the cliché of a Jewish penchant for materialism and conspicuous consumption: pointing a finger at anyone sitting near the stage, she would pass judgment on a woman's engagement ring, saying it was acceptable for "goyim" but mere "swimming jewelry" for a Jew.

At times, Rivers seemed to go out of her way to be incendiary. At one dinner party she hosted, Rivers asked everyone at the table to describe themselves with a single adjective. "The adjectives people gave were things like 'unstoppable,' 'triumphant,' 'superlative,' 'confident,'" recalled Jesse Kornbluth, who was one of the guests. "These were people who had willed themselves to be successful, as did Joan. So they get to me and I say, 'Ambivalent.' I remember Joan laughing at me and saying, 'Get over yourself! You're as ambitious as any of the rest of us kikes!'"

When Melissa married the horse trainer John Endicott in 1998, Rivers had his family crest embroidered on the bustle of her daughter's wedding dress. She was obviously proud that Melissa was marrying the kind of gentile who had a family crest—and yet she was also concerned that their son, Cooper, not lose his sense of Jewish identity. "The raising of her grandson worried her," Pogrebin said. "She really wanted him to be a Jew."

Such feelings didn't translate into being observant in any traditional way. When Pogrebin's *Stars of David* was made into a musical, the composer William Finn was asked to write a Joan Rivers song. "We had a meeting, and she was talking about not having a temple, and I said, 'I have a place you're going to love,'" Finn reported. "I took her to a gay temple."

On the night before Yom Kippur, Finn brought Rivers to the evening service at Congregation Beit Simchat Torah, a New York synagogue serving the LGBT and inclusive Jewish community. When she walked in, pandemonium broke out. "People were flying over their seats; they couldn't believe it was her," Finn said. "I've never been in a maelstrom like that—ever."

During the service, Finn was astonished by Rivers's familiarity with the liturgical prayers. "I asked her, 'How do you know how to daven so well?' She said, 'The way you're praying reminds me of my father.' She was so Jewish."

Although the service was lengthy, Rivers was game. "She's, like, eighty years old, and she stood for, like, four hours," said Charles Busch, who accompanied her that night. "I was bored out of my skull, and I sat down. She was like, 'If I can stand, why can't you stand?'"

Despite the solemn ceremony, Rivers remained her usual acerbic self. "I said I was very touched when this old lesbian in front of us held the Torah," Busch recalled. "Joan said, 'It would have been more touching if she'd washed her hair.'"

Although Rivers rarely went to temple services, she nonetheless saw them as meaningful. "She was more of a cultural Jew, but there was a very deep pride in it, and the traditions were important to her," said Dorothy Melvin, who became an Orthodox Jew in her later years.

One of the musical numbers written for *Stars of David* was a Rivers-inspired song called "High Holy Days." "In the insanity of her day, in the voraciousness of her career, this was when she described the pause, the once-a-year time that she dialed down and sat there and felt like it was where she should be," Pogrebin explained.

If Rivers was an infrequent temple-goer, her support for Israel remained a constant, and her views on that were absolutist. "There were no shades of gray in the question of Israel's existence or its politics," said Pogrebin. "Being Jewish was in her DNA, and it doesn't matter if she's praying or fasting or observing in any traditional way. She's 100 percent Jewish, and she owns that. Whether or not I agree with her extremism, I was refreshed by her unapologetic Jewishness. She thinks Jews are great in all the stereotypical ways—she thinks they're smarter, she thinks they make good husbands. It's a rah-rah Jew identity for her."

Rivers's passion for Israel was so ferocious it could trump all other considerations, as Andy Cohen learned when he booked her on his show, *Watch What Happens: Live.* She was scheduled to appear with Maksim Chmerkovskiy, who made his name on *Dancing with the Stars*—but Rivers apparently had an issue with her fellow guest.

"Before the show, I got word from Joan's team that she was going to eviscerate this guy on TV," said Cohen, who had no idea why Rivers would be hostile to him. "She was fired up in a way I had never seen her, and she said, 'Just watch!' I think she was just going to cut his dick off, so I did everything I could to keep them from interacting on the air. And then during the commercial break she said to him, 'Where are you from?,' and he said something about being pro-Israel. She turned on a dime, and they fell in love. She completely opened up to him."

Despite Rivers's loyalties, she sometimes expressed her sense of Jewishness in ways that others found disturbing. "I sent a Jewish friend who was in Auschwitz to see her show, and he was very offended by her joke that she lost her whole family at Auschwitz and she was standing in the gift shop for hours," her friend Margie Stern recalled.

In 2013, Rivers made a crack about the supermodel Heidi Klum on *Fashion Police:* "The last time a German looked this hot was when they were pushing Jews into the oven," she said.

The Anti-Defamation League assailed Rivers's remark as "vulgar and hideous." Its national director, Abraham Foxman, said, "Of all people, Joan Rivers should know better. There are certain things about the Holocaust that should be taboo. This is especially true for Jews, for whom the Holocaust is still a deeply painful memory."

Defending herself on CNN, Rivers said, "It's a joke, number one. Number two, it is about the Holocaust. This is the way I remind people about the Holocaust. I do it through humor."

Asked why she wouldn't apologize, she said, "For what?," and added that people should criticize anti-Semites instead of someone whose late husband lost his entire family during the Holocaust.

The following year Rivers ignited one of the biggest controversies of her career with an unrepentant attack on the Palestinian victims of Israel. In August of 2014, a TMZ reporter asked her about the Gaza conflict and noted that almost two thousand Palestinians had been killed. When he posted a video of her response, it caused a firestorm. "Oh my God! Tell that to the people in Hiroshima," Rivers said, raising her hands in mock horror. "Good. Good. When you declare war, you declare war. They started it. We now don't count who's dead. You're dead, you deserve to be dead. Don't you dare make me feel bad about that. They were told to get out. They didn't get out. You don't get out, you are an idiot. At least the ones that were killed were the ones with low IQs."

Describing the Hamas government as "terrorists," Rivers added, "They were reelected by a lot of very stupid people who don't even own a pencil."

The resulting furor was amplified by social media. The comedian Anthony Jeselnik tweeted that Rivers once told him "she would die before she'd ever apologize for a joke," but she did post a statement about the controversy on her Facebook page.

"I am both saddened and disappointed that my statement about the tragedy of civilian casualties was totally taken out of context," Rivers announced. "What I said and stand behind is, war is hell and unfortunately civilians are victims of political conflicts. We, the United States, certainly know this as sixty-nine years later we still feel the guilt of Hiroshima and

Nagasaki. The media, as usual, has decided to only quote the most out of context and inflammatory non sequitur rather than giving an accurate account of what my intentions were behind the statement. Along with every other sane person in this world, I am praying for peace. It is stupid and wrong and I am tired of bearing the brunt of attacks by people who want to sell newspapers or gain ratings by creating a scandal about me that is nonexistent."

Rivers's statement failed to mollify those who felt that humor was an inadequate excuse for crossing such a line. When she died the following month, thousands of people tweeted that she deserved her fate because of her remarks on Palestine, and *Variety* reported that "the hashtag #karma saw a large spike on Twitter for a brief period."

"Karma at work there. Without a doubt," one person tweeted.

Such controversies inevitably emphasized Rivers's combativeness, but her friends also saw her Jewish background as the underlying inspiration for great generosity, particularly when it came to her family. From childhood, Joan and her sister had a fraught relationship, and they took very different paths in life. "As far as Joan was concerned, her sister was the smart one, her sister was the pretty one, her sister was the beloved one," said Dorothy Melvin. "They were very different from each other. Roddy McDowall said, 'If you weren't related, you would never be friends.'"

And yet for most of their adult life, Joan took care of Barbara and her children. "Barbara was a young widow, and Joan was a Jewish girl, and as Jews we have an age-old obligation to make sure we always take care of family first," Melvin said. "That is the Jewish way of thinking—that you have to be extra kind to the widow and the orphan. In her DNA, Joan felt she had to take care of her sister. Deep down, Joan was a real Jew."

## Chapter Seventeen

# MEN ARE STUPID: BEAUTY AND BETRAYAL

In 2009, Rivers published a book called *Men Are Stupid...and They Like Big Boobs*, which she claimed was a piece of wisdom that Marilyn Monroe had personally imparted to her. Having gotten everyone's attention, Rivers subtitled the book with her own solution to this age-old dilemma: *A Woman's Guide to Beauty Through Plastic Surgery*.

In a subsequent interview, Rivers actually described the scene in which Monroe supposedly made her immortal remark. "It was a 1951 dinner party," said Rivers, who was a college student at the time. "My father was a doctor, and so was the guy who hosted the party. Marilyn was very shy, so they sat her next to the least threatening person in the room—me."

According to Rivers, timid little Joan Molinsky finally worked up the courage to tell the beautiful blond actress that she too was hoping to have a career in show business.

"Honey, let me tell you a secret," Monroe allegedly replied. "Men are stupid and they like big tits."

When Rivers told this story to an interviewer decades later, she added, "That's still true. Oh, my first agent, listen to this, this is in 1965: he told me that I was too old—too old!"

By 1965, Monroe had been dead for three years, having succumbed to a barbiturate overdose that was declared a probable suicide in 1962, when Rivers was still a struggling nobody trying to get unpaid gigs in Greenwich Village coffeehouses.

Valerie Frankel, who cowrote *Men Are Stupid,* doesn't know whether Rivers actually met Monroe. "If Joan said Marilyn said it directly to her, it was probably a joke," Frankel admitted.

But Rivers's personal guide to beauty was no joke. It began with an unapologetic statement of her worldview. "Okay, politically incorrect or not, let's face it: men are stupid," Rivers wrote. "They can't help it. They're wired to procreate, and Mother Nature has doomed the poor things. They are attracted to creatures that are their opposites, with hairless bodies, big boobs, slim waists, rounded butts—and this has become the beauty ideal many women aspire to achieve."

As far as Rivers was concerned, the way to attain this ideal was simple, and the reason for doing so was even simpler: "For many of us, having it all means getting a nip, or a tuck, or a little lift now and again," she said. "Why? Because it makes us feel good."

Nor did she believe women should be embarrassed to admit to such stratagems. After dedicating the book to "all the women who've felt they had to keep their plastic surgery a secret, who've lied about having had it, and who've felt shame about needing it, wanting it, or doing it," Rivers proclaimed that she herself felt no such shame about having needed it, wanted it, and done it.

"She called it maintenance," said Blaine Trump. "She started having little nips and tucks every year."

For Rivers, this hobby became virtually recreational. "Joan's idea of a vacation was to check into a hospital and get something done," said Lonny Price. "This was a sickness; she couldn't stop. I don't think it was anything rational. She was clearly addicted to plastic surgery. I think she always felt like the ugly girl. She was always screaming, 'Everyone does it! I'm the only one who talks about it!'"

In 2012, Rivers told Anderson Cooper she had undergone 739 cosmetic surgery procedures. She joked about having had so many that for every ten she did, she got one free, as in many rewards programs. "It's a little like coffee—you just keep going," she said.

Rivers later claimed that she was kidding and the real total wasn't that high, but she didn't deny how extensive her interventions had been.

"She once said there was not an original part of her body," reported Larry Ferber.

Her quest for self-improvement was so compulsive that Melissa felt compelled to stage an intervention on their reality show *Joan & Melissa: Joan Knows Best?* "At some point I think the risk outweighs the reward, so I wanted my mother to know how I felt about it, and I think I made myself pretty clear," Melissa said. "I also found out that most of my friends are weak, and she turned them very easily."

Joan chimed in: "They all said, 'You shouldn't do it! You shouldn't do it!' And I said, 'What if I pay for everybody in this room? What would you do?' Every single person accepted."

"Joan would say, 'Whatever makes you feel better about yourself, do it,'" Frankel explained. "Surgery made her feel better about herself. Whether or not it made her better by any objective scale, she liked it, so she did it."

She did it so often that she became very cavalier about the toll of such procedures. When Lonny Price was working on *Sally Marr* with Rivers, he found her blithe insouciance very disconcerting. "At one point she had a peel or something, and her face was falling onto the script in pieces," Price recalled. "I said, 'Joan, you have to go sit over there.' She said, 'Oh—okay.' I don't think Joan was embarrassed by anything."

Charles Busch had a similar experience while he was helping Rivers to develop the one-woman show she would perform in London. "One day she answered the door and her face had these horrible scabs all over it," he said. "She said, 'Oh, I just had a peel. But I can only work two hours today, because I have to do a show in Connecticut.' I was just shocked that she was going to do a show with big scabs on her face, but she said, 'I'll just cover them up with makeup.' Bob Mackie said, 'Oh, I love Joan—she shows up at fittings with blood still in her hair.'"

Confronted with such problems, Rivers's usual approach was to ignore them—or to dissemble, if necessary. "At one point she was on television and her eyes were tearing, and she said she had some kind of infection, but she was lying," said Price. "The truth was that she'd had some plastic surgery done. She said, 'They just pulled it too tight.'"

271

Some of her interventions were so dramatic as to be shocking. "When she had cheek implants, that took everyone aback," said Trump. "It changed the structure of her face, but she said, 'Oh, it will settle in,' and after a while it did."

Rivers seemed weirdly nonchalant about appearing in public during those interludes. "One night we were having dinner at the Carlyle and I remember being horrified," said Pete Hathaway. "It looked like she had golf balls under her skin. I had no idea why she would even go out."

Such disfigurements didn't even dissuade Rivers from going onstage. "She did a play at the Geffen theater that I helped her with, and she had so much filler you couldn't see her eyes at all, because there was so much built up around her eyes," said Charles Busch. "They were just like dark sockets."

Seemingly devoid of embarrassment, Rivers never lost her enthusiasm for correcting nature's oversights. "I've been the public (lifted) face of cosmetic enhancement since the Stone Age," she wrote. "My abiding life philosophy is plain: *In our appearance-centric society, beauty is a huge factor in everyone's professional and emotional success*—for good or ill, it's the way things are; accept it or go live under a rock...So why not do whatever you can to improve your appearance?"

*Men Are Stupid* offers quite an array of options. Its contents include information on temporary and permanent ways to plump up your lips; wrinkle-erasing treatments that include collagen, Restylane, Juvederm, and other fillers; mole removal; skin resurfacing peels and microdermabrasion; laser zapping and other procedures to deal with rosacea, freckles, broken capillaries, and acne scars; cellulite; laser body hair removal and head hair transplants; "full, mini, and feather" face-lifts; facial implants and revolumizing fat transfers; "boob jobs, boob jabs, lifts, reductions, and all you ever wanted to know about how to tweak a nipple"; nose jobs; liposuction; tummy tucks and "mommy makeovers"; eye lifts for drooping lids and brows; vaginal rejuvenation, butt lifts, and advice on "how to work out your vagina"; and even a discussion of "what the hell happened to Michael Jackson?"

Rivers resorted to many of those treatments, undergoing surgical procedures on her lips, breasts, nose, stomach, brow, eyes, and arms, in addition to getting regular injections of Botox, among other things.

"She had her boobs reduced a couple of times, she had tummy tucks, eye job, lid job, nose, cheek implants," said David Dangle. "She was big on chemical peels, dermabrasion, and fillers. I think she looked extraordinary for an eighty-year-old woman. Her skin looked flawless. She had lovely skin and she kept it nice and tight."

"She was having knee lipo when Edgar killed himself," said Sue Cameron. "She even had her hands done to hold up all the products on QVC. She had a laser peel, and she would add fillers and bleach them."

But no matter what she did, Rivers never felt she was good enough. "She was insecure," said Blaine Trump. "If you said, 'You look great!,' she'd say, 'Oh, come on!' She couldn't accept a compliment. I'd always say to her, 'Just say "Thank you,"' but there was always that insecurity. She never thought she was beautiful."

During the early decades of her career, Rivers resorted to surgical upgrades while still remaining recognizable as the person she had been at the beginning of her adult life. As she explained it, her need to improve her appearance was deeply rooted in her unhappy childhood, when Barbara was the pretty one and their mother scrambled Joan's brain with mixed messages, poking fun at her weight even as she maintained that "looks are not important."

But what scarred Rivers forever was the searing grief of being rejected by men. "No man ever told me I was beautiful," she said. And she never got over her pain at all the times men denied her the reassurance she craved.

"I think she got up every morning and hated herself and said, 'I've got to do something to make myself like myself better,'" said Shelly Schultz. "To invest so much of that in your face, to change your look, you must not have been happy with the way you look. She must have seen something that bothered her or she wouldn't have continued to do that. It must have been looking in the mirror and saying, 'Oh, that's wrong, let me get that tweaked.' Anybody who does that to her face doesn't have good judgment. Jocelyn Wildenstein was inexplicable, but Joan was right up there."

Jocelyn Wildenstein, the wife of art dealer Alec Wildenstein, became the poster girl for horrifying excesses in plastic surgery after undergoing what were rumored to be up to $4 million worth of procedures to make her look like a cat. The resulting face was so alarming that it earned her the nicknames Catwoman and the Bride of Wildenstein, but her efforts to please her cat-loving husband proved fruitless: he subsequently divorced her anyway.

"Joan had a primal wound," said Jesse Kornbluth. "Joan's hunger was to be loved, but no one was going to say, 'I can't wait to fuck Joan Rivers!' I think it was hard for her to get a guy, and I think she cared a lot. Sex is one level of validation of truth in a relationship; it's how you take a relationship's temperature. I think Joan felt great with a cock in her. For Joan, it was the ultimate validation that a guy liked her enough to fuck her."

Rivers always believed that youth and beauty conferred an unfair advantage, but as she got older, she was disconcerted to realize that some women kept attracting lovers, no matter what their age or the state of their face. "She was in awe of my mother, who had four husbands and was such a predator when it came to finding men," said Sue Cameron. "When my mother was around eighty-eight, I remember her complaining she wasn't having enough sex. Husband number four died when she was ninety-two. She had a boyfriend at ninety-five, when she died."

Fascinated, Rivers demanded to know how she did it. "My mother was a geisha," Cameron explained. "She said, 'You have to dumb down, serve him martinis.' Joan wasn't going to do that."

But Rivers's hunger for affirmation involved more than sex or romance; she saw her fixation on appearance as the quickest route to self-esteem. "Looking good equals feeling good," she wrote in *Men Are Stupid*. "I'd rather look younger and feel happy than look older and be depressed."

She credited her DNA for a good complexion, but she was candid about other strategies for improving her looks—and her penchant for turning them into products she could sell.

"My hair is washed every day and done every day," she said. "It's a luxury to have a guy come to my home and do my hair every single day. It takes forever, about an hour, but it's okay because we're good friends. I also put the Joan Rivers fill-in hair powder. We did an infomercial on it and it's our number-one-selling product on QVC. It's un-fucking-believable. For ladies with thin hair, it makes your hair thicker and takes the shine off the scalp. Men use it too. And it doesn't come out in the rain. I needed it for myself and that's how I came up with the idea. I was twenty years old and filling my hair in with a pencil. Again, DNA—my mother had thin hair. So my guy, Raymond Rosario, he does all my hairpieces. I'm very much into pieces. He does a lot of the Upper East Side ladies. He knows how to tease. He can take an old Jew and make her look like a WASP. When Raymond does my hair I can walk into the Knickerbocker Club."

As with the Joan Rivers fill-in hair powder, Rivers was endlessly inventive about monetizing her beautification efforts. She was even willing to turn them into programming highlights by exposing herself for all to see, as Larry Ferber discovered in a memorable episode of her daytime talk show that featured her latest surgery. "The show was so popular she made the cover of *TV Guide*," he said.

Rivers believed it was crucial for an aging woman to look youthful in order to remain professionally viable—and many of her colleagues in the entertainment business saw that, rather than romance, as her primary motive for undergoing cosmetic procedures.

"She knew her livelihood was to look young and hip," said Larry Ferber. "She didn't think she could look like an old lady and do what she did. When *People* magazine mentioned she turned sixty, she was furious."

If aging is inevitable, Rivers never accepted its toll. "I think it made her angry in her later years that women's bodies change," said David Dangle. "That pissed her off. She could wear anything at one point, but then the neck starts to go, and you can't show the upper arms."

Colleagues always admired Rivers for being a trouper who believed the show must go on, but she was so blasé about cosmetic intervention that she sometimes made significant errors in judgment. From 1997 to 2002, she was host of a nightly talk show on WOR Radio, and one night the program director, David Bernstein, was horrified when Rivers arrived at the studio.

"She walks in stiff-limbed, like a robot, and she's orange—her face, her arms, her legs," he recalled. "I said, 'What's happening?' She said, 'I had a little touch-up surgery today.' It was head to toe. I said, 'You can't work,' and she said, 'You hired me to work. You don't take a day off because you're not feeling well.' So she goes on the air, and I don't like what I'm hearing. She's slurring her words—not badly, but enough to catch my attention, and I don't think the show is making a whole lot of sense. So I go to the studio at the very beginning of the break, about ten minutes into the show, and said, 'I'm going to take you off today.' She said, 'Why?' I said, 'Because you're a little off today.'"

To Bernstein's surprise, Rivers was cooperative. "She said, 'If you say I'm off, I'm off.' She was so grateful—'Thanks for saving me, thank you for preventing me from embarrassing myself!' We just switched to a tape. It was the only time I thought, 'She can't be on the air. She doesn't sound like she normally sounds.'"

To onlookers, the results of Rivers's eternal tinkering were highly variable. "I thought at times she looked unbelievably great and at times the surgery had gone too far and she looked like a plastic surgery victim," said Sandy Gallin. "Some people would say she looked like a freak. But sometimes you thought, oh my God, she's seventy-eight years old and she looks unbelievable!"

And yet no matter how much she did to herself, it was never enough. "One day she was at the office of the jewelry company and she said, 'I look old, don't I?'" Ferber recalled. "I said, 'I'm not going to lie to you: you look a little older.' She said, 'No more surgery. I'm done.' A year later, she walked into Primola and I almost didn't recognize her. The surgeon got a little carried away."

In her later decades, that verdict was shared by a growing number of observers. "I ran into her at the airport, and I didn't see Joan anymore," said Dorothy Melvin, who had left her job as Rivers's manager and hadn't seen her in person in years. "The person I knew wasn't there in her face. We were both crying, and I was thinking, 'I don't know her.' I just wanted to scream at her, 'Stop!'"

On the cover of *Men Are Stupid*, Rivers gazes out at her readers with heavily made-up eyes stretched tightly upward on a taut, unlined face.

Her lips are pursed in a pout frosted with iridescent lipstick, her white-gold hair is artfully tousled, her torso is swathed in a white blouse, and her neck is obscured by an enormous collar of crystal jewelry. A woman of unguessable age—she was seventy-six the year the book was published—Rivers looks like some kind of almost-human confection whose entire appearance constitutes a living monument to artifice of every possible kind. She is wholly unrecognizable as the woman with the long, horsey face who appears in photographs taken at the beginning of her career. Gazing at the apparition on the cover of *Men Are Stupid*, it's hard to decide whether it should be stored in a wax museum or a giant refrigerator, lest the fembot cream puff begin to melt and droop before one's eyes.

Makeup was a crucial element of Rivers's look, and her approach evoked an archeologist's painstaking care with the stratifications of an ancient dig. "When I first went to see her about working on the book, she walked into the room in this bathrobe-y caftan with full makeup and hair," said Valerie Frankel. "It was layers and layers of makeup. She would sleep with her makeup on. She took it off once a week, but every morning she put eyelashes on. She bought eyelashes by the crate."

After Rivers died, the gossip columnist Cindy Adams described her friend's preferred style in the *New York Post*. "Joan never went out without the extensions, industrial-strength hair spray, lashes, makeup, perfect lipstick and assorted accessories," Adams wrote. "She flew commercially to California every Thursday for TV's *Fashion Police*. Makeup and hair was done in NY, even at 5 a.m., then reapplied in L.A. She lived the part. Did the job. 'I owe it to everybody to look great. And I never want it to end,' she said."

As for Rivers's wardrobe, Adams added, "She wanted clothes 'over the top.' Glitz and shpritz. Sequins with rhinestones. Paillettes over bugle beads. Nothing was too much."

And Rivers lived up to her vision, no matter how humble the occasion. On what Adams described as "a slow unspecial Monday," she and Rivers went to the Second Avenue Deli. "So what wardrobe goes with matzo ball soup?" Adams asked. "Miss Rivers selected a beaded jacket festooned with appliqued flowers. I said: 'Joan, that's a little much for a half-empty deli.' Joan said, 'Let them learn.'"

Although Rivers was pleased with the image she created, her appearance eventually grew so distorted that some people found it deeply disturbing. "I thought she carried it too far," said Liz Smith. "She became sort of alarming, just looking at her from afar."

"I saw her in recent years at a restaurant, and it was horrific," said Gloria Steinem. "On the television screen, it doesn't look so bad, but in real life it was shocking. She looked embalmed. I had to stop myself from going up and saying, 'Joan, stop it!' I do think it's self-delusion. It's like the frog in the water: it's a little at a time—and then you're cooked. Once you start, it's very hard to stop, because you have to keep doing it."

Others were more forgiving. "I think it made her look better," said the radio and television personality Joe Franklin. "Her eyes looked like slits, but the rest of her face was okay. She feared and hated getting older."

And Rivers's angst was also the source of her success. "If she was a beautiful rich woman, we would not have Joan Rivers; we'd have a pain-in-the-ass debutante somewhere," Bill Reardin said. "We had Joan Rivers because she had to overcome her looks and the fact that she didn't have money."

As surgery, fillers, and injections increasingly froze her face, Rivers also developed a predilection for sartorial choices that constrained the rest of her. When Abigail Pogrebin interviewed her for *Stars of David*, Rivers had just come from the annual luncheon gala to benefit Central Park's Conservatory Garden, which is traditionally attended by socialites in elaborate hats. Wearing a hat with an enormous brim and a skintight fuchsia-colored satin skirt, Rivers conducted the interview while perched precariously on a small ottoman.

Pogrebin was alarmed by how circumscribed Rivers's freedom of movement seemed, from head to toe. Her face was so arresting that Pogrebin found it difficult to focus on what Rivers was saying. "I couldn't get past it; it was hard to sit there and watch," she admitted. "It's like you're hearing a voice that's coming out of a mask. It was a challenge to see the person in there. She couldn't move her face. Everything was immobile."

So was her body. "She couldn't move because of the skirt," Pogrebin said. "She couldn't get in the door because of her hat. Everything was in this frozen state of what she, I guess, would consider perfection. I was surprised by the spontaneity of the interview, because there was nothing loose or relaxed about her body or face. Or her home—this was not a relaxed home."

Pogrebin saw such choices as a manifestation of Rivers's insatiable ambition. "It was part of the voraciousness: 'If this is what it takes, I'll do it, because I want to stay in it! I'm not done!'" she said. "It was about not getting offstage, not being finished, not sitting by the pool. It was about being laughed at and talked about, and being controversial. There's a desperation to not going offstage, to doing dive comedy acts. I felt like there was just a frenzy—but it's not as simple as someone who just needs the adulation. You have to look at the defiance."

Whatever career benefits Rivers derived from her preternaturally youthful face, she paid an ironic price that prevented her from achieving her most cherished goal. For female performers, artificial measures to make their faces look younger can also preclude the professional opportunities they were trying to preserve. Although acting remained Rivers's lifelong dream, she didn't seem to realize that the more she distorted her face, the less castable she was in the vast majority of roles.

"I didn't understand why she had to do that," said the producer Manny Azenberg, who felt that Rivers's choices in the years after *Broadway Bound* rendered her unusable onstage. "She became somebody else after all that surgery. It was so severe it changed everything for me. She could not have come back and played that part, because nobody in the 1940s would look like that. Anybody who looks like that can't be cast as a nineteenth-century woman or as a twentieth-century woman; you could only be cast as somebody who's had thirty-two operations."

But in comedy, the ceaseless interventions may have helped her to remain viable. "There's no question her career wouldn't have lasted the way it did if she hadn't had the plastic surgery," said Rick Newman. "From a producer and manager's point of view, I would say it was smart because it kept her looking young. Show business is a business where your physicality is very important, and there are very few older comedians who continue to be successful. It's a very tough business, and it's just hard to stay up there and sustain your career. Joan didn't look like an elderly lady, even though you knew she was eighty-one and had a lot of work. Yeah, she looked like a freak, but I think it really worked for her; she joked about it, and it kept her in the public eye. I can't think of anyone who has been able to sustain a career the way she did, year after year, decade after decade. She just kept reinventing herself."

Even in comedy, however, women are disproportionately penalized for aging. "It's different for men," said Newman. "Don Rickles is Don Rickles, even now."

Rickles may be pushed onto the stage in a wheelchair, but the men who book talent still favor women they perceive as sexually desirable. "When you're a woman of a certain age, it's infinitely harder than for the guys," said Kathy Griffin. "The stigma still exists that chicks aren't funny, and when you're sitting there with the male heads of this and that who sign the checks, it's easier if you're conventionally attractive. I wish I was twenty-five and hot; I certainly don't have the film and television opportunities that younger girls do. The number of jobs diminishes so greatly that I just create my own. Joan carved out a niche where she couldn't be replaced or replicated."

If Rivers's efforts to look younger were driven by professional goals, some men responded on a surprisingly personal level. "I had a crush on Joan Rivers from the time I met her in 1992," said Jeffrey Gurian, a dentist turned comedian who was nearly a quarter of a century younger than Rivers. "She was very glamorous, very elegant, and I really liked her style. She would come out in a coat made of white feathers; Joan was dressed to the nines. She looked like a queen, and I thought she was beautiful. I used to think, 'I wish I had the nerve to ask her out,' but I'd think, 'She's not going to want to go out with me.' I had to bite my tongue to keep from asking her out."

Gurian, who wrote jokes for Rivers and other comics, admired her endless pursuit of self-improvement. "My sense of the plastic surgery was that she was doing it for herself, not for what anybody might think of her," he said. "She may have started out as a plain-looking girl, but she created a beautiful woman. If that's what you look like at eighty-one, you've got to give her credit."

Rivers's views about superficial appearances could be as paradoxical as her other opinions. She mocked younger performers who refused to accept starvation diets and cosmetic interventions, and yet she could also show surprising compassion for someone else's vulnerabilities. When Jeffrey Mahshie, a costume design consultant who has worked for many fashion designers, appeared on a show that Rivers was shooting at Barneys in Beverly Hills, he was dismayed by the arrangement of the furniture. "I walked in to the set and said under my breath, 'Oh,'" he recalled. "Joan said, 'What?' I said, 'Nothing.' She said, 'No, what?' I said, 'The way the chairs are set up—that's not my best side.' She said, 'I totally understand,' and she had them flip the set for me."

Most stars would not have reacted to a guest's insecurity with such sensitivity, let alone rearranged the set. But this incident involved a man. When it came to other women's vulnerabilities, Rivers alternated between trashing their flaws and making jokes about the social forces that oppress them.

Aging did offer abundant fodder for new material: "The fashion magazines are suggesting that women wear clothes that are 'age-appropriate,'" Rivers said. "For me that would be a shroud."

She joked about menopause, once a topic women were ashamed to mention: "I had a friend going through menopause come to lunch today. Her hot flash was so bad it steam cleaned my carpet."

Some cracks revolved around her cosmetic procedures: "I've had so much plastic surgery, when I die they will donate my body to Tupperware."

Other complaints called attention to the things she hadn't fixed, as when she compared her neck to a turkey's wattles: "I saw what's going on under my chin. I don't want to be the one the president has to pardon on Thanksgiving."

Sagging breasts were a favorite topic: "My breasts are so low now I can have a mammogram and a pedicure at the same time," she claimed.

The indignities of age inspired some unforgettable images: "Old women are suctioned to the ground. Boobs, out of a brassiere, in the morning—it just goes. I use my left boob as a stopper in the tub."

Ever pragmatic, she chose to look on the bright side: "I like colonic irrigation because sometimes you find old jewelry."

No matter how taboo a subject had been, Rivers insisted on dragging it out into the spotlight. "I think she was great for aging women," said Caroline Hirsch. "She talked about things no one would ever say, from her dried-up pooch to dating a man who was crippled. What makes it all funny is that it's true."

Having spent decades making fun of her sex life, Rivers was undeterred by senior citizenship: "My love life is like a piece of Swiss cheese: most of it's missing, and what's there stinks."

"Don't talk to me about Valentine's Day. At my age, an affair of the heart is a bypass."

The aging process simply updated her lifelong shtick about being sexually undesirable: "My vagina is like Newark. Men know it's there, but they don't want to visit."

And: "The only way I can get a man to touch me at this age is plastic surgery."

And: "My best birth control now is just to leave the lights on."

Not to mention: "My sex life is so bad, my G-spot has been declared a historical landmark."

She also mocked her own attempts to remain sexually viable: "You know why I feel older? I went to buy sexy underwear and they automatically gift-wrapped it."

For anyone who knew what had happened to her romantic life, that last joke was particularly poignant. After nine years, Rivers's relationship with Orin Lehman was suddenly blown up by his gift of sexy underwear to another woman, Monique Van Vooren.

"Orin was at the store, and he was putting a charge for Monique on a credit card, and Joan got a phone call from the store, because it was a huge charge," Blaine Trump explained. "That's when it hit the fan. At that point, everything Joan and Orin did, they did as one, and her account handled Orin's accounts. Joan said, 'Monique Van Vooren? Are you kidding me?' Orin swore they were just friends, but she said he was cheating. She said, 'That's it.'"

Adding insult to injury was Orin's choice of paramour. A D-list singer and actress, the Belgian-born Van Vooren had been a fixture on the New York scene for decades—and she was six years older than Rivers. "Joan was so horrified that it was Monique, this face-lifted freak," said Pete Hathaway. "She dropped him like a hot potato. It was literally in one second, like—'That's it!'"

Rivers was as implacable as she was heartbroken. "He cheated on me," she told the *Daily Beast* in 2014. "His accountant called me. The lady he had been seeing had been making purchases using his money. The accountant thought it was me and was calling to tell me to go easy. I finished with him the very same day, which was stupid. He called me every single day for a year, but I was so hurt and so betrayed."

"The shutter came down," said her friend Martyn Fletcher. "She said, 'I would never forgive him. He let me down, and I'll never trust him again.'"

Rivers portrayed the breakup as having been her choice, but there were also rumors that Lehman had tired of the relationship. "I heard both that he dumped her and that she dumped him because he was cheating on her," Larry Ferber said.

In either case, Rivers saw no room for equivocation or ambiguity. "It goes back to being an old-fashioned girl," said Trump. "She really thought they had a fabulous relationship, and when he betrayed her, she said, 'I don't want to spend the rest of my life wondering, who's he doing now?' She traveled so much, she felt she would never be able to trust him again."

But the sacrifice left Rivers bereft. "She was so sorrowful," said Sabrina Lott Miller, Rivers's executive assistant. "She loved Orin to heaven and back, but she was not going to allow him to disrespect her. It was just like, 'I'm going to have to love you from afar.'"

When asked for public comment on the breakup, Rivers was venomous about anyone who might have been seeing Orin behind her back. "I didn't mention names, but I said 'two old European hookers,'" Rivers told Michael Musto of the *Village Voice*. "You know how many women have come forward and said, 'That's me!'? These old, old women who haven't seen a tampon in fifty years, groping for green cards—it's so distasteful…Trust me, this isn't my group. I've never been a felon. When was the last time you came to dinner at my house and I had Eurotrash hookers?"

Rivers's friends were furious about Orin's disloyalty, which even the men blamed on the delusional ego of the aging male. "At eighty-seven, they think they're twenty-two," Robert Higdon said disgustedly. "If someone gives them a wink, they think, 'I've still got it, and I'm going to take a run for it!'"

But Van Vooren may also have been a formidable romantic rival. In 1996, the actor and female impersonator Charles Busch was appearing in an Off-Broadway show called *Swingtime Canteen* when Van Vooren and a group of her friends visited him backstage.

"I had never met her before," said Busch. But he was aware of her name. He once went to a beauty supply store in the theater district to buy the face-lift tapes beloved by drag queens, only to be told, "We're all out—Monique Van Vooren has taken them all."

When Van Vooren visited his dressing room, Busch was "partly in drag," he said, "still wigged and made up in my character as a glamorous 1940s movie actress. I had removed my costume and I was just wearing my belted backstage kimono."

As the visitors complimented him on his performance, Van Vooren didn't say a word. "And then, just as her party was about to leave, she moved in closer and sensuously slipped her hand down my kimono, lightly caressing my bare chest," reported Busch, who is gay.

He was even more startled when Van Vooren whispered a memorable suggestion in his ear. "She purred intimately, in a very Marlene Dietrich manner, 'I would love to get you in a bathtub and bathe you and perfume you like a courtesan in a seraglio,'" he said. "I quickly extricated myself from the situation, but I found her extremely alluring, and if she was even remotely serious, I deeply regret not taking her up on it."

Whatever Van Vooren's feminine wiles, Rivers's friends also suspected that Lehman was suffering from impaired judgment. "I think Joan tried to hide the dementia from people," Higdon said.

Among Lehman's intimates, not everyone saw Van Vooren as the villain. Wendy Lehman was complimentary about his last paramour. "Monique was very nice with Orin when he was getting sick," she said.

But his ex-wife wasn't surprised by his infidelities. "Orin did misbehave," she said. "I think most men think they can have all of it. I think he had different lady friends and this and that. Oh, yes, I think so. Men always have a pattern."

As when Orin and Joan first got together, Wendy Lehman reserved her greatest disapproval for her ex-husband's lapse in appropriate etiquette with Van Vooren. "Orin should not have done that. He should not have made it embarrassing for Joan," she said.

But in a parting shot at Rivers, Wendy compared her unfavorably with her successor. "Monique Van Vooren was much more ladylike," Wendy Lehman said with delicate disdain.

When Orin died in 2008, at the age of eighty-eight, *The New York Times* mentioned his late first wife, Jane Bagley, whom he had divorced many years before she died in 1988, and Wendy, his second wife, from whom he was also divorced. The obituary added that he was also survived by "his companion, the actress Monique Van Vooren."

After Lehman's death, Rivers's eyes welled with tears when she talked about their breakup. "I refused to speak to him," she said. "I was really stupid and silly about it. I regret that now he's dead."

When the *Daily Beast* asked if they had ever reconciled, she replied, "Yes, to a point. I saw him a couple of times. When I see friends finishing a relationship, I say, 'Just be careful. Don't shut every door. What upsets you in July will not affect you that much in November.'"

By then Rivers had decided that any possibility of new romance was precluded by her self-consciousness about the physical ravages of age. Shortly before her death, the *Daily Beast* asked her if she was still interested in dating. "No, the hotel is now closed completely," she said. "I look so bad in a bathing suit I kick sand in my own face. I've reached the point in my life where you think, 'That's it.' You look at yourself and say, 'How can you get a minus-forty-four dark room, pitch-black and then some?' Maybe if Stevie Wonder called, I'd say 'Okay.'"

When the reporter asked if she ever got "horny," Rivers replied, "Yes, but it's not worth it. Old men have too many physical problems. And with younger men, as my mother always said, 'You need to be the good-looking one.' I miss being able to say to someone after a party, 'Can you believe what that person said?'"

The *Daily Beast* inquired whether men still flirted with her. "Yes, but it's the most disgusting thing when they say to an older woman, which I am, 'How's my gal doing?'" Rivers said. "Go fuck yourself. I've had more good times than you'll ever know, so don't you dare patronize me."

In the same interview, Rivers was also asked if she had recovered from what Edgar did to her. "I moved on to a point," she said. "I don't really remember what Edgar was like. I lived with Orin Lehman for eight years, and can't remember what he was like. You remember them but they all become fuzzy and wonderful. You no longer miss their sharp wit; you miss an idea. It changes tremendously, and probably for the better."

Time had given her a philosophical perspective on all of it—the loves and the losses, the triumphs and the disasters. "The only thing that's saving me is my age," she said. "Because I don't care. I've been up, I've been down. I've been fired, I've been hired. I've been broke. What are you gonna do to me? Not like me? I don't give a damn."

Although Rivers worked on her appearance until she died, attracting a man was no longer the goal of her efforts. "She wanted to look like a star," said Martyn Fletcher. "She said, 'The people on the street probably bump into a famous person once or twice in their life. I want them to say, 'She looked amazing!'"

Whatever else might be said about the way she looked, she was indisputably a star—and she knew how lucky she was to have achieved that and so many of her other goals. "I'm not bitching," she said. "If life is 100 percent, I've got 90."

## Chapter Eighteen

# BACK TO THE TOP: FIGHTING LIKE "A RABID PIT BULL"

When F. Scott Fitzgerald died in 1940, he left an unfinished novel called *The Last Tycoon*, a roman à clef about the film producer Irving Thalberg and his rise to power in Hollywood. Although Fitzgerald didn't complete it, the book became famous for a quote that many regarded as the writer's epitaph: "There are no second acts in American lives."

Fitzgerald was only forty-four when he died of a heart attack, but the acclaimed novelist had long since become an alcoholic screenwriter who mocked himself as a Hollywood hack.

Joan Rivers lived nearly forty years longer than Fitzgerald, and it's hard to imagine a more compelling refutation of Fitzgerald's dictum than the second half of her life. She was fifty-four years old when her husband killed himself and she discovered she couldn't find work. What she accomplished over the next quarter of a century would be a stunning achievement for anyone, but for an aging woman in an unforgivingly sexist entertainment industry it was unprecedented.

"She built an empire out of the dregs of her life," said the comedy club impresario Rick Newman. "She was down at the lowest point of her career, and she turned it all around through hard work and talent and endless perseverance. It's admirable—and astounding."

By any measure, Rivers created an astonishing array of successes during the comeback years of her late fifties, her sixties, and her seventies. "She lost everything, and we went from Edgar's death and the complete loss of her career to filling houses, publishing books, doing QVC, the daytime TV show, the radio show, a Broadway show—look at what we did in the thirteen years after Edgar died," said Dorothy Melvin, who was Rivers's manager during that period.

Rivers's second-phase career had many component parts, some of which were new challenges she accepted in response to setbacks. "When she lost the daytime TV show, things were not good, so that's why she had a radio show," said the radio personality Mark Simone.

Her opportunity opened up in 1996 with the death of Barry Gray, the iconic personality at WOR Radio. "I was called into my boss's office, and he says, 'So who's replacing Barry Gray?'" recalled David Bernstein, WOR's program director at the time. "I didn't know, but the one thing I knew was that that wasn't a good corporate answer, so I said, 'Joan Rivers.' I just pulled it out of my ass. I think it was her line, 'Can we talk?,' that made me think, 'Talk, talk, talk!' Joan Rivers was a talker, and I was an admirer and a fan. I knew she was well educated, and I thought she was a remarkable performer."

Bernstein also saw Rivers as the quintessential New Yorker. "To me, New Yorkers always have ups and downs," he said. "Nothing is ever always one way, and you expect that in New York. We're all in the soup together; we all survive this thing together."

Bernstein's boss was dismayed to learn that his program director didn't know Rivers, her agent, or her manager, and had talked to nobody about hiring her at WOR. Bernstein's assistant was equally exasperated. "She said, 'What the fuck did you say that for?'" he recalled. "She knew I was an idiot and had just pulled it out of the air."

Fortunately for Bernstein, Rivers never disdained a potential opportunity, and her QVC earnings gave her enough financial stability to accept less remunerative commitments. Bernstein finally reached her agent at William Morris and explained that he had a two-hour slot to fill for a syndicated national show that went on the air five nights a week, from Monday to Friday. "Joan was doing QVC and stand-up, but I said, 'I can give her a platform she never had before, and she can be really herself,'" Bernstein recalled. "He liked the idea, and we made an appointment with Joan."

Bernstein's pitch was calibrated to address the frustrations Rivers had experienced with her television shows. "I kept harping on how she had never been able to be herself, how everything she had done was monitored and adjusted, but this was talk radio live, and on the radio no one knew what she was going to say," Bernstein said. "She clearly liked to work and wanted to work, but I explained to her that this was not television or movies. I said, 'We'll never be able to pay you what you're worth. But I can give you something different—the freedom to be a live, touchable, approachable personality.' That's what mattered to her."

At their next meeting, Rivers went over her calendar to see how her other performing commitments would affect the radio schedule. "She had a date marked 'Red Ball,' and she said, 'Know what that is?'" Bernstein recalled. "I said, 'A painful condition?' She said, 'I'm taking the job.' My stupid, juvenile humor—that's what made her take the job. She said, 'If I can do my QVC stuff, then pay me what you want to pay me and I'll do it.'"

Ever the eager beaver, Rivers tried earnestly to fit in. "She was grateful to be there, and she wanted to make sure everyone knew she was not a diva," Bernstein said. "Every night she came in with M&M's and coffee for the staff. She liked to keep everyone happy, and she was responsible. She was always on time, and she even worked when she wasn't supposed to be there."

But the results were initially disappointing. "She didn't start out well, because she didn't know radio, and when there's no visual, you have to rely on voice timing and pacing," Bernstein explained. "Joan was doing the show as an entertainer; she was performing, but it was not dialogue from the heart. She was doing *The Tonight Show*, and that's not why people listen to talk radio. They like a person they trust and agree with and think will verify their own opinions. The jokes have to be told differently on radio; you make them part of the story, and tell them in a way that listeners can anticipate where you're going, so they will stay with it. On-stage, she's there with a smirk, but on the radio it's theater of the mind."

Three or four months into the show, Bernstein sat down with her to discuss her performance. "She knows there's a problem, but she doesn't know what it is," Bernstein said. "She was very bothered that she might not be succeeding the way she wanted to be. I said, 'You're not really going in the right direction. You have taken the direction of many great talk shows—you're being serious; you're discussing issues. This would be a great show if it wasn't hosted by Joan Rivers, but everyone who listens and calls in wants to laugh.' I wanted it to be about issues she felt strongly about, but I wanted her to have some fun with it."

Bernstein gave her several technical pointers on how to correct the moments when her performance went flat. Instead of fighting back, she was delighted to get such radio-specific instruction. "She said, 'This is phenomenal—fantastic! I've never heard that before,'" Bernstein reported.

Another breakthrough came when Rivers finally gave vent to genuine emotion on the show. "One night she came in and she had been doused with red paint by the PETA people," Bernstein recalled. "I think it was a fur coat Edgar gave her, and she was mad. I said, 'Go on the air and be mad, but you have to say why.'"

Rivers spent five years at WOR, with her show airing from 7 to 9 p.m. for the first two years and from 6 to 8 p.m. for the last three. She also continued to juggle appearances all over the country, but no matter where she was working, Bernstein found her to be as generous and unpretentious as she was in the studio.

"Only once did I ever see her use the star thing," he said. "We went to Montreal and Detroit, and we got snowed in. The next morning we go to the airport to get a commercial flight, and Joan says, 'Melissa hates when I do this, but if I have to pull the FFF, I will.' She meant 'Flash the Famous Face.' I'm thinking, 'That's about as humble as I've ever heard a celebrity be.'"

After meeting an airline agent who was also named Joan, Rivers—who always carried items from her QVC collections with her to press on strangers—pulled a wrapped piece of jewelry out of her purse, gave it to the other Joan, and succeeded in getting herself, Bernstein, and Dorothy Melvin on a flight.

"There were two seats in coach and one in first class, and Joan said to me, 'You ride first-class,'" Bernstein recalled. "I said, 'No way. I'll never live that down!'"

Rivers's generosity sometimes extended to unlikely recipients. During the summer of 1998, when the news media was preoccupied with the Monica Lewinsky scandal and its impact on the administration of President Bill Clinton, Lindsay Roth was a sixteen-year-old intern at WOR Radio. Rivers's show was on at night, but one day when she was also substituting as an afternoon host, Roth invented a reason to enter the studio during a commercial break.

"I really believe in making your opportunities, and if Joan Rivers is going to be there this afternoon, I'm going to get in there and meet her," said Roth, a bold girl who had been voted class clown in school.

"Who are you and what are you doing here?" Rivers demanded.

Roth was delighted. "It was challenging, but not unkind. It was not malicious at all," she said. "It was like, 'If you have the balls to come into my studio, I'm going to play with you a little.' I felt like, 'Okay, we're on!' She said something to me that was cheeky, and she threw in some double entendre. It was all about Monica Lewinsky. She was not treating me like a sixteen-year-old; she was treating me like any other person who worked there and walked in the door.

"I was quick, so I spit something back that was funny."

When Roth left the studio, a staffer came running after her to say, "Joan wants you!" To Roth's amazement, Rivers asked the sassy intern to appear on her show that night—a split-second decision that may have determined Roth's entire career.

"She gave me an opportunity, and at that moment she gave me a gift: she let me show her who I was," Roth said. "Someone else could have been scared by it, but I didn't shrink. I gave it right back to her."

On the show that night, Rivers bantered with Roth about the Lewinsky scandal. Her line of questioning revolved around what she saw as the central issue: "Would you *shtup* the president if you were in that situation?"

"There's some risk in putting on someone who's sixteen and has never been on the air before, but I didn't fuck it up," said Roth, who later became a television producer and novelist.

They maintained a long and cordial relationship that lasted until Rivers's death, and Roth credits her with altering the course of her life. "She gave me a chance, and if I hadn't taken her bait, my life would have been different," Roth said. "To me, she represented women who were successful in show business. She was a woman who was not playing a part, who was funny on her own, who used her brains. Because she was always kind, she also showed me that you don't have to be an asshole to make it in this industry. And you don't have to stop. She understood that as you get older, it's harder to stay relevant, and sometimes you have to shock the shit out of people."

David Bernstein, who also stayed friends with Rivers after both left WOR, was equally impressed with her efforts to stay relevant as the years went on. "When she got *Celebrity Apprentice*, I thought, 'Man, she's managed to get the gigs to keep her in the spotlight'—and then she wins the damn thing and she's the hottest name in showbiz!" Bernstein said with admiration.

And amazingly, she was. From its shameless beginnings to the vituperative histrionics of its middle to the dramatic ending with a triumphant win by a seventy-five-year-old steamroller, the *Celebrity Apprentice* saga offered the ultimate performance by the quintessential Joan Rivers—and a veritable primer on how to succeed at any cost.

In 2007, after seven seasons as *The Apprentice*, Donald Trump's NBC reality game show started inviting celebrities to compete in order to raise money for charity. The following year, the program went after Rivers as a contestant. "Donald called me and said, 'Would you talk to Joan? We want her for *Celebrity Apprentice*,'" Blaine Trump recalled. "He just thought she was terrific and funny and would add a lot to the show. He knew how competitive she was. When they agreed to have Melissa as part of the package, Joan said yes."

For Joan, that requirement was nonnegotiable. "She had been offered *The Celebrity Apprentice* the year before and she had turned it down," said Billy Sammeth, Rivers's personal manager at the time. "I'll give Joan this: she does still have class somewhere in there. You have to have the skill of a surgeon to go in there and find it at this point, but it's still there. Deep down somewhere is that little Jewish girl from Larchmont whose voice goes, 'No, this isn't right.' She told me, 'I'd rather kill myself than be on *Celebrity Apprentice.*'"

But Rivers's desire to create opportunities for her daughter ultimately triumphed over her aversion to the show, according to Sammeth, who related the saga to Kevin Sessums in a 2012 interview published by the *Daily Beast.* "Just like there's that little girl from Larchmont in Joan, there is another, bigger part of her now that is like Mama Rose in *Gypsy* when it comes to Melissa," Sammeth said. "So she tells me that she will do the show only if they'll put Melissa on it as well. At first they didn't want Melissa, not at all, and it became a pissing match to get her on with her mother. It got from the point of they were dead set against having Melissa on the show to what a great idea to have both Joan and Melissa on the show. I just thought, who all must have turned down this show for them to finally think it was a great idea to hire Melissa Rivers?"

Joan agreed to be a contestant in 2008, but despite the face-saving designation of God's Love We Deliver as her beneficiary, she was mortified when the agreement was finally reached. "So suddenly now Joan had to do the show," Sammeth said. "She said, 'I'm so embarrassed I am actually going to be on this. What am I going to tell people?' It was the week that Paul Newman had died, so I told her just to tell people she was a last-minute replacement for Paul Newman. Of course, by the end of the show they have all gone from being 'celebrity apprentices' to sleep-deprived killers, which is exactly what Trump wants. Trump is really the scum of the scum of the scum."

Kathy Griffin recalled Rivers as citing another motive: doing the show would enhance her ability to book club dates for her stand-up act. "Touring is directly correlated with how visible you are, and she said she did *Celebrity Apprentice* for the network face time," Griffin reported. "She said, 'That's going to translate into selling more tickets on the road.'"

The agreement to include Melissa produced many of the show's most memorable fireworks during season eight, when Joan and pro poker player Annie Duke were challenged to organize competing auctions. The season premiered in March of 2009, and Trump fired Melissa in an episode that aired the following month—which prompted her to storm out of the boardroom, verbally assault her teammates and the production crew, and refuse the obligatory exit interview.

In a recap at the website BuddyTV, the ensuing circus was described as "the celebrity meltdown of the century, when the Rivers women finally went off the deep end."

After clashing with Duke in earlier episodes, Joan had compared her to Hitler, and when Melissa was fired they both blamed Duke and *Playboy* playmate Brande Roderick, another contestant. Melissa reacted with a screaming rant that made her foulmouthed mother look like the Church Lady by comparison. "'They both f--ked me...like two little whore pit vipers! Whore pit vipers!' Rivers shouted at her mother," according to the website Reality TV World. Joan "had previously announced that she would quit the show if the younger Rivers was fired, as she packed her personal items and prepared to leave with her daughter," the account added.

The resulting fireworks included Joan denouncing various opponents as Nazis, scum, the devil, pieces of shit, stupid blondes, and white trash, while Melissa contributed to the insults with "lying f--king whores" and "f--king bulls--t."

"Now, I'm not one to judge, but overreact much? You're on a reality TV show. Don't pretend like you just unfairly lost your job," admonished the reviewer at BuddyTV. "There are plenty of articulate ways Melissa could have fought back, but she didn't say anything of value. Then Joan Rivers has to go off on Annie and Brande, who didn't do anything to demean Melissa in the boardroom. What did the two of them think? They could gang up on Donald Trump on his own show so that they would win without deserving to win?"

Reality TV World pointed out that, while the footage of Melissa's screaming match had been shot more than six months earlier, an April 2009 *New York Post* piece revealed that "time has apparently done nothing to change Rivers's mind about her behavior." "I said what a lot of women have wanted to say to those kinds of girls their entire lives," Rivers told the *New York Post*. "It was like being in high school all over again."

Melissa attributed her conduct to being tired. "Of course you don't ever want to lose your cool...But I'm human. I was exhausted. I just got pushed too far," she said.

"Rivers also attempted to suggest that, given [that] she eventually returned for an exit interview...in which she attempted to spin her behavior, she had somehow ended her...*Celebrity Apprentice* experience 'as a professional,'" Reality TV World added sarcastically.

Although her mother threatened to quit when Melissa was fired, Joan stayed and won the season. But she and her primary antagonist maintained their hostilities to the bitter end.

"In the season finale of the hit NBC reality show, the seventy-five-year-old Brooklyn-born Rivers showed heart, tears, and 'disgust' for Duke," the *Daily News* reported. "'You are a two-faced person,' Rivers told Duke, forty-three, in a live face-to-face smackdown...Duke fired back that Rivers would be fired from most Fortune 500 companies. She was especially miffed that the funny lady called her 'worse than Hitler' and suggested her friends were in the Mafia. 'She's an amazing lady, but she's not a nice lady,' Duke said of Rivers."

She was, however, shrewd. Never one to waste an opportunity to cash in, Rivers made sure her QVC line reaped the commercial benefits of her exposure on *The Celebrity Apprentice*. "They filmed it in the fall and it aired in the spring, but the final episodes are live," David Dangle explained. "We worked out with QVC that Joan would be wearing jewelry and clothing from her collection in each episode. She would come to QVC on Monday morning and sell her necklace she wore in the boardroom."

The response was overwhelming. "We ended up doing about $15 million in sales of *Celebrity Apprentice* jewelry in thirteen episodes," Dangle said. "We let the customers vote for what Joan would wear on her final episode. When she won, QVC broke into its programming. I sold the necklace she wore, and we sold $800,000 of that necklace in ten minutes of airtime. It was just fashion jewelry—black glass beads—but the necklace ultimately sold a million dollars' worth."

*The Celebrity Apprentice* also resurrected Rivers's status as a hot celebrity. "That was when everything changed," said Blaine Trump. "You could barely walk down the street with her. It was incredible to see the difference. Her career had gone through the roof, and it was really hard for her to go out and have a private dinner without ten people coming over to the table."

In their *Daily Beast* interview, Sessums noted that Sammeth's last act as Rivers's personal manager was booking her on *The Celebrity Apprentice*. "I find that show so vulgar I might have considered that a firing offense myself," Sessums said. "Donald Trump has Sonny Bono beat as a kind of used car salesman."

Sammeth saw the unholy alliance between Rivers and Trump as a simple one: both of them were dazzled by his fortune. "She's in awe of him because he has money. Power to her is money," Sammeth said. "But I'll tell you when Donald Trump showed his true colors to me. Joan took me to the Howard Stern wedding. We're at the table with Trump. He goes, 'Joan…'—he's always so serious and humorless—'Joan, you know who would have been a great booking for *Celebrity Apprentice* and the network wouldn't allow it? O. J. Simpson.'"

Rivers's relationship with Sammeth ended badly. "Joan waited until she won *The Celebrity Apprentice* and then fired me," he said. "All during the filming of the documentary, she was loving and civil to me. Five days after she won, I got an email from her business manager telling me I was fired and that she was moving in a new direction…Let's just say that Joan does not wear power well."

Sammeth also served as Cher's longtime manager, and he was eventually fired by her as well. He compared the experience of managing Cher to being a four-year-old holding the leash of a German shepherd. "The dog is dragging you down the street but you think that you're in control because you're holding the leash," he told Sessums. "That's what managing Cher was like."

When Sessums asked him for "canine comparisons" to Rivers, Sammeth replied, "I hate to besmirch the reputation of an innocent dog, but a lot of the time her personality is like a rabid pit bull."

After being fired by both Cher and Rivers, Sammeth retaliated. "He turned around and sued each of them for the commissions he said they still owed him," Sessums wrote in the *Daily Beast*. "He felt more than wronged by their firing. He felt shunned. He wasn't just humbled. He was heartbroken... He sued Cher for 15 percent of the profits of her *Believe* album. But in Joan's case he went one step further. Not only did he demand $179,000 in commissions that he said she still owed him, including 10 percent of the $200,000 she won on *The Celebrity Apprentice*, but also sued her for $2 million, claiming that his character was defamed by the documentary *Joan Rivers: A Piece of Work*, in which, he said, she and the filmmakers led the audience to believe that he just might be a drug addict because of his repeated disappearances for days at a time, which he insisted damaged his personal and professional reputations... He settled each case before they reached the courts."

Sammeth's view of Rivers as a rabid pit bull presents a striking contrast with the Rivers portrayed by the Trump family, a woman who is a stellar example of character and courage.

Donald's daughter Ivanka, who served as a boardroom adviser for *The Celebrity Apprentice*, shares her father's penchant for superlatives. "Joan said often that the show was incredible for her career at that specific point in time," said Ivanka Trump, the executive vice president for development and acquisition at the Trump Organization. "It certainly was a tremendous vehicle for her. She performed tremendously well, and she won."

Ivanka Trump sees the televised competition as the ultimate test of a contestant's mettle. "I think what is amazing about the show is that you can't be insincere under fire," she said. "With the grueling challenge offered by the show, people's character comes out. What you saw with Joan Rivers was tremendous heart, passion, and energy. She had more energy in her pinkie than the other teams did in the whole team. Joan is a very direct person, very head-on, and she wore her emotions on her sleeve. You'd know when she wasn't happy and when she was."

She attributed Rivers's eventual success to her innate ambition, as well as to the ability to strategize that she honed over a lifetime of challenges. "To be as accomplished as she was, you have to be competitive," Ivanka Trump said. "You have to have perseverance, endurance, and incredible natural drive to succeed. You also have to be highly original and view the world through a different lens. I think you have to have an incredible work ethic. It's grueling: many weeks of long days, often fifteen to seventeen hours, very long days that can go till one in the morning. You have to be incredibly versatile in your skill set. You look at who's won that show, and they are people who can take what they learned in life and business and adapt it to unusual situations. There's no career that prepares you for the diversity of tasks on this show, so you have to be incredibly creative. You don't always make friends, but you also have to be charming. She won people over."

Ivanka Trump is also effusive in her praise of Rivers's personal relationships. "She was very friendly with my aunt, Blaine Trump, and she was really central casting of the friend you want to have: wickedly funny, fiercely loyal, incredibly warm—an amazing friend," Ivanka Trump said. "Joan cared deeply about other people, and she was very protective of the people she let into her life. She was a very sincere, honest person."

In describing Joan's experience on *The Celebrity Apprentice*, there are virtually no points of overlap between Billy Sammeth's account and that of Ivanka Trump—except for one. Both acknowledged that Melissa was Joan's major concern from the outset.

"She's an amazing mother," Ivanka Trump said. "Clearly her family was her most important priority, and her daughter came first. She made that clear to everyone."

Long before *The Celebrity Apprentice*, Rivers had become as ferocious in pursuing opportunities for her daughter as she was for herself. But when an unlikely TV gig for E! Entertainment Television came along, neither of them ever dreamed that it would revitalize both of their careers—and transform an entire industry.

## Chapter Nineteen

# FASHION FORWARD:
# TRIUMPH OF THE MEAN GIRLS

When Rivers first started doing red-carpet commentary for televised awards shows, she didn't have any grand ambitions. "I just needed a job," she said.

She began the assignment alone, and then Melissa joined her in interviewing celebrities as they walked into gala events. The gig initially seemed like just another paycheck—and not a particularly promising one. "Joan Rivers started the whole red-carpet thing, but it was desperation that she managed to do this—and to bring along her daughter, which was not easy lifting," said the composer William Finn.

As a duo, Joan and Melissa first hosted the E! Entertainment Television pre-awards show for the Golden Globe Awards in 1994, and they started doing E!'s annual Academy Awards preshow the following year. When Joan began to use Melissa as her straight man, tag-teaming the red-carpet commentary became unexpectedly fun. "We had a great time together," Joan said. "We were the only ones that did it in the beginning, and we came up with the phrase 'Who are you wearing?' and all that stuff."

They also came up with an attitude that was more snarky than respectful, as a headline on a Bustle.com essay by Erin Mayer put it: "What Joan Rivers Meant to the Red Carpet—She Was the First Person to Not Kiss Celebrity Ass."

In truth, their approach was not unprecedented, as Jason Sheeler wrote in an *Entertainment Weekly* piece about Mr. Blackwell, "the original red-carpet bitch." A fashion critic and television and radio personality, Mr. Blackwell created an annual awards presentation called the "Ten Worst-Dressed Women" list, published the "Fabulous Fashion Independents" list, and wrote an annual Academy Awards fashion review.

"Mr. Blackwell felt Joan and Melissa had stolen his act, because they were able to push it that much further," said Sheeler, now the fashion news director at *Departures* magazine.

In doing so, Joan and Melissa never imagined they were developing a magic new formula for televised fashion coverage. "Melissa told me, 'We were just doing what we were doing at home, talking shit about celebrities,'" Sheeler recalled. "Melissa said, 'It's all about the viewer. We're there to say what the viewer was thinking.'"

Back in the mid-1990s, no one foresaw that their on-air jokes about celebrities' dresses would inspire a television franchise—let alone that it would gradually evolve into a major new entertainment genre, spawning an explosive growth in the corollary industries that service it.

"Up until that point, it was just Mr. Blackwell reviewing red-carpet fashion, but in the late 1990s, the convergence of satellite trucks and the twenty-four-hour news cycle happened, and people needed more content," said Sheeler. "People started looking, and people started caring. Joan ripped off Mr. Blackwell's shtick, but she was the big game changer. It was Joan Rivers that kicked models off the covers of magazines in favor of actresses. Before then, actresses were not thinking, 'I have to get dressed up to go out for groceries.' Today it's all about head to toe looks, but back then it was not in their job requirement to be fashionable, and a lot of actresses were aggressively unfashionable. To care too much about clothing would have made you silly. But Joan started asking 'Who are you wearing?,' and the actresses knew there were going to be live news cameras, and the cameras started panning down, and it was head to toe. The fashion companies began to see the availability of revenues, and stylists were dispatched to dress the celebrities, and slowly the supermodel died—and it can all be traced back to the 'Who are you wearing?' moment. Up until that point, nobody gave a fuck."

But when red-carpet commentary evolved into a major attraction, Joan and Melissa created a new E! television show, *Fashion Police*, which became a weekly program in September of 2010. It began as a half hour show in which Rivers and several panelists discussed the dos and don'ts of celebrity fashion, and it expanded to one hour in March of 2012.

Rivers had initially disdained the idea of hosting a series whose sole purpose was to dish about dresses. In a 2010 interview with NPR's *Fresh Air*, she said, "I didn't want to do *Fashion Police* because I thought, 'This is stupid, this is beneath me, who wants to talk about fashion?'"

When she did, the early reactions were often snidely dismissive. "It may come as a surprise today, but 'Who are you wearing?' was once a controversial line," Erin Mayer wrote. "Many believed that people didn't care about the fashion aspect of the red carpet and shrugged off Melissa and Joan's reporting technique, dismissing the famous phrase as shallow and trite. In an interview with *Chicago Sun-Times*, Joan Rivers said, 'When I first said it, *The New York Times* wrote that "this is improper grammar." They also snipped that not only was my English wrong, but that nobody was interested in what people wore on the red carpets at award shows. I thought, "*The New York Times* is wrong!" And I was right.'"

Although Joan cared about wearing stylish clothes, she was never known as a fashion insider with any particular breadth of knowledge—but that didn't stop her from claiming the territory. "Joan made a phony career for herself as a fashion expert, and because she would say and do almost anything, she made a big success out of it," Liz Smith observed. "The wonderful thing about Hollywood is that no one is sincere. Joan brought the whole concept of down and dirty to the red carpet, where the interviews are so idiotic. 'Oh, darling, you look so fabulous!' ('God, did she look horrible!') It's the same thing that goes on in the fashion world."

Rivers's enthusiasm grew as she realized such a show would give her a new freedom to say whatever she thought, no matter how spiteful. "I love [*Fashion Police*] because I don't have to stand on the red carpet and pretend I like something—it goes against everything I believe in—and smile and say, 'Don't you look nice?,' and the next day say, 'She looked terrible.' So I'd rather not have to do the first part,'" Rivers said in a 2010 interview with *Entertainment Weekly*. "It's so great. The next day you can really say,

'The dress is so low-cut, she could've sold advertising on her cleavage.' But if you say that to someone on the red carpet, that's it. You don't get them back, and you don't get any other clients of the PR person back."

At the outset, Rivers's approach to the show was startlingly unpredictable. "The very first year, it was so unscripted it really was like somebody's aunt winging it," said Charles Busch. "Joan was getting everybody's names mixed up. But eventually things became more scripted."

Rivers's spontaneity was particularly refreshing as stylists became de rigueur and celebrities grew less likely to make heinous sartorial choices. "When Melissa and I started, nobody else was doing this and nobody had stylists," Joan told *Entertainment Weekly*. "They all picked their own dresses. It was wonderful because you got to see the good, you got to see the bad. You got to see what a real person thought they look good in. These days they have a stylist and they have a PR person walking with them. God forbid you say something bad about it, they'll never let you talk to them again... If you had to tell everybody, 'Don't you look great!,' then we're not telling anybody anything."

Ever the entertainers, Melissa and Joan managed to compensate for the safe, boring choices of celebrities with their own bitchy commentary. "Some of the one-liners she wrote were so outrageous," said one Hollywood movie director. "There was a picture of a model in some designer dress that was pale gray and pink crepe, and it trailed down with a lot of fabric. Joan said, 'It looks like Clint Eastwood's balls—it's gray and pink and it drags on the floor.' Only Joan Rivers could say that and get away with it."

Alternately ingratiating and insulting, Joan and Melissa terrorized female celebrities with such features as "Starlet or Streetwalker." The attitudinal shift they brought to the red carpet generated so much audience appeal that *Fashion Police*'s popularity proved to have enormous commercial implications, generating money-making opportunities far beyond the show itself. "The comedienne transformed the red carpet into the highly lucrative circus we know today," the *Daily Mail* said when Joan died.

Calling her "a pioneer when it came to the way we report on how celebrities dress," the *Daily Mail* explained that Rivers had "invented a place for the celebrity stylist, paving the way for the likes of Rachel Zoe to guide famous faces in dressing better to avoid her acerbic commentary...This, in turn, sparked the development of a sartorial merry-go-round that is today of huge financial value to fashion brands and the celebrities who wear their designs. Before Rivers started critiquing the red carpet in the midnineties, little attention was given to what celebrities wore to awards ceremonies. But when the already successful comedienne and daughter Melissa were invited to cohost the E! Entertainment Television pre-awards coverage for the Golden Globes in 1994, everything changed...The resulting show was such a success that the pair continued to host the show annually as *Live from the Red Carpet* until 2003, cementing Rivers's position as a red-carpet critic to both love and fear. While her success inspired a whole coterie of TV fashion critics, Rivers always remained the grande dame—largely thanks to the fact that she was never afraid of what the A-list might think if she were to cast a negative opinion. And those opinions were so popular with viewers, they sparked the genesis of the red carpet as a TV event. Indeed, E!'s hugely popular *Fashion Police*, which launched in 2010 and was fronted by Rivers herself, is a direct result of that effect. Now, the right dress can make or break a star's career, and in turn, if a small label is lucky enough to dress a major celebrity for a high-profile occasion, their business can skyrocket. As a result, celebrities can be paid six-figure sums to wear a custom-made gown to the Oscars, and there is an entire industry built around making such partnerships happen."

In her 2010 interview with *Entertainment Weekly*, Rivers said, "I think what's happened in general is [the celebrities have] all got stylists."

But no matter how much professional advice an actress buys to help her create a flawless look, no one can count on being insulated from savage reviews, of her body if not her outfit—and some have spoken out to criticize what such attacks represent.

"There are shows like the *Fashion Police* that are just showing these generations of young people to judge people based on all the wrong values and that it's okay to point at people and call them ugly or fat," Jennifer

Lawrence told Yahoo! CEO Marissa Mayer while promoting *The Hunger Games: Catching Fire*. "We have to stop treating each other like that and stop calling each other fat."

Rivers struck back on Twitter. "WAIT! It just dawned on me why Jennifer Lawrence fell on her way up to the stage to get her Oscar," Rivers said, referring to Lawrence's stumble after being named best actress for *Silver Linings Playbook*. "She tripped over her own arrogance."

She didn't leave it at that. In what might be pop culture's most striking case of the pot calling the kettle black, the eighty-year-old Rivers picked an astoundingly ironic issue as another weapon to attack Hollywood's hottest young actress, who was twenty-three at the time. "She has been touched up more than a choirboy at the Vatican," Rivers told the *New York Post*.

Even when they're not being criticized, some actresses are fed up with the hysterical scrutiny, which often crosses the line into farce. Jennifer Aniston and Julianne Moore refused to put their hands in the E! network's mani cam, which was designed to allow carefully manicured celebrities to "walk" their hands down a miniature red carpet. Elisabeth Moss pretended to flip the bird toward the cameras at an E! broadcast, and Cate Blanchett demanded "Do you do that to the guys?" when a cameraman panned up and down her dress.

"Since I've been strutting the red carpet, things have changed a lot," Blanchett said. "The way women are asked about these red-carpet moments—oh my God, it's just a dress! [People] forget the fact that women are up there because they've given extraordinary performances...Let's not forget the work."

Knowledgeable observers see the significance of larger trends embedded in such spats. "A lot of these actresses don't understand the history of it," said Jason Sheeler. "Joan was tacky, and there was a lot of disrespect among actresses. But some actresses who used to bad-mouth Joan Rivers got cosmetic contracts because of Joan Rivers. So now we're in a world where the stars are being paid hundreds of thousands of dollars to wear a necklace for an hour at the Oscars—and that's the legacy of Joan Rivers. Jennifer Lawrence has a multimillion-dollar contract with Dior for red-carpet fashion, and she only has that today because of Joan Rivers, because nobody cared about actresses in gowns before Joan Rivers. From that moment on, everyone's game was upped, and actresses started being on the covers of magazines."

As Rivers let fly with whatever outrageous remarks popped into her head, her attacks helped to create a skyrocketing demand for the entertainment value of such content, and the show began to build a whole new audience that spanned several generations, drawing in hordes of unlikely new fans.

Chip Duckett, who produced Rivers's live New York shows for many years, compared the television show to the rapid-fire insults of her stand-up comedy act. "*Fashion Police* felt like the first time she was allowed to be that similar to what she did live, and that sort of take-no-prisoners humor on E! brought her a huge audience all over the world," he said.

"Everyone watched *Fashion Police*—all these people you didn't think knew what E! Entertainment was," said Robert Higdon. "I was amazed. The spring of the year before Joan died, we had lunch at Michael's with Deborah Norville and her husband. Joan and I walked back, and all these young kids were running up to her, wanting to pose with her and take selfies. She didn't turn one of them away. What would have taken us twenty minutes took us an hour and a half. At her age, sixteen-year-old girls loved her."

It would be impossible to quantify the cumulative impact of Rivers's nasty commentary, but the trends it encouraged undoubtedly helped to normalize the sexist cruelty that has become standard fare throughout popular culture. In cyberspace as elsewhere, women—both public figures and private citizens, no matter what their age or background—are routinely subjected to vicious criticism of every aspect of their appearance. For female public figures of any kind, venturing an opinion can instantly elicit horrifyingly misogynist threats of rape, dismemberment, and other harrowing forms of death from an army of trolls.

But for Rivers, her unexpected incarnation as America's oldest mean girl paid off in revenue as well as in new fans, boosting everything from her stand-up bookings to her QVC income. "*Fashion Police* was a gold mine for her, because it cemented her authority—she was 'the fashion police,' the lady who said people looked good or bad—and it grew the business," said David Dangle. "It was a great power base, it kept her relevant, and it gave her a younger viewer. When Kendall Jenner is worried about what Joan Rivers is going to say, that's amazing."

Rivers found her latter-day success so exhilarating that scaling back her schedule seemed out of the question. "I would say to her various managers, 'What happens when Joan wants to retire?' And they would say, 'You're joking,'" Dangle recalled.

If Rivers resisted the idea of handing over any torches, she grew increasingly paranoid about the lengthening parade of potential rivals coming up behind her, and she hated it when people asked about the younger women dogging her trail. No matter what her age, she wasn't ready to cede the spotlight.

Some would-be successors found her welcoming. "She could afford to be generous to me, because I wasn't in her league," said Margaret Cho. "I was never a threat to her, because I'm not white and I'm not fancy, so I guess she didn't feel she had to worry, and she was always loving and kind. But she was very jealous of Kathy and very threatened by Kathy, even though there was no reason to be."

"Kathy Griffin is just waiting for me to die so she can have my career," Rivers complained to her intimates.

Many of their peers saw Griffin as champing at the bit, and *Fashion Police* ultimately pushed her into overplaying her hand. When Rivers went into a coma after undergoing an endoscopy, Griffin allegedly began angling to replace her on *Fashion Police* before Rivers had even died.

"Two different people report that, while Joan was still comatose, another comedienne already pushed for her E-TV *Fashion Police* show," the gossip columnist Cindy Adams wrote in the *New York Post*. "Nice, right? No business like show business. Replacements begin when a star coughs."

In a subsequent column headlined "*Fashion Police* a Mess Without Joan Rivers," Adams named names. "Kathy Griffin—talented, able—made a grab for the job while Joan lay on life support. I know. I was right there in her hospital room holding my forever friend's hand…However, Griffin and an E! spokesperson have denied it. Nobody will confirm this, so don't try," Adams wrote.

Others subsequently claimed they did confirm the backstage maneuvering, including the writer Rich Juzwiak, who called Griffin's tactics "jaw-droppingly opportunistic even by Hollywood standards" in a post on Defamer.com. "Kathy literally called E! the day after Joan went into a coma and said, 'If she doesn't make it, I'd like the job,'" Juzwiak's source reported.

Griffin denied everything, telling Larry King that the rumor was "disgusting" and "not true."

"I would never take Joan's job. Joan and I had a different style," Griffin maintained.

"Never" didn't last long; before the year ended, Melissa Rivers, the executive producer of *Fashion Police*, announced that Griffin was joining the show, along with stylist Brad Goreski, who replaced longtime panelist George Kotsiopoulos.

The changes touched off another round of behind-the-scenes drama, with Defamer reporting that Griffin "had George fired because she didn't want the gay guy that had been laughing at Joan's jokes all these years sitting next to her," according to Juzwiak's source. "She wanted to bring her own guy in that would laugh at her jokes, and she knew Brad Goreski because they both had shows on Bravo."

Griffin was also criticized for failing to work as hard as her predecessor. Juzwiak's Defamer story quoted from another blog that noted, "While Rivers is said to have had about twenty jokes written and at the ready for every situation, Griffin apparently thought she could waltz in and 'wing it' and she simply BOMBED. (It's not about being mean, it's about being *funny*.)"

*Fashion Police* tried gamely to position the show as an ongoing homage to Joan, clearly figuring that was its best bet for survival. After Joan died, the program opened with guest panelists swearing a mock oath of allegiance with a hand on the so-called Book of Joan. Melissa, who assumed a regular on-camera role to anchor the show, continued to refer to its followers as "Joan Rangers." A new segment was called "What Would Joan Say?"

But Griffin looked supremely uncomfortable in Joan's chair, and the whole arrangement self-destructed after the show's Academy Awards episode, in which *Fashion Police* cohost Giuliana Rancic said that Disney star Zendaya's dreadlocks made her look as if she smelled like patchouli "or weed." Cohost Kelly Osbourne accused *Fashion Police* of racism and left the show, followed by Griffin. Although they portrayed their departures as acts of principle, some reports claimed that they quit because they were about to be fired.

Griffin spun her exit as an act of feminist solidarity and enlisted Lena Dunham to help craft her farewell. "I do not want to use my comedy to contribute to a culture of unattainable perfectionism and intolerance towards difference," Griffin said in a statement she posted on Twitter and Instagram. "I want to help women, gay kids, people of color, and anyone who feels underrepresented to have a voice and a LAUGH! That has been my platform for decades and my body of work speaks for itself…I discovered that my style does not fit with the creative direction of the show & now it's time to move on."

But the debacle left Melissa seething, and she finally went public with her opinion of Griffin's behavior in an interview with Hoda Kotb at New York's 92nd Street Y in the spring of 2015.

"My biggest complaint was the feeling that she kind of shit all over my mother's legacy in her statement on leaving," Melissa said. "And I know that was not the intentional reading of it, but that's how I felt…by calling the comedy and the style of it old-fashioned. It was like, 'I understand what you were doing, you're trying to save yourself, but don't crap all over my mother to do it.'"

Melissa also acknowledged that she had made a mistake in agreeing to Griffin as her mother's successor. "It wasn't a match, on a lot of levels," she said.

After Joan's unexpected death, the desperate scramble to continue the show had led to strategic miscalculations. "It was a very, very difficult time. I had a lot of conversations with everybody involved," Melissa said.

"It really shows that we were a family. We went back too fast, and when the matriarch died, the sisters started fighting."

As the show's executive producer, Melissa was torn between her filial grief and her professional responsibilities. "It was extremely frustrating, as I had to keep my eye on the franchise and the legacy of it and not get involved in the personal," she said.

But for Melissa, it was all too personal. "I felt like *Fashion Police* was this little jewel, and it was the last piece I had of my mother and I working together. I felt like all these people were so out of control, including the one who made the allegations of racism. They took the last thing I had and smashed it. I felt like I was Humpty Dumpty and I was on my knees gluing it back together."

The mess only served to remind all parties that Joan was unique and irreplaceable. "It never would have happened if she was alive," Melissa said.

But *Fashion Police* continued its tradition of being resolutely unafraid to offend, taking up such pressing topics as "Is camel toe the new booty?" and "What is a 'thighbrow'?" (Answer: "When a woman's bush sticks out from her panties.")

"'Bitch,' 'ho,' 'gold digger'—this is really a tribute to my mother, and those are many of her favorite words," said Melissa. ("Slut," "whore," and "stripper" were also mentioned.)

Since its audience was accustomed to an unpredictable array of eruptions from its star, the show recycled some of Joan's more outrageous on-camera moments to bolster its entertainment value after her death. When the new season started in August of 2015, the first show featured a medley of clips, an inordinate number of which involved Joan rasping out the word "pussy." In a dizzying montage, she also slut-shamed Rihanna, drunk-shamed Snooki, and talked about Betty White's bowel movements.

Men didn't escape unscathed. "This dress reminds me of so many of the men I've dated," Joan said. "Just another six inches would have made it all better."

She also didn't hesitate to name names. "I have seen baggy brown wrinkly things. I have seen Bill Cosby's balls," she said.

309

Ever happy to flout the demands of political correctness, Rivers relished ethnic clichés, as in a discussion of Jennifer Lopez's appearance. "This confirms my theory that Puerto Ricans are just rich Jewish Mexicans," Rivers observed.

Throughout her career, Rivers always worked out new material at small clubs in New York and Los Angeles, many of which no longer exist. During the last five years of her life the incubation process occurred at the Laurie Beechman Theatre, a no-frills room in the basement of the West Bank Cafe, a restaurant on West 42nd Street where Tennessee Williams, Arthur Miller, and Sean Penn used to be regular patrons and Bruce Willis once worked as a bartender. The theater, which opened in 1983, was originally called the West Bank Cafe Downstairs Theater Bar before being renamed for Laurie Beechman, a Broadway singer, actor, and cabaret performer. Rivers's comedic predecessors in that space included Lewis Black, who authored forty plays as the playwright in residence for fourteen years.

"The first night she performed here, she gets offstage and says, 'This is the room I've been searching for my whole life. How's the food? Let's eat,'" said Steve Olsen, who owns the restaurant and theater. "After that, we'd have a shrimp cocktail waiting for her in the wings, and then she'd eat risotto balls and have a glass of wine."

Rivers had scouted the theater as a potential place to work once before, but Olsen liked her much better the second time around. "She was a totally different person from the woman I had experienced briefly twenty years earlier," he said. "She had gone through a complete metamorphosis. She was kind, benevolent, respectful, charitable, and so grateful this time. She used to thank me for having her."

Rivers's arrival at the Beechman coincided with the start of the last triumphant phase of her career. "That was the beginning of her final cycle," Olsen said. "People go in and out of fashion."

And Rivers was back in fashion. "She was with us sometimes six to eight nights a month," said Kenny Bell, the theater's director of programming and special events. "She was doing two a week, and Tuesday and Wednesday were her nights. One time she did a doubleheader for us, of two shows in a night."

No matter how often she performed, audiences bought what she was selling. "There was never an empty seat," said Shelly Schultz.

But Rivers wasn't in it for the profits. "The deal was that she was doing it for charity," said Olsen. "She didn't make a dime here. She gave it all to God's Love We Deliver and Seeing Eye guide dogs for the blind."

Olsen was dazzled by her stagecraft. "She was awesome—unbelievable," he said. "She and Robin Williams were similar; they would take a deep breath and then let it out nonstop for an hour and twenty minutes. Joan was unbelievably funny, and she hit the mark all the time. It was a phenomenal experience having her around. Everyone just loved her."

He was equally stunned by her nerve. "She was an equal opportunity put-down artist, and there were times I'd listen to things she was saying and I just couldn't believe she was saying it—but it was funny," Olsen admitted. "She'd say, 'I love celebrity adoptions when it's a child from the Third World. He's living in a 90,000-square-foot mansion with three pools, hot, medium, and cold, but they want their kid to know where he comes from. Throw him in the closet with a jar of flies and don't close the door—that's his roots.' When I was in the hospital getting a kidney transplant, she sent me a card that said, 'Get well soon. Your staff is robbing you blind. Love, Joan.'"

For more than thirty years, Rivers kept a paper record of all her jokes on thousands of index cards, which she stored in walls of filing cabinets. In the documentary *Joan Rivers: A Piece of Work*, she showed the bank of card catalogs containing her jokes, which she refused to transfer to a computer; if it failed, she said, "you're screwed."

The archive helped Rivers to vary her content in any way she wanted, a process of selection that she always approached as if she were a novice facing her first time onstage instead of a veteran. "I prepare like a crazy lady," she said.

"She had so much material she could flip-flop any way she wanted, but she always had current humor," said Kenny Bell. "She didn't do politics, but she touched every headline. She made jokes about every single thing. There's no person on this earth who was safe. No matter who they were, they were targets."

Before she performed, Rivers taped cue cards on the stage to remind her of jokes she might otherwise forget. "The cue cards were taped all over the floor, handwritten in Magic Marker in big letters on white poster board," said fashion consultant Jeffrey Mahshie, who saw her perform many times over the years. "Some things remained uncannily the same. There was always a section of those older jokes, because that was her comfort zone. She would still do Helen Keller jokes—but there were Kim Kardashian jokes peppered in there. She did add, but she did not throw away."

Sometimes the results struck younger audiences as baffling. "She did an appearance in Dallas when I was at the *Dallas Morning News,* and it was like she grabbed the wrong set of index cards," said Jason Sheeler. "She started doing jokes about Amy Carter being ugly. The audience was all a bunch of gay men, and we're looking at each other and saying, 'Did she just do an Amy Carter bit from 1976? It's 2008, and you still think it's fair to call a kid ugly from 1976—the daughter of a president, who never asked to be in public or on television?' It was low-rent drag queen humor—it was just like, 'I'm going to call you ugly!' That's where she would always lose me, because it just wasn't funny and it wasn't smart. It was bizarre. It was weird."

In writing Rivers's books, her coauthors faced a similar struggle to keep her humor from seeming too dated. "I would try to liven it up with younger celebrities and make it more modern, but she would always go with the Cher joke and fall back on Barbara Walters," said Valerie Frankel, who coauthored *Men Are Stupid.*

Whatever the vintage of Rivers's jokes, she always seemed to win over her audience in the end. "She was hysterically funny," Mahshie said. "This is someone who made my jaw hurt because I laughed so much."

And Rivers enjoyed the hilarity as much as her audience did. "No one in the place laughs more than Joan," said Jason Sheeler. "She was always laughing the hardest. There were some times when she would get to the joke and she could barely get it out, like a kid who can't wait to tell you a story. She said, 'How does Michael J. Fox walk during an earthquake?' Then she walks straight across the room—and she just doubled over."

Because they understood what it took to deliver such an act, industry insiders were even more impressed by Rivers's capacity to sustain her rapid-fire pace onstage. "It was a billion one-liners strung together, and that's the toughest kind of act to do," said Mark Simone. "To remember four hundred disjointed one-liners, rather than do a monologue—there are only a handful of people who could pull that off. I actually thought she was getting better in her later years. She wanted to get better, tighter, faster. I think she wanted to see how good she could get."

No matter how often Rivers performed at the Beechman, her show continued to be a powerful attraction. "It was never advertised, but it was always sold out," Bell said. "The audience was so varied. It was old and young, gay and straight, housewives from Long Island and people from all over the world. Her audience was people from their late twenties on into their sixties, but toward the end the millennials started coming in because they knew her from *Fashion Police*."

Rivers had a simple explanation for why she still went to the trouble of playing small clubs. "She said, 'I think of something funny, and I write the joke. I deliver the joke, and I either fall on my ass or they laugh. And that's better than staying home and watching television,'" Olsen reported. "She couldn't get enough of it."

# Chapter Twenty

## DAUGHTER DEAREST: HOW TO SUCCEED IN SHOW BUSINESS

Even as a little girl, Melissa Rivers—whose original name was Melissa Rosenberg—never got the chance to be an ordinary kid. Growing up with Joan was like being sent to showbiz boot camp, and the lessons started early.

As conceptualized by Joan, the curriculum seemed designed to cultivate a precocious cynicism rather than to preserve any childlike innocence.

Some parents strive to help their children discover their own unique inner voice, and they pursue that goal by encouraging their offspring to pay attention to what they feel instead of worrying about what the rest of the world thinks. But for the child of Joan Rivers, the training in how to deal with life was guided by a cold-blooded focus on manipulating public perceptions. The ultimate goal was to create a favorable image, no matter how fraudulent it might be.

The fundamental nature of that approach was encapsulated in an anecdote that Joan's longtime manager Billy Sammeth told Kevin Sessums in their *Daily Beast* interview.

"I once took Joan and Melissa to the Palm Court at the Plaza when Melissa was around seven or eight years old," Sammeth said. "Two old Jews came up to Joan that day. They said something to Joan in Yiddish. Melissa was roaming around the room like a little Jewish Eloise, and Joan calls her over. Melissa traipses over and Joan told the old Jew to repeat what he had just said in Yiddish, and Joan and Melissa fell all over each other hysterically laughing. My eyes were falling out of my head thinking how smart this little girl is to already know Yiddish. So after the old Jews walked away and Melissa goes off to pretend she's Eloise, I turn to Joan and say, 'My word, Joan. I'm so impressed. Melissa knows Yiddish?' Joan goes, 'No. She doesn't know Yiddish and I don't know Yiddish. But anybody who's speaking to you in Yiddish is telling you a joke, so you laugh at the end of it. I've taught her that much so nobody will think she's stupid.' That was Joan in her fifties. She's almost eighty now and she still treats her daughter the same way."

But it wasn't enough to mold Melissa's behavior; Joan also started early in trying to remake Melissa physically, as she had done with herself. "She made her have her nose done," said Sue Cameron. "She wanted Melissa to be pretty, and by Joan's standards, she was also getting Melissa ready for a man."

Despite her parents' obsession with show business, Melissa was their top priority throughout her childhood. "Melissa was the focus of everything," said Dorothy Melvin. "Joan's career was the most important thing, but family and Melissa would never suffer because of The Career. Melissa was Daddy's girl, his little pride and joy, and with Edgar, she could do no wrong. He was crazy about her, and she was crazy about him. It was a happy household."

But it was far from an ordinary one. "When Melissa turned thirteen, she didn't want a religious ceremony, so they gave her a very formal lunch at L'Orangerie, where the first course was eggs in eggshells with caviar, followed by poached salmon with pureed sorrel sauce and cucumbers," said Cameron. "When Joan got up to give the toast, she said to two hundred people, 'I guess this is the right moment to tell you, Edgar—Melissa isn't yours.' People were screaming with laughter."

While she was growing up, Melissa experimented with various passions that might have provided an alternative to her mother's world. As a child, she was a dancer and an equestrienne who competed on the show circuits. As a student, she was an intelligent Ivy Leaguer who graduated from the University of Pennsylvania with a degree in European history.

But when her father committed suicide, that trauma shaped her life forever. "I have massive abandonment issues," Melissa said in a 2005 interview with her mother on CNN's *Larry King Live*. "I suppose they're getting better, because I can now talk about the fact that my big fear is, everybody leaves. Nobody's word is good. The last thing my father said to me was, 'I will see you tomorrow.' You know, that's the great lie of my life—the great lie told to me by the most important man in my life. 'I will see you tomorrow' was the last phone call we had. Obviously, you know, I didn't, so I have a lot of abandonment issues. There was a lot of anger. What's so alarming for me about suicide is, I really feel that the victims are the ones that are left behind, because it destroys your relationships, or can destroy, if you allow them to, with the living, with the survivors. Our relationship was almost destroyed because of Daddy's suicide. And that's something I think people don't talk about enough. The first thing you want to do…is point fingers and say, 'What if? If only. If you had done this, if I had done that.' And I think you get a bad case of what I now call 'the what-ifs,' or 'the if-onlys.'"

During the estrangement from her mother, "something terrible and traumatic happened to me," Melissa told *People* magazine in 1993. According to the magazine, "At a particularly vulnerable point—three months after her father's suicide—she began to date a fellow student at Penn and suddenly found herself 'in an abusive relationship.' At the time, she says, 'I was so far gone [emotionally] that I don't know if I was allowing myself to physically feel the pain.' She stayed with him through two ugly incidents—Melissa refuses to discuss the specifics—but the third time, she says, was the last straw. 'I realized that I had a lot more to offer than to have someone hit me,' she explains, 'and I just said, "This is it." It made me realize what I had—and the thing I had and will always have is my mother. She was right there for me.'"

The story went on, "Joan remembers Melissa's phone call well. 'She called me and said, "Mother, don't worry, he pushed my face into glass, but I didn't cut my eye." I wanted to take that son of a bitch and kill him, but I couldn't say that to her.' Nor could she tell Melissa not to go back to him. 'But I asked her to remember that if she did, she was opening a door to that kind of abuse for the rest of her life. This was her battle. I allowed her to make the choice.'... And Melissa was grateful. 'She didn't condemn me. She never asked me, "How could you have gone back to him?"' she says. 'She just said, "Okay, this is the situation. Let's deal with it."'"

When Melissa graduated from the University of Pennsylvania in 1989, Joan gave one of the commencement addresses. "In the middle of the speech, Joan broke into tears as she told the crowd, 'I'm so proud of my daughter,'" *People* reported.

The year after graduation, Melissa abandoned the tainted name of Rosenberg, adopted her mother's stage name, and embarked on her perpetually fraught journey as Joan's Mini-Me, the identity that evolved into her real career. Melissa Rosenberg was the tortured child of a man who killed himself in a hotel room a few blocks from his daughter's college residence in Philadelphia. Melissa Rivers became the hardworking, hardboiled successor to as much of her mother's formidable legacy as she was able to pass on—which turned out to be a great deal.

"Melissa wanted to be her own person, but Joan wanted her daughter to be with her, and once Melissa made the decision to go into show business, Joan was going to do everything she could to help her," said Dorothy Melvin. "Melissa is a sharp girl, and she's had a great education, but I think Joan pushed her more than Melissa might have wanted to be pushed. When it comes to family, Joan was very controlling."

In the years since then, Melissa has worked as an actress, a producer, and a television host who succeeded her mother as the anchor of *Fashion Police* in addition to serving as the show's executive producer. David Dangle now runs Joan's clothing and jewelry company and sells its products on QVC, but Melissa is co-CEO of the family business. Eight months after her mother's death, she also became an author when *The Book of Joan: Tales of Mirth, Mischief, and Manipulation* was published—just in time for a Mother's Day sales blitz.

Melissa's résumé includes appearances on such television shows as *Beverly Hills, 90210* and her costarring role in the infamous docudrama *Tears and Laughter: The Joan and Melissa Rivers Story*. Melissa also costarred as her mother's straight man in the on-air red-carpet commentary they pioneered in the early 1990s. Other credits include hosting the E! network television specials *Oh Baby! Melissa's Guide to Pregnancy* and *Oh Toddler! Surviving the Early Years*.

More recently, Melissa was a cocreator and coproducer of *In Bed with Joan*, which featured her mother interviewing another celebrity—Kathy Griffin, Kelly Osbourne, Margaret Cho, and RuPaul were among the participants—in Joan's bed for a YouTube Web series that uploaded a new video weekly.

But no matter what she did, Melissa was always dogged by the rude question of whether she was even suited to such a career. "She doesn't have the talent," said a friend of her mother's—one among many who expressed that view in virtually the same words.

Not wanting to be cruel, most won't say such things for attribution. An exception is Billy Sammeth, Joan's former manager, who is overtly derisive about Melissa. "Well, she's not my favorite girl for a lot of reasons. Mainly because I respect people with talent," he told the *Daily Beast* in 2012. "I'm not so sure, if you're talented yourself, you take on your mother's stage name. It's not Liza Garland, for God's sake. But Joan has gotten away during this phase of her career with bringing Melissa along with her. 'It's you and me, kid,' she seems to be saying."

Some friends wish Melissa had felt free to find her own path in life. "If I could go back and help Melissa make decisions, I would have told her, 'I don't know why you're trying to follow in your mother's footsteps—your mother is a complete original, and there's no way for you to hold a candle to her, so why are you even going in that direction?'" said Andrew Krasny, Joan's former assistant and a friend of Melissa's in their youth. "She should have been a lawyer or a doctor, but Joan wanted her nearby, and she wanted to be close to her mother, and this was a way she could. I'm sure Melissa wanted to prove to her mother that she was talented. Joan was very aware of the vicious side of the business, and she knew that the one person who would never screw her was Melissa, so why wouldn't she want her on board?"

Other observers believe Melissa doesn't get enough credit for her contributions, particularly on the red carpet and *Fashion Police*. "Joan was the comic, but Melissa was the brains behind everything, handling the business," said Jason Sheeler, the fashion news director at *Departures*.

Joan was always furious when anyone questioned Melissa's qualifications. "She really and truly loved her daughter," said the television and radio host Joe Franklin. "Somebody would say something stupid, talking about nepotism and how her daughter wouldn't be working if she wasn't Joan Rivers's daughter. You couldn't deny that, but she defended it. I actually saw her yell at such a person. She laced into that lady: 'How dare you!' She was a scrapper, and people feared her. They thought she was like a tiger who would bite them. They were afraid of crossing her."

That embattled stance characterized Joan's maternal approach from the outset. Melissa grew up in a household where the family ethos was: Fuck them before they fuck you.

Melissa tried valiantly to live up to her mother's expectations, but she often seemed as miserable as if she were trying to fit into the wrong-size shoes. "Melissa used to look so uncomfortable on *Fashion Police*," said the composer William Finn. "That was the only time I was annoyed with Joan. I felt that Joan was pushing her daughter to do something she wasn't equipped to do."

And Joan pushed with a ferocity that sometimes seemed deranged. "On *Celebrity Apprentice*, she was a mother bear protecting her cub," said Finn. "When someone did something mean to Melissa, Joan became unbelievably vitriolic."

But even when they disapproved, many observers also felt compassion, both for the ferocious mama bear and for the long-suffering daughter. "Joan was very appreciative of whatever I did to help Melissa," said Liz Smith. "Melissa was a nice, sweet girl, and I just wanted to be nice to her. I feel sorry for those kids; if the parents are stars, they can never come up to the parental stardom. I didn't know whether Melissa had any talent or not and didn't care, but I felt that Joan was always forcing her to have a career, whatever it was."

Unfortunately, Joan's efforts created the widespread impression that Melissa lacked the ability to succeed on her own—a judgment that elicited snarky comments from friends and foes alike.

Some of the mother-daughter collaborations were universally considered to be cringeworthy. When Joan created *Tears and Laughter: The Joan and Melissa Rivers Story*, friends and colleagues recognized that the movie would reflect badly on both of them, and its timing was also harmful for the Broadway run of *Sally Marr*. But Joan was desperate to help Melissa, and nothing else mattered. "Joan said, 'Missy needs the tape!'" Lonny Price reported.

At the time, Joan had another powerful motive for wanting to work with her daughter: they were estranged, and Joan wanted desperately to repair the rupture. "Melissa blamed Joan for Edgar's death, and Joan didn't know how to undo the anger," said Rivers's WOR colleague David Bernstein.

But she cared more about healing that breach than anything else. "Her biggest concern was reestablishing the relationship with Melissa," said Larry Ferber. "It was the only thing in Joan's life that was more important than her career."

Melissa was always the core of Joan's emotional life, and that never changed. "Melissa was her world, and she was a very nurturing mother," said Martyn Fletcher, who spent many holidays with them. "She would phone her all the time, and she would always try to include her in everything."

Joan made jokes about the frequency of her phone calls, which seemed excessive by the standards of most adult offspring: "My daughter and I are very close. We speak every single day and I call her every day and I say the same thing: 'Pick up, I know you're there.' And she says the same thing back: 'How'd you get this new number?'"

But Joan didn't think it was funny when other people joked about her attempts to shoehorn Melissa into every gig. Throughout the entertainment industry, people who wanted to work with Joan learned that she would pull every possible string to make Melissa part of the package—just as she had in refusing to go on *The Celebrity Apprentice* until the show agreed to take Melissa as well.

Mark Simone had similar experiences when booking Rivers for his radio show. "She would say, 'I've got to have Melissa on with me,' which nobody really wanted," Simone reported. "Melissa couldn't give you funny one-liners."

Some friends nonetheless believe that Melissa has paid her dues and earned those opportunities. "At risk of her own career, Joan added Melissa to everything she did, in order to give her game," said Sue Cameron. "It was very hard for Melissa. She knew very well that Joan was forcing her on people. But along the way, Melissa developed. She became very skilled. She's a very good producer, and she's come into her own with the acerbic wit, and she's really good. She now legitimately deserves to be on *Fashion Police*."

Other friends emphasize the benefits of having a parent who cared so much. "Joan was an amazing mother," said Blaine Trump. "Not only did she help with Melissa's career, but she gave Melissa a tremendous sense of self-confidence. Her mother did the opposite with Joan. I think she really wanted Melissa to understand that she could do anything. She worried about Melissa, and she always tried to give her guidance. I think Joan really felt her wisdom was something Melissa could benefit from, and she felt Melissa didn't get it. I think it started with the estrangement. The wounds heal, but there are scars."

But the downside of such helicopter parenting was that Melissa never really grew up in her mother's eyes. Joan always wanted to control what her daughter did, and that led to conflict. "There was a lot of disharmony, in terms of the choices Melissa made," said Andrew Krasny. "But she was able to be the best mother she could be, and to genuinely care about her daughter, who is entitled and rebellious and not as talented as her mother. I think Melissa did the best she could do."

Some observers think Melissa actually feels superior to her mother. "Joan has made her what she is, whatever that is. Joan Rivers's daughter, I guess is all, finally," said Billy Sammeth. "And Melissa is almost angry that she is Joan Rivers's daughter. Her attitude is, Joan is the embarrassment— she is the talent."

In "TV's Queen Bitch," a 2003 essay for Salon that described Joan as "unbelievably vile and crude," Carina Chocano noted the "seething familial resentment" that characterized many of Melissa's interactions with her mother on *Fashion Police*. Chocano suggested they launch a new reality show so "you'd get the unadulterated pleasure of watching Melissa gamely try to keep things clean, vapid, and obsequious as her mother lets fly increasingly revolting and mortifying remarks just so she can watch her daughter's face twist into a mask of pure hatred."

If Melissa was embarrassed by her mother, she never rejected her perennial roles as sidekick and dependent. Joan continued to feel responsible for supporting her daughter, even in middle age. "For many years, Joan's obsession was, 'I've got to keep working—I've got to make sure Melissa is taken care of,'" Trump said. "She said, 'Melissa doesn't have a husband—who's going to take care of her?' She never wanted Melissa to be worried about money—and with Joan, the sky's the limit."

As the family breadwinner, Joan didn't seem to realize that Melissa might be able to support herself—if not at the level to which she was accustomed. "She just wanted Melissa to be self-sufficient and not to have to depend on anyone," said Sabrina Lott Miller, who still works for the family.

But Melissa grew up with private schools and designer clothes, mansions and yacht trips—not to mention innumerable opportunities she enjoyed because of her mother's achievements instead of having to earn them on her own. "Melissa's been extremely well taken care of," said one friend. "She sort of lives in a fool's paradise."

Such privilege reached its apotheosis in Melissa's wedding—an extraordinary event even by the standards of the Gilded Age proclivities of the one percent. Over the course of a lifetime, Joan created a lot of elaborate productions, including her opulent homes and her lavish parties. But nothing ever came close to the wedding she gave her thirty-year-old daughter in 1998.

For the impatient mother of the bride, it had been a long wait. Melissa, who was working as an on-camera host for E! Entertainment Television, lived in Los Angeles, where "it's hideous to be single, because all the guys want to be with models and actresses," she said. "I can't compete with all those skinny, beautiful, tall people. I once went for two years without a date. I held the record. I was also a full-fledged psycho magnet. If there was a guy who would really be bad for me in a room, you could blindfold me and spin me around, and I would walk straight toward him."

A passionate equestrienne who spent her weekends competing as a jumper, Melissa met her future husband, a horse trainer named John Endicott, at a horse show in Palm Springs. She was immediately enthralled. "He was so sweet, so unaffected," she said. "It wasn't like, 'I'm an electrician, but really what I want to do is write a screenplay.' You can't get away from that in L.A."

A few months after they got involved, Endicott moved to Los Angeles and the couple started living together. "It just happened," Melissa said. "It was the old, 'You can stay with me until you find your own place.' It was never found."

They got married five years later. When Endicott flew to New York to ask Joan for permission to marry Melissa, Joan said, "What took you so long?"

Endicott had some appealing attributes. When Lois Smith Brady wrote up the wedding in the Vows column of *The New York Times*, she described him as looking "like the actor Emilio Estevez, with eyes as blue as little swimming pools."

But for Joan, what mattered was that her daughter had someone she could count on. "I wanted so much for Melissa to settle down, to find an anchor," she told Brady. "Family is everything. Everything. It's a rough, rough world out there, and you need your own little army."

Joan knew what it was like to have such an anchor, and she knew how it felt to lose it. "It was very important for her daughter to have someone to call when she landed in another country, because that's what Joan wanted for herself," Cameron explained. "In Joan's mind, it was for Melissa's own good."

So were Joan's ideas about how her daughter's nuptials should look—something she had fantasized about for years. "She will have a dream wedding," Joan told *People* magazine in 1993. "It will be very elegant and very formal. Black tie."

Melissa had other ideas, according to *People:* "'Oh, no,' counters Melissa. 'I'd rather run off to Vegas—that chapel near the Riviera Hotel.' The two laugh. They've played this song before. 'She doesn't have a choice,' Joan insists. 'It'll be something like the Metropolitan Club. Lester Lanin will play "You're the Top," and we'll two-step around the room.'... Melissa sighs and shrugs. 'There are some things in life I'm resigned to,' she says lightly."

When Melissa finally got married, Joan had her way. "This wedding is going to be romantic," she said. "I want it to be a fairy tale. No reality. I don't want one of those modern weddings with a Japanese flower and a candle on each table. This is over the top."

That didn't even begin to describe it. Published reports of how much money Rivers spent on the event ranged up to $3 million. "Joan wanted a royal wedding, a royal St. Petersburg wedding—Anastasia getting married," said Cameron.

In realizing that vision, Joan's friends suspected that her fantasies had won out over her daughter's. "Melissa would have been happy just eloping, but I think Joan was caught up in making it a big showbiz thing," said Dorothy Melvin.

Rivers commissioned the floral designer Preston Bailey to re-create a winter wonderland from *Doctor Zhivago* with a hundred tall white birch trees and thirty thousand white roses, hydrangeas, and lilies of the valley. The results were awe-inspiring even by the standards of the rich, famous, and jaded.

"The wedding was absolutely un-fucking-believable," said Pete Hathaway. "We walked in through a moonlit snow-covered birch bower, and it was so staggering I felt as if I should have been onstage at the Metropolitan Opera. Where the snow had drifted into the crotch of a tree, that was done with white roses and white orchids. I had never seen so many flowers in my life. I happened to be walking in at the same time as C. Z. Guest, and she turned to me and said, 'I have been to a lot of parties with some of the richest people all over the world, and I have never seen anything like this.'"

If anyone needed a reason for such extravagance, Rivers cited her heritage. "She was a Russian descendant," said Larry Ferber. "It was gorgeous. It was so over the top it was ridiculous."

"On the stairs leading up to the ballroom, there was a Russian soldier in a black fur hat holding a plate of hors d'oeuvres, mostly caviar," said Cameron. "Joan hung pictures to make it look like the Hermitage. They were projected all around the ballroom."

The actual ceremony was presided over by a rabbi, a minister, and a chaplain from the United Nations. The bride wore a Vera Wang gown of ivory duchess satin and velvet, adorned with gold embroidery and Swarovski crystals and accented with a sable muff. The mother of the bride wore a champagne-colored ensemble with sable trim, and she made sure she got her own moment in the spotlight.

"The doors fly open and there's Joan, dressed to kill, walking in to 'Big Spender,'" Larry Ferber said.

A flamboyant number sung to a striptease beat by the dance hall "girls" who taunt the paying customers in the Broadway musical *Sweet Charity*, "Big Spender" was sung at Melissa's wedding by the New York City Gay Men's Chorus as Rivers sashayed down the aisle. "Only Joan could have pulled that off," said the writer Annette Tapert. "It was a star turn."

After the ceremony, the wedding guests dined on lobster, Angus beef, and a five-tiered Sylvia Weinstock carrot cake in the Plaza Hotel ballroom, attended by footmen in powdered wigs and nineteenth-century French regalia. "Joan brought in china and crystal for five hundred people, because she didn't like what the Plaza Hotel had," Dorothy Melvin reported.

"She got nineteen hundred ruby, emerald, and cobalt glasses—very Czarist Russia," said Pete Hathaway. "Joan was in her element."

As for her advice on marriage, Rivers shared with *The New York Times* the wisdom she'd imparted to her daughter: "If it's a choice between cooking or cleaning or looking good, go get that facial. No man ever made love to a woman because she kept a clean house."

Despite all the hoopla, few believed the marriage would work. "Every single person at that wedding was thinking, 'This is never going to last,'" said Pete Hathaway. "The one thing they had in common was horses."

But Joan had her hopes. "She wanted Melissa to live happily ever after," said Sabrina Lott Miller. "Because of her upbringing, she wanted that for her daughter. I think she still felt like there was a chance."

Two years after Melissa got married, she produced the grandson her mother adored, who was named Edgar Cooper Endicott as an homage to the grandfather he never knew. For Melissa, that was a redemptive act: she wanted "to reaffirm my father's life by naming my son after him," she said.

Three years after that, Melissa and her husband were divorced, and the family unit became Melissa and Cooper and Joan, who commuted to Los Angeles and lived with her daughter and grandson part-time. Cooper was also recruited as a character in such family productions as the reality show *Joan & Melissa: Joan Knows Best?*

"Anything with Cooper and Melissa gave Joan a great deal of happiness, but with Cooper especially, she loved teaching him and opening his eyes to the glories of the world," said Blaine Trump.

Joan made a regular tradition of taking Cooper on trips, and one of their annual destinations was a dude ranch in Wyoming. "She hated the boots, she hated the plaid shirts, she hated the jeans, but she wanted to make sure Cooper had those memories," Miller recalled.

Although Cooper is growing up in privileged circumstances, his mother absorbed the family ethos of constant striving. The second-generation offspring of America's rich and famous often fail to emulate their parents' penchant for industry, but Melissa always earned respect for adopting her mother's work ethic.

The reviews of her behavior have been somewhat more mixed. "Melissa was not as nice as Joan," said one television producer who dealt with them both. "She was clearly more self-centered and entitled. Whereas Joan was lovingly abrasive, Melissa was unlovingly hostile. Children of celebrities like that have this barrier around them. When you watch her on *Fashion Police*, she seems unsettled and angsty, not happy with things."

Although Melissa did a creditable job of playing her mother in *Joy*, the 2015 David O. Russell movie about Miracle Mop inventor Joy Mangano, no one who knew the family saw Melissa as a latter-day incarnation of Joan.

"They were so different they were like chalk and cheese," said Blaine

Trump. "Joan thought of Melissa as a surfer girl; she loved the outdoors. Melissa was always a California girl with no interest in New York. Can you see Joan on a surfboard, swimming?"

After building a happier life for herself in New York, Joan retained sour memories of Los Angeles. "Joan always said about that community, 'They don't stab you in the back—they stab you in the chest,'" Trump reported.

Joan had been deeply imprinted with her mother's aspirations, and when Melissa grew up, Joan was pained by the gap between her daughter's taste and her own. "I remember going to Joan's house once for dinner and everything was so incredible, and she said, 'Who's going to want my finger bowls after I'm gone? Melissa's not going to want them. She's not interested in any of my stuff,'" Trump recalled. "They were very different. Joan always wanted to redecorate Melissa's house."

At Melissa's 5,000-square-foot house in the Pacific Palisades, "it's a very California lifestyle," Pete Hathaway said. And Joan's relentless bullying drove her daughter crazy.

"Joan used to stay at Melissa's when she was in L.A., three days out of every week," the *Los Angeles Times* reported. "They filmed the majority of their WE TV reality show, *Joan & Melissa: Joan Knows Best?*, there, as well as Joan's Web series, in which the comedian conducted interviews with celebrities from her bed. Joan complained about Melissa's house all the time—especially her bedroom, which she once compared to the nicest room at a Holiday Inn. Unlike Joan's New York City penthouse, an outrageously luxe space fit for Marie Antoinette, Melissa's home feels more lived-in. It's more shabby-chic than eighteenth-century France. There's a lacrosse net for Cooper in the backyard and a collection of snow globes in the kitchen."

Joan seemed to regard her daughter's adulthood as an annoying development that demanded unwelcome adjustments from a mother who was not willing to make them. It was one thing to recognize that your daughter had grown up—but quite another to let her lead an autonomous life.

Negotiating the contested territory between their individual lives—deeply enmeshed despite the three thousand miles that ostensibly separated them—would remain a lifelong project. Even when Melissa was herself a middle-aged parent, Rivers remained a mother who came into her daughter's home and—without even consulting Melissa, let alone asking permission—rearranged the furniture as she saw fit.

Such antics struck many observers as outrageous. "On *Joan Knows Best?*, when she lives with Melissa, she redecorates Melissa's house while she's gone," said fashion consultant Jeffrey Mahshie. "How did she not know Melissa is going to be pissed? Nobody really does that. At least Joan had a sense of fun. She saw entertainment value in everything. If it was going to entertain us to set Melissa up on a date, she was going to do it, even if it would irritate Melissa, because Melissa would get over it. Joan wasn't going to change."

Her exasperated daughter was eventually forced to accept the same conclusion. After one argument, Melissa accused her mother of not respecting her boundaries. The next day, Rivers announced that she had thought seriously about this. Momentarily excited, Melissa imagined that her mother was finally going to concede Melissa's right to self-determination.

That was not what her mother had decided, as Melissa explained in her memoir, *The Book of Joan: Tales of Mirth, Mischief, and Manipulation.*

What Joan actually said was, "Melissa, I acknowledge that you have boundaries. I just choose to not respect them."

Boundaries didn't survive on camera either. Both mother and daughter seemed endlessly willing to turn private moments into public fodder for one of their reality shows.

"Did you see the episode of *Joan & Melissa: Joan Knows Best?*...of Joan smoking pot and getting high?" Kevin Sessums said to Billy Sammeth in their *Daily Beast* interview. "Melissa had to go 'rescue' her and drive her home and stop for cheeseburgers because Joan had the munchies so bad."

Joan's boundary issues were equally apparent when it came to Melissa's sex life. "Some parents never talk to their children about sex. My mother never stopped," Melissa said.

She even tried to turn talk into training. "Joan would call and say, 'I have to find someone to teach Melissa how to give a blow job. She has to learn how to keep a man,'" Cameron reported.

Rivers was deeply impressed by long-standing rumors that Kris Jenner encouraged—or even masterminded—the sex tape that helped launch Kim Kardashian's fame and the family's fortune. "I begged Melissa to do a sex tape," Joan said. "I said, 'I'll even hold the lube.' Melissa is such a princess. She said, 'What will the thread count of the sheets be?'"

When Melissa turned down hundreds of thousands of dollars to pose naked for *Playboy* magazine, Joan was so irate she turned it into a bit. "The nerve of that bitch!" she shrieked. "She's been divorced for three years and I'm still paying off her wedding. I'm seventy-five fucking years old, standing on a red carpet saying, 'Who are you wearing?' Who are you? Five hundred thousand dollars, and she turns it down? Pull down your pants and show them the pussy!"

In private, Joan was doubly resentful that she herself had not been offered such a payday. "Nobody ever asked me to pose for *Playboy*," she complained.

Despite such skirmishes, Rivers's primary goal for Melissa remained the same one her parents had for her: to get her married off. "I think everyone has to have somebody," Joan said. "It bothers me when she doesn't."

Since her mother wasn't satisfied with most suitors, Melissa offered a typically sardonic response: "She wants me to be with the person she thinks I should be with."

"Joan was always dying to have Melissa marry a banker, a doctor, a lawyer—someone successful who would bring home the bacon—but that's not what Melissa has been attracted to," said Pete Hathaway.

Although Melissa had boyfriends, it was hard for men to compete with her primary relationship. "The fiber of Melissa's life was always about her mother," said Blaine Trump.

After Melissa grew up, Joan satisfied some of her maternal drive by channeling it toward other people. "She was like a mother, not just to me but to everybody," said Mark Simone. "She wanted to talk to everybody and find out about them. Did they have a wife? A husband? Could she fix them up? She was the biggest matchmaker you ever saw. She was always trying to fix me up."

If Rivers couldn't resist telling her daughter what to do, she was an equal opportunity bossypants who took the same approach with everyone else too. "When you'd introduce her to anybody, she'd say, 'The jewelry—good. But what you're wearing—not right,'" said Mark Simone. "And she was always right."

It would be difficult for anyone to follow such a larger-than-life mother, and Joan made it clear that her daughter had no hope of competing with her.

"Missy, you don't have to be perfect," Joan said on *Fashion Police*. "You know why? Because I already am."

Losing such a parent has been an immeasurable blow. "Melissa is still struggling to accept Joan's death," the *Los Angeles Times* reported the following year. "On bad days, she locks herself in her closet and screams and cries."

Slowly, however, Melissa is trying to find her own way. "My whole life cannot be about my mother's legacy," she said.

## Chapter Twenty-One

# THE TIME OF HER LIFE: FAME, FRIENDS, AND FUN

A dozen years before she died, Rivers went to "a stuffy dinner party" in Connecticut and met the woman she would thereafter refer to as her best friend. Most people don't make a brand-new BFF when they're senior citizens, but as Rivers later noted, "Marjorie was the only other person who laughed out loud when someone said Demi Moore was talented."

"We clicked," said Margie Stern, who had a long career as the owner of several Manhattan shops called Pizazz before dedicating her retail experience to job training for young people as part of a nonprofit charity. "I never expected to click with someone like Joan Rivers. I've been married forever, and I'm not a woman's woman, in that sense; I don't have best friends. But she always felt that I got her. We wanted to be sisters, and we called each other Sissy; it was a running gag. Things were riotous and crazy. Every time I saw her, we laughed from the minute she got in the car. That's what our relationship was: have a good time. Just have fun!"

Their relationship took off the way new friendships between two girls often do in elementary school, with ecstatic mutual appreciation and constant contact. "She couldn't spell worth a damn, but we pretty much emailed all the time," said Stern, whose husband, Michael, is a businessman who produced fragrances for Oscar de la Renta.

"I think they appreciated the fact that in their later years, they kind of found kindred spirits," said Ricki Stern, Margie's daughter.

Rivers already had friends and relatives who depended on her for professional or financial assistance, but Stern was different. "I don't have an agenda; I didn't need anything from her, and I never wanted her to do anything for me," she said.

Together, they found humor in everything. "One time I had just gotten a mailing about how to know if you have Alzheimer's, and we were making up a laundry list of things that were so stupid—just dumb things, but we were both so hysterical we couldn't walk," Stern said. "I had to sit down on the ground. I was laughing so hard I was going to wet my pants. We just had so much fun."

Rivers was known for playing practical jokes on her friends, but with Stern she redoubled her efforts. "When we walked down the street, she would approach total strangers and say, 'Who's prettier—her or me?' I never won. They always chose her," said Stern, who is stunning. "One time she had a gorilla deliver a birthday cake to me that said, 'Dear Margie, Happy eightieth birthday.' I was in my early seventies at the time. The gorilla whispered to me, 'You look pretty good for your age.'"

Stern reciprocated in kind: "On her birthday, I had a cake delivered to her house that said, 'Happy birthday, Mary,' with 'Mary' crossed out and 'Joan' written in—and with a piece taken out of the cake."

Every Sunday they had dinner together, often after attending a matinee. "One night I walked into Sarabeth's on Central Park South and everyone turned around to look at me," Stern recalled. "Joan stood up and said, 'Ruthie—over here.' She had told the waiter—in a very loud voice—'When Ruth Madoff comes in, don't talk to her about the case, because she's very embarrassed.'"

Bernie Madoff's financial misdeeds were dominating the news at the time, and everyone in the room thought the chic blond Stern was his wife. All the other customers spent the entire evening glaring at her.

When they ate together, the two women always split one order between them. "We had the exact same thing all the time, and we shared everything," Stern said. "At Joe Allen, we had one salad with cheese and ham, and she would have the cheese and ham wrapped up. We had one banana cream pie. At Sarabeth we had an egg white omelet with tomatoes and mushrooms and a side order of spinach with extra garlic. We would get extra biscuits and cookies, and she would take them home—'for the dogs,' but I think she ate them. We had the same wine, Pinot Noir."

Every year they went to the gift show at the Javits Center. "We would buy soap, candles, jewelry—everything in sight. We always had the best time," Stern said. "Two years ago I broke my hip a week before the gift show, and she said, 'I'll push you in a wheelchair. But if I find out you had your face done instead of breaking your hip, I'm going to fucking kill you.' So I got bandages and wrapped my whole head up. I opened the door—and there's Joan limping in with a walker. I was so excited that we were going to get her—and this was a total 'Gotcha!' She one-upped me by walking in all bent over. I was so hysterical I thought I was going to fall and break the other hip. It was always the one-upmanship—except how could you one-up Joan Rivers?"

Rivers had actually purchased the walker she used for the gag. "Even though she worked so hard for the money, it kind of blew away," Stern said. "Someone else might say, do you really need to spend a hundred dollars to make a joke? But the end result was worth everything. She totally cracked me up."

The next time she was to meet Rivers for dinner at Sarabeth's, Stern was waiting to cross the street at Central Park South and Sixth Avenue when two large young men accosted her. "They grabbed me under the arms, lifted me off the ground, and took me across the street," Stern reported. "I said, 'What do you think you're doing?' They said, 'Joan Rivers told us you couldn't cross the street by yourself and we should carry you across!'"

Both Stern and Rivers were patients of Dr. Gwen Korovin, the ear, nose, and throat specialist who was sued for medical malpractice after Rivers went into a coma during an endoscopy and died. Months before that, Rivers called Stern from the doctor's Upper East Side office and demanded that Stern join her there right away.

"Gwen is very thin and put together, and she wears chic little dresses," Stern said. "But Joan said, 'Gwen is wearing a sandal and her pinkie toe is sticking out from it—she has a malformed toe, and it's the most disgusting thing I've ever seen! You need to come over and see this immediately!'"

Stern refused. "So we go to the theater the following Sunday, and she gets in the car and crosses her leg, and I look down and see that she has taken a piece of cardboard and glued it on her so it was sticking out of her shoe. She painted it with red nail polish and made it look like a pinkie toe. Who would do that—and not say anything? I was convulsed. So then we get out of the car and she goes up to perfect strangers and says, 'What do you think—isn't this disgusting?' She went up to a Muslim lady who was totally covered with a mask and everything. She stopped everyone in the street."

At one point, Stern agreed to get a tattoo with Rivers for her WE reality show, *Joan & Melissa: Joan Knows Best?* "Joan chose a bee, like the Joan Rivers bee pin," Stern said. "She was doing it on her rear, and she said, 'I'm just going to pull down my Spanx'—and she jumps up and runs out of there. She completely panicked."

Although Rivers bailed on her, Stern was stuck with the results of her own commitment. "I would never have gotten a tattoo; I was doing it for her show," she said. "I got a snake on my wrist. I said, 'What does mine look like?' She said, 'It looks like a sick worm.'"

Rivers subsequently got a tattoo of 6M on her arm as a reminder of the Holocaust. In deference to the subject, she didn't show that on any of her reality shows, but everything else was fair game. "She was doing all these crazy things—she said, 'Let's do pole dancing!'" Stern reported.

When they went shopping, one of their favorite haunts was a place Rivers called the Hooker Store, because it had "kind of flashy stuff," Stern said. If she admired something, Rivers would press it on her. "You had to fight her off. If you said, 'I like your bracelet,' she'd be like, 'Here, take it.' I have two of her costumes. One is a huge hot-pink feather coat that William Ivey Long made for her. I always loved it, so of course she gave it to me. I wore it to the opening of the Metropolitan Opera. She was the best friend you could ever have."

Both women considered their unexpected bond to be an extraordinary gift so late in life, but Rivers also took care to maintain long-standing relationships. "You do a show with someone and when it ends, it's usually over and done," Bill Reardin said. "But I was friends with her for twenty-five years; it didn't go away. She kept in touch."

Even if a relationship ebbed and flowed, Rivers made sure it wasn't extinguished. "For several years after *The Joan Rivers Show*, I would see her all the time, and it was like nothing changed at all," said Larry Ferber. "The last five years of her life, we totally reconnected. She remembered my birthday. She sent me an email that said, 'Dear Larry, Happy birthday to you, / Happy birthday to you, / Happy birthday, dear Larry, / You're a good-looking Jew.'"

For a star of her stature, Rivers remained unusually open to making new friends as well as retaining old ones. Her taste for high society notwithstanding, she seemed anything but a snob. "I do a big party on Christmas Day, and last Christmas she came with a friend of hers who's a countess," said Charles Busch. "I'm on the left side of my building, and Joan gets mixed up and goes to the right side of the building and rings the doorbell. An older gay man answers the door in his underpants—and it's Joan Rivers and the countess. He says, 'Charles Busch is on the other side of the building,' and Joan says, 'Get your pants on—you're coming with us.'"

Finding romantic prospects was a lot harder than making friends. One episode of *Joan & Melissa: Joan Knows Best?* revolved around Joan's desire to make a sex tape while being stymied by the difficulty of locating a costar. Landing a leading man wasn't any easier in real life.

"She asked people to fix her up, and my mother called a lot of single men living in Newport Beach, a wealthy community south of L.A.," said Sue Cameron. "No one would go out with Joan. Every single man said they were afraid of her."

In New York, Margie Stern also tried to fix up Rivers, who dated one man for a while and then decided he was too cheap, because he let her pay for things. Another guy just seemed intimidated. "He didn't open his mouth the whole time," Stern said. "She was overwhelming—just bigger than life. Most men are threatened by that. You know how many men were terrified of her? My husband loved her, but he was always the odd man out. We would never let him talk."

Rivers was philosophical about the problem. "Men don't like funny, aggressive women; we know that," she said.

Her standards were also lofty. "She wanted to be married, she wanted to have a boyfriend—but she wanted the Duke of Windsor," said Mark Simone.

Rivers might have accepted the Duke of Windsor, but friends suspected that her interest in having a man had become limited, if not theoretical. "This is what Joan wanted a man for: she wanted a proper escort for social functions, and she wanted someone to be in bed with her on Sunday to read *The New York Times*," said Sue Cameron. "She and Edgar would sit and do that, and she also did that with Orin Lehman. It wasn't about sex. She never talked about sex. I don't even know if she liked it."

"I don't think she gave a shit about men," said Valerie Frankel, one of her ghostwriters. "She had had relationships, and she was fine with not having a relationship. She was in love with working."

Rivers always understood that about herself: "I love performing. It's like a drug for me," she said.

"I would say, 'Do you ever want to go out with anybody again?'" Blaine Trump said. "And she would say, 'No. I don't have time to think about a man in my life.' In the last chapter of her life, she was so busy with *Fashion Police* and Melissa and the business. There was one man who had a fortune and wanted to date her, and she said, 'I'm not going out with anyone. I'm too busy.' I think dating was off the table. She was too busy with her career, and she just loved her career."

Although comedy remained at the core of it, Rivers never stopped trying to expand the parameters. "Her love of the theater, of comedy, and of her business just pushed her forward no matter what happened," said Blaine Trump. "We went to the theater and went backstage, and she said, 'Don't you just love the way this place smells?' I thought, 'You've got to be kidding me!' But that was how deep her passion ran. She always said, 'I'd be happiest if I just dropped dead onstage.' She never wanted to be incapacitated or not able to remember her lines. At her seventieth birthday she said, 'I've got ten great years left, but after that, I don't know—it could be over.' She looked on the years from seventy to eighty as a really happy, productive period in her life."

Margie Stern's friendship brought a great deal of joy and fun to that era, but it also inspired an unexpected chronicle of Rivers's career that substantially enhanced the public understanding of her legacy. Margie's daughter, Ricki Stern, is a filmmaker, and when she and her codirector, Annie Sundberg, were looking for a new subject, Margie suggested Rivers.

"My mom said, 'You walk down the street and people come up to her and it's amazing to see how loved she is,'" Ricki Stern said. "When I met with Joan, I was amazed at how sweet and vulnerable she was. I thought, 'There's a lot more there. There's a person there who could be part of a very intimate feature documentary.' My background was in theater, and I understand the passion it takes to do that. You have to be open and vulnerable, but you have to learn to deal with constant rejection. Joan represented the hopes and dreams that all young performers have that carry them on. What Joan really wanted was to always have a place to perform, because her emotional happiness came from having the chance to play in front of a new audience. Being able to interact with the audience gave her the greatest joy. It was her oxygen."

To Stern's surprise, financing the documentary proved surprisingly challenging. "No one would fund it," she said. "That was so unexpected. People said, 'I just don't like her,' or 'She's not funny,' or 'People don't like old,' or 'I love her but she's not our demographic,' meaning that the demographics are young now and no one likes old comics."

Stern and Sundberg persevered, and they ended up making a fascinating film called *Joan Rivers: A Piece of Work*, which presented a vivid portrait of Rivers's peripatetic life and fierce obsession with performing. Released in 2010, it won widespread praise for humanizing a complex, contradictory character whose vulnerable side had not been glimpsed by most of her previous audiences.

"Filmed over the course of fourteen months, *A Piece of Work* begins at a low point in Rivers's career," Matthew Jacobs wrote in the *Huffington Post*. "She bemoans the white space in her datebook, which in her mind signals a lack of desirability. But that nadir, like so many of the comedian's others, turns into another success story. By the end, she's been invited to participate in an all-star George Carlin tribute, landed the *Fashion Police* gig, and won *The Celebrity Apprentice*. Rivers didn't reclaim the dominance she achieved during her days as a frequent Johnny Carson guest and the permanent guest host of *The Tonight Show*—when she also became a regular on the variety show circuit (*The Carol Burnett Show, Hollywood Squares, Saturday Night Live*) and was nominated for a Grammy for her 1983 comedy album—but no matter: Rivers had long ago secured legend status. By the time the documentary crew finds her, she has nothing left to prove, even if she refuses to take a day off."

Rivers didn't see it quite that way; no matter how old she got, she never allowed herself the luxury of thinking she had nothing left to prove. She took great care to preserve her public image as an ageless wonder who showed no sign of slowing down, and she refused to leave the house without full hair and makeup.

And yet she was astonishingly transparent in the documentary, appearing without makeup and exposing her deepest fears. "Making a warts-and-all documentary in one's late seventies is itself quite daring, and for that the movie is both touching and provocative," Jacobs wrote. "Rivers always wanted to be an actress but was never taken seriously once she developed her coarse comedic aura, so instead she sums up her career in one of the most evocative self-reflections of any timeworn celebrity: 'My life is an actress's life,' she says while tearing up. 'I play a comedian.' It's one of the documentary's saddest, most revealing moments."

Rivers's intimates were thrilled with the film, but they were surprised that it didn't get more attention. "It blew me away, but it got no recognition at all," said Margie Stern. "Joan said, 'It's because Hollywood hates me.'"

Although she allowed the filmmakers to chronicle her fear of obsolescence, Rivers was offended by any implication that her star might have faded. "At one point, I said to her, 'The film brought you back,'" recalled Margie Stern. "She said, 'I never went anywhere.'"

In actual fact, Rivers seemed to go everywhere, and the film crew that followed her around the country was exhausted by the demands of her daily schedule. "It was just so hard to keep up with Joan. She had more energy than any of us," said Ricki Stern. "The travel was brutal, but that was part of her DNA. She had two assistants, because nobody could keep going. After two days with Joan, we were done; we'd need a break. But she would sign books till her fingers were numb, and she would never turn down a fan. She had the traveling down to a science. She would roll her little beat-up rolling bag into a place and unpack her own bag and wash her underwear in the sink and hang it out to dry. She was not a prima donna."

Rivers's friends felt the same way. "We'd try to keep up with her, and after a ten-day tour, we'd be ready to go lie down in a darkened room for five days, but she'd be off on another plane," said Martyn Fletcher, who traveled with Rivers as her hair and makeup artist on tours overseas. "She always said, 'I'm so tired, I can't do this anymore,' so I'd say, 'Well, you could stop.' She'd say, 'Are you out of your mind?' She was too driven. She'd say, 'What am I going to do if I retire?'"

Daunted by her jam-packed schedule, her intimates just shook their heads. "I would say, 'Why are you working so hard?'" Robert Higdon reported. "She would say, 'I'll stop when I don't feel that wonderful feeling I feel when I walk out onstage.' Joan had to keep working; it wasn't a choice. It wasn't to pay the light bill, although she did have to do that, because she lived grand. She needed to perform. She needed to create. She needed to work. That was her fuel. That was her air. As much as she would joke that she wanted a man to take care of her, if Rockefeller had said, 'Marry me—I'll take care of you,' she would have snuck out of the house and done stand-up behind his back."

But in order to do stand-up, Rivers had to travel around the country, which was always hard for her. "She hated flying," said Sue Cameron. "She had to do it, but she was afraid of crashing, so she would take Valium and close the shades all around her and put on a blindfold and go out. It was very difficult for her."

No matter what the rigors of the road, she remained a trouper. "Lots of comedians are nasty or curmudgeonly when they're beyond the spotlight, but she was always so kind, and she had a great rapport with the crew," Ricki Stern said. "It was kind of a lovefest—very comfortable. She was always the life of the party. She had so much infectious energy, and she had an outrageous humor that would just bubble up. You were constantly looking at the other people in the room and going, 'I can't believe she just said that!' It was unfiltered. It might be what you were thinking, but you would never say it. It was always funny."

Although Rivers experienced the same kind of professional ebbs and flows during her seventies that most performers do at any stage in their careers, she enjoyed a remarkably successful decade overall. By the time she hit eighty, she was even more famous, wealthy, celebrated, and sought-after than she had been a decade earlier—a rare achievement for any entertainer.

"That's what I loved about the last few years of her life—she was hotter than ever," said David Dangle. "Who at seventy-five is earning more money and filling more concert halls than they ever filled? I found that fantastic. It's just thrilling."

And yet no matter how much she achieved, Rivers remained convinced that she was never accorded the recognition she deserved. The feeling of being unappreciated and overlooked had haunted her for decades.

When *Enter Talking* was published in 1986, it received what Rivers's coauthor, Richard Meryman, described as a "sneering" review in *The New York Times*. Meryman, a longtime *Life* magazine writer and editor, described the memoir as chronicling Rivers's "search for the stage character who brought her success." And yet when she achieved it, that persona "turned out to be the one that the entertainment establishment still mistakes for the true person and scorns," Meryman wrote.

To Rivers, her career always seemed like an endless replay of her childhood as a social reject who couldn't get into the cool crowd. "How many parties have you gone to that I've not been asked? How about 100 percent?" Rivers asked Larry King during one interview.

King asked her why that was so, since she was "pretty, vivacious—you add to a party."

"I'm the only person that isn't invited to the *Vanity Fair* party," Rivers said, referring to the star-studded annual Academy Awards after-party, a coveted event that was a particular source of bitterness to her. "The garbageman says to me, 'See you there.' I go, 'I'm not asked.' I was in *Vanity Fair* one year and they didn't invite me to the party."

"What's your thought as to why?" King asked again.

"A bad rep. I don't know!" she said glumly.

When Melissa Rivers published *The Book of Joan*, she was interviewed by Hoda Kotb at New York's 92nd Street Y. Melissa complained that her mother was never able to wangle an invitation to the *Vanity Fair* Oscar party, even though she originated the formula that made the red carpet into the spectacle it has become.

After the program, I emailed Graydon Carter, *Vanity Fair*'s longtime editor, to ask why Joan wasn't on the guest list. "We never banned her from the Oscar party," he replied. "We just never thought of inviting her or Melissa. They should have spoken up."

In fact, Melissa said they tried for years to get Joan into the party, enlisting friends like the late Dominick Dunne to beg for an invitation—all to no avail. Other reports have claimed that Carter didn't include Joan because he thought she was vulgar.

"She was always that girl with her nose pressed against the glass," said Charles Busch.

Despite her success, Rivers remained as insecure as she had always been. "When I was being honored with a Legend Award by Live Out Loud, which gives scholarships to LGBT youth, I asked Joan if she would give me the award," Busch recalled. "She said to me, 'I've never received an award for anything.' After the awards, she was talking to the gay kids, and she told them, 'One day you're up, and the next day you're fucking down. One day you're up, and the next day you're fucking down!' She never lost her sense of the precariousness of everything she had achieved."

Many show business veterans wondered why Rivers wasn't chosen for the high-profile gigs routinely given to less famous men with fewer credentials, as when Ricky Gervais hosted the Golden Globe Awards.

"I thought she should have hosted the Oscars," said one entertainment industry journalist. "She was dismissed in a way that was insulting to every woman who wanted to be a comedy host. Let's have Jon Stewart, Billy Crystal, David Letterman—everyone but Joan. It's as if she wasn't being taken seriously, even though she was the smartest and funniest person in the room."

"I'm never going to win anything," Rivers told the *Daily Beast* shortly before she died. "I'm too abrasive...But I think comics should be on the outside. If you're on the inside, it's over."

And yet all she'd ever wanted was not to be an outsider, so it rankled. "When they talk about the top women comedians, I'm never mentioned," she said. "Whenever they talk about women directors of successful films, I'm not mentioned. When they talk about any category, I'm not in it. So I think that's the problem: they don't know where to put me, so I'm nowhere. Maybe when I die they'll say it. The only time the critics were ever nice to me was after I was fired from Fox—after they had destroyed me. Then they came out and they said, 'She was the first to do this! She was the top woman in her field!' Only when they thought I was dead in my career did they give me the accolades. So I said to Melissa, 'When they cremate me, throw in all the obituaries, because they're going to be glowing.'"

In truth, however, Rivers's self-image as a wallflower sometimes prevented her from recognizing what a big star others considered her to be. "Hal Prince throws a famous Christmas party every year, with a lot of famous people," said David Dangle, referring to the renowned Broadway director. "It's all the world she loved. She said to me, 'I don't get invited to that party. I go as the guest of Arnold Stiefel, Rod Stewart's manager.' It was the highlight of her year, the most fun she would have, because it was famous Broadway people in Hal's gorgeous town house. She carved out her schedule around Hal's party. I was talking to Charles Busch, and I said that Joan never knew if she would be invited. He said, 'Are you kidding? She was the star of that party! Everyone in the room would drop dead when she walked in—it was like, "Oh my God, Joan Rivers is here!"'"

Rivers seemed oblivious to such reactions. "At one point she whispered to me, 'Can you believe we're here?'" Busch said. "She was by far the most famous person in the room."

But Rivers couldn't seem to register that fact. "They could have cared less if I came to that party," said Arnold Stiefel. "Joan Rivers was an event, but in her crazy head, she didn't know that. She wasn't able to process how beloved and how successful she was. She was always fighting the fight to be loved, and she just didn't understand the huge extent to which she had succeeded."

Although her insecurities never abated, Rivers recognized how much she had to celebrate during the last years of her life. "I think she felt extremely blessed in every way," said Robert Higdon. "I think she was happy, and I think she was very proud of her achievements."

Her success was doubly pleasurable because it was so hard-won. "One time we were on the boat off St. Barts, and we took a tender in, and the first person we ran into was Barry Diller," Pete Hathaway recalled. "This was before he built his big boat, and it absolutely thrilled Joan to see that her boat was bigger than his. She had risen from the ashes, and she was a big success. It still stuck in her craw about losing the Fox show, but she was the biggest survivor of all time."

No matter how great her success, Rivers kept working. "That's what gave her pleasure; that's who she was," said Margie Stern. "It was never about the money. Working was what turned her on and energized her."

But she was driven by fear as well. "She was never convinced that things were okay, because if things are so great today, 'Oh my God, what's going to happen tomorrow?'" said David Bernstein. "Things were taken away from her unjustly; she lost a show, she lost a husband, for a few years she lost the love of her daughter, her career was going bad—and she wouldn't let herself forget it, because if you forget about the bad times, the good times won't have the same meaning. She created her own paranoia. She couldn't help worrying that her career could crash tomorrow. She has been knocked down from that same perch so many times that whatever happens, she's determined she's going to get back on. It wasn't to convince other people; it was to convince herself."

Rivers's fellow performers also discerned a deeper need. "I think she had that compulsion to hear laughter," Larry King said. "No one gets a bigger kick in any form of show business than comedy. You can't force it, but when you hear laughter, there's no bigger high. You are creating laughter in others, and it's a giant 'I love you!' They're saying, 'You have made me feel good!'"

But no matter how many audiences she seduced, Rivers kept trying to generate new projects in television and theater. "She was desperate to come back on Broadway," said Margie Stern.

Rivers had high hopes for a show called *Joan Rivers: A Work in Progress by a Life in Progress*, which she performed at the Edinburgh Festival in 2008. To help her develop material for the show, Charles Busch did a series of interviews with her, and he was astonished by the flood of emotion his questions triggered.

"She held nothing back," he said. "It was tears and rage. She talked about Johnny Carson, and it was like he had tentacles reaching out, trying to destroy her. She was bitter, because he was trying to destroy her career—total, sobbing rage. When she talked about Edgar, there was love, guilt, rage—it was all very alive in her. She was sobbing about her mother's death, and the fact that her father literally wanted to have her committed when he found out she wanted to be a stand-up comic. She talked about her sister, about how Barbara was the beautiful one and the smart one."

The show Rivers put together was set in her dressing room on the night of the Academy Awards, and its premise revolved around her being elbowed out of her Oscar night red-carpet broadcasting job. Like *Sally Marr*, it seemed a glorified one-woman vehicle, despite a couple of minor supporting characters. The focus was on Rivers's trials and tribulations, from her husband's suicide to "her own suffering at the whims of sexist, ageist TV bosses," as Brian Logan wrote in *The Guardian*. "She tells us, climactically, that 'performing for you is my life, and no one has the right to take it away from me.'"

Most critics found the show unappealing. "To accuse Joan Rivers of ego is like complaining that the Pope is Catholic," Logan wrote. "It comes with the territory. But even by her standards, this is a remarkable exercise in self-mythologizing."

As with *Sally Marr*, Rivers had veered too far into her grievances, so the dominant tone struck audiences as one of anger. "I think she didn't understand why people didn't like it. She felt she was being open about her entire career, but so much of it was so bitter it ceased to be funny," said the theater writer David Finkle. "So much of it was her spewing bitterness about Johnny Carson. It was extremely bitter, and it wasn't good. She should have let it go."

With Rivers, the rancor always lurked just beneath the surface. "She was the most loyal person ever, and she was a warm person, but she was also a fucking angry person," said Andy Cohen. "She had to fight for everything she had. She had balls. But I saw her anger, and I would never want to get in her way."

The negative emotions were always tempered with a touching belief in the possibility of new opportunities. "She never gave up the bitterness, but she also never gave up the hope," said Sue Cameron. "She was never too proud to try."

But the anger continued to fuel her humor. A month before her death, Rivers made her last appearance on *Watch What Happens: Live*. "There was a New York *Housewives* reunion airing that night, and I asked her to do a little *Fashion Police* lead-in," said Cohen, the executive producer of the *Real Housewives* franchise as well as host of *Watch What Happens: Live*. "Joan was not a fan of *Real Housewives*, and she said, 'I'm going to say they all look like filthy whores.'"

Older people often lose interest in a rapidly evolving culture, but Rivers's passion for what was new and different never flagged. "She was always the first one to know about whatever the latest fashion or cosmetic treatment was," Blaine Trump said. "She was really interested in popular culture, in whatever the next thing was, moving forward. She just didn't live in the past."

As always, most of her cultural references were rude, as with her comments about a group of multicultural children on her Comedy Central roast: "Oh look—Brad and Angelina are having a garage sale!"

Rivers even understood that a performer who wanted a high profile had to keep up with the new social mores generated by changing technology. "She understood the Twitter world, where it had to be rapid-fire," said Mark Simone.

Shortly before Rivers died, George Hamilton did a commercial for CVS with her. "They paid us very well, but they said, 'Joan is getting slightly more than you. She had higher social media hits than you,'" Hamilton recalled. "That was my first moment of realizing that she'd already tapped into that."

But it was her cutting-edge humor that always surprised people the most. The last time David Bernstein saw Rivers perform, he was astonished. "She was doing a bit about how everyone's checking their cell phones all the time," he said. "She was lying on the floor, her legs spread, simulating intercourse as a woman who is checking her phone while she's having sex."

Rivers also continued to amaze people with her lightning-quick reflexes. "She could ad-lib about anything," said Mark Simone. "Believe it or not, some of the greatest comics can't ad-lib at all. She was very smart, and she did her own radio talk show for five years. She could ad-lib for three hours a day."

Josh Ostrovsky, a social media personality and entertainer who calls himself the Fat Jew, was introduced to Rivers the year before she died when he and a friend named Ben Lyons ran into her in the Sirius radio building.

"When we saw her, Ben said, 'I'm really excited for you to meet her, because I feel as if you're aspiring to be Joan Rivers—you're a foulmouthed Jew who loves self-deprecation,'" recalled Ostrovsky, a plus-size model who is known for such comments as his claim that his penis is the size of a rock shrimp. "I was wearing boat shoes and a short kimono with a loud paisley print that belonged to my grandmother. At the time, I had a very large, billowing Jewish Afro. But too many other people were growing Jewish 'fros, so I cut off the sides. I had cut off half of it, so it was almost like a Jewish flattop. It was definitely a stupid haircut. Ben introduced us, and Joan said, 'Oh my God, look at your hair!' I said, 'Do you like it?' She said, 'I guess you wanted to look like my vagina in the 1970s.' I said, 'Yes! That's exactly what I was going for!'"

Ostrovsky was dazzled by Rivers. "Lots of comedians can make fun of someone masterfully if they have some time to come up with something really witty and cutting, but to be able to do it right there on the spot, it honestly was awesome," he said. "I'm a guy who is considered edgy, and in seven seconds this woman was able to put me back on my heels. It's an art to be really funny and not give a fuck. She knew that her charm and her ability to say something cutting and gross would be lovable. It was like having a drunk Jewish aunt who would say whatever she fucking pleases, but your aunt would just say something mean. It's such a thin line between being mean and having the person hate you, or being mean and having the person fall in love with you. Comedy ages so poorly, and things become not hot in fifteen seconds. But the fact that Joan Rivers was able to adapt and change and stay relevant for forty years and be considered raunchy and edgy—that's insane."

If anything, Rivers actually grew bolder with age instead of toning anything down. "I would say, 'You know you're getting worse!'" Kathy Griffin said. "The last time I saw Joan live, I kept thinking, 'You can't say those things!' She was telling everybody to get out of there—'All the Asian women, go! You're stealing our men! All the lesbians—go!' No matter what she said, the audiences loved it. When I do a show and the audience gasps, I say, 'Puh-leeze—if you saw Joan Rivers, I'd be a nun novitiate in comparison.' That kind of laugh-with-a-gasp is unique to someone who is breaking ground."

If Rivers's riffs often shocked people, her fellow comedians were thrilled. "I believe it's really emancipating to see a humorist get up and say things that are 'wrong,' and it's emancipating for the audience to see an eighty-one-year-old woman stand onstage and say whatever the fuck makes you laugh," Griffin said. "It was always about getting the laugh, and as Joan got older, she gave less of a fuck. And there's nothing more fun than watching someone who doesn't give a fuck. As Gloria Steinem wrote on her Facebook, these younger women have opportunities that Joan couldn't even have imagined. They can't imagine Joan's battles."

Having survived what she did, Rivers felt there was little more to fear. "I've learned, when you get older, who cares?" she said. "I don't mince words; I don't hold back. What are you gonna do to me? Fire me? It's been done. Threaten to commit suicide? Done. Take away my show? Done! Not invite me to the *Vanity Fair* party? I've never been invited!"

According to Griffin, Rivers's general attitude alternated between complaint and gratitude. "Our conversations were half ruthless bitching—just vicious!—and half 'Aren't we lucky!'" Griffin said.

347

"She knew she was very fortunate," said Martyn Fletcher, Rivers's London hairdresser and friend. "We had the most amazing experiences together, and we both knew we were having amazing experiences. She never took it for granted. She got it that she was having a great life. She would say, 'Are we not having the best time?'"

But in public, Rivers preferred to keep such positive emotions a secret. "She liked the image of being irascible, bitchy, arrogant," said David Bernstein. "She was so protective of her image that anytime she did something benevolent, she wanted it hidden. I honestly believe she was a happy person, and I think a lot of the happiness stemmed from giving. I feel like she'd be mad at me for saying this, because it conflicts with the image, but she was a very benevolent individual."

## Chapter Twenty-Two

# THE FINAL MOUNTAIN: GATHERING SHADOWS

Rivers never stopped working, but the period when she was being filmed for *Joan Rivers: A Piece of Work* represented a relative lull before the success of *Fashion Police* goosed up her public profile one last time. She was still haunted by any sign that her career was dwindling, and the most poignant scene in the documentary is one in which Rivers talks about that fear.

"Her greatest nightmare was that she didn't have anything in her book," said Blaine Trump.

When her schedule got sparse, her resentment of younger competitors flared up again. "The older you get, the harder it is for you to hang on," Rivers told Larry King in one interview. "They're waiting for you to fall."

And by "they," she usually meant Kathy Griffin. The documentary showed Rivers "reminiscing about the 'good years,' when her schedule was full," Jackie Oshry wrote in the *Huffington Post*. "Jokingly, she attributes this slump to none other than Kathy Griffin. 'Not good...not good. We have no Vegas, no giant club dates—Kathy Griffin has taken all of those away.' Minutes later, when trying to reach someone on the phone, she jokes again, 'I'd get through faster if I was Kathy Griffin.'"

In 2009, Comedy Central presented a brutal roast of Rivers and chose Griffin as its host. She introduced the honoree to the audience as "a legendary bitch—Joan fucking Rivers!"

Grinning at the audience, Griffin said they could only hope that

Rivers would have "half as big a nervous breakdown as she did on *Celebrity Apprentice*. And she still won! You know why? Because Joan has got the biggest, maybe hairiest balls in this room!"

She was equally scathing about Rivers's appearance. "Joan Rivers is not an Orthodox Jew, but men still fuck her through a sheet so they don't have to look at that face," Griffin said. "Let's do what everyone is afraid to do—take a close look at Joan Rivers!"

Rivers absorbed such barbs, smiling through what often looked like gritted teeth. In her closing remarks, she said, "Kathy Griffin, you know what you are, darling? You are a thief! Yes. You stole my act, you stole my gays, and you stole the face of the Burger King. I am not happy with this."

While such insults come with the territory, the roast clearly rankled. "They said such mean, disgusting [things]," Rivers said later. "Oh sure, turn against the Queen...It's like Marie Antoinette. Yeah, like you're gonna do better with Kathy Griffin. Fuck you...When she lasts forty-five years, then go stand on my grave."

Rivers could dish it out, but she didn't like taking it, and she usually avoided putting herself in that position. "We never roasted her; we asked her all the time, but she always turned us down," reported Barry Dougherty, the Friars Club's press and public relations officer. "Comedy Central did, but Comedy Central pays, and we don't."

Dougherty thought Rivers was particularly sensitive about people making fun of her face. "She was tired of plastic surgery being the only subject they would come up with," he said.

She was also tired of feeling constantly threatened by hungry rivals who were just waiting for her to falter. "It wasn't that Joan disliked Kathy; she could just see the ambition dripping from Kathy's mouth," said Sue Cameron.

As Jonathan Van Meter wrote in *New York* magazine, "Even at this late stage in her forty-year career, Rivers is nowhere near ready to cede the stage to a younger generation. (As her former manager Billy Sammeth says in the film, 'Right now they see her as a plastic surgery freak who's past her sell-by date...But God help the next queen of comedy, because this one's not abdicating. Never will.') I am reminded of an email she sent me a couple of years ago, when she was at yet another low point in her career. I asked her what she thought of Kathy Griffin. 'I am her friend but also furious,' she wrote. 'She is the big one now. My club dates have simply vanished and gone to her. She will last as she is very driven. Like me, she wants it. But every time a gay man tells me, "Oh, she is just like you! I love her!," I fucking want to strangle them. But, please God, let someone give me credit. I feel so totally forgotten. The fucking *New Yorker* did this big piece on the genius of Rickles, who is brilliant but who hasn't changed a line in fifteen years. Meanwhile, I am totally "old hat" and ignored while in reality I could still wipe the floor with both Kathy and Sarah [Silverman]. Anyhow, fuck them all. Age sucks. It's the final mountain.'"

If Rivers felt ignored by the larger culture, her fellow professionals were still paying attention. "She was very hip," said Lisa Lampanelli. "Bill Cosby is square. Don Rickles does the same act he's been doing forever. But Joan Rivers wanted more and different. She was a young old lady, and that's cool as hell. I don't get how she had that drive: 'I'm going to figure out who the Kardashians are and make jokes about them.' It's not just talking about what she knows; it's staying current."

Even at the male bastion of the Friars Club, Rivers was acknowledged as unique. "She didn't fall by the wayside the way a lot of entertainers did," said Barry Dougherty. "These people have their peak and then they're done, but she managed to keep up with the world. A lot of people aren't aware the world has changed. They're stuck; they can't figure out how to make a new audience like them and want them. Joan did."

Working as hard as humanly possible to maintain that standard, Rivers gave her younger admirers a master class in a rare set of skills. "We were in a pretty small club—but she was in a club of one," Griffin said. "There is a world of difference between a lightly funny person who can be funny when they have a script and someone who can stand up and deliver an hour with a mouth and a microphone and nobody else but you."

Griffin regarded Rivers as the ultimate role model. In her final years, "Joan was busier than ever," Griffin said. "She had three shows on the air! She never lost that feeling that you gotta be chasing that next job. Joan's whole career was a marathon, not a sprint. I was always saying, 'How do you do it?' She said she still feels like she's holding on to the arm of the chair and white-knuckling it. She said, 'You hold on until your knuckles are white, and if you start to slip, you hold on to the ledge by your fingernails.'"

That grim determination was equally apparent to nonperformers. "If you hang on to that ledge and someone tries to push you off, you grab on with your claw," said Valerie Frankel, one of Rivers's ghostwriters. "That was what she thought being in the public eye was: hanging on for dear life."

Rivers's try-as-hard-as-you-can ethos was so rigorous it inspired others to step up their game. "I don't think I ever showed up at one of our dinners without Chanel head to toe," said Griffin. "Joan was not going to come over in sweatpants, and she would give me the once-over. So I would overdress—put on Chanel on top of Herrera on top of de la Renta."

Rivers maintained that rigor even at home. "If you went to dinner at Joan's house, she was always dressed to the nines," said Blaine Trump. "I just think she loved that feeling of being glamorous and pretty. It was part of the show."

Rivers's work ethic had always distinguished her from male peers with a greater sense of entitlement, but the difference became even more noticeable with advancing age. "I don't think there were that many male comedians who were hitting a club once a week just to keep that muscle agile," Griffin said.

Given the awful things Rivers said about other women over the years, her aversion to taking return fire seemed disingenuous; sometimes her attacks left real wounds. "Joan disliked me a lot—I don't have any idea why," said Lisa Lampanelli. "I got a call from Howard Stern one day, and he said, 'She called you untalented and said you're not funny.' She hates me, and I have never met her. She said I only made jokes about dating black guys. At the time, I was married and hadn't made jokes like that in seven years. I thought, 'She's misinformed.' It just hurt my feelings. I feel sad when I'm misunderstood."

Lampanelli let it go, but she finally erupted when Rivers renewed her hostilities. "Somebody tweeted to me and said, 'Hey, are you going to be roasting at the Joan Rivers roast?' I said, 'Unless I'm roastmaster I would rather not take the time.' Joan misunderstood it and said, 'Lisa Lampanelli said we offered her roastmaster and she turned it down, and that's just not true.' I said, 'You tell that fucking old cunt to get her facts straight.' That cunt lied about me on Howard Stern. Joan said nice things about Sarah Silverman and Kathy Griffin, but I'm closest to her age. Maybe she viewed me as more of a contemporary."

Rivers was more consistently kind to younger men, usually gay ones, and many of them adored her in return. "She was, like, my biggest champion," said the comic and actor Billy Eichner. "Whatever I asked her to do, she would do, and she was as helpful as anyone could be. She would drop off DVDs of mine with Letterman and Jimmy Kimmel and say, 'You have to see this guy.' She did things like that all the time."

But with everyone, Rivers took great pains to conceal the ravages of age. "She pushed herself to walk fast all the time, because she didn't want people to think she was old," said Margie Stern. "She never wanted to look like an old lady; she didn't want people to know her knee hurt or her back hurt. No one was supposed to see. It was all this positive outlook for the world. She was always moving; she didn't want anything to catch up with her. Life was catching up with her, but you never heard her complain. A lot of it was tied up in her ego. She wanted to be seen as strong, ready, professional. The woman was eighty-one years old, and she was slurring her words sometimes from total exhaustion, but she would never admit it. She wanted to be out all the time, and she never said, 'I'm tired.' She was older than I am, but I figured if she was going through life and not complaining, she was a role model for me."

Rivers's schedule was so brutal it seemed increasingly unreasonable. "The weekend before she went into the coma, she was in L.A. on Friday for *Fashion Police*," said David Dangle. "She flew to Toronto on Friday night. She was on the air till midnight on the Shopping Channel, and she was back on the air at 9 a.m. She worked throughout the day. She stepped off the set and the car took her to the airport and she flew to New York Saturday night. It's crazy. I do that trip and I'm a zombie for two days. She did a trip like that every day. She'd leave L.A. and fly to Seattle, leave

Seattle and fly to Florida. There were no Fridays and Saturdays. Every hour was booked. Every day was booked."

In 2012, Rivers performed forty-four comedy dates and fourteen Laurie Beechman dates, did one lecture, and went on a UK tour of thirteen more appearances. In 2013, when she turned eighty, she did thirty-eight comedy dates, twenty-four Beechman dates, and seven lectures. During the eight months that she lived in 2014, she performed twenty-six comedy dates and twenty Beechman dates and did three lectures. When she died at the beginning of September, she had another nine comedy dates, seven Beechman dates, one lecture, and a fifteen-gig UK tour scheduled for the remainder of the year.

"Here's a woman who was at the top of her game—at eighty-one," said the comic Brad Zimmerman, who often worked as Rivers's opening act.

"She was never more relevant than at eighty-one," echoed Judy Gold. "She knew more about popular culture than the average sixteen-year-old girl. She knew everything that was going on. I don't know half the people she was talking about."

In addition to personal appearances, Rivers was juggling the shooting schedules for three television shows: *Fashion Police*, *Joan & Melissa: Joan Knows Best?*, and *In Bed with Joan*, the weekly Internet show that Joan hosted from her bedroom at Melissa's house in the Pacific Palisades. Her schedule also included regular trips to Pennsylvania for appearances on QVC and the weekly shuttle back and forth across the country.

Rivers was still churning out books as well. In 2012, she published *I Hate Everyone...Starting with Me*—which purported to answer the immortal question "How do I hate thee? How much time do you have?" Starting with Rivers's version of the Golden Rule—"Do unto others before they do unto you"—she took on everything from ugly children, dating rituals, funerals, bad restaurants, First Ladies, closet cases, doctors, and feminists to hypocrites of all kinds. Her targets included Anne Frank and Stephen Hawking.

The book blurb on Amazon read, "Her career in comedy may have begun with self-loathing, but, after looking at the decrepitude around her, she figured, 'Why stop here when there are so many other things to hate?'"

Rivers even managed to turn the fake blurbs on the cover of the book into a publicity bonanza. Although *I Hate Everyone* made *The New York Times* best-seller list, she claimed that Costco canceled its order and banned the book because it featured raunchy parody quotes among the testimonials on the back cover. Costco apparently considered Marie Antoinette's alleged review to be inappropriate: "I don't like her. Let her eat shit."

Full of righteous indignation, Rivers showed up at a Costco store in Burbank, California, with handcuffs, a megaphone, and copies of her book. She handcuffed herself to a shopping cart and starting talking to the customers while autographing her book for fans. When the police arrived, it took them an hour to pry her out of the handcuffs because Rivers had thrown away the key. This gave her enough time to sell about a hundred copies of the book.

"It was a scene right out of *Law & Order: STD*," she said delightedly. "I was giving special prices on my book. I was undercutting Costco!"

After being released, Rivers finally agreed to leave the store, and the police decided not to file charges. But Rivers insisted the incident constituted a violation of her constitutional rights.

"This is very frightening and it is truly about the First Amendment," she told KABC-TV. "This is America, and I don't want to see censorship. This is a store that sells three hundred rolls of toilet paper at the same time. And I say any customer that buys three hundred rolls of toilet paper deserves a funny book to sit on the toilet and read."

Lest anyone question her understanding of constitutional law, Rivers said she should be able to interpret it as she saw fit. "This is a First Amendment issue—let the people choose," she told the *Daily News*. "And if I'm misreading the First Amendment, that's my right to misread it. That's what makes this a great country. I'm never changing my cover. Did Anne Frank give her book a happy ending? It's not about money. I'm considering myself now the Jewish Rosa Parks."

Rivers turned eighty the following year, but she managed to publish yet another memoir, *Diary of a Mad Diva,* the year after that. Five months after her death, the recorded version won her a posthumous Grammy Award for Best Spoken Word Album.

Despite her determination to keep going, Rivers was too shrewd a businesswoman to make the mistake of so many executives who refuse to plan for their succession. During her last years at QVC, she gradually began to shift responsibility to David Dangle so he could carry on the business—an important priority because of her desire to keep providing income for Melissa and Cooper.

"Joan positioned it as 'David and I,'" Dangle explained. "They put me on the air in the middle-of-the-night shows—never prime time, never daytime, but she always kept the name out there so the customer knew who I was. Joan and I signed off on every piece she made, and four or five years ago, we started putting me into some daytime shows. She was getting the customer to know me and like me, instead of saying, 'Who is this dude?' She knew one day she wouldn't be here, and Melissa was very clear that she didn't want to do it, so Joan was laying the groundwork for the day when she wouldn't be here. She wanted the business to continue; there was too much money at stake. It took the pressure off her to have to sell."

Although Rivers's QVC business had been a consistent success for years, her friends saw it as one more example of the fact that she was perpetually denied her due—in business as in the entertainment world. "She was a mogul, but there was never a story on her in *Forbes*," said Sue Cameron.

Nor did Rivers think of herself as someone who had made it and might therefore be able to relax. Despite a steady income from the QVC sales, she never stopped worrying about money. "She always thought she was going to be poor," Cameron said. "She thought if she stopped for one second, she would be homeless."

When someone referred to Rivers as "well-off," she demurred. "No, I've always been salaried. I've never owned anything. I've done very well, lived very well," she said. But when pressed, she added, "Sweetheart, I'm still working at Indian casinos in Omaha."

Surrounded by rich friends, Rivers still saw herself as a working girl. "She had this magnificent duplex, but she never had a ton of money," said Barbara Walters. "She was not a huge earner. I mean, okay, don't cry for me, Argentina. She wasn't poor. But she never felt that."

And having money remained one of her greatest pleasures. "She was so grateful and happy," said Cameron. "She had limousines. She had boats. She could go to Europe whenever she wanted. And she earned it all herself. Nobody gave it to her."

But Rivers kept insisting she couldn't afford to retire. "I don't have money to do that. I could pull my living in and live okay, but I don't want to live okay," she said. "I'm very happy to live in my penthouse, very happy I can pick up a check, very happy to have a great life, and be able to spread my wealth a little bit."

Spread it she did. "Joan lived very high on the hog, and there were tons of people on her payroll," said Pete Hathaway. "There were cooks, maids, butlers, assistants, hairdressers, makeup artists—and she was paying all these expenses for Melissa, and for Barbara and her kids."

Joan's generosity also extended to coworkers. "There was a young engineer whose wife was sick, and he was having money trouble," said Mark Simone. "She put $10,000 in an envelope and gave it to the station manager and said, 'Give it to him, but don't let him know where it came from.' She was putting a lot of the children of friends and relatives through college."

But it was her familial responsibilities that weighed on her most heavily. "She supported a lot of people, including her sister and her entire family," Cameron said. "I sat with her one month when she was writing checks for all the people she was supporting, and there were so many checks for her to sign it was just stunning. She just gave away money to people. Her sister's husband died, and Joan picked up the entire cost of that family for decades. They went through long periods of not talking; they weren't talking when Barbara died, but Joan kept writing the checks. She felt guilty about her sister, because Joan made it and her sister didn't. I think she resented supporting her—and also got pleasure out of it, because her sister was the favored one. But Joan was in control, because the person with the money is the one in control."

Although Barbara had a law degree, she had stopped working and become a stay-at-home mother by the time her husband, who was a decade younger, died in 1977, at the age of thirty-seven. "Joan tried to protect Barbara, but she never quite recovered from the loss of her husband at such a young age," Robert Higdon said. "That was one of the first things she said to me when I met her—she said, 'My husband died.' Barbara did have a meltdown after that, and Joan felt completely responsible for taking care of her. Joan had a big nut with that family. Her biggest fear was not to be able to take care of everybody she needed to take care of."

Despite that generosity, Joan's friends saw her sister as envious and ungrateful. "Barbara was very jealous of her sister," Dangle said. "Her husband died, but that doesn't mean you have to be an angry harridan. It was abusive."

"Barbara was a bitch," said another one of Joan's friends. "Joan was the earth mother to all these people who used her."

No matter how extensive Joan's largesse, Barbara managed to make herself look like the poor relation. "Joan was always handing over these five-year-old $100,000 mink coats to her sister, but Barbara would arrive in some stained *schmatta* and a raincoat," said Pete Hathaway. "Joan was fantastic to Barbara, but the time I began smelling a rat was when Joan sent her interior designer, Louis Malkin, down to fluff up Barbara's house—and Joan was picking up the tab."

Barbara died in June of 2013, two nights before the gala celebration that had been planned for Joan's eightieth birthday at the Metropolitan Club. Joan canceled the bash, which had a guest list of three hundred.

The following year, the *Daily Beast* asked her how losing her sister had affected her. "There goes your link to your childhood," Joan replied. "She was the memory bank of our family. I have no one to call up and say, 'Do you remember that time Daddy punched out our neighbor? Do you remember the time that Mummy bought the mink coat and didn't tell Daddy?' I am trying to be a good 'mother' to her children, but they're in their thirties. We weren't very close, but we were sisters. We fought, we made up. I miss not having 'my sister.'"

The loss also intensified her own sense of impending mortality. "Now that I reflect back on it, I think she knew she didn't have long," said Robert Higdon. "Losing her sister made her aware; that was a big bell that went off. Her biggest fear was that she would have a stroke and be a burden to Melissa. In the world of show business, when do you turn your light off? When do you say it's time to walk off the stage? She wasn't ready to do that, but she wanted to be the one to make that choice. One of her biggest fears was that she could become insignificant. It never happened."

"She wasn't neurotic about dying, but she thought about it a lot," said Margie Stern. "I think it was always tied in to her vision of who she was. She was terrified of losing it. She said, 'I'm just so scared of forgetting my lines.' We had dinner on the Sunday night before the Thursday when she went into the coma. We were talking about a friend who was going gaga. Joan always said, 'I don't want to be incapacitated. If I can't get up and work and do my act, I don't want to live.' She said, 'I want you to save the sleeping pills for me. Just put me down; that would be it. I'm eighty-one years old. I've had a fantastic life.'"

Rivers talked constantly about such concerns. "In the last year of her life, she would ask me how old my mother was when she started to lose it," Blaine Trump reported. "She felt that her mother started to lose it, and she would say, 'I just don't want to be around if I lose it.' She said, 'The greatest thing that could ever happen to me would be to die onstage.'"

Rivers had tried to prepare for the inevitable. "It's in my will: I'm not to be revived unless I can do an hour of stand-up," she said.

As her fears grew, she also made some practical changes. "She sold her house in Connecticut; it was like she was preparing," said Trump. "She didn't want Melissa to be burdened with that. And she was talking about selling her apartment and moving into the Pierre. It was closing in."

If Rivers lived in a bubble, she found it very painful to be reminded of the harsh reality. "When she did *Hot in Cleveland*, where she played Betty White's sister, she was so upset, because she said, 'We really are old ladies!'" said Sabrina Lott Miller. "It brought her in full view of her mortality. She would look in the mirror and say, 'Who's that old lady staring back at me?' She just hated that."

And yet Rivers kept looking for new ways to ratchet up her career, even in the final weeks of her life. "We had dinner on August 14, and we were sort of celebrating Joan's birthday in June and Aileen Mehle's birthday," Trump recalled, referring to the columnist. "Joan was talking about all of her projects. I was exhausted just listening to her schedule. I said, 'Joan, I don't know anybody who works as hard as you.' She was really on fire; I felt like she was at the top of her game. I can't imagine a woman who says she wants to die onstage saying, 'I'm done.' If she wasn't busy, she was bored. She loved the creative process, and she always had ten ideas for a new show."

Inspired by *Judge Judy*, Rivers and Andy Cohen were developing an advice show that would feature Rivers as the tart-tongued dispenser of wisdom. Cohen was amused to discover that it wasn't her only new venture. "As I was pitching this show, my agent kept finding out about other things she was pitching," he said. "I thought it was hilarious. The bitch was out there. She was not done."

To Rivers, departing the stage remained inconceivable. "One of her maxims was, 'When you retire, you expire,'" Joe Franklin said. "In her mind, if you retired, you'd die."

The last year of Rivers's life brought a milestone event that marked the end of a long and bitter estrangement. When Johnny Carson retired in 1992, Jay Leno took over *The Tonight Show* and hosted it until 2014—but he maintained Carson's ban on booking Rivers as a guest throughout those years.

The exile seemed grossly excessive. "My agent would call maybe every two years and say, 'People commit murder and they're out in twenty years—what is it?'" Rivers said.

But when Jimmy Fallon succeeded Leno as host in February of 2014, he invited Rivers to appear on his first show, which coincidentally occurred on the forty-ninth anniversary of her first ever appearance on *The Tonight Show*. "It's about time!" Rivers said. "I've been sitting in a taxi outside NBC with the meter running since 1987."

Rivers appeared with other stars that included Robert De Niro, Will Smith, Lady Gaga, Mariah Carey, Kim Kardashian, Sarah Jessica Parker, and U2, and Fallon's gesture meant a great deal to her. "I thought, how darling, and sweet, and sensitive," she said. "I was so emotional."

"She was so crazily, overwhelmingly touched that Jimmy Fallon had her on his first show," said Andy Cohen. "That was huge for her—major, major. She told me the car dropped her off at the wrong entrance to Thirty Rock, and it was the same one she used to do *Johnny Carson*. She said, 'Thank you,' and started to cry."

Rivers turned eighty-one that June, and she made more headlines over the summer. "Rivers has been very active lately," Deadline.com reported in August of 2014. "Last month she stormed out of an interview with CNN's Fredricka Whitfield, after Whitfield called Rivers's trademark fashion blasts 'mean,' and asked Rivers if she was concerned the fur she was wearing on the cover of her new book might offend animal rights activists. 'You're not the person to interview someone who does humor,' Rivers snapped as she exited."

During the interview, Rivers was exasperated by the familiar charge that she hurt celebrities' feelings. "You really think Nicki Minaj cares I didn't like her dress?" Rivers said.

Whitfield pointed out that *Diary of a Mad Diva* contained jokes about the deaths of Casey Anthony's baby and Princess Diana, among other sensitive subjects. Rivers replied that "life is very tough" and jokes give people "a vacation for a minute from horror." But when Whitfield mentioned that Rivers was wearing fur on the cover of her book, Rivers erupted. "Are you wearing leather shoes? Then shut up!" she said.

It was at this point that Rivers astonished Whitfield by walking off the set. "Are you serious?" Whitfield asked.

She was indeed. Rivers complained afterward that the CNN interviewer "was a news reporter and not an entertainment reporter. She did not seem to understand we were talking about a comedy book and not the transcripts from the Nuremberg trial. Every question was an accusatory one designed to put me on the defensive. She seemed to miss the point that *Diary of a Mad Diva* is simply a very funny book, and as Winston Churchill said, if you can make one person laugh, even for a minute, it's like giving them a little vacation."

Rivers described Whitfield as "very judgmental, very nasty, very opinionated, very negative," and then added, "It was like my wedding night, ya know?"

Although Rivers denied that the whole flap was a publicity stunt to promote her new book, she milked it for all it was worth. "She shrewdly kept the spotlight trained on herself—three days later stopping by David Letterman's CBS late-night show, where she began to poke fun at June Allyson—America's sweetheart circa 1940—and Dave walked out in protest, leaving Joan to interview herself," Deadline reported.

Rivers had made a joke about losing an endorsement deal for Depend adult diapers. "Letterman then calmly removes his jacket and walks offstage, pretending to be grossed out by the joke, but Rivers proceeds by interviewing herself. 'How's your sex life, you old bitch?' she asks, before responding with a joke about vaginal dryness," *Rolling Stone* reported. "When it becomes clear that Letterman is riding out the gag for the long term, she even throws to commercial like an old late-night pro."

Generating a steady stream of such controversies to keep people talking about her, the obstreperous eighty-one-year-old seemed full of life, and her penchant for causing trouble was undiminished. "This summer alone, she first raised hackles in July when she called First Lady Michelle Obama 'transgender' and implied that President Obama is gay," *Variety* reported.

Looking back on those months, her friends were divided about what was really going on in Rivers's mind. "She was just exhausted," said Sue Cameron. "It was too much for her. She said, 'I can't fly back and forth across the country every week.' She knew it was too much now, and she was taking steps to lower the stress. She said, 'I think I want to buy something on the San Juan Islands off Seattle. Would you like to live there with me?' She wanted complete isolation and nature, but close enough to a major airport so she could get back to New York. She'd never even seen the San Juan Islands, but she was going to live there."

Others scoff at the idea. "There were all these fantasies, and she would throw things around, but that didn't mean one thing," said Margie Stern. "She was tired, but she wouldn't have left New York."

Her coworkers didn't believe she would ever have gotten off the merry-go-round voluntarily. "She had so much energy," said the Beechman Theatre's Kenny Bell. "She would say, 'Don't get old—aging sucks,' but the energy she had would give forty-year-olds a run for their money. She was an inspiration. If you could get old like her, it's not so scary."

But the unrelenting activity was driven by the same desperation that had always hounded her. "Her whole life, she was chasing something," said Mark Simone. "Even when she walked, she was running. Bob Hope created this character, and he was happy for the rest of his life. Not like Joan. She was never satisfied. She was always running to grab something. She was always trying to do something else."

Her friends understood why. "I think probably the answer to Joan is her mother," said Lonny Price. "Is it too simple to say she didn't get enough love from her mother? It's such a cliché, but it's true."

While virtually everyone admired her energy, some saw Rivers's example as a warning. "She seemed to me a cautionary tale about not getting your identity and your self-esteem from performance, from fame, from money, from work," said Lisa Lampanelli. "It's the deep hole that therapists talk about. What do I fill my deep hole with? Fame? Possessions? Relationships? Money? No, that didn't work. It's about filling the hole with something else besides work. When I watched the documentary, I thought, 'Oh—I have to be careful about that.'"

Others preferred to emphasize the satisfaction she derived from her achievements. "I think she was happy," said Ricki Stern. "She enjoyed her life. Anger fuels everything, but in her everyday life you didn't see anger. But you knew her whole thing was, 'Life isn't fair, so you power through it with comedy.' She was very sensitive to life's unfairness, and the way she processed it was through humor."

Rivers may never have caught what she was chasing, but she made the most of the journey. "She loved life," said Andrew Krasny. "I don't think I've ever met anybody who loved living as much as she did."

## Chapter Twenty-Three

# GRAND FINALE:
# SUDDEN EXIT, PURSUED BY BEAR

For Joan Rivers, August 27, 2014, seemed like an ordinary day. She had scheduled a minor surgical procedure for the following morning, but she had been as busy as ever all week, even though it was the tail end of the dog days of summer—a time when even Manhattan slows to a torpid crawl.

"I was with her in Toronto for two of the last five days before she went into the coma, working till midnight," said David Dangle. "The day before she went into the clinic, she had a meet and greet for Time Inc. A friend who saw her said she was white-hot—he'd never been so entertained."

Rivers appeared at the event in the Time & Life Building to promote *Diary of a Mad Diva*, and that night she performed at the Laurie Beechman Theatre. "She was full of life," said Kenny Bell. "She had to get up early the next morning for the procedure, but she was in such good spirits."

In her act, Rivers joked about her own mortality. "She said, 'I could drop dead right now, and you guys would be so lucky. You'd be invited to every dinner party in town, and you could say, "I was right there! One minute she was talking about vaginas, and the next minute she was on the floor!"'" said Shade Rupe, a longtime fan who was in the audience that night. "If you had me guess her age, I'd say she was in her fifties. She was so on. She didn't miss a step, she didn't go ditzy, she didn't forget anything, and her timing was amazing."

When Bell said good-bye to Rivers after the show, they were both exhilarated. "We were laughing so hard she was practically dancing down the street," he said.

"She killed that last show of hers; she really nailed it," said Steve Olsen, the owner of the Beechman. "Joan knew about cycles, because she had so many setbacks, but she died on top. She left here at nine thirty at night, after her final performance ever, and twelve hours later she was in a coma."

Rivers had every intention of keeping up her usual pace during the days to come: she was planning an appearance the following night at the Count Basie Theatre in Red Bank, New Jersey. But August 27 turned out to be the last day of her functional life. The next morning, fate intervened in the form of a catastrophic medical mishap that resulted in her death on September 4.

When Rivers suffered cardiac and respiratory arrest while anesthetized for a routine procedure at Yorkville Endoscopy, many people assumed that she was undergoing yet another cosmetic surgery. The actual truth was as ironic as it was poignant: she was just trying to diagnose a lingering problem with the asset that had carried her to fame and sustained it for half a century.

Always raspy, her voice had seemed particularly hoarse of late, and Rivers was concerned enough to pursue treatment. Before she was anesthetized at the clinic, she signed a written consent form allowing for an upper endoscopy, which examines the digestive tract, and a possible biopsy.

Even before the procedure began, those charged with her care had allegedly engaged in curious irregularities that may have violated regulatory and medical protocols. The medical personnel who gathered in the room for Rivers's endoscopy included Dr. Lawrence Cohen, the medical director of the clinic; Dr. Renuka Bankulla, an anesthesiologist; and Rivers's longtime ear, nose, and throat specialist, Dr. Gwen Korovin. Dr. Korovin's presence that day may have cost Rivers her life.

In early 2015, Melissa Rivers filed a malpractice suit against Yorkville Endoscopy. According to the complaint, Dr. Korovin was not licensed to perform any medical procedures at the Yorkville clinic and should not even have been allowed into the room. After Rivers was sedated, Dr. Korovin performed a transnasal laryngoscopy, which examines the back of the throat and vocal box—even though that procedure had not been discussed.

"The complaint says Bankulla raised questions given that Rivers had not authorized the additional procedure—but Cohen ignored the objections and allowed Korovin to go on with the laryngoscopy," the *Washington Post* reported. "The complaint notes that during the laryngoscopy, Bankulla had trouble keeping Rivers's oxygen saturation at a safe level, and her oxygen dipped again during the endoscopy. The doctors 'failed to properly observe and monitor Joan Rivers's vital signs which were deteriorating,' it states, adding that her blood pressure and pulse were also dropping. When the endoscopy was done, Korovin wanted to do another laryngoscopy. Again, a concerned Bankulla raised objections."

Dr. Bankulla had ample reason for concern. "The anesthesiologist warned that the cords were extremely swollen, and that they could seize up and Ms. Rivers would not be able to breathe," *The New York Times* reported. "'You're such a curious cat,' Dr. Lawrence Cohen, the medical director of the clinic, Yorkville Endoscopy, scolded the anesthesiologist, according to the suit...Dr. Cohen dismissed the anesthesiologist's concern as 'paranoid' and let Dr. Korovin proceed, the suit said, with disastrous results."

After Rivers died, various news organizations published rumors that one of the doctors also took selfies of his unconscious patient, a charge later affirmed by court papers filed for the lawsuit. The complaint alleged that Dr. Cohen snapped photographs of Rivers and Dr. Korovin with his phone, saying that Rivers would "like to see these in the recovery area." Rivers did not at any time "authorize Cohen to take photos of her while under sedation and while undergoing medical procedures"—but no one in the room objected, according to the lawsuit.

Rivers never made it to the recovery area. Her heart rate slowed to dangerous levels, a condition called bradycardia, and her oxygen levels also dropped as she suffered from "an airway obstruction and/or laryngospasm,' a closing of the vocal cords," *The New York Times* reported. "But, the court papers say, Dr. Bankulla did not demand a 'crash cart,' which might have had a drug like succinylcholine to relax her muscles and allow insertion of a breathing tube, then waited several minutes before calling for help. When she did, two other anesthesiologists arrived, and one of them tried to administer oxygen through a mask, to no avail. Dr. Bankulla looked around for Dr. Korovin to punch a hole in Ms. Rivers's throat—an emergency cricothyrotomy that she should have been trained to do as an ear, nose, and throat doctor—but Dr. Korovin had fled the clinic, according to the suit."

According to ABC News, "The lawsuit language is blunt: Korovin, it said, 'abandoned her patient, Joan Rivers.'"

After Rivers went into cardiac and respiratory arrest, further time allegedly elapsed before critical measures were taken. "Twelve minutes after the doctors called 'code blue,' someone dialed 911 for an ambulance," the *Washington Post* reported.

Rivers was rushed to Mount Sinai Hospital, where she was placed in a medically induced coma. She died a week later without having regained consciousness. The New York medical examiner subsequently determined that Rivers died from brain damage due to lack of oxygen.

The subsequent lawsuit accused the doctors at the clinic of being "reckless, grossly negligent, and wanton" and of having abandoned Rivers "when emergency procedures were necessary to save her life." The complaint also alleged that "none of the medical personnel at Yorkville Endoscopy who were present during the procedures performed on Joan Rivers possessed the knowledge, training, and ability to handle the medical emergency."

In her family's view, Rivers ironically suffered from substandard care because of her fame. "The lawsuit says that Ms. Rivers was in part a victim of her own celebrity, receiving treatment that violated protocol because her doctors were starstruck and trying to please her," *The New York Times* said. "Dr. Korovin, an ear, nose, and throat doctor to a number of well-known actors and singers, was Ms. Rivers's personal physician, and did not have privileges at the clinic. But Dr. Cohen, the medical director, allowed her in, Mr. Bloom, the lawyer, said on Monday. The court papers say Dr.

Korovin fled the clinic when it became clear that Ms. Rivers was in trouble because she knew she was not supposed to be there, and 'wanted to avoid getting caught.'"

"'Joan Rivers needed a doctor, not a groupie,' Mr. Bloom said."

Melissa Rivers characterized the behavior of everyone concerned as inexcusable. "The level of medical mismanagement, incompetency, disrespect, and outrageous behavior is shocking and, frankly, almost incomprehensible," she told the Associated Press.

In response to the suit, Dr. Bankulla filed papers saying that she had taken every lifesaving measure at her disposal, that a crash cart was available, and that Rivers "was being adequately oxygenated with mask ventilation."

When Joan was first hospitalized, her medical emergency instantly became big news, but the dire nature of her condition was not made public. Informed of what had happened at the clinic, Melissa and Cooper immediately took a morning flight from Los Angeles to New York, arriving at Mount Sinai Hospital at around 8 p.m. Joan was already receiving messages of love and support from her admirers. "Get well my friend," Kathy Griffin tweeted.

"I'm thinking about you and sending lots of love your way," Ellen DeGeneres tweeted.

Later that night, Melissa released a statement that said, "I want to thank everyone for the overwhelming love and support for my mother. She is resting comfortably and is with our family. We ask that you continue to keep her in your thoughts and prayers."

When Joan's condition was upgraded from critical to stable, her intimates were briefly hopeful. "In the beginning, we thought maybe there was a chance," said Margie Stern, who rushed to the hospital as soon as she heard about the situation. "They put her into this deep coma, but I thought she would wake up. I was optimistic."

Over the next few days, the information given to the public seemed confusing. "My mother would be so touched by the tributes and prayers that we have received from around the world," Melissa said in a statement released on Friday, the day after Joan went into the coma. "Her condition remains serious but she is receiving the best treatment and care possible. We ask that you continue to keep her in your thoughts as we pray for her recovery."

On Saturday, TMZ reported that Rivers was on life support.

On Sunday, August 31, Melissa issued a statement saying that her mother remained in serious condition, but "our fingers are crossed."

By September 1, the Monday of the Labor Day holiday weekend, some news outlets were reporting that doctors had started to bring Rivers out of her medically induced coma. "The waking-up process has begun and will take until Tuesday," one source told the *Daily News*. "There is real concern that the part of the brain that controls motor skills may have been compromised, leaving her as either a vegetable or in a wheelchair."

Reports the next day painted a very different picture. On Tuesday, September 2, E! said that a source "close to the situation" had described Joan as "making small but positive steps."

"She's getting better," E! claimed, citing the same source. But Melissa released a qualifying statement, saying, "At this time she does remain on life support."

The following day, Melissa issued another statement: "My mother has been moved out of intensive care and into a private room where she is being kept comfortable. Thank you for your continued support."

Although many people suspected that Joan was brain-dead, the heartbroken vigil at her hospital bedside became increasingly theatrical. Joan was moved to a larger suite that was "decorated by celebrity wedding planner Preston Bailey with flowers, bows, plants," according to Cindy Adams of the *New York Post*. As Joan lay in bed covered by a white faux mink blanket, Melissa had her mother's hair and makeup done while a CD of *Oklahoma!* played in the room.

"It was just surreal," said Sue Cameron. "Joan was wearing a pink and gold caftan, and she looked gorgeous. She looked like she was ready to get up and go on in Vegas."

QVC's Michael George was surprised and touched when Melissa included him in the select group of friends and associates who were summoned to say a personal good-bye at the hospital. "I was honored and sad when the family invited me to be at her bedside, and it was a very moving moment for me," George said. "I felt I was there on behalf of the QVC family, so we could say our farewells. It really meant a lot to me."

Those who were invited felt grateful to Melissa for her inclusiveness. "She could have gone in the other direction and said, 'Fuck all of you, I've had to share my mother with you my whole life,' but she continued to share her mother with us," said Andrew Krasny, who joined the inner circle at the hospital. "To me, that's the most generous thing Melissa has ever done."

But on September 4, Melissa made the heartbreaking decision to take Joan off life support. "I made sure she was in no pain and surrounded by those that she loved and loved her the most," said Melissa, who climbed into bed with her mother before Rivers passed away.

Martyn Fletcher was among the close friends in the room when Joan died. "What I found so moving was that there was such love that surrounded her," he said. "Everyone in that room absolutely adored her. It would be lovely to think that she knew. It was such a defining moment."

Melissa released a statement bearing the news: "It is with great sadness that I announce the death of my mother. She passed peacefully at 1:17 p.m. surrounded by family and close friends. My son and I would like to thank the doctors, nurses, and staff of Mount Sinai Hospital for the amazing care they provided for my mother. Cooper and I have found ourselves humbled by the outpouring of love, support, and prayers we have received from around the world. They have been heard and appreciated. My mother's greatest joy in life was to make people laugh. Although that is difficult to do right now, I know her final wish would be that we return to laughing soon."

Rivers's death inspired an avalanche of reactions from around the world, but it also provoked some unsettling thoughts about cosmic justice. Margie Stern couldn't help but remember Rivers's glee in making fun of Gwen Korovin's toe with her cardboard fake toe sight gag. Joe Franklin, the former radio and television host, recalled a different joke.

"When Julie Andrews had a problem with her vocal cords, Joan did a vicious attack in her nightclub act, and made all kinds of funny voices,"

Franklin recalled. "I said to her, 'Joan, you're pretty severe.' The funny thing was that she had her own vocal cord problems. Talk about karma!"

Rivers's funeral was held on September 7 at New York's Temple Emanu-El, the largest Jewish house of worship in the world. Known for its wealthy, powerful congregation, the temple is located at 65th Street and Fifth Avenue, three blocks from Rivers's apartment. Stately and vast, it seats twenty-five-hundred people—more than the august Saint Patrick's Cathedral, fifteen blocks south on Fifth Avenue.

For Melissa, the job of organizing an appropriate farewell was a colossal task, but her mother had already made many of her wishes abundantly clear. In her 2012 book, *I Hate Everyone…Starting with Me*, Rivers applied show business standards even to the challenges posed by death.

Rivers disapproved of anyone who shortchanged the dramatic potential of their demise. "I hate people who die of natural causes; they just don't understand the moment," she said. "It's the grand finale, act III, the eleven o'clock number—make it count. If you're going to die, die interesting! Is there anything worse than a boring death? I think not. When my time comes I'm going to go out in high style. I have no intention of being sick or lingering or dragging on and on and boring everyone I know. I have no intention of coughing and wheezing for months on end. One morning you'll wake up and read a headline: 'Joan Rivers Found Dead…on George Clooney's Face. Clooney Was So Bereft All He Could Say Was, "Xjfhfyrnem."'"

Rivers regarded death notices as a lively source of entertainment. "I love the obituaries," she wrote. "To me, obituaries are just wedding announcements without the pictures. I read the obituaries carefully, the way Lindsay Lohan reads her Miranda rights."

Rivers was equally enthusiastic about funerals, which she saw as a fashion opportunity. "I love funerals!" she said. "To me a funeral is just a red-carpet show for dead people. It's a chance for mourners from all walks of life to accessorize basic black, and to make a fashion statement that is bold enough to draw attention away from the bereaved but subtle enough so that no one knows that it's happening. And it's a great way to have quiet fun."

371

But she envisioned her own send-off as anything but quiet. "When I die (and, yes, Melissa, that day will come; and, yes, Melissa, everything's in your name), I want my funeral to be a huge showbiz affair with lights, cameras, action," she said. "I want Craft Services, I want paparazzi, and I want publicists making a scene! I want it to be Hollywood all the way. I don't want some rabbi rambling on; I want Meryl Streep crying, in five different accents. I don't want a eulogy; I want Bobby Vinton to pick up my head and sing 'Mr. Lonely.' I want to look gorgeous, better dead than I do alive. I want to be buried in a Valentino gown and I want Harry Winston to make me a toe tag. And I want a wind machine so that even in the casket my hair is blowing just like Beyoncé's."

Rivers also advised skipping the usual platitudes. "I hate people who try to make you feel better," she said. "Like the neighbor who says, 'Don't forget, the first part of "funeral" is "fun!"' Or the minister who says, 'He's in a better place now.' I'm tempted to yell out, 'No he's not. He had a house in the Hamptons. What's wrong with you?'"

She even provided a sex tip for seniors about the social opportunities created by an opportune death. "As I get older, I'm going to a lot more funerals, and let me tell you something, it's a great pickup scene," she said. "A graveside funeral is live eHarmony for the bereaved."

As for her own funeral, Rivers made some specific demands that included a list of those who should not be invited: Michelle Obama, whom she had called a "tranny"; Adele, whom she referred to as "fat"; and Chelsea Handler, whom she described as a "drunk" and a "whore." Handler spent several years in a romantic relationship with Ted Harbert, the CEO of Comcast Entertainment Group, which oversaw E! Entertainment Television, the home of Handler's show, *Chelsea Lately*—and Rivers never let her forget it. "The girl made it on her back fucking the president," she said.

But the list of those who did get invited to Rivers's funeral was long and stellar. It included Donald and Melania Trump, Barbara Walters, Kathy Griffin, Hoda Kotb, Kathie Lee Gifford, John Waters, Joy Behar, Sally Jessy Raphael, Sarah Jessica Parker, Matthew Broderick, Alan Cumming, Kristin Chenoweth, Cindy Adams, Chuck Scarborough, Bernadette

Peters, Robin Quivers, Diane Sawyer, Geraldo Rivera, Steve Forbes, Michael Kors, Carolina Herrera, Rachael Ray, Judge Judy Sheindlin, Billy Bush, Rosie O'Donnell, Whoopi Goldberg, record producer Clive Davis, Tommy Tune, fashion designer Dennis Basso, television bandleader Paul Shaffer, Dr. Mehmet Oz, Andy Cohen, Barry Diller, and Rivers's *Fashion Police* panelists Kelly Osbourne, Giuliana Rancic, and George Kotsiopoulos.

The guests included personal friends as well as bold-faced names. "There were dozens of QVC people there, from hosts to crew members—a great cross section of people," said Michael George. "It was quite unlike any funeral I've ever been to, but it was just an amazing event, to spend an hour or two laughing nonstop. It was just what she would have wanted. It was so true to what she was."

Arriving at Temple Emanu-El, the funeral-goers found crowds thronging five deep behind the barriers erected along Fifth Avenue. In lieu of sending flowers, mourners were asked to donate money to God's Love We Deliver, Guide Dogs for the Blind, and Our House Grief Support Center.

Inside the temple, Preston Bailey had arranged cascades of white lilies and orchids in great profusion. Although Rivers had visualized her own appearance in an open casket, she ended up being cremated, so mourners were deprived of the wind machine blowing her hair "like Beyoncé's." Other entertainment abounded, however.

The Broadway musical theater star Audra McDonald sang "Smile," and Hugh Jackman performed Peter Allen's song "Quiet Please, There's a Lady Onstage." The New York City Gay Men's Chorus serenaded the audience with "There Is Nothing Like a Dame," "Big Spender," and "That's Entertainment!" The Pipes and Drums of the Emerald Society, a unit of Irish-born members of the New York City Police Department, played "Amazing Grace" on bass drum and bagpipes—and then followed that with rousing renditions of "New York, New York" and "Give My Regards to Broadway."

The eulogies elicited as much laughter as they did tears. Inside Edition host Deborah Norville talked about Rivers's secret mission to hide the ashes of her late friend Tommy Corcoran in a vase at Buckingham Palace.

Not content with stashing his remains there, she secreted another batch of ashes under a rosebush at Highgrove House, the private residence of Prince Charles and the Duchess of Cornwall in Gloucestershire.

Melissa's eulogy included a humorous letter she had written to her mother.

Mom,

I received the note that you slipped under my bedroom door last night. I was very excited to read it, thinking that it would contain amazing, loving advice that you wanted to share with me. Imagine my surprise when I opened it and saw that it began with the salutation, "Dear Landlord." I have reviewed your complaints and address them below:

1. While I appreciate your desire to "upgrade" your accommodations to a larger space, I cannot, in good conscience, move Cooper into the laundry room. I do agree that it will teach him a life lesson about fluffing and folding, but since I don't foresee him having a future in dry cleaning, I must say no.

Also, I know you are a true creative genius (and I am in awe of the depth of your instincts), but breaking down a wall without my permission is not an appropriate way to express that creativity. It is not only a boundary violation but a building code violation as well. Additionally, the repairman can't get here until next week, so your expansion plan will have to be put on hold.

2. Re: Your fellow "tenant" (your word), Cooper. While I trust you with him, it is not okay for you to undermine my rules. It is not okay that you let him have chips and ice cream for dinner. It is not okay that you let him skip school to go to the movies. And it is really not okay that the movie was *Last Tango in Paris*.

As for your taking his friends to a "gentlemen's club," I accepted your rationale that it was an educational experience for the boys— and you are right, he is the most popular kid in school right now— but I'd prefer he not learn biology from those "gentlemen" and their ladies, Bambi, Trixie, and Kitten. And just because I yelled at you, I do not appreciate your claim that I have created a hostile living environment.

3. While I'm glad to see you're socializing, you must refill the hot tub after your parties. In fact, you need to tone down the parties altogether. Imagine my surprise when I saw the photos you posted on Facebook of your friends frolicking topless in the hot tub.

I think it's great that you're entertaining more often, but I can't keep fielding complaints from the neighbors about your noisy party games like Ring Around the Walker or naked Duck, Duck Caregiver.

I'm more than happy to have you use the house for social gatherings, but you cannot rent it out, advertise as "party central," or hand out T-shirts that say "Fuck Jimmy Buffett."

In closing, I hope I have satisfactorily answered your complaints and queries. I love having you live with me, and I am grateful for every minute Cooper and I have with you. You are an inspiration. You are also thirty days late with the rent.

Much love, Melissa

But for most of those in attendance, the funeral's high point was provided by Howard Stern, who opened his remarks by saying, "Joan Rivers had a dry pussy."

"At first, the words just hung there, as no one knew exactly what to do," Margaret Cho wrote in a *Huffington Post* piece called "Joan Rivers Put the 'Fun' Back in Funeral."

"Of course I started laughing hysterically, and everyone else, remembering who we were there to honor, followed suit. Howard Stern actually choked back tears as he continued—'Joan's pussy was so dry it was like a sponge—so that when she got in the bathtub—*whooooosh*—all the water would get absorbed in there! Joan said that if Whitney Houston had as dry a pussy as Joan's, she would still be alive today...'"

Stern described Rivers as a "big sister" and the "best friend in the world," as well as the "crazy aunt at a bar mitzvah."

"I hope Joan is somewhere chasing Johnny Carson with a baseball bat," he concluded.

The high-risk gambit won rave reviews. "With Howard Stern, she certainly had the kind of funeral that nobody else could have gotten away with," said Barbara Walters. "Nobody would have laughed more than Joan—and Joan was so dirty. She was at heart a prudish Jewish girl, but she had what a lot of people would call a filthy mouth."

Rivers's friends were thrilled with every aspect of the service. "It's exactly what Joan would have wanted," said Dorothy Melvin. "It was show business. People were laughing, people were crying, and Joan liked a show. She loved drama. She loved Broadway. She liked it big. She would have loved every single moment of it."

"It was a great send-off," said Martyn Fletcher. "She'd be furious she missed it."

"I think Joan would have sobbed," said Andrew Krasny. "I don't think she realized how globally loved she was, and how she changed the course of so many people's lives—and how many people had her sense of humor."

Her intimates knew only too well that Rivers felt unappreciated throughout her entire life. "She would never have believed the outpouring," Robert Higdon said. "She never believed she was loved. She would have been shocked. She never would have believed the tributes. I was just awestruck by the whole thing. She had no idea the world would respond that way."

Among showbiz veterans, some were struck by the sudden recognition of what her career had represented. Rivers was a fixture of the culture for so long that she had become like wallpaper—a perennial part of the scene that everyone took for granted until she was gone. "The interest in her is way beyond anything anybody understood," said Mark Simone. "She had been there every moment of everyone's life. A year ago she wasn't the hottest thing on earth, but she is now."

Even that didn't move old-timers to forgo their characteristic cynicism, and some noted that the effusive testimonials omitted the less appealing aspects of a more complex picture. "After my book on Johnny Carson was published, Joan got in touch and said, 'I loved the book. I really appreciated how you dealt with Edgar'—that I didn't knock him," Henry Bushkin reported. "And I didn't say she was a cunt. That was the eight-hundred-pound elephant at her funeral service."

But no one could deny Rivers's significance, no matter how they felt about her. "She was a polarizing figure, but whether you loved her or hated her, you respected her," said Lindsay Roth.

Rivers even earned praise from those she had victimized. "Watching Joan Rivers do stand-up at age eighty-one was incredible: athletic, jaw-dropping, terrifying, essential. It never stopped. Neither will she," tweeted Lena Dunham. "I told [comedian Marc] Maron I'd have a zinger when Joan died. But I didn't think she ever would. She felt eternal, and anyway, zingers are her territory."

This didn't stop Dunham from firing one off: "That being said, Joan is gone but a piece of her lives on: her nose, because it's made of polyurethane."

Knowing that Rivers had feared being incapacitated, her intimates were consoled by the fact that she never endured such an ordeal. The believers among them imputed their own meaning to the way her life ended. "As it was, she went out on such a high; she just went to sleep without knowing," Higdon said. "In some ways it was God's way of saying, 'Well done.' He blessed her, in a way, with her departure. She would always say, 'I don't know what you mean about God's grace,' but I think she finally found it. Walking out of her service, I thought, there's nothing unfinished here."

And yet there were slights that stung, despite all the accolades. The Broadway League, which represents the interests of theater owners and producers, initially refused to honor Rivers by dimming the lights on Broadway, the traditional posthumous tribute after the death of a theater world notable. Since Rivers was a playwright, a Broadway actress, a Tony Award nominee, and a constant theatergoer, the omission seemed curious. When the decision was challenged, the explanations only raised questions about whether a double standard undervalued Rivers's contributions compared with those of famous men.

Charlotte St. Martin, then the executive director of the Broadway League, initially claimed that Rivers did not meet the criteria for the honor, which was supposedly reserved for people who had been "very active recently in the theater, or else…synonymous with Broadway— people who made their careers here, or kept it up." The league had accorded that honor to Robin Williams, who starred in one play, *Bengal Tiger at the Baghdad Zoo*, in 2011, and performed a stand-up special, *Robin Williams: Live on Broadway*, in 2002.

St. Martin's comments prompted a wave of social media outrage, spawning the hashtag #dim4joan. The Broadway League finally reversed its decision, citing the public outcry: "Due to the outpouring of love and respect for Joan Rivers from our community and from her friends and fans worldwide, the marquees of Broadway theaters in New York will be dimmed in her memory tonight, at exactly 6:45 p.m., for one minute," the league announced on September 8.

The next affront was delivered the following February during the Academy Awards ceremony, which omitted Rivers from the "In Memoriam" segment honoring those who died the previous year. "That was such a snub," said Sue Cameron. "All her friends were just furious."

Robin Williams, Mickey Rooney, and Mike Nichols were included in the segment, but so were numerous executives, writers, and members of the production community whose names were unknown to those outside the industry. Since Rivers was a screenwriter, a director, and an actress in Hollywood feature films, she seemed more than worthy of mention, even without considering her contribution to the red-carpet phenomenon. "Rivers, per IMDb, boasts thirty-eight acting credits to her name in a career that spans sixty-three years," *People* magazine reported.

Fans were not mollified when the Academy issued a statement claiming it simply didn't have room for all "the many worthy artists and filmmakers we were unfortunately unable to feature."

"Dear @TheAcademy: It was really shameful that you didn't include #JoanRivers in your 'In Memoriam' tribute at the #Oscars. That was wrong," one fan tweeted. Another added, "Omitting Joan Rivers from that 'In Memoriam' was genuinely disrespectful."

Rivers's friends were even more outraged. "The Oscars were totally offensive," said Robert Higdon. "Thank goodness she was recognized at the Tonys."

The Tony Awards did include Rivers in the "In Memoriam" segment, which featured Josh Groban singing "You'll Never Walk Alone" while pictures of departed notables flashed onscreen. But in other industries where Rivers had worked, the recognition of her contributions remained curiously inconsistent. She was included in the "In Memoriam" tribute at the Emmy Awards, but excluded at the Grammy Awards—even though she had won the year's Grammy Award for Best Spoken Word Album earlier that very day.

Elsewhere, however, interest in Rivers's life remained intense. "When she died, we had an absolutely overwhelming and immediate response from the QVC customer base, from Facebook posts to calls to customer service," Michael George reported. "I was amazed at the employee response. There was a very gut response of empathy and sadness and sympathy. I received so many beautiful letters from employees who had worked with Joan, and others from QVC people who never met her but felt connected to her."

QVC management was initially unsure of how to respond to her death, despite Rivers's plan for Dangle to succeed her. "It was so unexpected; everyone just thought she would go on forever," George said. "We wrestled with whether to continue the business, but the feedback from customers was to continue it, and I'm glad we did. Sales have remained strong. David had appeared with her quite frequently, and occasionally hosted by himself, so the customers knew him and his connection to Joan. As long as Joan Rivers Worldwide wants to work with QVC and our customers are responding, we would see that business continuing."

By the middle of 2015, Dangle felt confident about the changeover. "The transition has been smooth," he reported. "We had a better first half of the year this year than we did last year. The customer is saying, 'I miss Joan so much, but I'm so glad I can still buy the jewelry.' Now Joan is making money for her daughter—and she's not even here."

Rivers's former coworkers proved equally devoted. A month after she died, Bill Reardin helped to organize a reunion of staffers from *The Joan Rivers Show*, and about forty people flew to New York to celebrate their former boss, while colleagues in Los Angeles participated on FaceTime.

Many felt very emotional about her loss. "The day she died, I was sitting in my car in front of preschool, and I just couldn't stop crying," said Randi Gelfand Pollack, the show's booker. "There was such a connection."

Most had maintained that connection, even though decades had passed since they worked with Rivers. "The last time I saw her, she said, 'Come to see my show,' and after the show we talked until one thirty in the morning," said Larry Ferber.

He was on a cruise in Alaska when he got a text saying that Joan had gone into cardiac arrest, and he was so upset he considered canceling a speech he was scheduled to give about his years in the entertainment industry. "I thought, I don't think I can do this," said Ferber, who had titled his speech "Could They Talk" in homage to Rivers. "And then I thought, Joan would have said, 'Get off your ass and go to work!' So I did."

But the loss left him feeling bereft. "When she died, I cried," he said. "I lost a good friend. She was one of a kind. There's nobody like her. She's irreplaceable."

Virtually all of Joan's close friends felt the same way, and many wept while being interviewed about her, months after her death. The loss was most devastating for Melissa, but one consolation finally emerged with the resolution of her malpractice suit against the clinic and the doctors who had presided over Joan's fatal procedure.

In May of 2016, the Rivers family announced that an agreement had been reached in order to avoid protracted litigation and the doctors accepted responsibility for Joan's death. The dollar amount was not released, but news reports described it as a multimillion-dollar settlement.

"Melissa Rivers said in a statement that she was happy to be 'able to put the legal aspects of my mother's death behind me and ensure that those culpable for her death have accepted responsibility for their actions quickly and without equivocation,'" *The New York Times* reported. "She said she hoped no one had to go through what her family had endured and vowed to 'work towards ensuring higher safety standards in outpatient surgical clinics.'...The lawyers for the Rivers family, Jeffrey Bloom and Ben Rubinowitz, said they did not reveal the amount of the settlement because they wanted to focus on improving patient care. But they said it was 'substantial.'"

A spokesperson for Yorkville Endoscopy said, "Our thoughts and prayers continue to go out to the Rivers family. We remain committed to providing quality, compassionate health care services that meet the needs of our patients, their families, and the community."

In an interview with *Entertainment Tonight*, Melissa Rivers added, "I hope that this sparks conversation about care and policy at ambulatory surgical centers. If talking about what happened to my mother can help even one other family, it will have been worth it."

## Chapter Twenty-Four

# LEGACY:
# LAUGHTER AND LIBERATION

Long before Rivers died, knowledgeable observers were describing her legacy in sweeping terms. "It's impossible to overestimate her impact, both because she redefined what was possible for women in comedy and because she's been a role model for so many," Roz Warren wrote in *Revolutionary Laughter: The World of Women Comics*, which was published in 1995.

Although that was true even then, the next two decades brought transformational changes to the culture as well as to Rivers's career. By the time she died, many of the hottest names in comedy were women. Tina Fey and Amy Poehler had hosted the Golden Globes; Ellen DeGeneres and Whoopi Goldberg had hosted the Academy Awards. Sarah Silverman, Whitney Cummings, Kathy Griffin, and Margaret Cho made HBO specials, and Griffin has also made sixteen stand-up specials for Bravo, breaking the Guinness world record for the number of aired TV specials by any comedian on any network in the history of comedy.

After turning down the chance to replace Jon Stewart as host of *The Daily Show*, Amy Schumer won an Emmy Award for her own Comedy Central show, *Inside Amy Schumer*. She also wrote and starred in the movie *Trainwreck*, which has grossed more than $100 million.

Even more impressive was the $300 million gross of *Bridesmaids*, the 2011 movie that Kristen Wiig cowrote and starred in with Melissa McCarthy, Maya Rudolph, and Rebel Wilson. Since then, McCarthy's box office performance has been so stellar that *Forbes* headlined one recent story "Can Melissa McCarthy's Career Survive All These Hit Movies?" In the last three years alone, her films have included *The Boss, Identity Thief, The Heat, Tammy,* and *Spy,* among others. "Comedy is a man's world, but it's changing with these emerging stars like Melissa McCarthy, who's hysterical," said Larry King.

If that represents the view of a man in his eighties, women half his age have a different perspective. "Women run comedy now," Sarah Silverman said in the Comedy Hall of Fame documentary *Joan Rivers: Exit Laughing.*

Virtually all of Rivers's successors acknowledge their debt to her. "Her existence changed everything for women in comedy," Silverman said.

"I can't think of a female comic who wasn't influenced by her," added Judy Gold. "I think she opened doors for everybody."

When Amy Schumer made the cover of *Vogue* in July of 2016, Jonathan Van Meter described Rivers's influence on her. "Just after Joan Rivers's death in 2014, Schumer gave a hilarious and moving speech in which she essentially said that Rivers was the reason she got into comedy. 'I carried her with me for as long as I can remember,' she said that night onstage, choking up," Van Meter reported.

When he interviewed Schumer for the cover story, her first words were about Rivers. "When I heard she had died, I was like 'Well, *that's* not possible.' It really fucked me up," Schumer said.

But for most people, the full recognition of Rivers's impact was a long time coming. "She had this insanely diverse career that people didn't recognize until she was gone," said Chip Duckett, who produced Rivers's live shows in New York for nearly two decades. "She was such a chameleon, but when they looked at the whole of her career, a lot of people woke up to the fact that she had been such a trailblazer in so many ways."

Throughout that career, Rivers remained on the cutting edge of the culture instead of being relegated to the dusty past that had claimed most of her chronological peers. When Joan died, Sarah Silverman said she watched *Fashion Police* every week and was stunned by how much Rivers got away with in her commentary. "They were the most hard-core jokes on TV," Silverman said. "You just can't believe that she's saying them."

The following month Silverman paid tribute on *Saturday Night Live* in a sketch that featured Rivers arriving on the celestial stage. "Heaven—are you serious?" said Silverman as Rivers. "Me in heaven? I guess I should be here—I'm practically a virgin. The last time someone was inside me it was Melissa."

Such cracks seemed eminently appropriate, given Rivers's sixty-year track record of talking about what did and did not enter her vagina. On any family tree of comedy, performers like Silverman and Amy Schumer are direct descendants of Rivers. In an interview with *The Guardian*, Margaret Cho described Rivers as one of her "comedy parents."

Back in the 1960s, Rivers began skewering the double standards that judge women more harshly than men, and today's younger comics are continuing that trend. Amy Schumer regularly sends up sexist values on her television show, *Inside Amy Schumer*, and some of her sketches have become instant classics—including one in which Tina Fey, Julia Louis-Dreyfus, and Patricia Arquette mocked the cutoff date that determines when a woman has passed her "last fuckable day," as decreed by men. Another much-acclaimed segment, a parody of *Twelve Angry Men*, skewered Hollywood's warped body expectations for women at a trial in which an all-male jury debated whether Schumer was hot enough to appear on television.

"I don't think she's protagonist hot," said Kevin Kane.

"But Kevin James is?" John Hawkes asked.

"She's built like a lineman, and she has Cabbage Patch–like features," said Paul Giamatti. "Her ass makes me furious!"

And yet no matter how strenuously she made fun of ageism and sexism, Rivers continued to reinforce the rules of a male-dominated culture—whereas many of her successors make a point of defying them. When Schumer signed a $10 million book contract for her memoir, she was forthright in declaring that she was thirty-four years old and weighed 160 pounds—and neither of those facts rendered her undesirable, because she could still "catch a dick anytime I want."

Schumer refuses to subsist on Altoids in the name of beauty, and she is vocal about her rejection of such self-martyrdom. "I am very into making up my own rules," she told *Vogue*. "Like, I don't want to play the game and succeed at it. I want to redefine it."

Schumer isn't the only one. When Mindy Kaling's book *Why Not Me?* hit number one on *The New York Times* best-seller list, Kaling tweeted that her ass was so big it split her skirt and she had to be sewed back into her dress in order to continue shooting her television show, *The Mindy Project*.

From TV, movies, and stand-up to the book industry, women comics have sparked a burgeoning market for such subversive content. Tina Fey reportedly received an advance of up to $7 million for her 2011 book, *Bossypants*, which sold 3.5 million copies.

But Rivers went to her grave still horrified by the refusal of such women to conform to the strictures that she herself had worked so hard to obey. Appalled by Lena Dunham's penchant for disrobing on her TV series, *Girls*, Rivers protested that Dunham was "the first fat girl naked on television" and that viewers watched her with "their hands over their eyes." Rivers also complained that if she ever had to see Dunham's "ass, boobs, or tattoos" on TV again, HBO should be charged with crimes against humanity. Since Dunham was free enough to "have her fat ass on display," Rivers added, why wasn't she "free enough to have a fucking salad once in a while?"

The contrast between Rivers's values and those of Dunham provide eloquent testimony to a distinct cultural shift among the younger generation. In her HBO special, *Amy Schumer: Live at the Apollo*, Schumer refers to herself as a garden gnome, a fat tumbleweed, Gilbert Grape's mom, "one of those inflatable things outside a car wash," and super bloated, among other descriptions. "I'm not a real woman—I'm just harvesting organs for one," Schumer said.

Schumer "isn't afraid to say insulting things about herself," Mike Hale noted in *The New York Times*. "But she doesn't do it with the self-mocking edge of a Joan Rivers. It's a comfortable kind of self-deprecation, born of insecurity but delivered with a confidence that takes the sting out and gives the listener a smug feeling of complicity."

Younger women now claim the right to poke fun at anything they want. "The breadth of my genius lies in my range, from in-depth sociopolitical commentary to jokes about shitting your pants," Cho said. "You have the entire human experience in there—a combination of being insightful and crass."

But Rivers got there first—and in challenging the prevailing restrictions of her time, she played a major role in expanding the ability of the entire culture to deal with the realities of women's lives. When she started out, Ed Sullivan wouldn't let her use the word "pregnant" on camera despite her bulging belly. Such taboos exerted a toxic influence on women's lives, according to Dr. Anna Fels, a psychiatrist at Weill Cornell Medical College and author of *Necessary Dreams: Ambition in Women's Changing Lives*.

"Cultural silence about any subject conveys that it is disturbing, shameful, ugly, frightening—and important enough to need a cover-up," said Dr. Fels. "Cancer used to be one such subject. Another was the sexual and reproductive experiences of women. Words like 'vagina,' 'menstruation,' or even 'pregnancy' were banished from common speech as 'dirty words.' Women didn't know what their sexual organs looked like or even where they were. To be socially prohibited from mentioning, let alone discussing, their bodies, and particularly their sexuality—women's identities were diminished. They in effect existed in a verbal purdah."

By using her wit to defuse such fraught subjects, Fels said, "Rivers began to change all that."

When Rivers first shocked people by mentioning unmentionable secrets like abortion, she was just trying to grab the attention of her audiences. But in doing so, she helped to liberate herself and everyone else from the societal stigmas imposed on women because of their gender. "She talked about the fact that once you tell the truth and let it all out, you don't have to be afraid ever again," said Mark Simone.

As any visitor to comedy clubs can attest, women today have plowed through every line of demarcation that used to prevent them from sharing their experiences and airing their grievances. Susie Essman's act includes jokes about blow jobs, G-spots, menopause, hot flashes, night sweats, thinning vaginal walls, and vaginal dryness. Female stand-ups routinely get onstage and talk about peeing, pooping, and farting. Amy Schumer discusses her urinary tract infections so much that they should get second billing at her engagements. After Tig Notaro was treated for breast cancer, she took off her shirt and performed topless, revealing her double mastectomy scars, in *Tig Notaro: Boyish Girl Interrupted*, her HBO comedy special.

"There's not that big a boundary between men and women anymore in terms of the material they can do," said Catch a Rising Star founder Rick Newman. "To some of the audience, the double standard still exists, but nothing is sacred in comedy."

And over time, the cumulative impact of such incremental acts of defiance is incalculable. "This is how you turn the world around—through humor," said Ricki Stern, who directed *Joan Rivers: A Piece of Work*.

Indeed, some analysts credit female comics with having moved to the forefront of cultural change. "Comedians Are Leading the Feminist Movement," proclaimed the headline of a 2015 Mic.com essay by Dr. Marcie Bianco, an adjunct associate professor at Hunter College. "These comedians use satire to cut to the bone, and misogynists are too busy laughing to realize they're bleeding to death."

Female comics are also expanding their scope. Thirty or forty years ago, Rivers was unusual in trying to work as a director, screenwriter, playwright, and producer in addition to being a performer. Today such multiple roles are commonplace. "Everything's changed," said the long-time club owner Caroline Hirsch. "Comedy was always the boys' place, and now the women are rising. There are an amazing amount of women coming up through the ranks. They write their own jokes, they think outside the box, and they all want to produce. It's much more permissive—of language, of content, of how women dress. The content can be anything— Amy Schumer is allowed to say 'pussy' on Comedy Central. Comedy has opened up a whole new world of what's acceptable for women to say, and Joan kind of started it. She broke the ice there. When Howard Stern talked about Whitney Houston's vagina at Joan's funeral, that was Joan's joke. Here she is, making fun of a dead person, which should be taboo— but it's not. Looking back, Joan seems like even more of a role model, because she broke through when it was even harder to do."

Long gone are the days when women in stand-up struggled in vain to be heard. "I spend a lot of time in comedy clubs, and there are just as many women waiting to get up and get stage time as men," said Barry Dougherty of the Friars Club.

Gender barriers remain indisputable. The sexism is most obvious among the old guard. When the Friars Club held a ninetieth birthday party for Jerry Lewis, the *New York Post*'s Page Six reported that the "starry guests" included Robert De Niro, Jim Carrey, Richard Belzer, Chazz Palminteri, Jeff Ross, and Freddie Roman—"'but not a single woman,' noted a guest."

Nor has television changed as much as might have been expected. When Rivers got her own show on the new Fox network in 1987, she was the first and only female host of a late-night talk show. In 2015, a year after she died, *Vanity Fair* featured a photograph of late-night talk show hosts that prompted this analysis in the *Huffington Post*:

"If you needed any more proof that late-night TV is still a man's world, look no further than *Vanity Fair*," wrote Emma Gray. "Ten men in suits (eight of whom are white) sit sipping whiskey for a recent story under the headline 'Why Late-Night Television Is Better than Ever.' The answer is certainly not diversity of any kind. It's common knowledge that late night is something of a boys' club. After all, there are exactly zero women hosting late-night shows on major networks right now. And women who are involved with late night, like Grace Helbig, who replaced Chelsea Handler on E!, are nowhere to be found on *Vanity Fair*'s cover. And it's not just the hosting gigs that primarily go to men. The majority of staff writers on late-night TV shows are—you guessed it—of the dude (and pale) persuasion. Even Stephen Colbert—who wrote an essay for *Glamour* which acknowledged that late night is 'a bit of a sausagefest' and detailed how he hopes to celebrate women's voices—only has two women on his writing staff of nineteen."

But such imbalances now provoke outrage rather than passive acquiescence. "The 100 percent male, 80 percent white *Vanity Fair* image didn't go unnoticed by women and men on Twitter, who began calling out how tone-deaf it was," Gray reported. "The men featured in the *Vanity Fair* story are generally excellent comedians. It's great to celebrate the accomplishments of men like Stephen Colbert, Jon Stewart, and Larry Wilmore, while looking forward to seeing what newcomers like Trevor Noah might do. But the *Vanity Fair* piece doesn't even acknowledge the staggering gender gap until its final two paragraphs. 'What's conspicuously missing from late-night, still, is women,' writes David Kamp. 'How gobsmackingly insane is it that no TV network has had the common sense—and that's all we're talking about in 2015, not courage, bravery, or even decency—to hand over the reins of an existing late-night comedy program to a female person?'"

The dial has moved slightly since then; in 2016, Samantha Bee got her own show on TBS and Chelsea Handler returned to late night on Netflix. Despite such incremental changes, however, "it's not quite enough," Gray concluded dryly.

If the major networks are still a white boys' club, Rivers's influence has nonetheless permeated the culture in myriad other ways. Her stardom inspired countless women to follow her into the entertainment business, and many were particularly encouraged by the fact that she wasn't beautiful. Rivers's appearances on *The Tonight Show* marked the first time the comic Cory Kahaney ever saw a woman telling jokes on television. "She wasn't that pretty, but people laughed, and they loved her," Kahaney said in a posthumous tribute to Rivers at New York's Museum of Jewish Heritage. "I was a Jewish girl and not that pretty, and it gave me a vision of a possible future. I was so grateful for that."

To such girls, Rivers's success proved that other qualities could compensate for physical attractiveness if a woman was shortchanged by fate. "She gave little outcast Jewish girls the permission to have a dream—to dream that you can do it," said Judy Gold. "I'm a Jewish girl from New Jersey, and there was Barbra Streisand, Joan Rivers, and Bette Midler. They were not conventionally beautiful; it was all talent, tenacity, and hard work. Joan was a hero to me. I felt I could do it because she did it—against all odds."

Kathy Griffin grew up in an Irish Catholic family, but she felt the same way. "I knew when I was two that I wanted to do this," she said. "It was pretty much my first thought: I want to be a comedian someday. I looked to everyone, but I related to Joan the most. She was the biggest, and she could roll with the big boys. Obviously sexism is alive and well—it's still all middle-aged white guys signing the checks and doing the hiring and firing—but I watched this petite woman really roll with Johnny Carson, the toughest of all the boys' clubbers. That was the first lesson she taught me. Of all the women who went before us, she's the one who broke the glass ceiling for me. She stood up to the guys when the guys really hardcore fucked her. Who had her back? Nobody."

Rivers's career gave younger comics an ongoing master class in how to succeed and stay relevant, and many fellow performers were particularly inspired by her resilience. "She's the poster girl for perseverance," Sarah Silverman said in *Joan Rivers: Exit Laughing*. "Her whole lifetime was a lesson."

Because Rivers shared her struggles with such candor, her story provided a compelling illustration of the fact that life is full of unexpected challenges, and survival depends on how you deal with them. "The attitude was, adversity makes you stronger, and you do not give up, and in the end you fucking win," said Chip Duckett, Rivers's longtime producer.

Duckett was particularly influenced by Rivers's courage and zest for daily life, even in the face of adversity. "She lived every day, wanting to keep going, wanting to be active regardless of her age," he said. "It made me take stock of how fortunate I am, which I don't think I was always aware of until I saw how she felt about it."

Many of Rivers's former colleagues cite her as a professional role model who had a lasting impact on their careers. "What I learned from Joan Rivers was, always know how to reinvent yourself," said Larry Ferber.

"No one reinvented themselves better or more often than Joan," said Judy Gold.

For Rivers, that trait was rooted in perpetual insecurity. "It's a struggle every day," she said in the documentary *Joan Rivers: Exit Laughing*. "It's quicksand. If you don't reinvent yourself, you're gone. I'm always just looking for another door to go through."

In doing so, she demonstrated the importance of enterprise over and over again. "Some of the other things I learned from Joan were, act on good ideas. Don't sit on your ass and wait for it to come to you. Move!" said the former *Joan Rivers Show* producer Marlaine Selip.

Rivers's longevity also made a big impression on her successors, particularly the tremendous success she achieved in her seventies. "I find that so inspiring," said Sarah Silverman.

But Rivers's influence wasn't limited to those in show business; innumerable fans absorbed unexpected wisdom from reading her books and observing her life story. When Rivers died, Laura Haefeli was a college student aspiring to a career in comedy and working as an intern at *Saturday Night Live*. "Of any comedian, she was most herself, and I've had a hard time being myself," said Haefeli, who grew up in a Catholic family and identifies as gay. "She did what she loved doing, and she got a lot of shit for it until the day she died. She definitely paved the way and showed me that I can do what I want and be who I am and go into the field I want. As long as you're working hard and doing what you love, that's all that matters, and she worked harder than all of them."

Men and women, gay and straight, young and old—all were affected by Rivers, whose range is suggested by how disparate her audience had become. Haefeli is in her early twenties; Bill Boggs, an Emmy Award–winning television talk show host, is now in his seventies. Over the course of several decades, Boggs interviewed Rivers several times, and he never forgot the ferocity of her drive for success.

"She said to me, 'You have to want it more than food. You have to want it more than your family,'" he recalled. "Here's a woman who slept in her car—she was that dedicated."

Boggs sees Rivers's relevance as extending far beyond show business. A motivational speaker who lectures about success all over the country, he is the author of *Got What It Takes? Successful People Reveal How They Made It to the Top—So You Can Too!* "Anyone who wants to accomplish anything in life should look at Joan Rivers, at the tunnel vision she had and the sacrifices she made," Boggs said. "She is a role model for everyone."

In June of 2016, Christie's auctioned off The Private Collection of Joan Rivers, a selection of possessions that ranged from Chanel and Judith Leiber handbags to diamonds to costume jewelry and "tons of china, service for all New York," as Melissa put it. "My mom never saw a tag sale she didn't like."

The auction raised a total of $2.2 million, with a portion of the proceeds going to Guide Dogs for the Blind and God's Love We Deliver. The highest bid went for a nineteenth-century Fabergé frame, which sold for $245,000.

Before the auction, the value of the Tiffany silver dog bowl engraved with the name of Spike—the Yorkshire terrier Rivers credited with having saved her life when she contemplated suicide in 1987—was estimated at $500 to $800.

The dog bowl sold for $13,750.

# UPDATES FROM THE AFTERLIFE: "YOU *WERE* FAT, YOU BITCH!"

On the one-year anniversary of Joan Rivers's death, my cell phone pinged in the middle of the night. Sue Cameron was emailing from Los Angeles to tell me she had just seen a psychic and enjoyed a long chat with Joan.

When we spoke the next day, Cameron assured me that she had consulted this medium before, the woman wasn't a charlatan, and she always relayed information from the dead that she had no way of knowing in real life. "She works for various law enforcement agencies," Cameron explained. "She doesn't predict anything; it's just whoever shows up to talk. She channels them. A lot of people come in."

Cameron had actually scheduled the session to reach out to her late mother, "but I was secretly hoping that Joan would come in," she said. "And she did."

I wasn't surprised to hear that Cameron thought so. Joan's close friends were well aware of her fervent belief that spirits could survive death and communicate with the living.

As a headline in the *New York Post* put it a few days before the one-year anniversary of her demise, "Rivers believed in ghosts." According to the gossip columnist Cindy Adams, "Joan's spectral fetish was strong. One holiday she wanted her hotel room changed. Upset, she told me, 'I feel a distinct extra presence here. Curtains ruffled. I suddenly felt a chill. Like I'm not alone.' Once, when accommodations couldn't change, her grandson moved into the room. Another vacation in an old-fashioned historic inn, she jammed a chair against her door. 'The closet moved,' she said. 'It slid in toward me. Not just once. Here's something otherworldly. I feel it. Who knows what went on long ago? I'm not comfortable. I want out.'"

Many of Joan's friends experienced similar incidents. "She said she felt the presence of ghosts, and she was frightened of them," said Blaine Trump. "She really was crazed on the subject."

Rivers was far from alone in that belief: 18 percent of adults in the United States say they have seen or been in the presence of ghosts, according to a 2009 Pew Research Center survey, and 29 percent have felt in touch with someone who has already died. In 2013, a poll by the *Huffington Post* and YouGov found that 45 percent of Americans believe in ghosts, or that the spirits of dead people can come back in certain places and situations.

Rivers saw dead people everywhere. "She was nuts about ghosts, and she always slept with the lights on," said Robert Higdon, who recalled her wearing a miner's headlamp to bed so she could illuminate her surroundings while they were on safari in Africa.

"Wherever we were, there was a ghost," Higdon said. "I had a country house in Middleburg, Virginia, and she said it had a ghost. Her dog knew it. She said, 'Spike can tell there's a ghost here.' At Malcolm Forbes's château in Normandy, she was staying in Malcolm's room, and my room was cut through there with a secret passageway. I had to sleep with the passageway open all night, because she was afraid a ghost was going to get her."

When Rivers and her grandson went to Colonial Williamsburg, the historic site proved a particularly fertile ground for apparitions. "She saw two or three ghosts," Margie Stern reported. "One was a black man in the mirror. When she went to the administration, they said, 'Are you in room X? A lot of people have seen ghosts on that floor.'"

At home in Manhattan, Rivers had calmed down about ghosts after exorcising her apartment, but anxiety often overwhelmed her when she traveled. "To me it was crazy, but she just was so nervous about it all, to the point where if she got to a hotel and felt something was off, she would change hotels," Trump said. "She was really scared."

During one visit to Scotland, Rivers and Trump were heading for a house outside Edinburgh, "and somebody said, 'I hope you're not staying at such and such house, because that house is possessed,'" Trump recalled. "Someone else said, 'Whatever you do, don't stay in room number one!' We got to the house, and they said, 'Miss Rivers, you're in room number one.' Joan was just crazed. I said I'd switch rooms with her and she said no."

But she knew how upset Rivers was, so she eventually decided to keep her company. "In the middle of the night I went and knocked on Joan's door, and the two of us slept in her room." Trump imitates herself lying rigid in bed, staring straight up at the ceiling in wide-eyed alarm, with the covers drawn up to her chin.

Notwithstanding her terror, Joan couldn't resist acting like a Jewish mother even with an ancient Scottish ghost. "She said, 'This woman is trapped in this house. I really want to free her,'" Trump reported. "We did a cleansing of room number one before we left. She did this whole ceremony with a bowl of water and a mirror, and she said a prayer for the woman, because she wanted to release her spirit."

Despite her fear of ghosts, there was one spectral visitor Rivers didn't seem to mind. After Orin Lehman died, she claimed that his spirit often came to hang out with her. "For a long time she saw Orin Lehman sitting in his favorite chair in her living room," said Margie Stern. "She would just say, 'He's there.'"

Some wraiths may be tortured souls seeking escape from eternal purgatory, but Rivers's own spirit is apparently a busybody who likes to check up on everyone. Before she died, she told Pete Hathaway, "I'm dying to see my mother again." In life, she often visited him at his historic nineteenth-century home in Salisbury, Connecticut. "She definitely came back to this house after she died," he said.

As a gift for her Connecticut house, Hathaway once gave Rivers a four-leaf clover made of horseshoes, and after she died he asked to have it back as a memento of their friendship. Several weeks later, he hung it on a wall.

"The next morning, I came downstairs as the sun was coming up, and I heard a knock on the front door," he said. "I thought, how odd—who the hell is knocking on my door at five thirty in the morning? I heard it again, and I opened the door and there was no one there. I had set the sprinkler the night before, and everything was wet. No one had walked down the path, because there would have been wet footprints going onto the dry bluestone. As I turned around, I happened to see the four-leaf clover, and I thought, Joan was just here. I think she was saying, 'I'm glad you finally got the horseshoe out of the box and hung it up.'"

When Hathaway told Rivers's assistant what had happened, he imitated the mysterious knock, a distinctive pattern of raps as specific as Morse code. "Jocelyn said, 'A chill has just gone up my spine. When we were traveling, that was the knock we used to do on each other's doors to be let in. That was Joan,'" Hathaway reported.

About three weeks later, "I was minding my own business early in the morning and I heard high-heeled footsteps going up and down the halls and into the bedrooms," he said. But when he investigated, "no one was there."

That was the last time Hathaway felt Rivers's presence. "She's never been back," he said wistfully.

Some of Rivers's friends are disappointed that she hasn't visited them. "I'm waiting for her to come back and talk to me," said Margie Stern.

Sallie Ann Glassman had better luck. Shortly after Rivers's death, Glassman was climbing Choquequirao, an Incan site in southern Peru, when Rivers suddenly appeared on the path ahead of her. "She points to her eyes and to my eyes and makes the gesture, 'I see you,'" Glassman said. "It was enough to stop me in my tracks, but then she sort of dissolved right in front of me."

Since returning to the United States, Glassman has seen Rivers again "many times," she said. During one session with a medium, Glassman reported, "Joan said, 'I'm right here.' She put her hands on my face and said, 'I've got this. You've been guiding me; now I'm guiding you.' She expressed her frustration that she was trying to communicate with her loved ones, and they don't know she's there. Joan is trying very hard to let Margie Stern know she's not just going to disappear on her."

Sue Cameron also got quick results when she consulted her own psychic and Rivers showed up immediately. She seemed to be reexperiencing the last day of her conscious life. "She was sitting in the waiting room at the Yorkville medical center," Cameron reported. "She said, 'I have a premonition this isn't going to go well.'"

(Cameron later called Melissa to ask if her mother had actually said that before undergoing her procedure, and Melissa replied, "That's absolutely right.")

During Cameron's session with the psychic, Rivers seemed her usual self. Even when faced with brain death at the Yorkville clinic, she had apparently remained preoccupied with her eternal quest for new jokes, and her first thought was that the accident could provide fresh material. "When she stopped breathing, she came out of her body and watched all of it," Cameron said. "She said, 'Oh—I could really turn this into a bit!'"

Cameron wasn't surprised by the fact that Rivers had made an appearance via a psychic; she had always expected to survive the death of her body. "Joan absolutely believed in heaven—there's no question about it," said Cameron. "She talked a lot about hanging out with people in heaven, and she nominated candidates for hell."

Her intimates also assumed that Rivers would relish the chance to tell off her dead husband when she finally got to confront him again. In a tearful bedside farewell at the hospital, Cameron had even teased her comatose friend about such a scenario. "I said, 'I feel sorry for Edgar, because he's about to see you,'" she recalled wryly.

But other friends may have had a more accurate sense of Rivers's growing detachment as the years went on. "I once asked her what she'd do if she saw Edgar in heaven, and she said, 'I'd nod politely—and walk on by,'" said Robert Higdon, adding that they both burst out laughing at the thought.

When Cameron saw the psychic, she learned that the spectral Rivers was avoiding her late husband, as promised. "I asked if she's seen Edgar. She said he's in a small library with lots of books, and he stays in there all day and reads, and she doesn't go in there," Cameron said. "At the

Ambazac house, they had a small room that was a den, with all the books, and Edgar stayed in there all the time and read books. Melissa re-created that room in her house, so I think Edgar's in Melissa's house now."

To Cameron's relief, Rivers seemed at peace with the circumstances of her death. "She was tired and ready to go," Cameron said. "She was so tired of having to be Joan Rivers. She said it was such an ordeal to keep the Joan machine going. She said over and over, 'I'm exhausted. I'm done! I don't want to be Joan anymore.' I said to her, 'It was medical malpractice! I want to kill Gwen Korovin!' She said, 'Don't bother. She'll get a reality show, and that'll kill her.' She displayed no anger. I don't think Joan would have chosen to go this way, and she certainly didn't want to leave her family, but she was just bone-tired exhausted."

Rivers did regret the pain her sudden death had caused her friends. "She said she was devastated when she saw how grief-stricken her loved ones were," Cameron said. "When she died, there was a point where I couldn't stop crying, and I went to the Santa Monica pier. I was holding on to the railing, just crying. She actually described that. Nobody knew that—but Joan knew."

But as always, her family was her main concern. "Joan said, 'All I care about is that Melissa and Cooper are happy,'" Cameron said. "She knew Melissa was doing well, and she was so happy she gave her this life. She said that she didn't love doing reality television, and she did it for Melissa. She wanted to leave Melissa a safety net. She said the only downside of being dead is that she likes to have an impact, and Melissa can't hear her. When I told that to Melissa, she said, 'Believe me, I hear her!' I said, 'We all do!'"

Indeed, Rivers is actively keeping tabs on her friends, and she seems particularly interested in surgical procedures. "She asked me, 'Do your feet fit in shoes now?'" Cameron said. "This is stunning, because last January I had a foot operation on a toe that had a bone spur on it, just so I could fit in shoes!"

Rivers also kept track of what happened to a sentimental object her daughter had bequeathed to Cameron, who was touched to receive a token of her deep friendship with Edgar when Rivers's apartment was sold.

"Joan described exactly the scarf of Edgar's that was in her drawer in New York that Melissa gave me a couple of months ago," Cameron reported.

For her, the whole conversation felt much like the ones she and Rivers shared in person for so many years. "She said, 'Can you believe I did QVC?' It was very funny. I wasn't crying during this part; it was like I was talking to her. We were laughing."

As for Rivers's eternal reward, it turned out that her version resembles a cruise on Lake Tahoe. "Whenever she would have a gig at Harrah's, they would give her a boat and a captain and food, just to go around Lake Tahoe during the day, and she loved doing that," Cameron said. "The hotel would give us tuna sandwiches and fruit, and we would have lunch on the boat. She just loved being out on boats. When Edgar died, the first thing she did was charter a boat in Greece. That's her go-to thing—charter a boat."

Rivers apparently arranged something similar in the great beyond. "She said she was spending a lot of her time on boats, because she loves the wind in her hair," Cameron reported. "She said it's fabulous, because now she doesn't care if her hair gets messed up. She's happy. She's out cruising—no personal appearances, no makeup, messy hair, floating on the water. She's thrilled. Believe me, she's fine."

Since Rivers felt she never got her due on earth, Cameron was comforted to hear that Joan was overwhelmed by the response to her death. "She was at the funeral, and she said she had no idea how much she was loved. She said, 'I cannot believe all the love! I never knew.'"

But Rivers couldn't resist a minor dig about the most celebrated performance at the service. "She made a joke that she could have written Howard Stern's speech better," Cameron said. "That's so Joan!"

Whatever her quibbles, Rivers was gratified to learn that she left such an enormous mark on the world she lived in. She had spent her entire life feeling judged and found wanting, and nothing—no amount of applause, fame, money, or love—was ever sufficient to fill the aching hole inside her. Her insatiable need for approval drove her until the day she died.

But in the end, she created a more outsized legacy than the icons she admired and envied. The session with the medium left Cameron with the sense that Rivers understood what she had achieved and that the larger world had finally recognized it as well.

Rivers left her life the way she lived it: at full throttle. She'd told so many of her friends that she didn't want to stick around in an impaired state, and she managed to do exactly what she loved doing until the last day of her life.

"She had no ailments," Bill Reardin said. "She was in such good physical shape. She had such energy. She never had people say, 'She looks old and tired.' She went out on top."

It was the way she wanted to go, and Rivers's last words to the psychic struck Cameron as a reassuring sign that her friend's driven spirit was resting in peace at last.

"I'm so grateful," Rivers said. "What a life!"

That sounded like a fitting epitaph for an extraordinary career, but Cameron suspected that Rivers had more to say. Before she died, she made it clear that she planned on settling some scores in the great hereafter. "She absolutely believed she was going to go and confront Elizabeth Taylor," Cameron said.

Rivers was looking forward to delivering her final message: "You *were* fat, you bitch!"

# ACKNOWLEDGMENTS

Many authors thank their agents for helping them with a book, but this one literally wouldn't exist without David Kuhn, because it was his idea. My deepest gratitude to David for pushing me to take on the extraordinary life story of Joan Rivers, who not only entertained me while I was writing about her but will forever inspire me with her courage and determination.

Thanks also to Judith Clain and her team at Little, Brown for their support and enthusiasm, which were much appreciated.

I owe an enormous debt to the friends and family, former coworkers, and other colleagues of Joan Rivers who gave their time and shared their experiences with me. My deepest thanks to Melissa Rivers, Sabrina Lott Miller, Sue Cameron, Dorothy Melvin, Liz Smith, Margaret Cho, Gloria Steinem, Judy Gold, Kathy Griffin, Larry King, Barry Diller, George Hamilton, Barbara Walters, Lou Alexander, Blaine Trump, Ivanka Trump, Shelly Schultz, Andrew Krasny, Lisa Lampanelli, Caroline Hirsch, Cary Hoffman, Henry Bushkin, Arnold Stiefel, Sandy Gallin, Bob Colacello, Josh Ostrovsky, Jesse Kornbluth, Annette Tapert, Jenny Allen, David Finkle, Rick Newman, David Bernstein, Margie Stern, Ricki Stern, Michael George, David Dangle, Robert Higdon, Pete Hathaway, Martyn Fletcher, Abigail Pogrebin, Mark Simone, Barry Dougherty, Pat Cooper, Kip Forbes, Kenny Bell, Steve Olsen, Andy Cohen, Billy Eichner, Lonny Price, Manny Azenberg, Erin Sanders, Sally Koslow, Rob Koslow, John Erman, Jason Sheeler, Larry Ferber, Marlaine Selip, Bill Reardin, Ann Northrop, Steve Garrin, Molly Haskell, Chip Duckett, Valerie Frankel, Charles Busch, William Finn, Karen Pearl, Bill Evans, Jeffrey Mahshie, Sallie Ann Glassman, Jeffrey Gurian, Jeff Cubeta, Lindsay Roth, Laura

Haefeli, Dr. Anna Fels, Randi Gelfand Pollack, Leslie Stevens, and the late Wendy Vanderbilt Lehman, Lynn Grefe, Danny Schechter, and Joe Franklin, along with all the other people who shared their memories with me, including those who requested confidentiality. Thanks also to Jocelyn Pickett and to Jane Klain at the Paley Center for Media for her invaluable research assistance.

A special thanks to Bill Boggs, who first introduced me to the world of professional comedy in 1969, encouraged me to do this book, and shared his expertise as well as his experiences with Rivers. I am also very grateful to my other friends—you know who you are—for their unflagging support, and particularly to Carrie Carmichael for her extraordinary generosity during the months I was holed up writing.

Finally, my deepest thanks to my long-suffering computer guru, otherwise known as my son Nick, who bails me out of my all too frequent technological emergencies with unfailing skill and the patience of a zen master. But my debt to my wonderful children extends far beyond such practical help; I am immeasurably grateful to Emily and Nick for giving me an irresistible reason to get up in the morning even when I can't figure out what the hell else I'm doing. A lot of wonderful things have happened to me over the years, but you two are far and away the best, and I love you with all my heart.

# NOTE ON SOURCES

In reporting *Last Girl Before Freeway,* I conducted interviews with Joan Rivers's family, friends, staff and other employees, colleagues, former coworkers, business associates, fellow performers; with insiders in comedy, television, radio, theater, and other parts of the entertainment industry; and with people who knew Rivers in different capacities. These interviews, many of them in multiple sessions, took place during the period from September of 2014, when Rivers died, through the spring of 2016, when the book was completed. In addition, I have quoted Rivers's own words from her books, including the memoirs *Enter Talking* and *Still Talking;* from her jokes and other works; from published print interviews, documentary and other filmed and video interviews; from archival and historical sources, including books about related topics, print and other press coverage; and from Rivers's performances, television and radio shows, and other appearances throughout her career.

# INDEX

Note: The abbreviation JR refers to Joan Rivers.

Rosenberg, 4–5, 58, 72, 77–81,
85, 87, 88, 93–94, 96, 97–98,
101–02, 139–41, 148, 174–79, 181,
184, 186, 209–10, 225, 286, 336,
343, 344, 397–98; need for approval, 399; personality of,
208–09, 213, 216, 296, 337;
political opinions of, 256, 257–62;
pranks and practical jokes of, 88,
161, 332, 333–34; pro-choice
views of, 251, 252; relationship
with daughter, 93–94, 98, 119,
139, 184, 189, 191–92, 194, 196,
216–18, 228, 237, 242, 271,
292–94, 295, 298, 314–30, 343,
356, 357, 398; romantic
relationships of, 192, 200, 210,
335–36; stage name of, 9, 31, 317;
suicide contemplated by, 3–4;
therapy of, 194; unpredictable
anger of, 101, 214, 344, 345; work
ethic of, 209, 222, 298, 326, 339,
343, 349, 351–54, 356, 360,
362–63, 364, 365, 390. See also
acting; aging; beauty; fans;
legacy; money and wealth; plastic
surgery; reinvention of career;
stand-up comedy; weight
Rivers, Melissa: adolescence of,
119–20, 315; birth of, 5, 79; and
*Celebrity Apprentice*, 292–95, 298,
319, 320; childhood of, 314–15;
and Barry Diller, 185; education
of, 131, 139, 191, 315, 316–17,
322; and *Fashion Police*, 302, 303,
307–09, 317, 318, 321, 322, 326,
330, 336; and father's suicide,
182, 183, 191–92, 316, 320; as gift
to Johnny Carson, 87–88; and
JR's death, 369–70; and JR's eulogy, 374–75; and JR's funeral,
371–72, 374–75; on JR's medical
condition, 369; on JR's premonition about endoscopy procedure,
397; on Orin Lehman, 247; malpractice suit against Yorkville

Endoscopy, 365–68, 380–81; marriage to John Endicott, 265, 326;
Pacific Palisades house of,
327–28, 354; and red-carpet commentary, 299–301, 303, 317–18;
relationship with father, 92–94,
139, 177, 179, 180, 181, 182, 193,
315, 316, 326; relationship with
mother, 3, 90, 93–94, 98, 119, 139,
184, 189, 191–92, 194, 196,
216–18, 228, 237, 242, 271,
292–94, 295, 298, 314–30, 343,
356, 357, 398; romantic
relationships of, 329; wedding of,
265, 322–25
Riviera Shore Club, New Rochelle,
32–33
Rosenberg, Anna, 70, 86
Rosenberg, Edgar: adjustment to
California, 92, 94, 97, 98, 101–02,
148; ambition of, 71, 72, 73–75,
85, 92; childhood tuberculosis of,
74; credit for JR's career, 5, 119,
131; family background of,
73–74; as father, 92–93; funeral
of, 163, 182, 183–84, 189, 201;
health of, 139, 149, 187; JR hired
as comedy writer for, 69, 70–71;
JR's engagement to, 71–72; and
JR's estrangement from Johnny
Carson, 131, 135, 138, 144, 146,
150, 154, 156, 159, 160, 162–63;
and JR's Fox show, 139, 149–50,
166–67, 168, 171, 172, 173–78,
181; JR's marriage to, 4–5, 58, 72,
77–81, 85, 87, 88, 93–94, 96,
97–98, 101–02, 139–41, 148,
174–79, 181, 184, 186, 209–10,
225, 286, 336, 343, 344, 397–98;
as JR's unofficial manager, 74–76,
85, 94–95, 98, 106, 118, 138, 141,
142, 144, 146, 147–48, 154, 156,
159, 160, 186, 187, 188, 220;
personality of, 75–76, 77, 92,
94–95, 118–19, 140, 149–50, 166,
167, 178, 179, 180; as producer,

# ABOUT THE AUTHOR

Leslie Bennetts is the author of the national bestseller *The Feminine Mistake* as well as a longtime *Vanity Fair* writer and former *New York Times* reporter. At *Vanity Fair* she wrote many movie star cover stories in addition to articles on subjects ranging from priest pedophilia to U.S. antiterrorism policy, and she was the first woman ever to cover a presidential campaign at *The New York Times*. Bennetts has also written for many other magazines, including *New York*, *Vogue*, *More*, *The Nation*, and *Glamour*. She lives in New York City.